W9-AFO-359

From King's College To Columbia, 1746–1800

Columbia University Press   *New York*   *1976*

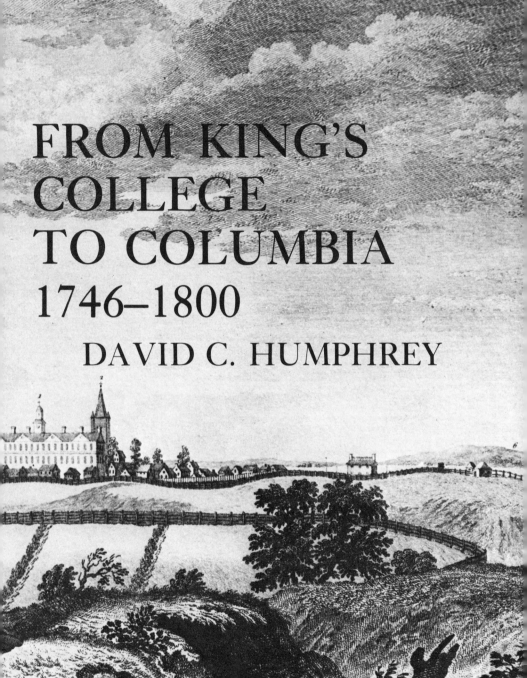

FROM KING'S COLLEGE TO COLUMBIA 1746–1800

DAVID C. HUMPHREY

Title page
Southeast View of New York City with King's College at the Center
Trinity Church is behind the college, the Hudson River is on the right, and Staten Island is in the distance. Known as the "Palm Tree Print," the picture was drawn "on the Spot" in the 1760s by Capt. Thomas Howdell of the Royal Artillery. The engraving is by P. Canot.
CREDIT: COLUMBIANA, COLUMBIA UNIVERSITY

Chapter 1 appeared in slightly different form as "Urban Manners and Rural Morals: The Controversy Over the Location of King's College," in *New York History* 54 (Jan. 1973): 5–23. Chapters 13 and 14 appeared in slightly different form as "The King's College Medical School and the Professionalization of Medicine in Pre-Revolutionary New York," in *Bulletin of the History of Medicine* 49 (Summer 1975): 206–34.

Library of Congress Cataloging in Publication Data

Humphrey, David C   1937–
  From King's College to Columbia, 1746-1800.

  Bibliography: pp. 373–91
  Includes index.
  1. Columbia University—History. I. Title.
LD1249.H85   378.747'1   75-41351
ISBN 0-231-03942-5

Columbia University Press
New York   Guildford, Surrey

Copyright © 1976 by Columbia University Press
Printed in the United States of America

LD
1249
.H85

To Janet

162302

PREFACE

COLLEGE HISTORIES have generally not been among the more successful historical works. They are often narrow, and occasionally self-serving. Frequently they ignore a major constituency at a college, the students. In any case, there are inherent limitations in what can be accomplished by writing the history of a single college. And with King's College the problem is complicated by a scarcity of primary sources. I have tried to meet a number of these problems head-on. Collective biographies of students and trustees aided immensely in gauging the character of the college and in measuring its development. So have comparisons with the histories of other colleges, particularly Princeton, as has extensive research on related institutions, particularly the Anglican church. I have devoted one chapter to examining the social experience of the undergraduates, another to hypothesizing about the college's political and intellectual impact on them. And I have suggested a way of thinking about how the college reflected and affected its cultural setting. My main goal, however, has not been particularly different from that of many other college histories: to understand how the college developed—and why it developed as it did.

I am grateful to a number of people who have helped me during the past several years. Clarence L. Ver Steeg of Northwestern University suggested I undertake this project and guided and supported me throughout it. Janet G. Humphrey aided me in the research, carefully edited several drafts, made innumerable suggestions which I followed and a number which I did not, proofread ad infinitum, and sustained me during some trying times. Well before I started this project M. Halsey Thomas, then curator at Columbiana, eased my labors immeasurably by discovering many essential documents from Columbia's past, by editing and publishing a number of others, and by compiling an excellent general catalogue of alumni and officers. The manuscript has also benefited by his editing. Several of my colleagues at Carnegie-Mellon University have suggested improvements in the manuscript or have helped me in other ways. I would particularly like to thank Irving H. Bartlett and Joel A. Tarr for their thoughtful criticism of my work and for their continuing encouragement. Harold L. Burstyn, now of William Patterson College, gave chapters 13 and 14 a careful reading, while Eugene D. Levy did the same for chapter 1. I am also indebted to Lawrence A. Cremin of Columbia University for his comments on the manuscript and his support, and to the National Endowment for the Humanities for a research grant which made it possible for me to complete this project.

The staffs of many libraries and historical societies assisted me in innumerable ways. I am especially grateful to Arthur Breton, formerly of the New-York Historical Society; George Jones of the Darlington Room, University of Pittsburgh; Kenneth Lohf, Alice H. Bonnell, and the late Charles W. Mixer of Columbia University; and Ann Deklerk and Dorothy Kabakeris of Hunt Library, Carnegie-Mellon University. My thanks also to Joanne Zuri and Angela Napoleone for their help in preparing the manuscript for publication.

Finally, I would like to thank Bernard Gronert of Columbia University Press for his help and cooperation. I have enjoyed working with him. And I am especially indebted to Agnes Mc-Kirdy of Columbia University Press, whose careful and thoughtful editing of the manuscript improved it immensely.

Pittsburgh, Pennsylvania   DAVID C. HUMPHREY
September 1975

CONTENTS

ILLUSTRATIONS

From King's College To Columbia, 1746–1800

1.

THE SHAPING OF KING'S COLLEGE

INTRODUCTION

IN MARCH 1745 James Alexander, a distinguished member of the New York bar, signed a will which bequeathed £100 to a college "to be erected in the Province of New York" and £50 to a college intended for New Jersey. In so doing, it turns out, Alexander provided us with the earliest surviving document to mention plans at mid-century for either college and the only evidence that a proposal was afoot in 1745 to found a college in New York. The New Jersey college foundered on the rock of denominational rivalry before the year was out. Anglicans and Presbyterians quarreled over its control, and the governor refused to grant a charter.[1] Just what happened to the New York project in 1745 remains a mystery.

The following year, 1746, proved to be a more fruitful one for higher education in America. On October 22 a new acting governor chartered the College of New Jersey, now known as Princeton University. The next day New York assemblymen authorized the preparation of a bill (it became law on December 6) to raise funds by public lottery for their own provincial college, soon to be chartered as King's College and now known as Columbia University.

The College of New Jersey opened in 1747. Seven more years passed before classes started at the College of New York (as King's was also known). Plans for the college almost died at first from a lack of public interest. In the 1750s they barely survived the intensity of public attention. During these crucial years various individuals and interest groups discussed and often clashed over the shape of the college. Where should it be located? Who should control it? Who should attend? What should they learn? On some questions the range of agreement permitted a smooth resolution of differences. On other issues the conflict became so bitter that it threatened to destroy the project and left many New Yorkers disgruntled about the outcome. Out of the deliberations and controversies emerged an institution that failed during the 1760s and 1770s either to dissipate the ill will of its antagonists or to fulfill the expectations of its friends. If some New Yorkers hailed King's College as a bulwark of order and prosperity, others castigated it as a tool of tyrants. If its supporters sought to transform it into the Oxford of the New World, its enemies sniped at it for two decades, then cheered when its president was hounded out of town by a Revolutionary mob. In the 1780s New York politicians fought anew over its role in the republic. Yet, the vicissitudes of King's College and the divisiveness it inspired are factors which in retrospect make it an intriguing subject of study and at the same time provide an illuminating view of the tensions besetting American society during the second half of the eighteenth century.

1.

THE CONTROVERSY
OVER LOCATION

IN THE CLOSING DECADES of the twentieth century it is difficult to imagine Columbia University situated in rural New York. Americans today, however, can readily sympathize with some of their eighteenth-century forebears, who contended that the "Goodness of the Air" and moderate cost of living in New York's countryside offered a more suitable setting for the college than New York City, with its "bad" people and its innumerable "tippling Houses." The city also had its enthusiastic defenders in the "grand Debate" over the college's location that began in 1747. By 1753 the conflict had stimulated much "laborious Enquiry" and provided "a copious Fund for private Conversation." At least one observer blamed the controversy for retarding the "great Work" of founding the college. Some of the contenders, their Yankee appetites whetted by expectations of rising land values and a ready market for farm goods, took less than a genuine interest in the problems of higher education. The leading spokesmen for both sides, however, sincerely believed that the college's setting was inextricably intertwined with its character and function.[1]

Proponents of a rural college never organized an effective campaign. What strength they had reflected the appeal of their arguments and the prominence of the men who propounded them, like Cadwallader Colden and Reverend James Wetmore. Colden mounted the most potent challenge to the New York City interests that dominated the college movement. His credentials at mid-century were imposing: botanist, physical scientist, author of a noted work on New York's Indians, senior councillor of the province, and principal political adviser to Governor George Clinton from 1746 to 1750.

For Colden, as for many New Yorkers, the city's capacity to corrupt students weighed against an urban location. The risk of moral debasement seemed especially perilous in light of the future careers expected of students who would be educated at the college. The college's principal supporters anticipated that it would train the magistrates, legislators, judges, lawyers, clerics, and doctors who would guide the fortunes of New York in the years ahead. Leadership was, in their eyes, the key to the colony's future prosperity. Peaceful harbors, fertile soil, and rivers penetrating the backcountry provided the raw materials of a nation's greatness, but the achievement of communal well-being was fundamentally a moral process in which men shaped their lives and the lives of their posterity for good rather than for evil. Through the wisdom of their decisions, through the heroic character of their actions, through the model they provided for their inferiors, leaders of talent and virtue could bring glory to a people. Leaders who lacked these qualities could bring a nation to its knees.[2] Did it make sense, then, to place the college in an environment where New York's most promising youths might be "debauched by bad Company and Examples"? Colden believed that a college in the countryside would free impressionable youngsters from the city's "many temptations to idleness" and "worse vices." [3]

Colden also hoped that a rural location would permit a college to teach agriculture. He himself engaged in botanical research at his country estate near Newburgh, in the Hudson River valley some sixty miles north of New York City. His investigations nourished his appreciation of agriculture as a science. A professor of agriculture could conduct experiments, correspond with noted farmers, and communicate to New York's future leaders knowledge about a field which Colden regarded as the "foundation of the Wealth and wellfare of the Country." [4]

His conviction that the location of the college would shape the educational experience of its students prompted Colden's concern about how a college in the country could recreate the city's virtues while escaping its limitations. New York City's outstanding attribute, according to some of its advocates, was its gentility. If taverns and prostitutes abounded, so did gentlemen of sophistication and learning. Colden may not have condoned the snobbery of one city proponent in the "grand Debate," who pointedly remarked that England's rural academies were surrounded by "illiterate Artificers" whom the students learned to look upon as "tasteless unpolish'd Clowns." But Colden did worry about how students at a rural college could gain "that advantage of behaviour and address" which they would acquire in the city by "general conversation with Gentlemen." His solution was a training program in gentlemanliness: oblige students to use the manners of "well bred Gentlemen," teach them dancing and proper carriage, and have them "declame or dispute or Act plays," so that they would lose the bashfulness that frequently gave students an awkward appearance.[5]

It is hard to tell just when Colden decided that Newburgh offered the ideal setting for New York's first college. Early in 1744 he launched a campaign to establish an Anglican (Church of England, Episcopal) mission and "a public School" there. He had his eye on a 500-acre tract, fronting on the Hudson, which the province had granted in 1719 to a group of Lutherans to support their minister. Since most of the Lutherans had moved away—or so the Anglican Colden claimed—he declared that New York should regrant the tract to Anglican residents in the area. Reverend Samuel Johnson, Colden's good friend and later the first president of King's College, thought the plan had excellent prospects for promoting "religion and learning." [6] In the fall of 1744 the London-based Society for the Propagation of the Gospel in Foreign Parts (SPG or Society), the missionary arm of the Church of England, learned of Colden's proposal through Hezekiah Watkins, Johnson's and Colden's nominee as missionary to Newburgh, who arrived in London in 1744 for ordination. The Society promptly appointed Watkins missionary to Newburgh and queried Governor Clinton of New York about procuring the 500 acres. In addition,

Colden arranged with two New York City lawyers to pursue the matter with the provincial government, but the colony's involvement in King George's War (1744–1748) and protracted feuding among New York politicians delayed any action on it.[7]

The SPG considered the tract of land almost exclusively as a home base and a source of income for its missionary, but Colden remained interested in establishing a school there. In December 1748 he sought to convince the SPG of the land's suitability for a "School or Colledge." The tract was "near the center of the Province," he argued, easily accessible by boat, and "in the most healthy part of the Province"; no place seemed "more convenient for a Colledge." Of course, Colden knew by that date that the founding of a college in the colony was a real possibility, since the provincial assembly had conducted two lotteries that had raised more than £3000. Indeed, Colden recommended that the SPG persuade King George II to instruct New York's governor not to assent to "any act of Assembly for erecting a Colledge in this Province," unless the king specifically approved it. An Anglican himself and Governor Clinton's closest political associate, Colden did not expect to find to his liking a college sponsored by the assembly, which numbered several influential Presbyterians and Dutch churchmen among its members and which had been fighting with the governor for the past two years. The SPG, advised Colden, should see to it that New York's college "be put upon a proper Foundation." [8]

By 1748 the lawyers representing Colden and his associates had drawn up a petition to the governor for the 500 acres, to be used for an Anglican cleric and a "Semenary for Learning." But months passed without any positive action. In 1749 the New York City Lutheran church challenged the petition, claiming that the land should be given for the use of the city's Lutheran minister. Colden gained time when the assembly dallied over organizing a college. But time proved of little value. SPG officials ignored the suggestions Colden had sent them, and, in 1750, Colden himself virtually retired from New York's tumultuous political scene.[9] By 1751 the lawyers handling his case had submitted a revised petition to the governor, which no longer mentioned a seminary of learning, though it did include provision for a schoolmaster to teach children in the Newburgh area.[10] Whether by this date Colden had given up the idea of locating the college at Newburgh is difficult to say. In any case, on March 5, 1752, two days after Governor Clinton finally ordered the attorney general to prepare letters patent transferring the 500 acres to the Anglicans, the vestrymen and wardens of New York City's Trinity Church voted to give the college a valuable and attractive piece of land for a campus in New York City.[11]

Some proponents of a rural location for New York's college backed Westchester County, Long Island, or Manhattan Island north of the city as a setting, mainly for reasons that would warm the heart of any modern suburbanite. These areas, they contended, combined the benefits of rural living with the advantages of nearness to the city.[12] The most outspoken group advocated the Boston Post Road, which, now disguised primarily as U.S. Route 1, journeys through such Westchester County towns as New Rochelle and Rye on its way from New York City to New Haven, Connecticut. The identity of the "Post Roaders" remains largely a mystery, since the newspaper articles they wrote were signed with pseudonyms and the cryptic initials that colonials found so engaging. However, the key figure of the group more than likely was Reverend James Wetmore, Anglican cleric of Rye.

James Wetmore was the kind of dedicated, aggressive Anglican parson who reminded dissenters just how much they disliked the Church of England. A Connecticut native and a Yale graduate, Wetmore preached at the North Haven Congregational church for four years before defecting to episcopacy in 1722. By mid-century he could look back on almost three decades of zealous service to "the Church," most of it as minister to Rye's Anglican parishioners. When plans for a college in New York surfaced in the mid-1740s, Wetmore marshaled a battery of reasons in a 1747 newspaper article why the college should be located in Rye, including the urgency of being "near a settled Church" (his own, of course).[13]

Wetmore did not voice what may have been the most compelling reason behind his preference for Rye. Having divided his life between Connecticut and New York, Wetmore had promoted the expansion of the Anglican church in both colonies. He expected New York's college to become the first Anglican college in the northern colonies and alma mater for the Anglican clerics and laymen who would sustain the church in the future. A college located at Rye could compete with Yale for the sons of Connecticut's Anglican families at the same time that it conveniently serviced New York's Anglicans, who were concentrated in New York City, Westchester County, and Long Island.

In his public defense of Rye, Wetmore joined other Post Roaders in emphasizing the special appeal of a rural location that was readily accessible yet at a "convenient Distance" from New York City. Whereas it would be difficult to restrain students at an urban college from "Vice and neglect of their Studies," a suburban college provided the "Retirement" and the visual setting ("Sea, Hills, Dales, Fields, Woods, Plains, &c") that would stimulate philosophical reflection. While an urban college would have to import food and firewood, a suburban college could rely on nearby farms and forests. And it could be reached easily from the city by students, trustees, visitors, and supplies.[14]

Since Long Islanders could (and apparently did) make a similar case, the Post Roaders stressed their "central" location in the province and the advantages of being on the same side of the water as the city. City residents could journey to a college situated at Rye both by land and by a gentle water voyage along the coast. In contrast, the Post Roaders conjured up unpleasant images of New York City's most prominent citizens heading home from commencement at a college on Long Island's north shore, crowded on a ferry boat among horses, chairs, and "a Throng of rude and troublesome Companions," crossing open water with the wind high. One day the inevitable calamity would strike, and the "whole Company" would be "thrown into the Sea and drowned." Proponents of the Post Road deliberately directed their arguments at New York City's leading citizens, since they knew it was imperative to convince the city elite of the Post Road's virtues. To soften objections of Long Islanders the Post Roaders emphasized that a ferry operated regularly between Rye and Oyster Bay (its "danger" was not discussed).[15]

The Post Roaders' trump card was the cosmopolitan exposure their location would give the proposed college. First, it would minimize the problem of isolation that Colden had thought to overcome through programs of dancing and play-acting. Despite its rural setting, a Post Road college could offer its students "the Advantage of the Conversation of learned Gentlemen, who frequently travel that Road from *Boston, Connecticut, New-York* and *Philadelphia.*" Second, the Post Road provided more visibility to the public than other rural locations. Since New Yorkers expected their college to serve as "one of the publick Ornaments of the Colony," as concrete testimony to New York's cultural maturation and self-sufficiency, it obviously would not do to hide such an important symbol. Situated on the Post Road, the college would not escape the "Observation of Gentlemen who travel through the Country, as well Strangers as our own People." [16]

One Post Roader went so far as to suggest a particular eight-acre lot in Rye as most "fit and suitable for the College." Yet, Wetmore and probably other Post Roaders were not overly sanguine about achieving their goal. Like Colden, they realized that wherever the college was located it would bolster the surrounding area's prestige and economy, and that this very fact gave the college a strong appeal to other New Yorkers besides themselves. They also knew that if the "principal gentlemen" of New York City wished the college placed in the city, it would be difficult and perhaps undesirable to thwart them. [17]

Benjamin Franklin once noted that the founders of the Academy of Philadelphia, after lengthy discussion, located their school in the city rather than the country because the majority of the Academy's prospective financial backers wanted it there. [18] The arguments of Cadwallader Colden and James Wetmore withered in the face of similar pressure: the wealthiest and best-organized proponents of the college preferred an urban location. From its origins in the mid-1740s to its culmination in the mid-1750s, the movement to found a provincial college was dominated by a small but powerful group of New York City lawyers, merchants, and politicians—men like Joseph Murray, Henry Cruger, Paul Richard, James Alexander, Benjamin Nicoll, William Smith, Sr. and

Jr., William and James Livingston, John Chambers, and Edward Holland. The provincial assembly's handling of the project reflected their influence. Assemblymen from New York City prepared and introduced the initial legislation in 1746, calling for a public lottery to raise funds for a college. The city's assemblymen also prepared and introduced additional lottery bills in 1747 and 1748 as well as a 1751 act that created a board of ten lottery trustees. The 1751 act named eight city luminaries and two rural New Yorkers as board members and charged them with managing the lottery funds and receiving proposals for the college's location. The two rural trustees did not participate in the board's deliberations. When, in 1753, the legislature authorized the trustees to organize the college, they decided to locate it in New York City.[19]

The trustees and their urban confederates made little effort to justify publicly their preference for New York City. Several of them probably shared William Livingston's belief that "the most superficial Thinker" should realize that "the College ought to be plac'd in or near this City. . . ."[20] This conviction, nourished by their personal identity with the city and their pride in its growth, also reflected several practical considerations. The majority of the trustees and their urban allies expected to manage the college through a private board of governors. To locate the college outside the city, however, would make this plan impractical and might endanger the urbanites' control of the institution. Even if assembly-appointed governors managed the college, as William Livingston and William Smith, Jr., proposed, the job would be simplified by placing the college in New York's political center. New York City also provided a meeting ground for the colony's many religious groups. A city location pleased the Anglicans who predominated among the founders, since so many of the Anglican families who were likely to patronize the college lived in or near the city. Nor could any other town offer students such a variety of churches to attend. The best Rye could do was an Anglican church one-third of a mile from the campus and a Presbyterian church a mile away, an arrangement that could not have cheered the numerous Dutch Reformed church members who supported the college project.[21]

If most of the leading advocates of an urban location shunned a public defense of their position, one of them enthusiastically spelled out the advantages of a city campus in a pamphlet published in 1752. Its author was Reverend William Smith, a young Scot and a devoted Anglican who had migrated to New York the year before. Why should we "send our Youth into the Depths of Woods, to perform their Collegiate exercises, in the unambitious Presence of inanimate Trees?" he asked. New York's future leaders should learn to "unite the Scholar with the Gentleman" and "ought to know Men and the World." Put students in the country—away from the "Sight of Men"—and they will "contract" an "aukward Bluntness." Put them in the city—"where the polished and learned Part of the Province are their Judges"—and "at one and the same Time, they can learn the *Belles Lettres*, Breeding, and some Knowledge of Men and Things. . . ." [22]

Smith handily parried the objections to an urban location. The expense of firewood, he suggested, bothered only the short-sighted. Within a short time the woods about a country college would be cleared, requiring the use of imported firewood; in any case, " 'tis the Opinion of many, that in less perhaps than half a Century, Coal will be the cheapest Fuel. . . ." As for the city's immorality, Smith believed this factor should not deter the parents of half the students, since about that proportion would be city residents anyway. Nor should parents from rural New York fear for the corruption of their sons. The students would live within a college building, where their access to city life would be carefully regulated by college authorities. [23]

Smith had a point about the building, of course. The founders of New York's college never planned to loose the students upon the city, where they could exploit its social opportunities at will. Indeed, a college building provided the answer to several problems, though Smith himself did not explore them. Teen-age boys would be separated from their parents, which apparently some founders considered "an advantage." Yet they would live within a controlled environment—in some ways resembling a family— which permitted the college to inculcate the proper virtues in students at the same time that they took advantage of the city's

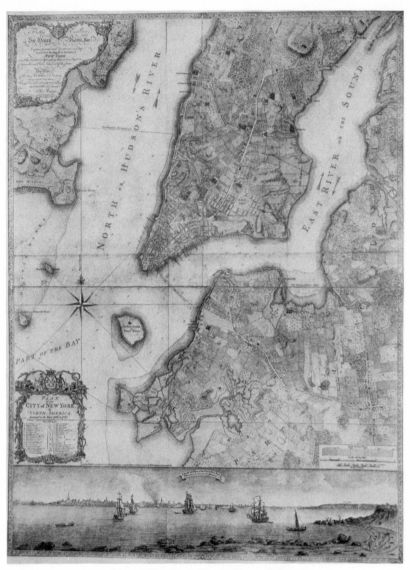

Map of New York City by Bernard Ratzer
The map was drawn in 1767 and published in 1776. The engraving is by Thomas Kitchen.

CREDIT: COLUMBIANA, COLUMBIA UNIVERSITY

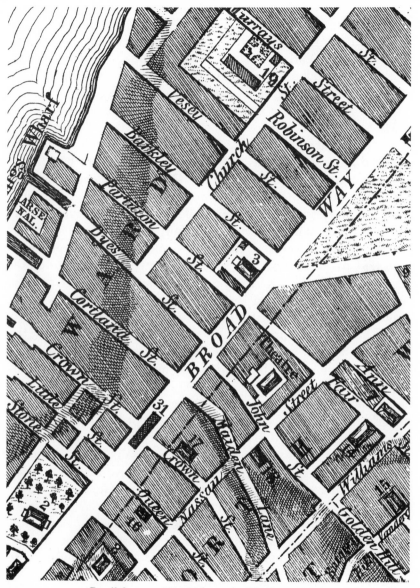

Detail from an 1854 Lithograph of the Ratzer Map.

King's College, on the corner of Murray St. and Church St., is marked by number 19 on the map. Trinity Church, then as now located at the head of Wall St., is marked by number 2. Because of landfill projects the Hudson River is now several blocks from the site of the former campus.

CREDIT: COLUMBIANA, COLUMBIA UNIVERSITY

cosmopolitanism. Moreover, a well-constructed college building placed in New York City should satisfy those New Yorkers who regarded the college as a provincial showpiece. New York City residents were all the more eager to have a college to serve as a civic "ornament" after the Academy of Philadelphia opened in 1751.[24]

The construction of an attractive building in New York City required funds and land as well as enthusiasm; but the city's leading residents were equal to the task. During the college's first decade they contributed more than £13,000, much of which was used to defray some £10,000 in building costs. However, it was the vestrymen and wardens of Trinity Church, whose membership included several of the college's most vigorous supporters, who first paved the way for an urban location. In 1752 they offered the college "any Reasonable Quantity of the Churches Farm"—a sizable tract in the city's west ward, which had been granted to the church in 1705. Even at this early date it had been considered an appropriate site for a college.[25] At mid-century the tract was no less appealing, running between Broadway and the Hudson River, a few hundred yards north of Trinity Church, near the city's center yet far enough away to seem "out of Town" and to provide more than ample space for a pleasant campus. A majority of the trustees soon decided to accept Trinity's offer, the only one they received. Their decision surprised no one, particularly since four of the trustees were Trinity vestrymen. Eventually the church agreed to give the college a five-acre lot, which today is bordered by Church Street on the east, Greenwich Street on the west, Murray Street on the north, and Barclay Street on the south. The college remained in lower Manhattan until 1857 when it was relocated at Madison Avenue and Forty-ninth Street. In 1897 Columbia moved to its present site on Morningside Heights.[26]

Early in 1753 William Livingston, one of the college trustees, publicly admonished New Yorkers to stop amusing themselves with disputes about where to locate their college and get on to a more serious issue: who was going to control it. Livingston, a Presbyterian, was extremely apprehensive that a single religious denomination might gain control of the college—which was exactly what Anglicans like Colden, Wetmore, and the Trinity Church vestrymen had had in mind for some time. Livingston's warning and the Anglican response triggered more than three years of public and political furor, known as the "King's College Controversy." Livingston succeeded masterfully in shifting the focus of debate from the location of the college to its control. Virtually no major figure questioned any longer the wisdom of placing the college in the city.[27] Whereas Colden remained aloof from the struggle, Wetmore closed ranks with his urban compatriots in the crusade to win Anglican control of the college.

The "King's College Controversy" dwarfed the relatively mild quarrel over the college's location. Yet, the failure of Colden, the Post Roaders, and other New Yorkers to dislodge the proponents of an urban location meant that, whatever the outcome of the struggle for control, the college's character had in an important way already been settled. From the very first day of classes in 1754, the college's urban location would influence its appeal to parents, the nature of its undergraduate life, and its impact on New York society and politics.

2.

THE KING'S COLLEGE CONTROVERSY: THE ANGLICAN BID FOR CONTROL

IN OCTOBER 1754 President Samuel Johnson of King's College wrote despairingly to his stepson that "amidst all this buzz & Confusion really I am almost crazy & know not what to say or do. . . ." The previous summer Johnson had accepted eight boys into the college's first class and started instruction. Now, three months later, the provincial legislature still balked at granting the college a charter. Fearful that "those indefatigable wretches" who opposed the charter would triumph, Johnson refused to resign his pastoral post in Stratford, Connecticut. His parishioners were becoming impatient at his indecision. Johnson smarted as he contemplated the possibility of losing both the college and his pastorate, a prospect some dissenters * anticipated with glee.[1]

While Johnson pleaded with his stepson for advice, William Livingston weighed the prospects of resolving Johnson's dilemma for him by quashing his college. James DeLancey, lieutenant governor of New York, had indicated in a conversation with Living-

---

* The term "dissenters" refers here and elsewhere in the text mainly to Presbyterians and Congregationalists, which were the two non-Anglican groups that Samuel Johnson and his Anglican associates had primarily in mind when they used the term. They did not usually apply the term to the Dutch Reformed.

ston that he was not prepared to approve the college charter, but Livingston wondered if a "consummate Politician" like DeLancey could be trusted. Livingston rested his hopes with the General Assembly. If the assembly refused to appropriate any money for the college, the dearth of funds could render the charter inoperative. Meanwhile Livingston would promote his own proposal for a college, one in which Anglican clerics like Samuel Johnson—or any clerics for that matter—would have little say.[2]

New York City harbored some 13,000 souls in 1754. Probably many of them knew something of Johnson's struggle with Livingston, not because news traveled so fast but because the battle lasted so long and aroused such intense feelings. It erupted in March 1753. By March 1756 it was still not over. It may seem strange that plans for a college could generate such sustained hostility, but this was a measure of how important the issues were to the men who debated them.

To Livingston and Johnson the roots of the King's College Controversy reached far into the past. Johnson stirred in Livingston historical memories of Archbishop Laud and the age-old intolerance of England's established church. Livingston provoked in Johnson the fear of chaos that eighteenth-century "free thinkers" generated with mounting intensity in the breasts of Christianity's staunchest guardians. Each man believed that the survival of fundamental values was at stake, for both men were trapped by an expectation that the proposed college would mold the outlooks of future political and professional elites.

Samuel Johnson, like James Wetmore, Cadwallader Colden, and the Trinity Church vestry, anticipated long before the college opened in 1754 that it would become a bulwark of the Anglican church. By 1750 Johnson was even referring to the projected institution as an "Episcopal College." Johnson's hopes reflected his reading of the political situation in New York, his faith in the zealous Anglicanism of his New York associates, and his belief in the legitimacy of the cause. Several of New York's leading Anglicans, in turn, were counting on Johnson by 1750 to head the college.[3] Their choice seemed utterly sound. No other Anglican priest in the colonies could touch Johnson's reputation as an intellectual, educator, and religious leader.

At mid-century Samuel Johnson could look back on a career that was strikingly similar to that of James Wetmore. Both men grew up in Connecticut, graduated from Yale in 1714, became Congregational clerics, defected to episcopacy in 1722, and journeyed to London for ordination as Anglican priests and for appointment as missionaries of the SPG. While Wetmore located in New York, Johnson settled in Stratford as minister to the only organized body of Anglicans in Connecticut. By the time Johnson accepted the presidency of King's College, he had emerged as the forceful leader of a growing Anglican enterprise in Connecticut that already numbered nineteen churches and ten priests.[4]

A tall, rather corpulent man, Johnson was fifty-three years old in 1750. One clerical associate later recalled that his countenance was "majestic and commanded respect," yet there was also something "pleasing and familiar" about it. If he appeared "grave and composed" in the pulpit or at his desk, he was "often warmed and animated by his subject." Friends found him a cheerful, agreeable, and instructive conversationalist, and much the gentleman. His sons knew him as an affectionate, extremely solicitous father, one who expected much of them and set clear-cut boundaries for their behavior but who also paid heed to their "natural genius and inclination." [5]

Johnson liked to think of himself as an inquisitive, assiduous, open-minded scholar. He wrote in his autobiography that he "was impatient to see to the bottom of everything" and devoted as much time as possible to his "beloved studies." For more than three decades Johnson kept a list of the books, pamphlets, and magazines he read, a list which numbered more than fifteen hundred titles by the 1750s and which embraced, among other writings, the best that Englishmen of his age had to offer in philosophy, theology, belles lettres, history, journalism, and works on education.[6] Johnson systematically related what he learned to what he knew, seeking a coherent world view. Upon his discovery of Bacon, Descartes, Newton, and Locke as a young man, he rejected much of what he had previously learned at Yale. Yet his

Samuel Johnson, President of King's College 1754–1763
The painting by an unknown artist hangs in the King's College Room, Columbia
University.
CREDIT: COLUMBIANA, COLUMBIA UNIVERSITY

realization that their ideas could lead to religious skepticism and
freethinking set him in search of a way to reconcile science with
religion. Through his commitment to Berkeleian immaterialism
and, later, through his fascination with the antiscientific ideas of
John Hutchinson, Johnson gradually subordinated his scientific
beliefs to the intellectual demands of religious orthodoxy.[7]

The process reflected the quandary of a man whose genuine intellectual curiosity was matched by his deeply conservative social and political instincts. In Johnson's eyes religious orthodoxy sanctified patterns of individual behavior and of social and political organization—personal humility, social hierarchy, submission to monarchical authority, and the like—patterns that were the buttresses of "order and rule." A disregard for religious orthodoxy thus invited an age of republican unruliness and of turbulent relationships among egotistical individuals. Living in a colony where, it seemed, revivalism, popular participation in government, and social striving were already feeding at the roots of the social order, Johnson responded occasionally with anger to what he considered an immediate, not an abstract, danger. Nothing, commented an Anglican priest about Johnson, was "apt to excite his indignation" so much as "the licentiousness of an unprincipled age, with respect to religion and government." [8]

Although by mid-century Johnson had lived his entire life in Connecticut, his intellectual, ecclesiastical, and educational pursuits had led to many warm friendships with distinguished residents in other colonies and across the seas. He conversed and corresponded with Bishop Berkeley about the philosophical intricacies of immaterialism and helped persuade Berkeley to endow two graduate fellowships at Yale. He exchanged ideas with Cadwallader Colden on Berkeleianism, Newtonian science, and moral philosophy, and tutored one of Colden's grandsons. Benjamin Franklin consulted him on curricular matters, invited him to head the Academy of Philadelphia, and printed his *Elementa Philosophica*, the first philosophy text published in the colonies. Johnson corresponded frequently with the bishop of London and the archbishop of Canterbury on the status of the Episcopal church, while Anglican clerics from Boston to Philadelphia admired his efforts to transform the church into a thriving institution. Many of the same clerics had profited by his skills as a teacher.

Johnson's reputation preceded him when he moved to New York in the 1750s. So did a group of Anglican clerics who bowed to his leadership. Back in the 1720s when James Wetmore first arrived in the colony he found ten clerics laboring for the Anglican church in the pastoral vineyards of New York and New Jersey, but only one of them had been raised and educated in the colonies. Three decades later ten "foreign-born" missionaries still presided over Anglican churches in the two colonies, but American clerics, most of them New Englanders, now held three ministerial positions in New York City, ringed the city in posts at Newark, Elizabethtown, New Brunswick, Rye, and Hempstead, and served Hudson River valley parishioners at churches in Newburgh and Albany.[9] The King's College Controversy would turn out to be a process through which this group of American clerics, under Johnson's leadership, achieved cohesion and direction and transformed New York City into a center of northern colony Anglicanism.

Underlying the formation of this community and its doggedness about founding an Anglican college in New York were both the successes and the failures which Johnson and an associate, Timothy Cutler, had experienced in Massachusetts and Connecticut as they battled the established Congregational church, members of which controlled both Harvard and Yale. Cutler had served as president of Yale for three years when, in 1722, he joined Johnson and Wetmore in converting to episcopacy. Purged from Yale within five weeks, Cutler became minister of Christ Church in Boston. Both Cutler and Johnson believed that the future expansion of the Anglican church in the northern colonies depended on attracting and educating an indigenous clergy. At first it was a problem of numbers—so few British-born and educated clerics ventured to the wilds of New England. Then Johnson and Cutler soured on those who did. Three British-born clerics in Massachusetts, all Low Church Anglicans, began criticizing Cutler's High Church ways, his plans to Anglicanize Harvard, even his support for the appointment of a colonial bishop. In the 1730s and 1740s Johnson's dislike for "foreign-born" missionaries burgeoned when several of them attacked the kinds of adaptations, like concessions to the power of lay vestries, that he judged necessary to build an effective Anglican church in Puritan New England.[10]

Despite their agreement on the importance of developing an indigenous clergy, Cutler and Johnson emphasized different tactics. When Cutler's thoughts drifted across the Charles River to his alma mater in Cambridge, he contemplated how Anglicans might undermine Congregational control of Harvard and seize it themselves. Johnson supported Cutler's attempt to gain a seat on Harvard's board of overseers, and he joined Cutler in insisting to the bishop of London that if Congregational control of Harvard were not infiltrated or abrogated, Harvard would "forever stand in the way of our Church's growth. . . ." [11] But Johnson took a different tack toward his alma mater in New Haven. He bypassed the issue of Yale's control and concentrated on luring its sons to the bosom of the mother church.

Johnson preached at New Haven, welcomed Yale graduates into his home for instruction in Anglican theology, and planned the construction of an Anglican church at Yale's doorstep. Should a Yale alumnus decide to become an Anglican priest, often it was Johnson who located a congregation for him and then persuaded the SPG to appoint him a missionary and provide a stipend. [12] Primarily due to Johnson's tireless evangelism, 5 percent of Yale's 447 graduates in the classes of 1725 through 1748 became Anglican priests, almost all of them at churches in New England and the middle colonies. By mid-century Johnson could justifiably boast to Benjamin Franklin that he had "never been without pupils of one sort or other half a year at a time, and seldom that, for thirty eight years. And thank God, I have the great satisfaction to see some of them in the first pulpits, not only in Connecticut, but also in Boston and New York. . . ." [13]

Yet, Johnson and his clerical colleagues realized that their failures overshadowed their achievements. Anglicans had not dented Congregational control of either Harvard or Yale. Cutler soon wearied of his fruitless struggle for a seat on Harvard's board of overseers. Nor did he have much impact on Harvard undergraduates. Only 2 percent of the students in the classes of 1725 through 1748 became Anglican priests—about half of them well after leaving Harvard—and several took positions outside New England and the middle colonies. At both Harvard and Yale 95 percent of the undergraduates in the classes of 1725 through 1748 were non-Anglicans. Johnson's plans for a church in New Haven encountered numerous obstacles. When an Anglican cleric tried in 1738 to clear a plot for the church, a mob of Yale students and townspeople threatened his life. Ten years later construction of the church remained an elusive goal.

In the mid-1740s both Johnson and James Wetmore thought they detected a "growing disposition" toward Anglicanism at Yale, but this heartening prospect slipped temporarily into the background when Presbyterians founded the College of New Jersey (later Princeton) in 1746.[14] It was maddening enough that dissenters now controlled the only college in the middle colonies as well as the two colleges in New England. It was galling that a royal charter could be granted to the likes of Reverend Jonathan Dickinson and Reverend Aaron Burr, whom Johnson and Wetmore regarded as "the most bitter Enemies of the Church." [15]

Dickinson and Burr, like their Anglican opponents Johnson and Wetmore, had graduated from Yale and become dissenting clerics, but the defection of the latter two to episcopacy created a gulf that widened during the 1730s and 1740s, when the Great Awakening swept through the northern colonies. Whereas Dickinson and Burr hailed the religious revival from their pulpits in northern New Jersey, celebrating the inward experience of *"new Birth"* and attacking the formalistic notions of their High Church critics, Wetmore and Johnson condemned the revival and its proponents (the New Lights and the New Sides) as menaces to social order, true religion, and the church as an institution. Regeneration, contended Johnson, resulted not from a sudden infusion of grace into a passive individual but from a lifelong devotion to Christian virtue. During the 1740s Wetmore and Johnson both published pamphlets which unmasked what they considered to be Dickinson's theological delusions.[16]

How deplorable, then, that Dickinson and Burr should become the first two presidents of Princeton and should commit their institution to training New Side and New Light ministers. The College of New Jersey "will be a fountain of Nonsense," grumbled Johnson in 1747. How appalling, too, that it should be located only a few miles from New York City (at Newark from 1748 to 1756), where it could provoke questions about the need for a separate college in New York.[17]

During the next several years Johnson, Wetmore, and their clerical associates in the middle colonies employed a variety of tactics—most of them fruitless—to combat Presbyterian influence at Princeton. They questioned the legality of Princeton's charter. They urged the archbishop of Canterbury and the SPG to lobby for the appointment of an Anglican governor of New Jersey, who would pose an obvious threat to the college.[18] They considered placing a "popular, discreet and prudent Missionary" near Princeton to gain the "Affections" of the students. Their most successful tactic was to intensify their efforts to turn the college proposed for New York into Princeton's denominational rival. "I wish it [New York's college] may take effect Speedily," Johnson wrote Cadwallader Colden in 1747, "that you may not suffer the Jersey College . . . to get a head of it." Despite the dissenters' success in retaining control over Harvard and Yale and in outflanking the Anglicans in New Jersey, Johnson looked optimistically on Anglican prospects in New York. The defeats elsewhere only raised the stakes.[19]

It was at this point that the community of American-born Anglican clerics began to form in New York and New Jersey, providing Johnson with the makings of an interest group which would campaign eagerly for an Anglican college. Taking up new clerical positions in the area between 1743 and 1751 were Samuel Seabury at Hempstead on Long Island, Henry Barclay and Samuel Auchmuty at Trinity Church in New York City, Thomas Bradbury Chandler at Elizabethtown, New Jersey, and three other American-born clerics. In 1754 Samuel Seabury, Jr., joined them as rector at New Brunswick, New Jersey. Including Wetmore, they had all graduated from Harvard or Yale, and most of them had grown up in New England. Four of them had studied theology with Johnson, and all respected his leadership. With their Anglicanism steeled in the hostile religious climate of Massachusetts and Connecticut, they anticipated creating their own religious stronghold in New York, freed from the dominion of

"Puritanism, Independency, and New Lightism." [20] In pursuing this goal during the King's College Controversy they also benefited during 1753 from the polemical talents of William Smith, the young Scot who earlier had articulated the reasons for locating King's College in New York City.

The intensity of clerical involvement in the King's College Controversy reflected the Anglican churchmen's basic assumptions about the college. They expected New York to establish a single provincial college. Either Anglicans would control it or a rival religious group would. They considered pleas for a nonsectarian college to be either a deceptive tactic used to disguise sectarian goals or else the odious mouthings of rank freethinkers, who hardly deserved to be entrusted with the grave responsibilities of collegiate education. Moreover, they believed that whoever controlled the college would have a profound impact on the outlooks and values of the political, judicial, and religious leaders of future years. Thus the specter of Princeton. Dissenters "will be trusted with the Education of our Youth," lamented some New Jersey Anglicans, "they will endeavour to warp them from all other Principles, and Form them according to their own, and in the nixt Age, if not sooner, we shall have an Assembly entirely Independent [Presbyterian], and then, what becomes of the Church . . . ?" An Anglican college in New York, in contrast, would "rear up good men for Church & State," men who were the "growing hopes" of the Episcopal church's future prosperity. [21]

The education of "Church scholars" would not serve simply to promote the expansion of episcopacy. True, a plentiful number of properly educated Anglican statesmen and clerics could work wonders for the church, particularly in New York. Less than one-seventh of New York's churches at mid-century were Anglican, but the Church of England enjoyed the advantages of a royally appointed governor and council, an influential group of Anglicans in the provincial upper class, and the public funding of Anglican ministers in four counties. No doubt enticing visions of the future in New York danced before clerical eyes: the conversion of the backcountry, the stationing of a colonial bishop in New York City, perhaps even a colony-wide Episcopal establishment. [22] Yet, the meaning of an Anglican college reached more deeply. Beyond the growth of the Episcopal church lay the salvation of the society.

The clerics—above all, Samuel Johnson—regarded Anglicanism as a source of the spiritual and social values which alone could arrest the pernicious drift of colonial society. As one cleric put it, Anglican principles, when "heartily imbraced [,] do more thorowly dispose Men to the Love of peace and Order, and a consciencious Submission to a lawfull Authority, than any other[s]. . . ." In contrast, it seemed to Johnson that dissenters, especially evangelical dissenters, adhered to "conceited notions" in religion and "republican mobbish principles and practices in policy," with each man "thinking himself an able divine and statesman." The results were "perpetual feuds and factions" and "wild extremes" of "free thinking." By "laying a foundation for sound learning and true religion in the rising and future generations. . . ," Johnson hoped to "stem the torrent of irreligion and vice which seems coming on like a flood that threatens to lay waste all before it." [23] A corps of enlightened Anglican leaders could restore respect for political and religious authority and thereby assure social peace and unity.

It was James Wetmore who first sketched a plan for Episcopal control of the College of New York. He announced in an anonymous newspaper essay in 1747 that he expected the "Rectors of the established Parishes" and three political figures to manage the college and select additional trustees. Since New York governors had traditionally interpreted the colony's Ministry Act of 1693—which provided public support for six pulpits in four of New York's southern counties—to mean support for Anglican ministers, Wetmore's point was obvious. Just as ministers of the Congregational church (the established church in Connecticut) ruled Yale and Church of England clerics managed the various colleges at Oxford and Cambridge, so the six "established" priests in New York should run the College of New York. Wetmore also confided to the SPG that he thought the bishop of London (or a colonial bishop, if that day ever came) should license the college's faculty and trustees, doubtless not unlike the manner in which diocesan bishops in England licensed all grammar school masters.[24]

Wetmore seemingly ignored the pitfalls of transplanting patterns of church control over education from either Connecticut or England. Most residents of Connecticut had, until recently, recognized the special status of the Congregational church, while episcopacy retained its traditional supremacy in England. But the bewildering variety of religious communicants in New York never had agreed that the Anglican church deserved special favors, regardless of how New York governors chose to interpret the Ministry Act. New York City alone at mid-century embraced Anglicans, Dutch Reformed, Presbyterians, Quakers, French Calvinists, German Lutherans, Anabaptists, and Jews. Also, Wetmore may have misconstrued the generally amicable relations between Anglicans and non-Anglicans in New York during the previous four decades to mean that non-Anglicans accepted Episcopal precedence. Denominational conflict had been extremely rare outside the four southern counties covered in the Ministry Act—only eleven SPG missionaries served white settlers in those areas from 1700 to 1775. Within the four counties interdenominational tensions were low, with non-Anglicans frequently sending their children to study with SPG schoolmasters and even attending Anglican services on occasion.[25]

How would a sectarian college fare in a religiously pluralistic colony? James Wetmore watched expectantly while Princeton fenced with antagonists in New Jersey, where religious diversity was only a mite less pronounced than in New York. Like Wetmore, Burr and Dickinson looked to Yale for inspiration in planning their college, as one sees in the sectarian makeup of Princeton's governing board. In 1747 the College of New Jersey's trustees consisted of nine Presbyterian ministers and three Presbyterian laymen, an arrangement that hardly charmed the colony's many Anglicans, Quakers, and Dutch Reformed. Powerful enemies were just what Princeton could not afford at that moment, since its charter of 1746 was legally vulnerable. As Burr admitted, it was likely "to meet with Difficulty" since it had been issued by a "Superannuated" acting governor "without Consent of Council." [26] Two factors saved the day. First, the 1746 charter explicitly guaranteed "Equal Liberty and Advantage of Education" to students of all religions—the first college charter to do so. Princeton's leaders used the concession effectively to dramatize the "catholic" character of their college, draw attention away from their exclusive control, and thus defuse some of the religious hostility toward Princeton. Second, the king appointed a new provincial governor in 1747 who was sympathetic to Princeton and who persuaded the reluctant trustees to loosen their viselike grip on the college. In 1748 the trustees agreed to a second charter which expanded the percentage of lay trustees, added an Anglican and a Quaker, and made the governor of New Jersey the ex officio president of the trustees. Although modest, the changes helped win approval of the new charter, but some New Jersey politicians still complained that there were "to[o] many of the presbaterian Clargey Concerned." As a result Princeton could not persuade the legislature to approve a college lottery and so had to resort entirely to private fund raising.[27]

By observing Princeton, Wetmore and his fellow clerics learned that there were important benefits to be gained by balancing Anglican control with explicit toleration for non-Anglican students. A declaration of religious tolerance could serve to project a public image of "catholicism" and thus muffle religious opposition. Princeton offered a second lesson, but the clerics ignored it— denominational control and public financial support might be incompatible in a religiously pluralistic society with no established church. The clerics chose, instead, to take the opposite tack, to insist that the Anglican church *was* established in New York and that this fact justified Anglican domination of a publicly financed institution. In a colony where Anglicans comprised less than one-fifth of the citizenry, the clerics grounded their campaign on an unpopular premise.

Johnson, Wetmore, and their associates were quite prepared to plead their case before any audience, but they relied on powerful lay allies to provide the political authority, social prestige, and economic resources which could transform clerical rhetoric into substantive achievements. The clerics forged their major alliance with the leading parishioners of Trinity Church in New York

City. Founded in 1693, when most New Yorkers belonged to the Dutch Reformed church, Trinity had prospered with the Anglicization of the city. By 1749 a new chapel was needed to accommodate its many communicants, whose numbers were swollen not only by immigrants but also by converts from the Dutch Reformed, French, and other "foreign" churches in New York. Even an antagonist like William Livingston believed at mid-century that Trinity had the "most numerous and richest Congregation in this City." Patronized by royal officialdom and by a majority of the city's wealthy lawyers and merchants, Trinity could boast a vestry of "first" citizens.[28]

For his part, Samuel Johnson enjoyed impressive personal ties to the Trinity Church leaders. In 1746 the vestry called as their new rector the Reverend Henry Barclay, Johnson's close friend and former student. An even more vital link was Benjamin Nicoll, scion of the prominent Nicoll family of Long Island and Johnson's stepson. Johnson had raised the boy from age eight, and their affectionate relationship carried into Nicoll's adulthood. Now Nicoll was cultivating a promising legal business in New York City, where his prospects were not impaired by his marriage in 1747 to the daughter of the mayor. Sitting on the Trinity Church vestry were several of Nicoll's professional associates, his father-in-law, and, as of 1751, Nicoll himself. When Johnson reported in 1750 that the "gentlemen" of New York expected him to preside over their college, there was no question where Johnson's "gentlemen" worshiped on Sundays.[29] The King's College charter of 1754 would soon name eleven Trinity vestrymen—half the vestry—as governors of the college.

Two vestrymen, John Chambers and Joseph Murray, combined with Benjamin Nicoll to form a skilled and influential trio of Anglican lay leaders. Chambers—whose older brother distinguished himself as a rear admiral in the British navy—grew up in New York, established a successful law practice, accumulated an "ample fortune," and married into the heart of the New York elite. Through his friendship with Governor Clinton he won appointments to the provincial supreme court in 1751 and the provincial council the next year. Chambers served as a vestryman and warden of Trinity Church for forty years. Joseph Murray migrated to New York from Ireland by his mid-twenties, set up a lucrative law practice, married the daughter of New York's Governor William Cosby, and gained a seat on the New York Council in 1744. He served on the Trinity Church vestry for thirty-seven years and at his death in 1756 bequeathed to King's College his extensive library and an estate worth £10,000.[30]

The alliance of Trinity laymen and Anglican clerics hinged on their mutual esteem for Anglicanism as a pure faith and a source of conservative social values. Joseph Murray, for instance, regarded Princeton with almost as much chagrin as did Samuel Johnson and James Wetmore. In 1745 Murray had supported the initial movement to found a college in New Jersey, but by 1747 he was questioning the validity of Princeton's charter. During the intervening period he had watched with dismay while New Jerseyites rioted in protest against ejectment suits brought by the East Jersey Proprietors (one of whom was Murray). The nucleus of the rioters was the Newark and Elizabethtown congregations of Jonathan Dickinson and Aaron Burr, the very men who had just gained a dominant voice in the College of New Jersey.[31] Murray turned his attention to founding a college whose leaders placed a high value on political authority and social order. Murray himself was childless, but for some of his Anglican associates the issue was charged by their expectation of educating sons, grandsons, and nephews at a college which espoused their own religious, political, and social beliefs and which conferred on its alumni the prestige derived from affiliation with the established church in England. The small percentage of Anglicans in New York troubled the laymen no more than it distressed the clerics. The people who counted were those who could afford to patronize the college, whether by giving funds or by enrolling sons, and Anglicans abounded in those circles.[32]

Yet clerical and lay perspectives on the religious character of New York's college were by no means identical, and the disparity proved a source of tensions within the Anglican camp during the King's College Controversy.[33] For most laymen the stakes were not as high as they were for the clerics. In their roles as fathers, religious communicants, and community leaders the laymen favored Anglican control of the college; but, unlike the clerics' situation, an Anglican "preference" would contribute little to their personal careers, their social prestige, or their political influence. Nor were their feelings about the college stirred by the pessimism that troubled the clerics. The laymen were concerned about preserving social order and a "true publick Spirit" in the face of emerging capitalist values. But they hardly viewed the colonies as tottering on the brink of moral and social collapse. A college served to ensure a prosperous future through capable leadership, not to ignite a moral reformation "from above." [34] What better proof that the urge for profit had not destroyed men's community impulses than their own participation in the college project. They were not, it seems clear, driven by the "anxiety, tension, and frustration" about colonial society that has been ascribed to some college founders and that characterized Samuel Johnson's thinking. [35]

Most of the clerics had grown up in the rivalrous religious climate of New England. They measured their success by the number of converts they won over from competing denominations. The laymen, however, had spent most of their lives in the relatively tolerant atmosphere of New York City. They achieved success in their legal and commercial careers by shutting out religious differences and cooperating with men of any faith. Politicians, like James DeLancey, learned to contend with an electorate comprised mainly of non-Anglicans. True, John Chambers almost matched James Wetmore in the parochialism and rigidity of his religious loyalties, but Joseph Murray and Benjamin Nicoll tempered their Anglicanism with a respect for each of New York's religious groups. An Anglican "preference" in the college struck the laymen as a reasonable return for their proffered and prospective gifts of land and money, but they were less convinced than the clerics about the wisdom of pegging Anglican domination on a touchy and legally fuzzy point like the establishment of the Anglican church in New York. The laymen also were more prepared than the clerics to share the management of the college with repre-

sentatives of other religious groups. Throughout the college movement several laymen collaborated with a small but influential
group of Dutch churchmen.[36]

Finally, vestrymen—not clerics—ran Trinity Church, and some
of them expected a college to operate the same way. Their respect
for the clerics did not diminish their suspicion of high-flying notions of clerical power. James Wetmore proposed that six Anglican clerics dominate the college board of trustees. The laymen
believed that lawyers, merchants, and politicians could better represent the delicate mixture of civic and church concerns that stimulated their interest in the project.[37]

Anglican intentions to dominate King's College dated from the
first lottery bill in 1746, but Nicoll, Chambers, Murray, and their
fellow vestrymen had little visible impact on the project until
1751. Late that year the provincial legislature finally authorized
ten trustees to manage the lottery funds and accept proposals for
the location of the college. Just as urbanites controlled the board
of trustees, so did Anglicans. The seven Anglican members included four vestrymen—among them Chambers, Nicoll, and Nicoll's father-in-law—as well as Cadwallader Colden and James
DeLancey. Apparently Samuel Johnson was sufficiently encouraged to turn down an invitation, extended at the urging of
Benjamin Franklin a year and a half earlier, to become head of the
Academy of Philadelphia.[38]

The Anglican grip on New York's college tightened in March
1752 when the Trinity Church vestry made its offer of several
acres of church property for a campus. Trinity attached no explicit conditions to the gift, but, as the vestry and the clergy of
New York later insisted, they "always expected that a gift so valuable . . . would be a means of obtaining some privileges to the
Church. . . ." In August Johnson fretted that the project proceeded "very heavily," but by October he anticipated that the
college would "be soon established." [39] An anonymous newspaper
essayist—actually Reverend William Smith—hinted boldly at the
drift of Anglican plans in November. Smith contended that the
governor (an Anglican) should charter the college, that the trustees
named in the charter should elect Samuel Johnson the first presi-

dent, and that Johnson should double as minister to Trinity parish's new chapel. During the same week the General Assembly, nearing the close of its session, resolved that at its spring session it would take the establishment of a college "into Consideration." [40]

Early in 1753 William Livingston and William Smith, Jr., launched a series of newspaper essays which insisted that the College of New York should be nondenominational and publicly controlled. The two men later claimed that their "reflections" were triggered by the "clandestine designs" of a "small juncto" of churchmen who "privately conspired" to procure a charter placing the college almost entirely in Anglican hands. "The subversion of this fastidious babel, was owing to his late excellency governor *Clinton;* who boldly refused a patent, for so odious a monopoly." [41] Whether their charge was true or not (it is difficult to tell), Livingston and Smith knew that some action on the college would take place soon and that they had better do something if they hoped to forestall the Anglicans. "The Case is this," Livingston confided to a friend in February. "Our future College . . . is like to fall without a vigorous opposition, under the sole management of Churchmen. The Consequence of which will be universal Priestcraft & Bigotry in less than half a Century." When Livingston publicized his sentiments, Reverend Samuel Seabury promptly countered in the *New-York Mercury* that a "Preference" in the college "must of Necessity be given to some one Denomination among us . . . ," and "what Denomination has an equal Title to this Preference with the *Established Church?*" Three years of public wrangling and private scheming lay ahead. [42]

3.

THE KING'S COLLEGE CONTROVERSY: THE CHALLENGE OF THE "REFLECTORS"

WILLIAM LIVINGSTON, a tall, angular young man, had just turned twenty-three when the New York legislature initiated the college project in 1746. William Smith, Jr., Livingston's most spirited confederate in the upcoming struggle with the Anglicans, was a mere lad of eighteen. Both youths took an immediate interest in the college; and both quickly predicted its demise. "The Generality of our Assembly-Men are persons of no Education and have no *Taste* for *Letters*," explained Smith, probably taken with his success in earning a Yale degree at age seventeen. Livingston was cheered by his own prognosis that political bickering would "greatly delay if not wholly prostrate" the college project, since he feared that Yale, Princeton, and a college in New York could not operate so closely together "without clashing & interfering with each others Interest." Both youths thought Princeton would "turn to a better Account," and their confidence is understandable. The seven Presbyterians who founded Princeton in 1746 included Smith's father, Livingston's older brother, and the minister of the church to which Smith belonged and which Livingston joined in 1752. If Anglican clerics privately condemned Aaron Burr and Jonathan Dickinson as "bitter enemies" of the Church of England,

Livingston and Smith knew them as family friends and peerless religious leaders. Samuel Johnson's son must have chuckled when his good friend Smith assured him in 1747 that "Mr. Dickinson's merit has procured him universal Esteem. . . ." [1]

Religious and family ties inspired a loyalty to Princeton that influenced Livingston and Smith throughout the King's College Controversy. But their affection for Princeton did not outweigh the provincial pride rooted in their New York upbringing. Livingston spent his youth in Albany, while Smith grew up in New York City. Both men graduated from Yale, clerked in New York City law offices, and by 1750 had become law partners in the city. Livingston quickly discovered his own immense talents with a pen, a facility with words that he did not hesitate to turn on himself—"spindle Shanks" he once called himself, one of those "ordinary fellows . . . whose noses hangs parallel with their chins." Nor was Smith unadept with a pen. Within the space of a few years Livingston became New York's first poet, Smith its principal historian, and both men publishers of its first essay-journal. Neither man lacked awareness of his own exceptional talents—"self-consciously clever" is the way one historian has described them. [2]

Like so many laymen who supported the college project, including its Anglican sponsors, Livingston and Smith were deeply impressed by New York's recent growth and its prospects for future glory. After all, by 1749 the colony had 73,000 inhabitants, almost 50 percent more than in 1731. From 1749 to 1756, while New Yorkers debated the location and control of their college, the population would grow another one-third, to just under 100,000. New Yorkers were enjoying the fruits of a burgeoning commercial life. Several indices of commercial growth and prosperity climbed sharply at or just previous to mid-century—the volume of exports to England, the number of vessels registered in New York, the prices of agricultural commodities. The volume of imports from England between 1748 and 1752 exceeded by more than three times the level two decades earlier. "Every Thing . . . conspires to make *New-York* the best Mart on the Continent," insisted Smith in an essay on the colony's "Superiority in several Instances, over some of the neighbouring Colonies." [3]

Smith's booster spirit could not, however, overcome his conviction that New York was culturally inferior. "This *Province* above
any other," he lamented in the *New-York Weekly Journal*, "has felt
the Miseries of Ignorance, and they still remain our sorest Afflictions. A sordid thirst after Money, sways the Lives of our People.
. . . ." Livingston concurred: "[O]ur Gentry are nothing better
than wealthy, distinguished, illustrious & exalted Block heads." [4]
Obviously, the two men were engaging to some degree in rhetorical flair. Cadwallader Colden, James Alexander, and William
Smith, Sr., were widely read, intellectually curious men, as were
other members of the gentry. When Benjamin Franklin proposed
in 1743 the formation of a learned society to promote "Useful
Knowledge," New Yorkers such as Joseph Murray, James DeLancey, and several of their associates quickly indicated a desire to
join. Livingston and Smith soon belonged to a "Society for improving themselves in useful Knowledge" in New York, and a second such club met regularly in the city in 1749.[5] By 1750 the
provincial gentry numbered among its ranks some forty college
educated laymen, and other members of the gentry were well
versed in the liberal arts and sciences.[6]

Yet, Livingston's and Smith's hyperbole did not seem excessive
to those colonial critics who judged New Yorkers against the
Olympian figures of classical Greece and Rome or the cultural
grandees of the mother country. James DeLancey was no Pericles,
James Alexander no Newton. When compared to ancient Athens,
New York did appear to have a "Cloud of Darkness" hanging over
it, a cloud which a college could help to "burst & breath through,"
or so declared one patron of the College of New York. In a short
time New Yorkers would "see a tast for learning rearing its head,
Learned Men Courted, Invited, encouraged & revered, the publick Seats of Justice [,] Magistracy & Legislation fill'd, honourably
fill'd with Men of our own Country. . . ." [7]

Livingston projected a similar vision of the future in a brief
pamphlet he published in 1749. Should New York carry through
on its plans for a college, he could see "a glorious multitude of
Statesmen and Heroes, Philosophers and Orators rising before"
him. New Yorkers would forswear their compulsion to amass "su-

William Livingston
The painting is by Albert Rosenthal after Charles Wilson Peale.
CREDIT: COLUMBIANA, COLUMBIA UNIVERSITY

perfluous Riches" and instead enrich "their Minds with the inestimable Treasures of Knowledge." Soon the colony would be distinguished less for the "barbarous Ignorance" of its past than for
the enlightenment which was drawing it into the circle of "polite"
European nations.[8]

While grandiose visions of the future dominated Livingston's pamphlet, he also took the opportunity in it to praise New York's assemblymen as the *"properest Persons"* to organize the college, and he directed a few caustic words toward Governor Clinton of New York, Cadwallader Colden, and the Anglican clergy. But the rhetoric was mild, especially for a man of Livingston's political verve and of his antipathy toward the Anglican church and its clergy. Indeed, he and Smith remained remarkably silent about the religious character of the college until early 1753. Then Livingston confessed that the threat of Anglican control had "long been the Subject of my thoughts," although neither he nor Smith had publicly responded to newspaper essays in 1747 and 1751 which proposed prominent roles in the college for Anglican clerics. Livingston was even content to work quietly with the seven Anglicans who were appointed along with himself and two others to the board of lottery trustees in 1751.[9]

Livingston and Smith thus astonished the Anglican clerics by opening a campaign in 1753 for a nonsectarian college. Theirs was a "pernicious" scheme, charged Samuel Johnson, designed to wrest the college "out of the Church's Hands"—which, of course, was exactly right. But the two lawyers offered more than a contrivance to diddle the Anglicans. They sketched an innovative plan for organizing a college in a pluralistic, secularizing, and politically representative society. In 1754 they incorporated their ideas in a charter and pressed the provincial legislature to turn their model into the College of New York.[10]

Livingston and Smith found in the *Independent Reflector* a perfect vehicle for introducing their views to the public. Already the weekly essay-journal, published under Livingston's editorship since November 1752, had created quite a stir in New York City. During March and April 1753 Smith and Livingston directed a literary fusillade toward *"Our Intended* College"—anonymously, of course—and explained why the college must be nondenominational and publicly controlled. The problem was simple. The institution would have a momentous impact on the public welfare and thus it must be managed in the public interest. How dangerous to bestow absolute control of the college on a body of private gentlemen, particularly should members of one religious group predominate. They would discourage free intellectual inquiry and, unchecked, impose their sectarian sentiments on students who one day would "unavoidably affect our civil and religious Principles" in their posts "on the Bench, at the Bar, in the Pulpit, and in the Senate." A college originally founded to make young New Yorkers "more extensively serviceable to the Common-Wealth" would actually become an "Engine of Persecution, Slavery and Oppression." And what of religious groups shut out from control of the college? Were they to help finance it, send their sons there, and then stand meekly by until their lives were ruled exclusively by devotees of a rival denomination? Clearly a "Party" [sectarian] college would spark widespread dissension and would be "indifferently stocked with Pupils." [11]

To Smith and Livingston the solution was as inescapable as the problem was obvious. First, the college should be incorporated not by a royal charter from the governor and his council (centers of Anglican strength) but by an act of assembly, the political body which best represented the variety of religious interests in New York. Second, the legislature should retain control over the college, by reserving the right to fire recalcitrant trustees, to name all new trustees, to reject the trustees' choice of president, and to void any bylaws passed by the trustees. Third, the act of incorporation should bar the establishment of any particular "religious Profession" in the college, exclude divinity as a formal subject of study, authorize informal and "free Conversation upon polemical and controverted Points in Divinity," and allow faculty and students to attend "any Protestant Church at their Pleasure." Finally, students should have legal recourse through the courts if the president and trustees should violate the rights guaranteed them in the act of incorporation.[12]

This intellectually bold and tactically clever proposal suited the goals of its authors nicely. As Presbyterians, Livingston and Smith had witnessed with a jaundiced eye the growing strength of Trinity Church and its success in luring wayward sheep away from rival denominations in New York City. As dissenters, they genuinely feared that lusty Anglican appetites threatened the political and religious rights of most New Yorkers. As eighteenth-century enlightened rationalists, they distrusted *"High Church"* priests who self-servingly converted the "pure and simple" religion of Jesus into a "Divinity Shop" of "superstitious Rites," "Bows and Capers," and elaborate doctrinal distinctions.[13] And as ambitious young men, confident in their abilities and unawed by their elders, they relished an opportunity to make a political and intellectual splash. Their proposal met these concerns and did so on the plane of high principle. In the name of liberty and equity, they challenged the Anglicans and captured public attention.

Their essays on the college might have attracted less notice had they not been introduced into a journalistic caldron already simmering with anticlericalism. Several weeks earlier Livingston had reproached the "little Popes" of all religious denominations in the first of a series of anticlerical articles in the *Independent Reflector* and the *New York Gazette*. "I never doubted," remarked Livingston about the "prodigious noise" touched off by his journalistic blast, "that the Generality of Priests in all Ages and Countries, were actuated by the same spiritual Pride, the same tempestuous Zeal for Baubles and Conundrums, and the same Impatience under Correction." The Anglican clerics, who realized they were Livingston's primary target, promptly counterattacked in the press, despite one parson's opinion that combating the "Reflectors" (as the Anglicans called their opponents) with serious argument was like "charging a cannon for the destruction of a vermin." [14]

When Livingston and Smith channeled their anticlericalism into an impassioned indictment of sectarian education, Anglican clerics responded within the context defined by the earlier quarrel, stepping up their defense of the clergy, the Anglican church, and sound Christianity. Reverend Samuel Seabury accused the Reflectors of seeking to "pull down" the Episcopal and Dutch Reformed churches, "aggrandize" the Presbyterian church upon their ruins, and "engross the sole Government of our College." Samuel Johnson worried more about the far-reaching challenge to Christianity posed by a "free thinking latitudinarian seminary" where "no sort of religion was to be taught" at all. Convinced that their antagonists in New York and their competitors at Princeton were working hand in glove, the clerics wondered out loud why a sectarian college was a blessing in New Jersey but a curse in New York. Could it be that the *Independent Reflector* sought to undermine plans for a college in New York in order to protect Princeton's educational hegemony? [15]

From April through October 1753, Seabury, Johnson, Wetmore, Reverend William Smith, Henry Barclay, and Thomas Bradbury Chandler contributed essays regularly to the *New York Mercury*. We "were like to be trod upon by our most inveterate enemies . . . ," the clerics explained, no doubt frustrated that animosity toward the Anglican church had seemingly dogged them from New England into the middle colonies.[16] Livingston, William Smith, Jr., and an occasional collaborator matched the clerics week after week, mainly in the *Independent Reflector*. John Morin Scott, a fellow Presbyterian, Yale alumnus, and New York City lawyer, helped Livingston and Smith out the most, forming with them an able triumvirate.

On a few points florid rhetoric magnified the actual distance separating the two camps. The Anglican clerics readily conceded that "all protestant Youths should be admitted on a perfect Parity" with full toleration of their religious beliefs. The triumvirate, in turn, proposed to require attendance at daily religious services within the college walls. A "regular and due Discipline" was impossible without it, argued Smith, Jr. Yet, while Smith maintained that a college "ought to be a mere civil Institution . . . without any Intention to teach Religion," Samuel Johnson never wavered from his conviction that the chief goal of a college was to give children "a truly Christian education" by teaching them Christianity's "most wise principles and its most pure and holy practices." And while the clerics stood firm in their contention that the "Established Church" should have a "Preference" in the college, the Reflectors denied that Anglicanism was established in New York and continued to insist on a nonsectarian institution.[17]

Just how fundamental a conflict it was became obvious as each side appealed to history, authority, and first principles. The *Independent Reflector* drew on a tradition of radical dissent rooted in the English civil war of the mid-seventeenth century and iden-

tified chiefly with the libertarian writings of John Trenchard and
Thomas Gordon in the 1720s. The Anglicans invoked the authority of the High Church Tories whom Trenchard and Gordon had
attacked—defenders of Crown and Church like William Oldisworth and William Hume.[18] In other words, Livingston and
Smith drew on the left wing of early eighteenth-century English
political thinking, the clerics on the right wing. The intellectual
debt was so explicit that each side saw fit to reprint pamphlets
from the earlier struggle. Well aware that Livingston and Smith
had modeled the *Independent Reflector* on Trenchard and Gordon's
Independent Whig, the clerics came out in June with *An Answer To
some late Papers, Entitled, The Independent Whig* . . . , penned by an
Anglican clergyman in 1723. Livingston, Smith, and John Morin
Scott responded in September with the publication of Thomas
Gordon's 1720 essay, *The Craftsmen* . . . , adding a virulently an-
ticlerical preface which condemned the clerics' "dark and horrible
Plot for usurping the sole Rule of the College." [19]

Week after week the Reflectors and the clerics confronted New
Yorkers with the sharp differences in their conceptions of the
state, the relationship of state and church, and the religious and
political implications of denominational pluralism. Where the Reflectors argued that government originated from a compact among
men and that citizens retained the right of resistance, the clerics
insisted that God himself "put" men under government and
"made it their Duty to be obedient to Rule and Order." Ridicu-
lous notions about the "Origin of Power in the People" were just
what one might expect from the "whimsical Noodles" of their opponents, cried the clerics. Where the Reflectors contended that
religion was primarily a matter of individual conscience and had
"nothing to do with the Interest of the State," the clerics maintained that religion had always been the "Magistrate's principal
Care." Was there "any Thing so friendly to Government as Religion, or of so much Use and Importance to make Men good Citizens . . . as to plant the Fear of God in their Hearts . . . ?" [20]

To the Reflectors, a myriad of sects clashing over theology and
ritual only confirmed one's ultimate dependence on individual
conscience. To the clerics, denominational pluralism vindicated

clerical authority. It pained and disgusted them to envision a world turned "loose, to wander in Search of Truth, without a Guide, among all those dangerous Sects and Opinions laid before us." [21] To the Reflectors, only a balance of power among churches would preserve the liberty of each group and a stable order among them all. Give one church superior authority and it would tyrannize the rest. Fear and resentment would burgeon among the dissenting groups and result in perpetual chaos. To the clerics, the key to stability lay in benevolent power, not in a balance of power. The scramble for preeminence would end only when the state recognized one church as superior and—in the Church of England's case—relied on its historical record of benevolence toward dissenters.

By the fall of 1753 it must have been obvious to New York newspaper readers how serious a division separated the warring factions. The Anglican clerics themselves could not help but think that their stature as leaders had been seriously impugned. Month after month the triumvirate berated their character and questioned their function. The clerics conceived themselves to be the spiritual fathers of the community, coordinate with and just as indispensable as the political fathers. The Reflectors declared them dangerous to the state, irrelevant to education, and superfluous to religion.

It was thus a controversy that swirled around the college, although often not dealing directly with it. Yet the college remained the hard, immediate, vital issue. The triumvirate warned that an Anglican victory would encourage a full church establishment by inviting encroachments in other areas and by placing the education of New York's youth in the hands of imperious men. "Shall we who were Priest-ridden and Priest-beggar'd at home, tamely submit to the cumbrous Yoke here . . . ?" [22] The essential nature of the college seemed to hang in the balance. The clerics envisioned a college whose organization and educational message would reflect in several respects the values and conceptions of High Church Anglicanism. The triumvirate unveiled plans for a college without clerics, a college whose organization and educational message would reflect the precepts of radical ideology. Who could doubt that the outcome of the struggle would have a great bearing on the character of the college and its educational impact.

The journalistic battles of 1753 ended only when Anglican politicians threatened the printer of the *Independent Reflector* with a loss of official business and then succeeded in closing the press to Livingston and his fellow "scribblers." With the opposition silenced—"tyrannically suppressed" in Livingston's words—the clerics soon put down their own pens.[23] The press war had aroused quite a clamor in the city and heightened public consciousness about the college. Non-Anglicans responded enthusiastically to the triumvirate's attacks on Anglican lust for dominion, probably more so than to the much-heralded virtues of a free college. As one Presbyterian clergyman later told William Smith, Jr., he applauded efforts to foil "the ambitious Designs of a high-Church Faction for in-grosing the College." Such "vile Encroachments of our Liberties" must be prevented. But he also objected to a free college, since no "Scheme of Religion" was to be "publickly taught" and "every College Law must have the Assembly's Sanction." Who "can imagine that our Assembly, Scarse one of them brought up at the feet of Gamaliel, knows what Laws are necessary for a College!!" [24]

Despite the heat generated by the press war, the Reflectors soon learned that their acerbic prose was having only a minor impact on the politicians. Behind the scenes, plans to found a college gradually unfolded once the assembly reconvened. In July 1753 the legislature authorized an additional college lottery and voted the lottery trustees £500 per annum for seven years to pay a faculty, starting in 1754. In October the situation brightened even more—at least from an Anglican perspective. Governor Clinton stepped down, and his replacement immediately committed suicide (for reasons not related to the King's College Controversy). Lieutenant Governor James DeLancey, who favored an Anglican college, became acting governor, a position he held for the next two years. That same month Samuel Johnson visited New York City to consult with Anglican leaders about the conditions under which he would accept the presidency of the college, if, as the Anglicans expected, the position were offered to him.[25]

Up to this point the college trustees had done nothing more than lend out the lottery funds at interest and view the land offered by Trinity Church. No meetings had been held since April 1752. Now they set May 1754 as a target date for opening the college and decided to name a president and a "second master." But at the trustees meeting on November 22, 1753, William Livingston stole the march on the Anglicans by proposing Samuel Johnson for the presidency and then submitting the name of Chauncey Whittelsey, a Congregationalist, for the second position. The trustees unanimously approved the compromise, probably several of them wholeheartedly. But John Chambers and perhaps others did so because they really had no other choice. They wanted Johnson, but to accept Johnson and reject Whittelsey would risk a public hubbub and would sustain Livingston's contention that the Anglicans desired nothing short of exclusive control. Anglican lay leaders on both sides of the Whittelsey question had had enough public furor. They even vetoed James Wetmore's plans to publish additional essays on the Church of England's establishment in New York.[26] The Anglican clerics, however, were not in such an accommodating mood. Indeed, they were emboldened by Trinity Church's decision to contribute £150 per annum toward Johnson's salary, officially for his services as assistant minister.

On the surface Chauncey Whittelsey seemed an innocuous choice for "second master." He was a New Haven businessman, not a cleric, and an Old Light unsympathetic to the Great Awakening. While a student and tutor at Yale in the 1730s and 1740s he had impressed Johnson as an "extraordinary" scholar and Livingston as an excellent teacher.[27] Yet, Johnson did not relish the prospect of sharing his college with a Connecticut Congregationalist, particularly one who preached occasionally (in fact, Whittelsey felt strongly enough about his preaching to forego his business career for the pulpit a few years later). Johnson did not veto Whittelsey. But he did express his displeasure to his New York allies, and he held out hopes that Reverend William Smith or "some worthy fellow" at Oxford or Cambridge might get the second spot. Reverend Henry Barclay and John Chambers, more vehement in their opposition to Whittelsey, tried to quash his invitation from the trustees, and, when that failed, sought a way to make the post objectionable to him. Meanwhile, neither Johnson nor Whittelsey would accept the position offered him until the college took on a clearer shape.[28]

The trustees did not open the college in May 1754, but they came close. They met several times that month and agreed on such issues as a temporary location (Trinity Church's new schoolhouse) and a public announcement outlining the college's goals, curriculum, and policies on admissions and religion. The announcement was prepared by Samuel Johnson, who spent part of April and most of May in New York City, consulting several times with Chambers, Murray, and company, and consenting tentatively to head the college.[29] When the announcement appeared in the press early in June it must have convinced some New Yorkers that the threat of Anglican oppression was illusory. Johnson pledged that the college would not "impose on the scholars, the peculiar tenets of any particular sect of Christians," but would "inculcate upon their tender minds, the great principles of Christianity and morality in which true Christians of each denomination are generally agreed." Students were to attend religious services on Sundays, but they could do so at any place of worship approved by their parents. Daily worship at the college would consist of "a collection of lessons, prayers, and praises of the liturgy of the Church," mostly, however, "taken out of the Holy Scriptures" and only such as were "in the best manner expressive of our common Christianity." The Anglicans had taken a similar stand in 1753. Indeed, earlier in 1754 Johnson had ardently defended the religious liberties of college students against the incursions of President Thomas Clap of Yale, who had barred Anglican students from attending the newly built Anglican church in New Haven. Now Johnson, speaking as head of the College of New York, publicly committed himself on the eve of the college's opening to a position that seemed eminently more liberal than Clap's and equal in its tolerance to anything propounded by Princeton. If Princeton claimed to be a "catholic" institution, certainly the College of New York could claim no less.[30]

The Anglicans, however, had already bungled the issue on another front. During the numerous "private consultations" early in May the Anglican leaders, probably at the behest of hard-liners like Barclay, Chambers, and Wetmore, decided to insist upon two stipulations in the college charter they were then drafting: the president must always be an Anglican, and the daily worship services must be based on the Anglican liturgy. On May 14 the Trinity Church vestry officially made these stipulations a condition of their gift of land. Two days later the trustees approved the charter draft, with one trustee dissenting—William Livingston. He blasted the charter with twenty reasons why it was unjust, unwise, and illegal. Within days he and Smith had mounted a new campaign against "Trinity Church College." [31]

Livingston undoubtedly would have raised a fuss about any charter drafted by the Anglicans. But to demand a religious test for the college presidency played right into his hands. There were thirty-five Presbyterian churches in New York at mid-century, and their communicants thrived on their historical identity as the defenders of religious conscience against an oppressive Anglican church. [32] In the *Independent Reflector* the year before Livingston had succeeded in arousing the anxiety of Presbyterians about an Anglican college by appealing to their folk memories of "Afflictions" and "fiery Trials" endured by "pious Predecessors" in the name of "Liberty of Conscience." "And will you endanger that dear-bought Toleration," he asked his Presbyterian readers, "for which they retired into voluntary Banishment, for which they agoniz'd, and for which they bled?" Now Livingston had tangible evidence to substantiate his warnings of a renewed Anglican attack on their liberties, for nothing so symbolized to Presbyterians the arbitrary nature of Anglican rule than the infamous Test Acts, which required all English officeholders to take communion in the Church of England. To "suffer any Sect to introduce such Tests for any Civil Office," exhorted Livingston, would gradually reestablish "that antient Yoke of Bondage to escape which our Forefathers abandoned their native Country and were prosecuted for their noble opposition like the most flagitious Malefactors." No matter how vociferously Anglicans might insist that King's College was just as catholic as Princeton, Livingston could always point out that there was not a "Syllable" in Princeton's charter that "looks like appropriating it to any particular Persuasion of Christians." Princeton's trustees could name even an Anglican churchman to the presidency, should they so chose.[33]

While the Anglicans strengthened Livingston's hand, they gained little themselves. Their candidate for the presidency had already won the job, and their draft of the charter left the college in Anglican hands even without the two controversial stipulations, since it created a self-perpetuating board of governors dominated by Anglicans. But the Anglicans, jarred by the *Independent Reflector*'s challenge in 1753, feared that their small numbers and New York's religious diversity made them vulnerable to attack, if only at some indefinite point in the future. Why not use Trinity Church's gift of land as a quid pro quo and secure a legal preference for the Church of England while they had the opportunity. With DeLancey in the governor's chair, and Chambers, Murray, and Edward Holland on the council, approval of the college charter should be an easy matter. Anglican prospects in the assembly were less certain, but there were indications that the assemblymen would surrender the lottery funds.[34] In any case, the charter was valid without the assembly's assent, a point that Samuel Johnson used to reassure his anxious son late in May. Yes, replied his son, but the college depended on the assembly for "support & principal encouragemt.," and should the Reflectors organize a "party" in the assembly against the Anglicans, the results could be devastating. Johnson himself recognized another soft spot in Anglican planning when he commented that Acting Governor DeLancey provided "only a buttress, not a pillar." [35] The most influential political figure in mid-century New York, DeLancey retained his power by juggling successfully a complex set of political interests. Backers of an Anglican college expected his support, but DeLancey realized it was a risky issue. He knew that with so few Anglicans in the electorate he could soon dissipate his strength in the assembly over a minor question if he were not careful.

Anglican calculations misfired before the month was out. Their petition for a charter passed the council, but two councillors, seizing an opportunity to splinter DeLancey's political following, gave the Anglicans "no small surprise" by protesting vehemently against it. The acting governor hesitated to grant the charter. Livingston and Smith soon gave him additional reason for pause. Knowing the "Governors Fondness of Popularity," they figured that DeLancey would hold off issuing a charter "till he had an opportunity of knowing the opinion of the House at their next session . . . ," scheduled for mid-August. If they could turn the assemblymen against the charter in the meantime, DeLancey might reject it.[36]

Angling to build up constituent pressures on the assemblymen, Livingston and Smith sounded an alarm against ecclesiastical tyranny throughout the rural counties of New York, where the Anglicans had "but a slender Influence." They lined up agents in each of these counties, relying heavily on Presbyterian ministers and Presbyterian assemblymen, and canvassed part of the backcountry themselves. With "all possible Industry" they distributed anticharter propaganda and circulated petitions which damned the "Party College" and called for a "Free" one. When the assembly convened in August, Smith reported gleefully that the Anglican charter was "the most unpopular Thing in the World." Livingston predicted that the assembly would incorporate its own college, basing it on the proposals in the *Independent Reflector.* Actually, anticharter sentiment in the assembly fell short of both men's expectations, but it was strong enough to dissuade DeLancey from granting the Anglican charter, at least until "the Heat of the people was a littled abated."

That, of course, was just what Smith and Livingston would not allow. As soon as the assembly adjourned until October they renewed their campaign in the backcountry. By September the Anglicans were so exasperated with Acting Governor DeLancey that they charged him with duplicity.[37] Some of the Anglican clerics could not understand why a statesman should pay heed to "a few forced Petitions, from distant Counties, signed by ignorant People, that know not what they are about." Livingston retorted that the "Voice of the People is the Voice of God." [38]

Despite DeLancey's laggardness, Johnson had opened the college in July. Soon he was meeting regularly with eight students, "the majority of whom were admitted, though utterly unqualified, in order to make a flourish," snickered Livingston. Johnson, however, did not regard a charterless college as much of a flourish, and his humor was not helped by the lack of an assistant. Seriously ill, Whittelsey lingered in New Haven, waiting for his disease and the turbulence in New York to abate. Johnson himself departed for Connecticut on September 1, when he learned that his son had been "seized with a violent fit of sickness." He stayed two months. To say the least, it was an inauspicious beginning for King's College.[39]

James DeLancey could not sit on a political fence indefinitely. When the assembly convened in mid-October he realized that tensions had not eased and that support for the college charter was slipping. The issue was proving distressingly attractive to political antagonists who saw an opportunity to undermine DeLancey's power. Earlier in October DeLancey had bowed to pressure from the Anglicans and agreed tentatively to go ahead with the charter. Joseph Murray, John Chambers, and the acting governor then had worked out a new draft which retained the controversial stipulations but sought to make the charter more palatable to its enemies, probably by broadening representation on the board of governors—"bait . . . to prevent my opposition," Livingston called his own nomination to the board.[40] When DeLancey saw the drift of events in the assembly he decided to act. On October 31 he called a meeting of the council, won approval of the new charter, and signed it himself two days later. Barclay communicated the delightful news to Johnson and even put in a good word for DeLancey, since he had given them "a good majority of churchmen" on the board of governors. On November 10 Johnson returned to New York City and resumed classes.[41]

Despite the Anglican victory, no one believed the crisis was over. DeLancey himself refused to turn over the charter to the new board of governors, thus leaving the college for the time being in control of the lottery trustees. Perhaps DeLancey did so to mute the anger of his opponents while he inveigled the assembly into confirming the charter and transferring the lottery proceeds to King's College. In any case, it was plain that he had a fight on his hands on both counts. Already the assembly had come close to censuring the lottery trustees for exceeding their authority in petitioning for a royal charter. Early in November Livingston's brother introduced a bill in the assembly to establish a "free college," organized along the lines suggested by the *Independent Reflector.* Let the Anglicans have their "Trinity Church College," the Reflectors seemed to be saying, but do not confuse it with the provincial college first proposed by the assembly in 1746—"Trinity Church College is set up in opposition to the College of New York. . . ." [42] Only the latter, a nonsectarian, publicly controlled institution, deserved public support and provincial identity. Livingston and Smith suspected that the "free college" bill would never get by the Anglican-controlled council, but should it pass the assembly it would at least solidify opposition in the lower house to public funding for King's College. The Reflectors set their sights on preventing King's College from collecting the several thousand pounds raised by assembly-authorized lotteries since 1747. Success on this score plus a refusal by the assembly to confirm the royal charter would dim any chances of public support for King's College in the future. [43]

The opposing forces soon realized that neither side had the strength to push through its measures. The assembly adjourned in a stalemate, and the controversy shifted to the press. In mid-November the publisher of the *New York Mercury* had reversed his former policy and opened his columns to all parties in the conflict. The Reflectors promptly launched a new weekly essay series— "The Watch-Tower"—which ran in the *Mercury* for twelve tempestuous months. Livingston assumed the major burden of writing, seeking to keep "the Province warm" until the assembly reconvened. [44] When the Anglicans assembled their own team of penmen, with the clerics aided this time by Benjamin Nicoll and John Chambers, the publisher of the *Mercury* found himself besieged by the ferocious scribblings of both camps. Each side reviewed the college movement—Livingston its perversion by "Church Bigots," the clerics its disruption by advocates of "Anarchy and Confusion." Livingston compared the *"Party College"* in New York unfavorably with Princeton's catholic design. This infuriated the clerics, who would have thrilled at having the control over King's College that Presbyterian clergymen enjoyed at Princeton. Livingston himself became enraged when Nicoll publicly accused him of falsifying the minutes of the lottery trustees. Livingston "raves about like a Madman," reported one Anglican, and "says that one Town can't hold him [and] ye Author of that Peice." [45]

While each faction maligned the other, they both began cultivating the Dutch Reformed. The Anglicans emphasized the parallels in the organization of the Church of England with that of the Reformed Church of the United Netherlands (to which the Dutch Reformed churches in New York belonged)— a "sisterly *Relation*," the Anglicans called it. The "Watch-Tower" cursed such a "pretended *Affinity*," argued that the two churches differed widely in "Constitution, Doctrine, Discipline and Manners," and condemned "all Episcopalian Pretenders to Sisterhood, as Enemies to the Purity and Prosperity of the *Dutch Church.*" [46] The reason both sides curried favor with the Dutch Reformed was simple. They believed that the Dutch held the balance of power and that an alliance with them could bring victory in the assembly. The Dutch, however, had ideas of their own about organizing a college.

4.

THE KING'S COLLEGE CONTROVERSY: THE DUTCH AND THE DENOUEMENT

A "STEADY FRIEND AND MOST GENEROUS BENEFACTOR" to King's College—so reads the tombstone of Paul Richard, a prosperous New York City merchant and politician who died in 1756. The tombstone can be found at Trinity Church, as one might expect of a man who gave £500 to "Trinity Church College." [1] But in life Richard was a member and officer of the Dutch Reformed church. Death cut short his efforts in behalf of King's College, but other members of the city's Dutch church backed the college from its founding to its closing. Only three men attended more than 70 of the 108 meetings of the college governors from 1755 to 1781. All three belonged to the Dutch church, one of them its senior minister and the other two former deacons. [2] Indeed, for a time in the 1750s it seemed that King's College might become a center for training Dutch Reformed clergymen.

Like New Yorkers of other faiths, Dutch church people participated in the college movement in a variety of ways: through votes in the assembly on lottery bills and other college legislation, through purchases of lottery tickets and signatures on petitions, through conversations in homes and taverns about the college's location and control, and in a few cases through private gifts of money and publication of newspaper essays or pamplets. Among the leaders of the project Dutch churchmen figured prominently: as sponsors of assembly legislation affecting the college from 1746 through 1753, as two of the more active members of the board of lottery trustees which organized the college, and as one-fourth of those governors who actually managed the college in the 1750s once Acting Governor James DeLancey delivered the charter to them.[3]

What distinguished these Dutch Reformed gentlemen from some of their fellow churchmen was their willingness to work closely with the Anglicans. They were, as Reverend Henry Barclay of Trinity Church called them, "good friends." [4] They did not feel threatened by an Anglican preference in the college, nor did they judge such a preference detrimental to the colony's future. The Anglican church, like the Dutch church, served the cause of humanity and religion, a common purpose which overshadowed doctrinal and organizational differences. Any number of factors could have muted the "good friends' " sense of Dutch Reformed distinctiveness. Most of them traced their ancestry back to Scotland, Germany, and France, not Holland. Most had prospered as merchants in a community where religious boundaries melted before business alliances, friendships, and marriages, and where English had replaced Dutch as the principal language in politics and business. Some probably found an appealing figure in Reverend Henry Barclay, whose Dutch ancestry, Dutch wife, and command of the Dutch language helped him mediate between the Anglican and Dutch churches. Even Johannes Ritzema, the Dutch-born and educated dominie (minister) of the Reformed church in New York City, developed a cordial relationship with Barclay and supported the Anglicans throughout the King's College Controversy. Amidst the howl generated by Smith and Livingston in the summer of 1754, Ritzema enrolled his only son in the college's first class. Other Dutch Reformed families, including many of actual Dutch extraction, followed suit during the college's first decade. From Samuel Verplanck in 1754 through Henry Rutgers in 1763, probably close to one-third of the matriculants at King's College came from Dutch Reformed families.[5]

Samuel Verplanck (B.A., King's College, 1758)
Verplanck was a member of the first class at King's College and a fifth-generation descendant of one of New York's early Dutch settlers. The portrait is by John Singleton Copley.
CREDIT: COLUMBIANA, COLUMBIA UNIVERSITY

William Livingston and his confederates realized early in 1753 that to defeat Anglican plans they must mobilize the Dutch Reformed—the largest religious group in the colony—against a "Church College." Yet the task posed its difficulties. Barclay's pro-Anglican "good friends" were prominent members of the

New York City congregation, the biggest, wealthiest, and most influential Dutch congregation in the colony. Moreover, James DeLancey numbered several Dutch politicians among his following in the assembly.[6] Characteristically, the Reflectors took to the press. Their initial effort, from Barclay's partisan viewpoint, was a "Malicious Slandrous Peice." Written in Dutch ostensibly by a Dutch Reformed clergyman, it exhorted all congregations (according to Barclay) to "take up arms" against the Anglicans or else suffer the "Utter Destruction" that would inevitably result from Anglican control of the college. Barclay penned a reply in Dutch, while Samuel Seabury publicly labeled the piece an "impudent and scandalous Forgery" and warned of a Presbyterian scheme to undermine the Dutch church.[7] Occasional appeals to the Dutch punctuated the remaining months of 1753, with each faction warning of the other's lust for "Dominion" and emphasizing the harmony of its own church's doctrine and organization with those of the Dutch Reformed church.

In the fall of 1753 the Reflectors tried a new, less direct means of enlisting Dutch support. William Smith, Jr., used the *Occasional Reverberator*, a short-lived companion journal to the *Independent Reflector*, to warn the Dutch in New York City that their church was "continually declining" in numbers and influence because it clung exclusively to the Dutch language. With English prevailing in the political, commercial, and social life of the city, Dutch had become so "Useless" that many Dutch youngsters did not understand it. Smith cautioned that unless services were conducted in English at one of the two Dutch churches in the city, young communicants would continue to flee to other denominations.[8]

Smith articulated a genuine problem in the Dutch church. Church members lamented that "their Youth daily fall off to other Churches," and some agreed with Smith that the explanation lay in the "prevailing Use of the English Language" outside the church. In fact, William Livingston himself had earlier switched to the Presbyterian church when he could no longer understand Dutch sermons.[9] However, the prospective fruits of introducing English language services also meshed nicely with the Reflectors' goals in the King's College Controversy. They expected the use of English to stop the flow of Dutch churchmen to the Anglicans, who, Livingston noted resentfully, had "grown numerous by their acquisitions from the Dutch." Moreover, a revitalized Dutch church could serve as a counterweight to Trinity Church and thus help preserve the "Ballance of Power" which the Reflectors considered the key to religious liberty and order. Finally, Livingston believed that only the Dutch language stood between a "firm Coalition" among Dutch churchmen and Presbyterians. Once the language barrier was removed, they could meet on the common ground of rigorous Calvinism and together keep the Anglicans in check.[10]

The triumvirate probably encouraged language reform through private channels as well as the press, especially through Livingston's brother, Philip, a deacon in the city's Dutch church. In any case, eighty-seven members of the Dutch church signed a petition in February 1754 which briefly restated Smith's case from the *Reverberator*. But, according to Livingston, a "dissenting part" of the congregation and several Dutch ministers were "warmly bent on opposing it," so its advocates postponed the matter "in Expectation of a more favourable Juncture." Dominie Ritzema vowed that, rather than see an English minister in a Dutch pulpit, he would lay his head upon the block and say, "Cut it off." [11]

By the end of May 1754 the triumvirate had little to show for their efforts. The two Dutch Reformed lottery trustees had voted solidly with the Anglicans on every issue, including the Anglican draft of the college charter, and the assembly had as yet shown no signs of disaffection toward the project. Samuel Johnson was optimistic that the "Dutch friendship" would pay off in assembly approval of the charter, while William Livingston lamented the "Supiness & Inactivity" of the city's Dutch congregation in the face of Anglican imperiousness.[12]

The triumvirate finally made some headway in the fall when Dutch churchmen in parts of rural New York signed some petitions against the Anglican charter.[13] But this accomplishment paled in significance before a dramatic turn of events in New York City. The consistory of the Dutch Reformed church in the city (its ruling body—ministers, elders, deacons, and churchmasters) decided to petition the assembly for a Dutch professor of divinity in the new college. The decision to petition reflected a convergence of two developments. On the one hand it grew out of a conflict no less crucial for the future of the Dutch church than the controversy over language. The Dutch churches of New York and their respective consistories were subordinate to the Classis of Amsterdam (the governing body of the Dutch Reformed churches in the Amsterdam district), which had sole authority to ordain candidates for the Dutch Reformed ministry in the American colonies and reviewed (if it did not make) all significant decisions affecting the colonial churches. Just as Samuel Johnson and his fellow Anglican clerics lobbied for a colonial bishop who could ordain candidates for the Episcopal ministry and make ecclesiastical decisions on the spot, so some Dutch churchmen wanted to organize a local association which could respond quickly and personally to Dutch church problems and ordain prospective ministers without their undertaking an expensive, time-consuming, and hazardous voyage to Holland. In 1747 the Classis of Amsterdam agreed to the formation of a coetus (an association of ministers and elders from member churches) in the colonies, but it was subordinate to the Classis of Amsterdam, and its powers were so limited that some of its members soon called for a full-blown American classis. The proposal made no mention of formal education for prospective ministers who were to be ordained by the new classis, but the implication was obvious.[14] American-born ministers would soon fill most colonial pulpits as an American classis weakened ties to Holland and the supply of ministers from the fatherland dried up. American ministerial candidates would hardly relish a voyage to Holland for study when they no longer needed to go there for ordination.

On October 1, 1754, the consistory of the Dutch church in New York City flatly rejected the proposal for a classis, apparently fearful that a local classis could intrude in the consistory's affairs much more efficiently than one in Amsterdam. The New Light sympathies of Theodore Frelinghuysen, the leader of the proclassis forces, stiffened the opposition of some members, who looked dimly on his revivalistic brand of Calvinism. Nor did some church officers, including the two Holland-born ministers, like the prospect of severing their close connections with the fatherland, the kind of sentiment that earlier spurred opposition to the introduction of English. Orthodox Calvinism and a Dutch identity seemed safer in present hands.

It seems contradictory, then, that at the very meeting in which the consistory rejected the classis they also resolved to petition for a Dutch professor of divinity in the College of New York. The explanation lies in the consistory's expectation that they would control the professorship. It would expand rather than contract their autonomy, permit them to nominate a professor whose theological beliefs accorded with their own, and provide an alternative to and possibly preempt any plan instituted by an American classis, should its formation gain approval. The consistory anticipated only one college in New York, and its Dutch professor of divinity would be at their beck and call, not Frelinghuysen's. Despite their stand against a classis, they had no trouble understanding that many prospective ministers would prefer to study in New York rather than, "at a vast expense to the parents, be obliged to reside several years in Holland. . . ." [15]

If the consistory's proposal reflected their antagonism toward a classis, the decision also was prompted by their growing distrust of the Anglicans. By October William Livingston's brother, Philip, had spent weeks sowing seeds of distrust among the Dutch toward Anglican plans for the college. Livingston singled out the church's second minister, Lambertus Deronde, and convinced him, as well as several key laymen, that unless the Dutch Reformed church moved quickly it might be shut out from any influence in the college. The triumvirate cooperated behind the scenes. Petitioning the assembly for a Dutch professorship of divinity was a "most refined Peice of Policy," William Smith, Jr., later noted, "and I incouraged the first mention of it. . . ." Either the petition would pass and thus breach the Anglican grip on the college, or else the Anglicans would squelch it and incur the wrath of the Dutch, a split which the triumvirate had been promoting for months.[16]

Meanwhile, the consistory had appointed a committee to draft a petition, but two committee members, Ritzema and Paul Richard, opposed the idea. The Anglicans had managed at just that point, after weeks of dickering, to persuade Acting Governor DeLancey that he should sign the college charter. The Dutch petition could disrupt their planning, particularly if it were addressed to the assembly instead of DeLancey, who considered himself the appropriate authority. John Chambers suggested that the Dutch wait until DeLancey signed the charter and then petition the newly created governors of the college for the Dutch professorship. Ritzema and Richard agreed to cooperate. They made their case at a consistory meeting on October 16. Philip Livingston, however, had already stacked the cards against them. At the annual elections for the consistory held that same day, Livingston "so managed the Voters" (William Smith, Jr.'s, words) as to keep out friends of the Anglicans. Livingston gave Deronde a petition to the provincial assembly drafted by William Smith, Jr., and Deronde cajoled the new consistory into accepting a modified version of it. On October 25 this petition was formally introduced into the assembly.[17]

The decision of the Dutch to bypass DeLancey irked the acting governor, but, much to the relief of the Anglicans, he skirted the issue and signed the royal charter for the college a week later. Now the Anglicans, assured of control over the college, agreed with two Dutch assemblymen on a compromise which would give the college the lottery funds and the Dutch their professorship. A bill was drawn up with "great hopes" that it would win the support of other Dutch assemblymen. But now some of the Dutch were reluctant to ally themselves with a college so firmly in Anglican hands, and the triumvirate was determined to prevent the Anglicans from securing the lottery proceeds. Samuel Johnson painfully reported early in December 1754 that the Reflectors had "made such a stir among the Dutch" that the Anglicans had given up on the compromise bill for the current session of the assembly. Throughout the early months of 1755 the press war continued unabated, with each side wooing the Dutch, but the legislature focused its attention on the more urgent issues raised by the outbreak of the French and Indian War (1754–1763).[18]

In May 1755 the issue moved off dead center when DeLancey finally delivered the charter to the college governors. They held their first meeting and hammered out a new strategy with DeLancey and Ritzema. DeLancey himself (with the council's approval) issued an additional charter, giving the consistory the right to appoint a Dutch professor of divinity. The Anglicans hoped this concession would placate the Dutch and thereby extricate the lottery funds from the grasp of the assembly. But when the college governors petitioned the assembly for the funds, the assembly confounded the Anglicans by postponing consideration of their petition indefinitely.[19] "The Reflectors Triumph!" Johnson's youngest son admitted sourly. William Smith, Jr., later noted with more enthusiasm than accuracy that "universal Joy possessed every Breast upon this Occasion. . . ."[20]

Obviously the additional charter had not had the anticipated impact. The Reflectors could claim some of the credit, but growing dissension within the Dutch church also undercut Anglican strategy. Throughout the spring of 1755 Theodore Frelinghuysen berated the Anglicans for Arminianism and for monopolizing the college. The Dutch must arouse themselves from their "Infatuation, Stupidity and Lethargy," cried Frelinghuysen, and sever their ties with the "High Church College" in New York. Otherwise the Anglicans would "promote their domineering Sway" by enticing Dutch youngsters from the church of their fathers. The leaders of Princeton at least were less grasping and more sound theologically. But the Dutch had "no Business" with either college.[21] Frelinghuysen asked representatives from all Dutch congregations in the colonies to meet in May, so that they might ratify plans for an American classis and a Dutch academy. On the very day that the governor and council of New York approved the additional charter, Frelinghuysen's convention commissioned him to seek funds in Holland for the first Dutch university in the new world.[22]

"This effectually thwarted the design of Rev. Ritzema," the proponents of an American classis and seminary wrote triumphantly to the Classis of Amsterdam a few months later. Ritzema, however, was not through. The consistory of the New York City

Dutch church was little more enthusiastic about Frelinghuysen's classis in 1755 than it had been in 1754. Along with several other churches, the New York City Dutch church withdrew from the Frelinghuysen-dominated coetus, which approved plans for a classis and seminary, and formed a rival association, known as a conferentie. Ritzema immediately enlisted the clerical members of the conferentie in support of the Dutch professorship at King's College. But the thorn in Ritzema's side was now his own consistory.[23] They controlled the professorship, and they would not fill it. Instead they censured Ritzema for his part in procuring the additional charter.

Elected the previous October under Philip Livingston's watchful eye, the consistory had never appreciated Ritzema's habit of collaborating with the Anglicans nor his desire to seek a professorship from the college governors rather than from the provincial assembly. The Anglican flavor of the King's College charter only heightened their wariness. Despite the assembly's failure to act on the October 1754 petition for a professorship, the consistory considered it still a matter to be worked out between the assembly and themselves, if there was to be a professorship at all. A minority, which favored an American classis and seminary, was unalterably opposed to the professorship at King's College regardless of who granted it. Ritzema thus exasperated his consistory when, without consulting them, he blithely arranged for the professorship through the additional charter from DeLancey. It nettled them all the more that the charter neither provided a salary for the professorship nor protected its holder from arbitrary removal by the Anglican-dominated board of governors. The consistory was hardly prepared to cooperate with the Anglicans and pay for the favor themselves.[24]

The Anglicans were not about to pay for the professorship either. Its establishment had not brought them victory in the assembly. And without the lottery funds the financial future of King's College was uncertain. The Reflectors hoped that Sir Charles Hardy, the new governor of New York who arrived in December 1755, would call for assembly elections which might give the Reflectors the edge they needed to resolve the legislative stalemate in their favor. Instead, Hardy gave "new life" to the Anglicans by subscribing £500 to the college.[25] The time seemed ripe for a compromise, so the Anglicans proposed to forego the £500 per annum for seven years appropriated by the assembly in 1753 in return for the lottery funds and assembly confirmation of their charter. Livingston responded by gathering up a bundle of anticharter petitions to present to the assembly and by blasting the scheme in a special issue of *The Watch-Tower*.[26] The Anglicans dropped the idea. The issue once again slipped into the background and remained there throughout most of 1756.

At long last in November 1756, Samuel Johnson was able to report to his son that the "party struggles about the college" were now "at an end." Wearied by the protracted conflict, the contestants agreed to divide the lottery proceeds between the college and the city of New York, the latter to use part of it for a "pest house" (a lodging for the crews of "infected vessels"). "It rids us of a bone of contention, by dividing it between the two pest houses," commented William Smith, Sr.[27] The Reflectors abandoned their "free college," the Anglicans their hopes for assembly confirmation of the college charter.

Johannes Ritzema, however, would not relinquish his quest for a Dutch professor of divinity, a goal the Classis of Amsterdam unwittingly encouraged by ridiculing Frelinghuysen's proposed independent seminary as a "queer" notion. In 1758 the conferentie assured their superiors in Amsterdam that "our Academy established at New York prospers remarkably . . ." and that they would use their "privilege" to call a professor of theology "at the first opportunity." In the mid-1760s Ritzema almost persuaded the college governors and the conferentie each to provide £200 annually for a divinity professor, but the arrangement fell through. Ritzema appealed for support from the Classis of Amsterdam in 1769, but the classis rejected the idea as "impracticable" and criticized Ritzema for being "too strongly attached" to the Anglicans. At no time could Ritzema convince his own consistory to endorse his efforts, in part because of their fear that "the Dutch churches would run the risk of being, with their Confession, absorbed by such a Union. . . ."[28]

By 1771 it was too late. The conferentie reunited with the Dutch Reformed churches of New York and New Jersey to form a general convention, virtually independent of Amsterdam. The "Articles of Union" stipulated that professors of theology called by the convention "shall not stand in any connection with English academies. . . ." [29] In any case, Ritzema's opponents had succeeded in founding their independent college. Sparked by Theodore Frelinghuysen in 1755, the campaign for a Dutch seminary reached its climax in 1771 with the opening of Queen's College, now known as Rutgers University.

5.

"CHURCH COLLEGE" OR PROVINCIAL COLLEGE?

"[W]E STOOD as long as our legs would support us, &, I may add, even fought, for some time, on our Stumps," reminisced William Livingston at the conclusion of the King's College Controversy. Samuel Johnson thanked God that the "jury tryal" was over and that "all opposers stop their mouths." Livingston felt "Vanquished." Johnson was optimistic that his college would "flourish & be a great public Blessing." [1] The outcome, however, could not be measured in simple terms of victory and defeat.

The charter of 1754 was a case in point. Livingston condemned it as a "partial bigotted and iniquitous plan." It was not exactly what James Wetmore had hoped for either. Wetmore had expected that Anglican clerics serving in the six "established" parishes could control the college board of governors and that all governors and faculty would be licensed by the bishop of London. Instead, the bishop of London was denied any authority over the college and, much to Samuel Johnson's dismay, was even removed from the list of governors when the lay authors of the charter revised their draft in October 1754. [2] As for clerics from "established" parishes, the charter but precisely *one* of them on the board—the rector of Trinity Church—and then neutralized his presence by giving ex officio membership to the senior ministers from the Dutch Reformed, Lutheran, French, and Presbyterian churches in New York City. In fact, besides President Samuel Johnson and the archbishop of Canterbury, Trinity's rector was the only Anglican cleric among the forty-two governors. Where Congregational ministers ruled Yale and Presbyterian clerics held a majority of the seats on Princeton's board of trustees, Anglican parsons had little say in the deliberations of the King's College governors.

Even Johnson's power was narrowly circumscribed in the charter, especially when compared with the prerogatives given the president in other college charters. For instance, the authors of the King's College charter followed Princeton's charter on many points—in some cases word for word—but they added a clause reserving for the governors the right "to appoint what books shall be publicly read and taught in the college," a stipulation not found in the charters of Princeton, Harvard, or Yale. Nor was Johnson given the power to preside over governors meetings, a privilege enjoyed by the president of Yale, and, in the absence of the governor of New Jersey, by the president of Princeton. The Anglicans used these limitations on presidential power to assure New Yorkers that the religious test for the presidency should not be considered a grave imposition on their liberties. The president himself would be checked by the governors, who would prevent "his ingrossing too much Power." [3]

If the clerics were less than thrilled with the college charter, they probably were just as perturbed about Benjamin Nicoll's contention that the president need not be an Anglican. Nicoll argued that the religious test would be "no bar" to a Dutch churchman, "moderate" Presbyterian, Lutheran, or French churchman whom the governors regarded as a "proper person" for the presidency.[4] The allusion was to the English practice of "occasional conformity," by which dissenters regularly held political office, despite the Test Acts, through taking communion according to the Anglican prayer book once a year. Nicoll's point was the kind that rankled dissenters rather than mollified them. But it bespoke a flexibility which James Wetmore did not admire, just as it probably irked Wetmore to find that close to a third of the governors were not Anglicans.

The distance between Wetmore's expectations in 1747 and the outcome codified in the charter of 1754 reflected the comparative moderation of the Anglican laymen who guided the college project and their responsiveness, albeit begrudging, to the political pressures generated by the triumvirate. The result was a governing board which, in its interdenominationalism as well as its control by laymen, differed strikingly from that of Princeton. The College of New Jersey's charter of 1748 named Presbyterians to all but two of the twenty-four trustees' positions. Attendance patterns at governing board meetings sharply reveal the contrast between the two schools. From 1758 through 1761 eleven Presbyterian clerics and three Presbyterian laymen attended half or more of the board meetings at Princeton; during the same period of time at King's College half or more of the board meetings were attended by three Anglican clerics, nine Anglican laymen, five Dutch church laymen, and the principal ministers of the Dutch, French, and Lutheran churches in New York City.[5]

The governors of King's College could thus point to a variety of factors which supported their contention that the religious character of the college did not violate its standing as a community institution—the interdenominational makeup of the board and its domination by laymen, the board's control over the president, the clause in the charter guaranteeing "Equal Liberty and advantage of Education" to students "of any Religious Denomination," Samuel Johnson's public pledge that students could worship at a church of their choice on Sundays and that he would not "impose on the scholars, the peculiar tenets of any particular sect of Christians," and the absence of religious tests for faculty or governors.[6] Added to this was the unique position of public officials on the governing board. Whereas no previous college charter had named more than one public officeholder an ex officio trustee, the King's College charter gave ex officio membership to the first commissioner for trade and plantations, the mayor of New York City, and nine provincial officials. Counting both ex officio governors and those appointed by name, the original governing board included the governor of New York, the majority of his council, a quarter of the assemblymen, all three supreme court justices, and the treasurer, secretary, and attorney general of the colony. Little wonder that Anglican founders of King's College regarded it as a public institution!

None of this carried much weight with the triumvirate. The

Anglicans judged their charter against Princeton, Yale, and their own initial expectations and decided it was remarkably generous. The triumvirate measured it against their "free college" and their goal of wresting the college from Anglican hands and labeled it a fraud. After all, Anglicans controlled the board of governors and the presidency. Most of the ex officio officeholders were Crown appointees and Anglicans, not elected officials beholden to the voters. Claims of interdenominational representation masked the fact that only two of the forty-two governors were Presbyterians. As for the religious liberty of the students, they might worship on Sundays at a church of their choice, but the other six days they would attend services conducted by Samuel Johnson out of the liturgy of the Anglican church. Moreover, the "second master" turned out not to be Whittelsey (who was as reluctant to teach at King's College as the Anglicans were to have him) but Samuel Johnson's son.

By marshaling facts like these it was not hard for men of the triumvirate's propagandistic skills to generate a deep resentment against King's College. The way the Reflectors told it, the Anglicans had given not an inch on their despicable plot to monopolize the school. The Anglicans themselves unwittingly cooperated with the triumvirate by chattering about the "Established Church" in New York and by inserting a religious test in the college charter. One result of all this was the termination of public financial support for the college. Even the Anglicans realized that King's College would depend exclusively on private sources of income once the seven-year appropriation ended. Lack of money, however, did not turn out to be the college's affliction. Some Anglican supporters had believed all along that a "preference" for the Anglican church would help attract contributions from prosperous Anglicans, especially in England.[7] They were right. By the mid-1760s King's College had the largest endowment of any American college. "But what will a seminary without students, though richly endowed[,] avail us?" asked William Smith, Jr.[8]

Behind the denial of public funds lay a more serious problem—the provincial assembly's failure to confirm the charter and to confer on the college the legitimacy it desperately needed after three years of public contentiousness. The King's College Controversy was simply dropped, not resolved. In the eyes of many non-Anglicans the college emerged from the struggle as the "little dirty contracted party project" that the triumvirate said it was.[9] Even when religious tensions eased, opponents of the college withheld their approval. No Presbyterian attended a governors meeting until after the American Revolution, despite the appointment of Livingston and the minister of the New York City Presbyterian Church ex officio. Nor did the Frelinghuysen wing of the Dutch Reformed church moderate its hostility. This combined with the coolness of the consistory of the New York City Dutch Church seriously weakened the impact of the endorsement given King's College by Johannes Ritzema and several Dutch Reformed laymen. Samuel Johnson had felt just as antagonistic toward Yale while raising his sons in the 1730s and 1740s, but, as he noted of his oldest boy, "I am obliged to send him to a dissenting College, or deny him any public education at all. . . ."[10] New Yorkers had the luxury of a choice and neither Yale nor Princeton nor, after 1770, Queen's College, was far removed.

A college expected to stimulate a public spirit thus fell victim to divisiveness. Except in a handful of cases, Presbyterian families refused to enroll their sons at King's. Nor was the college well patronized by Dutch Reformed families outside New York City and environs, where in many areas support for Ritzema and the conferentie was relatively weak. The college "makes indeed a most contemptible Figure," William Livingston noted with satisfaction a decade after the King's College Controversy ended, at a time when the entire undergraduate body numbered about twenty-five students. "I rejoice," Livingston continued, "that I have been greatly instrumental in giving it the *fatale vulnus* [fatal wound] in its first origination."[11]

Livingston's wound did not prove fatal. But his success in convincing New Yorkers that King's College was a "Church College"—not a provincial college—seriously hampered efforts to make it a thriving institution. So did the ineffectiveness of the college's affiliation with the Anglican church. The clerics and the governors expected that its position as virtually the only Episcopal college in the colonies—William and Mary they dismissed as "almost at the southern End" of the American colonies—would attract Anglican students from many colonies, including the West Indies.[12] Their hopes proved unrealistic. With its administrative head in London, its missionaries scattered along a four-hundred-mile stretch from Massachusetts to Delaware, and its parishioners scanty in number compared with the dissenters, the Anglican church in the northern colonies was ill equipped to generate much support for a church college. In New England Anglican clerics were simply so enmeshed, physically and psychologically, in the innumerable local problems they confronted each day in their parishes that they found it taxing to unite effectively in almost any kind of campaign. Parishes were too large, catechists and schoolmasters too few, and the hurdles erected by the Congregationalists seemingly unending. Anglican clerics in the middle colonies generally operated in a more favorable political climate, but in the rural areas the burden of duties meant that their horizons, like those of their brethren in New England, often extended no farther than parish boundaries.[13]

Clashes between clerics and vestries also fragmented Anglican efforts, as did conflict among clerics, especially a coolness mixed with occasional bitterness in the relationships between foreign-born and colonial-born clerics. Angered by Samuel Johnson's success at monopolizing the SPG's ear on the appointment of new missionaries, one foreign-born cleric urged the SPG to preserve a "just Ballance between yᵉ Europeans and American's" in the clergy. Upon learning of plans to found a college in New York, he reacted not with enthusiasm but with skepticism, noting that the "multiplication of such small seminaries" would "not advance learning to any remarkable pitch." [14] None of the ten foreign-born Anglican clerics in New York and New Jersey in 1755 participated in the founding of King's College. Nor did American-born clerics, outside an active handful in New York, southern Connecticut, and northern New Jersey, show much concern for the project. Johnson even had a difficult time getting Connecticut colleagues to fill his Stratford pulpit while he struggled in New York City during the summer months of 1754 to start up the college.

One Connecticut cleric publicly censured Johnson for neglecting his church and contended that Johnson had no need to leave it.[15]

Internal squabbling and a pervasive parochialism thus impeded the development of a sense of common purpose and coordinated action. Even a figure of Johnson's vision admitted that he was "a stranger to the affairs of the Church beyond [south of] New Jersey." A persistent shortage of priests also hampered the creation of an effective Anglican church and intensified the burden on its missionaries. "[W]e want ministers extremely, there being more than two churches to each minister," complained Johnson in 1752. Fifteen years later the problem had not improved. "The Church of Christ is starving for want of spiritual Teachers," lamented one New York cleric, who noted that "several missions in this province and the neighbouring provinces were vacant. . . ." The clerics blamed the crisis on the lack of a colonial bishop, who could ordain candidates without their having to "brave Neptunes blasts, the smallpox, and the enormous Expence attending an European voyage." [16] The reasons for the shortage were more complex than that, but a resident bishop would have undoubtedly eased the problem. A bishop also could have mediated quarrels, disciplined wayward priests, diminished the communications problems and the time lag that impaired the Anglican church's transatlantic decision-making process, and in other ways possibly brought more efficiency, direction, and cohesion to the church's efforts. Dissenters and some entrenched Anglican groups—lay vestries, for instance—realized this and managed to block the appointment of a colonial bishop.

As it was, the Anglican church proved a weak reed on which to lean. Its inability to attract ministerial candidates posed a serious shortcoming in an age when a college education had more bearing on the preparation of a minister than on any other occupational role. President Myles Cooper of King's College observed in the mid-1760s that he hardly knew of "more than two or three, on this Side the Water, that seem to be intended for Orders. . . ." From its opening to the American Revolution, the college educated less than twenty boys who eventually entered the Anglican priesthood, about one per class. Clerical candidates of other faiths avoided the college, many of them repelled by its reputation as an Anglican institution. In contrast, Princeton graduated some two hundred twenty boys in the classes of 1748 through 1778 who joined the clergy, about ten per class.[17]

Princeton had the advantage of appealing to religious groups in the northern colonies which far outdistanced the Anglicans in size and in the attractiveness of their ministerial ranks to young men, but Princeton's success lay in its ability to capitalize on its potential constituency. Encouraged by a network of New Light and New Side clerics who esteemed Princeton as the educational fountain of evangelicalism, students who later entered the ministry flocked there in sizable numbers from Massachusetts, Connecticut, New York, New Jersey, and Pennsylvania. Princeton drew fewer students from the southern colonies, but more southern graduates of Princeton joined the clergy than did students from all colonies at King's College.[18] One need only read the minutes of the Presbyterian synod of New York (of New York and Philadelphia after the "union" of 1758), whose members came from Pennsylvania, New Jersey, New York, Delaware, and Virginia, to sense the sturdiness of New Side support for Princeton. The synod, for instance, established a scholarship fund for prospective ministers at Princeton and exhorted member congregations to raise money annually for the college.[19]

Anglican clerics did nothing of the sort. Nor, outside New York City and the surrounding area, did they and their lay associates recruit students for King's College.[20] Indeed, only seven Anglican clerics—three Trinity Church ministers, three of Johnson's associates from southern Connecticut, and Thomas Bradbury Chandler—sent their sons to the college. Those colonial Anglicans who attended college from the 1750s to the 1770s thus were scattered among the several American "nurseries of learning." Episcopal ministers did gather at King's on occasion for clerical conventions or to receive honorary degrees, but the college had little more success attracting Anglican students from outside New York than Presbyterian students within it.

The administrative center that might have transformed King's College into an intercolonial Anglican institution was two thou-

sand miles away and strikingly unsuited to the task. At first ecclesiastical officials in London had a devil of a time simply keeping
the various colonial colleges straight. In 1754 the bishop of London wrote Johnson how thrilled he was that Princeton had turned
out to be an Anglican college, with Johnson at its head. A few
months later the archbishop of Canterbury congratulated Reverend William Smith (who had recently been named a master at the
Academy of Philadelphia) on becoming president of King's College.[21] The confusion was soon corrected, but it reflected the ecclesiastics' distance from the issue and its elusiveness within their
expansive purview. The SPG, after all, ran a far-flung missionary
operation that extended from Nova Scotia to Georgia to the West
Indies and that embraced clerics, schoolmasters, and catechists
ministering to whites, blacks, and Indians. SPG officials had not
participated in the founding of King's College, had no authority
over it, and were content to leave its management in local hands.
Not that they failed to recognize its religious kinship. In 1759
they gave £500 sterling to King's College, a generous gift that
eased the financial burdens of the college's first years. But the
SPG developed few plans to exploit the opportunities afforded by
an Anglican college, and when they did so, they formulated them
to suit the imperial perspectives of ecclesiastical and political officials in London. In the 1750s imperial considerations dictated
that King's College could best serve as a vehicle for converting the
Indians.

From 1754 to 1763 the overriding imperial concern was the
Great War for Empire (known in America as the French and Indian War, in Europe as the Seven Years War), which erupted
with the clash of English and French forces on the American frontier. The struggle focused attention on several Indian tribes,
among them the Six Nations in New York, whose allegiance appeared to have a crucial bearing on the outcome of the war in the
American colonies. Could not the colleges of New York and Philadelphia, inquired the SPG of Samuel Johnson and Reverend
William Smith in 1756, educate a number of Indian children in
the Christian religion, who then might evangelize their fellow
tribesmen? The archbishop of Canterbury put the issue to John-

son more bluntly. Attempts to convert the Indians could "counteract the artifices of the French papists, and do considerable services, religious and political at once. . . ."[22] Johnson sympathized with the idea, but he had little desire to divert his energies and the college's small resources from the main job of training a political and professional elite. He politely rebuffed the SPG with an explanation that "nothing can be done with the Indians so long as the war continues. . . ." The war's conclusion found Johnson and his associates no less reluctant about educating Indians at the college. Henry Barclay discouraged a proposal that Joseph Brant study at King's College with the observation that he could "hardly be a Day without hearing his Countrymen in general heartily cursed as deserving to be all extirpated. . . ."[23]

With the SPG working at cross-purposes and Anglican ministers outside New York City area unsupportive, Johnson and his clerical colleagues relied on their lay allies in New York City to build an influential Anglican church college. Even this coalition showed signs of deterioration. The seemingly endless months of contention over the college left Johnson resentful toward "the gentlemen at the helm" of the project, whose "want of vigor and activity" he blamed for the protracted "confusion and altercation." Johnson singled out James DeLancey as the bête noir. He "is every day so overwhelmed with w[i]ne etc. as to be scarcely capable . . . of business . . . ," Johnson reported to his sons in 1755. DeLancey felt no less bitter about the college, his support of which he believed had seriously jeopardized his political standing. He declined to attend any meetings of the governors, claiming at one point that he had contributed enough to the college by the loss of his reputation.[24] Trinity vestrymen on the board attended meetings regularly, but they were unwilling to undertake any grandiose schemes. On the other hand, the input of Anglican clerics into the board's decision-making had been severely limited by the composition of the governors and their control over Johnson, both factors which, from Johnson's perspective, made it difficult to gain the governors' cooperation. Friction between Johnson and the board eventually triggered a movement, led by James DeLancey's brother, to oust the president. However, at the close of the King's College Controversy the relations between Johnson and most of the governors remained relatively amicable, with Johnson's stepson always prepared to smooth out ripples of dissension. And three years of controversy had fashioned an especially effective working relationship among Johnson and his fellow Anglican clerics in and about New York City.

King's College emerged from the controversy over its control neither a nonsectarian provincial college nor an intercolonial Anglican college. In many respects it resembled its urban neighbor to the south, the College of Philadelphia. The latter has been hailed as the only nonsectarian college in the colonies, with King's usually labeled an Anglican institution. In operation the differences were slim. At both schools Anglican laymen comprised about two-thirds of the governors, while clerics had little or no say on the boards. (Not a single practicing cleric served on Philadelphia's board during the 1750s.) Both schools were headed by Anglican ministers, who promoted the interests of the Church of England at their colleges and based college religious services on the Anglican liturgy. Reverend William Smith, provost at Philadelphia, assured the SPG in 1756 that "the Church, by soft and easy Means, daily gains Ground" in the college. "We have Prayers twice a day, the Children learn the Church-Catechism, & upon the whole I never knew a greater Regard to Religion in any Seminary. . . ." [25] At both schools, too, the Anglican propensities of the college heads were moderated by the presence of non-Anglicans among the trustees and students, by the secularism of the Anglican governors, and by the cosmopolitanism of the presidents themselves.

The parallels would have been more striking had either a Dutch professor of divinity or Chauncey Whittelsey gained a secure position on the King's College faculty. William Smith tried to maneuver the College of Philadelphia into the Anglican camp, but his efforts were countered by Francis Alison, the vice-provost, a Presbyterian minister whom the trustees hired initially in 1752 to head their academy. The Old Side Presbyterian synod of Philadelphia approved Alison's appointment because they expected him to "promote the good of the . . . church"—in other words, they

hoped Alison would educate ministerial recruits more suitable
than the evangelical products turned out at Princeton.[26] If the
College of Philadelphia was nonsectarian in origin, it was multi-
denominational in operation. Anglican influences predominated,
much to Alison's despair on occasion, but he retained an important role on the faculty until the American Revolution closed the
college. This duality of religious interests, not their absence, gave
the College of Philadelphia its special character. The vehemence
of Anglicans in New York, especially the clerics, and the recalci-
trance of the triumvirate thwarted the creation of a similar arrangement at King's College. The result was to limit both the
college's appeal to prospective students and the richness of its intellectual life.

6.
HIGHER EDUCATION FROM AN ELITIST PERSPECTIVE

ABRAHAM AND ANN COCK of New York City could not have been prouder of their "Little boy," Billy, who in 1769 was twelve years of age. Perhaps William's behavior was "a Little wanting," admitted his stepmother, but he was "of a very good Disposition and not of wild turn as many Children are. . . ." Seldom was he "five minutes in a day without a book in his hand." Billy's parents praised their only son with a certain urgency, because they were entreating John Tabor Kempe, attorney general of New York, to let Billy clerk in his law office. Abraham Cock's "whole happiness seems to Depend upon placeing his Child under you . . . ," Ann Cock explained to Kempe.[1]

Kempe replied cautiously, apparently agreeing to take the boy but emphasizing for the moment Billy's need for a sound education. Kempe knew that the colony was already "well supplied" with lawyers—or so contended the New York Bar Association. Its members hoped to upgrade the profession and enhance their personal prospects by restricting entry to a select number of broadly educated and affluent apprentices. Bar association regulations allowed members to accept an apprentice only if he studied at least two years in college, served a five-year clerkship, and paid £200 to his master. Although the New York Bar Association disbanded in 1770, there remained in effect a provincial supreme court order of 1767 requiring all lawyers who practiced before the court to have clerked for three years if they had a B.A., five years if they did

not.[2] Kempe's personal feelings about the value of a college education were reflected in his role as one of King's College's most conscientious governors.

So the Cocks sent Billy to study at King's College, first with the
grammar school master, then in the Bachelor of Arts program.
They did not do so gladly, since Billy had already attended a
school in New Jersey. Both the boy and his parents were eager
that he get on with his career, and they did not quite see the need
for so much additional schooling. Nor could they readily afford
the heavy expense. Abraham Cock was a cooper who had prospered making and repairing casks, barrels, and tubs. He owned
three lots in the New York City and had his own "negro man."
But the costs of higher education and a law apprenticeship were
burdensome for an artisan, and the Cocks sometimes ran short of
ready funds. The squeeze came early in 1773 when Abraham
Cock fell seriously ill. He "Bleeds night & Day," Ann Cock reported to Kempe, and there were "very Little hopes of his recov-
ery." Despite the calamity, nothing seemed to disturb either of
them so much as "Billy not being Bound." [3]

By fall the Cocks had "not mony . . . in the house for the Support of the family." In November 1773 Abraham Cock died. The
executors of the estate sold his house and lots to pay his debts.
Billy, however, remained at King's College, while his stepmother
moved to Albany and earned money by keeping "a house for
Boarders." Cock graduated from King's College in 1775, served
his apprenticeship (with Kempe, presumably), joined the New
York bar, and became register of the court of chancery and a New
York assemblyman.[4]

Despite the many quarrels over issues of control and location,
the principal proponents of King's College could have reached
agreement rather easily on the significance and appropriateness of
Billy Cock's educational experience. Underlying their religious,
geographical, generational, and occupational divisions was a solid
bond of elitist values that shaped their conceptions of who should
attend King's College and why.

Consider, for instance, how the founders of King's College
might have viewed the reasons why William Cock "made it." A

major factor was his family's economic resources, including the accumulated assets that carried the family through financial crises. Whatever Billy's talents, his family could never have contemplated a college education and a clerkship had Abraham Cock not prospered in his trade. The college, proclaimed William Smith, Jr., was "for the Education of all who can afford such Education." The governors of King's College concurred, welcoming all students whose "fortunes enable and inclinations induce them" to attend.[5] Those youths without the requisite funds received no aid from the college. One of Billy Cock's classmates lost his father in 1773 and dropped out of school. "My Father was at a Considerable Expence in fitting and Keeping me in King's College," wrote this boy. Now his mother had six children, "all unsetled and some quite young with a very small Estate." [6]

That it was the Cock family's economic resources which transformed King's College and a clerkship from obstacles into opportunities for young Billy was a "fact of life" the founders of the college accepted but did not celebrate. Instead they emphasized the importance of talent, virtue, and knowledge in making good leaders. Men were to be esteemed not according to "the Money they are possessed of" but according to their merit. William Cock undoubtedly displayed the appropriate characteristics. He was studious, hard working, tractable, and "Extremely anxious" to become a lawyer.[7] Four successful years at King's College enhanced his reputation for talent and virtue. Only one slip marred his record of good behavior at college—the evening during his sophomore year when he and several other students ill-used one of the professors by *calling* [him] *Names* in the Dark." When Cock and his fellow culprits publicly acknowledged their offense, the affair was dropped before it reached the college governors. Matters of discipline were not trifling concerns. George Rapelje, in the class behind Cock's, pleaded with the governors to reinstate him after his expulsion for abusing the same professor with the "most indecent Language." "Gentlemen," Rapelje addressed the governors, "your Sentence of Expulsion will be an almost insuperable Obstacle to my being received into any Employment . . . , for who will receive me after having imbibed such prejudices against me?"[8] Anglican clerics in New York and New Jersey went so far as to formalize a process for screening out clerical aspirants with poor behavior records. In 1769 they agreed to recommend for orders only candidates who had attended college and could produce a certificate of "good Behaviour" from the president.[9]

Thus, economic resources and a reputation for talent and virtue smoothed Billy Cock's passage toward his goal of becoming a lawyer. So did John Tabor Kempe's willingness to sponsor the boy, a concession that apparently grew out of Ann Cock's social connections. Kempe served as Billy's educational adviser, hired him as an office boy while he pursued his studies, undoubtedly oversaw his progress at King's College, and apparently took him on as a clerk at a time when clerkships were hard to come by.[10] Kempe's sponsorship was not the kind of advantage that founders of King's College emphasized in their public pronouncements about rewarding talent and virtue, but it was not an unusual phenomenon in a society where personal connections opened so many doors. Indeed, one founder proposed, as will appear later, that the college itself sponsor selected deserving students whose talents could be put to public use and whose families lacked the money to finance a college education.

William Cock's path to success seems to suggest that a college education was nothing more than a hurdle that boys with plentiful funds, special talents, and records of good conduct might surmount. However, proponents of the college expected undergraduates to undergo a profound educational experience which would "enlarge the Mind, improve the Understanding, polish the whole Man, and qualify them to support the brightest Characters in all the elevated stations in Life. . . ." For a boy like William Cock this meant transforming an awkward youth into a man of "genteel Distinction," equipping him to become a "compleat Lawyer," instilling in him the values appropriate to responsible leadership, and developing his elite identity.[11]

King's College students would, first of all, acquire the attributes of English gentility without the "charge or hazard of stirring one foot" from their homes in the New World. The "noble Charms" of rhetoric and poetry would "improve the Temper" and "soften the Manners," assuring that they would become pleasing companions rather than unruly rowdies. The classics would enrich their minds with the "politest furniture" and afford an "agreeable entertainment" much superior to billiard tables and drinking matches. "Practical arts" like geography, surveying, and agriculture would help round out their knowledge, so as to permit participation in every kind of discussion. King's College alumni would not, however, become lettered fops or cloistered scholars. The goal was gentility without insipid punctilio, learning without pedantry.[12] Nor would they become men of leisure. They would serve as judges, lawyers, ministers, and statesmen—positions in which manners had great bearing, for who could revere the judge unadorned "with a dignified Mein and Deportment." [13]

Images of English gentility blended with conceptions of English professional standards. "Strange!" noted William Livingston on the preparation of lawyers, "that five Years spent at a Lawyer's Office in [the] running of Errands, should be sufficient to usher Men into a Profession the most complicated, difficult, extensive and accurate of all others." The practice of law demanded breadth of vision, depth of knowledge, a "quick Perception, a clear Judgment, and tenacious Memory." By preventing men of "dull Parts and no Education" from crowding the field, New York lawyers of "Sense and Breeding" used bar association agreements to upgrade standards of practice as well as to protect their interests.[14]

The conception of the "compleat Lawyer" attracted New York's most prominent attorneys at mid-century. Well before the founding of King's College William Smith, Sr., with whom both William Smith, Jr., and William Livingston clerked, incorporated his ideas on the "compleat Lawyer" into a course of study for his apprentices. "The Sciences necessary for a Lawyer," according to Smith, included "the Languages," geometry, geography, history, logic, rhetoric, divinity, and the "Law of Nature and Nations." Livingston was so impressed by the program that he adopted it for his own apprentices.[15] Joseph Murray and John Chambers each brought to his practice a breadth of knowledge that helps explain their enthusiasm for King's College. Murray was noted for his

legal erudition, and he and Chambers had two of the largest libraries in mid-century New York. Chambers's six hundred volumes included legal and religious works, classical and European
history and literature, and scientific and philosophical writings by
Pascal, Bacon, Locke, and others. Four younger shining lights in
the profession, Livingston, Smith, Jr., Benjamin Nicoll, and John
Morin Scott, all of them Yale graduates, gave their assent to the
concept of the broadly educated lawyer by favoring a requirement
that all law apprentices have a B.A.[16]

Since proponents of the "compleat Lawyer" were men of such
stature in the community, they had an impact that went beyond
the law profession. Their educational ideas were translated into
community institutions, King's College among them, and they
prompted men in other fields to value a liberal education. William
Livingston and William Smith, Jr., did so explicitly, by publicly
condemning "poor Tools in the Pulpit" and "Mountebanks and
Quacks in Physic" as well as *Pettifoggers* in our Courts." "I hope
the two rising Colleges," wrote Livingston in reference to King's
College and Princeton, "will give us some Security against the
Increase of all these Pests of Society. . . ."[17] Several New York
doctors in the 1750s, influenced as well by European modes of
medical education and practice, shared Livingston's desire to upgrade professional standards. The "complete Physician," they believed, not only mastered the several dimensions of medical
knowledge, from physiology to botany. He first "laid the Foundation" in the liberal arts and sciences, for only those "whose minds
were prepar'd by the study of the learn'd languages, cultivated by
the belles lettres, & enrich'd with the knowledge of Philosophy
. . ." would find their way through the "dark & intricate wind-
ings" of medical science.[18] However, a decade passed before there
emerged a group of physicians with the internal strength and community prestige to have much impact on the preparation of doctors, a shift which resulted in the founding of the King's College
Medical School in 1767. Anglican clerics, on the other hand,
needed no advice from Livingston and Smith. Requirements for
ordination already assured some measure of professional education, and the clerics were not about to recommend candidates who

had failed to immerse themselves in the "sublimer parts of learning and true wisdom." [19] The clerics, like the lawyers and eventually the doctors, were committed to training an indigenous professional elite which would give not an inch to European
professionals in the profundity of its knowlege, the sophistication
of its intellectual skills, and the nobility of its values.

Notions of gentility and the complete professional shaded into a
third conception: the virtuous leader. Professional men, opulent
merchants, substantial landowners, and successful politicians all
shaped the character and direction of community life through
domination of their occupational sectors and through control of
community political and social institutions. The major proponents
of King's College themselves exemplified the pervasive influence
of the elite. Of the leading lay figures—some twenty-five lawyers,
merchants, and politicians—all but four held major political or
judicial positions in New York or New Jersey at some point during their careers, more than half of them sitting on the New York
Council. They also had considerable say in the operation of New
York City's principal churches, especially Trinity Church, as well
as of civic institutions like the New York Society Library. Positions of such consequence were not, at least in theory, plums to be
picked by victorious participants in an open contest where attributes like shrewdness and craft counted as much as talent and
virtue. The community and especially the elite had a vested interest in the fitness of decision makers. An education in virtue provided one means of improving the chances that the responsibilities
of leadership would be discharged properly.

An education in virtue also signified, above all, an indoctrina-
tion in those values esteemed by the elite, a process that was all
the more important for boys who did not grow up in elite families. The inculcation of values like patriotism, public spirit, and
service to society prepared the way for public leadership. Exposure to a succession of heroic models dramatized the significance of these values, for history abounded with examples of the
"Alteration & Improvement, that one or two Men, of Superior
Talents & true greatness of soul, have made in a State. . . ." The
context of decision-making was defined by instilling values such as

order and tranquility, the security of life and property, liberty with respect for law and authority, and reverence for God and the British constitution. And prospective leaders were schooled in familiar yet crucial personal attributes like honor, industry, frugality, and piety. To be sure, proponents of the college did not all agree on the implications and relative significance of these values. Samuel Johnson and his fellow Anglican clerics stressed the prerogatives of authority and the duty of obedience by the "unthinking" multitude. The triumvirate, on the other hand, celebrated the virtues of liberty and underscored the dangers of imperious and unchecked rulers. To them, the cultivation of a veneration for liberty in the leader himself provided one way to protect the liberty of all.[20]

Training a young boy like William Cock to become a man of taste and manners, a "compleat Lawyer," and a virtuous leader could not help but foster an elite identity, just as it was intended to do. King's College students would quickly learn, if they did not realize it initially, that they were special people with "greater advantages" than most New Yorkers and, in turn, that society had "higher expectations" of them. Their "Vertue & great Abilities, [when] improved by Study & a proper education" would distinguish them from the mass of men and establish a sounder claim to positions in the professions and as political leaders than could either birth or sheer wealth. In contrast, those "design'd for Mechanic Professions, and all the remaining People of the Country" required an education better suited to their "proper Spheres."[21] One could readily justify a liberal education for those "whose Stations in the Commonwealth give great Weight and Force to their Examples . . . without supposing that all Ranks and Sexes must immediately become Cultivators of the Muses, and proceed learned, polite and virtuous. . . ."[22]

The elitist perspective shared by the founders of King's College precipitated widespread agreement among them on the purposes of higher education and on the manner of determining who should attend the college. However, the founders did vary in the degree to which they worked out a systematic conception of elite education; and behind the variations lay some important differences in how they viewed the relationship of the college to society. The fate of Edward Antill's plans for the college illuminates the distinctions. Antill's membership in the colonial elite rested securely on a foundation of wealth, heritage, political influence, and family connections. He owned an extensive estate in New Jersey, held a seat on the New Jersey Council, and was married to the daughter of the colony's late Governor Lewis Morris. In 1757 Antill decided to turn over to King's College £800 New York currency and a mortgage worth over £1,000. He did so with a specific purpose in mind.[23]

Edward Antill believed that the "Strength & Glory" of the state depended on its success in discovering youths of "superior Talents & Noble Principles" and educating them to "manage the publick affairs." Already New York could boast advantages such as its location "in the middle of the American Provinces," its opulent merchants, and its many products for trade. Should the colony take steps to exploit the talent in all ranks of its young people, it could become the "Metropolis & Mistress of America." Antill's solution was a teacher corps made up of talented poor boys. A tutor should be hired to instruct a group of poor children and identify those of marked ability. The college would "set them a part for a more liberal Education," turn them into "Able Masters," deploy them throughout the colony, and use them to identify other qualified youths and prepare them for the college. "Here will be a constant Succession of Men," Antill explained to Samuel Johnson, whose efforts would stimulate a "general Tast for polite Learning. . . . You will soon have a Sufficient number of Sensible judicious Men, rise up from among yourselves, capable & worthy of filling the different Seats & Offices of your State. . . ."

Unlike many of his fellow founders, Antill thus doubted that the college could fulfill its function by educating only those students who could afford to attend. The children of the rich were not always "of great Abilities." They did not readily apply themselves to their studies. And the state could not depend upon them "to undertake such employments as are Necessary for the publick Good." In contrast, poor boys could be compelled to keep "close to their studies" and "behave themselves well, on pain of being turned down to more Servile employments. . . ." And their incentive to succeed was much greater, since they had "no other views & prospects than those that arrise from the Improvements they make in knowledge & Vertue. . . ." They provided perfect candidates for a teacher corps which could tap the reservoir of talent at all levels of New York society, and undoubtedly they could excel in leadership posts themselves.

Edward Antill's proposal was distinguished by its integration of poor boys into the mainstream of the college's operation and by a generous gift of capital with which to launch the plan. But Antill shared several key ideas with other founders, particularly Reverend William Smith, William Smith, Jr., and Samuel Johnson. First, graduates of the college would not only enter but monopolize both the professions and the "publick Seats of Justice [,] Magistracy & Legislation." Second, parents and educators should sort out those boys with the appropriate talents and inclinations for these elite roles at an early age—about eight or nine—and groom them for the positions they would be expected to assume upon completing their education. Third, the selection and education of elite candidates should be systematized, with the state providing some degree of supervision and support. And fourth, instituting such a process was crucial enough to the prosperity of the state to justify an ample and prompt investment of money, talent, and energy by its citizenry.[24]

Reverend William Smith worked out the most elaborate procedure for training elite candidates. Confining the first stage of his plan to New York City, he proposed a two-track system that embraced boys of "all Ranks and Conditions." They would study together for three years at an English school, until age nine. Then those youngsters "designed" for the professions and the "chief Offices of the State" would undertake a five-year program emphasizing Latin and Greek at the Latin school, followed by four years of college, while the rest of the boys pursued a six year nonclassical, "more compendious" course at the mechanic's school (to be called, remarkably enough, *"Barnard-College"*). The college students would finish at age eighteen, the rest at fifteen. Operating on the assumption that children were the "Property of the State" and should be educated "according to the Intention of the State," Smith suggested several steps to achieve a "uniform Scheme of Education . . . in every Part of the Province" for both of the "two grand classes" of students. Once the city system began functioning, all private schools in or near the city would be "supprest." Then the college and the mechanic's school would educate "gratis" several masters (much like Antill's teacher corps) and send them into the backcountry to oversee a colony-wide educational system. Each township would establish an English school, each county a Latin school, while "higher education" remained in the hands of the college and the mechanic's school in New York City. Local public funds would help support the various English and Latin schools, with the higher institutions benefiting by lotteries and gifts. Smith was vague about student charges, but, apart from the gratis education for prospective masters, he did not propose any plan for free education or scholarships.[25]

There is nothing especially remarkable about the fact that the governors of King's College ignored Smith's ideas. His scheme was sweeping and expensive, and Smith himself did not linger in New York to promote it but instead moved on to the College of Philadelphia. The rejection by the governors of Edward Antill's plan (but not his money) raises a more substantial question, since a gift from a figure of his prestige should have encouraged at least token experimentation. The governors' nonaction takes on added interest in light of their decisions on such issues as student fees and the length of the B.A. program. Their policies suggest an educational viewpoint that varied in several respects from that of men like Antill and Smith, despite the underlying elitist perspective shared by all of them.

The deliberations of the governors were dominated by New York City merchants and lawyers, men who in many cases had supported the college project from the beginning. However, they were not men who readily committed their educational views to paper, unlike the triumvirate, Reverend William Smith, and other founders who were either missing from the ranks of the governors or of small voice. The governors' rhetorical reticence could have

stemmed from several factors. Few of them had had "any opportunity of a collegiate Education" (Johnson complained that most
were "intire Strangers to such an affair"), and fewer still were men
of letters. Yet they did not doubt the value of a sound liberal education.[26] What they lacked was a systematic conception of educational reform which justified elaboration on paper. Their thinking
was relatively informal and personal as well as scrupulously tempered by practical considerations.

They agreed, for instance, that the opportunity to acquire a liberal education would raise the quality of leadership in New York
and contribute to the future prosperity of the colony, but they did
not jump from this assumption to an expectation either that they
themselves should comb the youth of New York to find the most
talented prospective students or that their alumni would monopolize the political and professional elite. A college created new options for New Yorkers. Bar associations might realistically demand that prospective attorneys obtain a college education. SPG
missionaries could construct a sounder case for a colonial bishop
now that they had an "Episcopal College" to train ministers on the
American side of the Atlantic. Parents, especially Anglican
parents, now had a suitable and convenient place to educate their
children in the liberal arts and sciences. To what extent New
Yorkers exploited these options depended on innumerable individual and group decisions which the governors felt were not theirs
to supervise.

This attitude meshed with the tendency, stronger in the governors than in some other founders, to view King's College from the
parents' side of the educational fence. The governors hailed the
college not only for what it promised the colony but for what it
provided the gentry—an opportunity to give its children "advantages" that seemed only proper for the gentry to have at its disposal. How appropriate that a prominent New York merchant
should specify in his will that "if any of my sons shall desire a liberal education at the College of the City of New York, they are to
be permitted." Or that a letter of recommendation for the son of
another civic luminary should note that the boy enjoyed "the advantage of a liberal Education in the Colledge of New York,

where he has received the degree of Master of Arts." [27] A father whose son had the requisite talent and inclination might consider college as a way to achieve any number of goals, from maximizing the boy's career options to qualifying him for a specific profession, from bolstering his elite credentials to imposing the stringent discipline neglected by indulgent parents, from giving him a dose of polite culture while he waited for an opening as an apprentice to providing an extended opportunity for maturation before he made a career decision. To the governors of King's College these were not abstract issues. More than half the matriculants during the college's first six years were their own sons and nephews. This inward kind of perspective, however, did not provoke an aggressive quest for students.

In the early nineteenth century authorities at many colleges pared tuition fees, established scholarship funds, and in other ways sought to attract both a sizable student body and a cadre of poor boys. They did so to triumph over the intense competition for students generated by a flood of college founding and to project a democratic image in a society which frequently denounced colleges as rich men's institutions.[28] The governors of King's College would have frowned on the management of these schools. To them, a college was neither a popular institution nor a charity institution. It offered advantages to those boys who could afford them, advantages that popular access would dilute. One faculty member went so far as to boast publicly (and incorrectly) that the students at King's College were, "in general, the Sons of Gentlemen of independent Fortunes." [29] Yet the governors did not conceive their college to be the exclusive preserve of the rich either. They were probably not even averse to remitting tuition for selected poor boys at some future point. However, to them financial soundness and academic respectability came first. The students would follow.

In this light, the failure of the governors to greet Edward Antill's proposal with enthusiasm makes sense. So does their policy on student fees and the length of the B.A. program. Once the lottery trustees located King's College in New York City, costs became a troublesome issue. The cost of living was higher in the city

than the country, notably the price of food, which was by far the
biggest item in a student's budget. The French and Indian War
aggravated the problem. The use of New York City for a distribu-
tion center and a troop concentration point stimulated inflation,
and prices remained at a high level in the 1760s despite an economic recession in the city. The governors responded by setting
the steepest rates for tuition, room, and board of any college in
the colonies—in 1764 they were 50 percent higher than at the
college's nearest competitor, Princeton.[30] "I Did expect tell Last
year to have sent my sons to Kings College . . . ," lamented one
New Yorker, but "to my surprise I found the board near or about
5 Shillings per week Dearer then in the Jarseys and the tuition
about one third Darer and for this reason with regreat I have sent
them there for the present." [31] Undoubtedly many other fathers
shied away from King's College for the same reason, which would
help account for the small size of the student body throughout
most of the college's brief history.

The irony of all this is that by the mid-1760s King's College
had the largest endowment of all the colonial colleges. It exceeded
Princeton's ill-managed fund by six times in 1768.[32] Unlike the
trustees of Princeton, the governors of King's College had the patience to conserve capital and build an endowment which would
pay off in the future. But the other side of their patience was their
lack of a compelling mission which required immediate results.
Princeton was managed by ministers who were trying to save
mankind and who needed a flow of new clerics to do it. They
rushed their institution into operation, graduated the first class a
year later, and conscientiously sought large numbers of students
through low fees and scholarship funds. The founders of King's
College dallied for years over organizing the college, then the governors graduated the first class four years after it opened, refused
to risk financial adversity by charging competitive fees, and
spurned the idea of financial aid to needy students. Even after ac-
cumulating a substantial endowment the governors balked at
bringing their fees more into line with other colleges.

The governors' policy on the length of the B.A. program reflected no more willingness to bend academic than financial stan-

dards for the sake of appealing to students. The college instituted a four-year curriculum and regularly placed almost all incoming students in the first class. Undoubtedly Samuel Johnson took the lead in this instance, and the governors did not hesitate to follow. On other issues Johnson berated the governors for their want of "Spirit & vigor." For example, the governors' dilatoriness over establishing a grammar school exasperated him, since he considered it the key to assuring a steady flow of qualified entrants to the college. Like the founders of Princeton, Johnson thirsted to turn out men who could "stem the torrent of irreligion and vice" then engulfing colonials.[33] But Johnson's sense of urgency did not diminish his reverence for learning. He could not imagine accomplishing the goals of a college education in less than four years, especially since so few students were adequately prepared when they entered the freshman class. Nor could a man with his respect for Oxford ignore Bishop Berkeley's advice that if "terms for degrees" were the "same as in Oxford and Cambridge, this would give credit to the College, and pave the way for admitting their graduates *ad eundem* in the English universities." [34] Princeton, as usual, worried more about attracting and graduating students. The college set up a four-year program but "frequently" accepted students "After the first Year," in some cases even in the senior year. An attempt in the late 1760s to require four years of residence provoked such discontent that the trustees dropped the plan for its "inexpediency." One cleric condemned this plan as an effort to educate only "gracious, holy, humble (and I may add rich) youths for the ministry. . . ." [35] The College of Philadelphia adopted a three-year B.A. course from the outset and openly admitted that, with "the present great demand for young men of education," it could not "retain" youths for four years, "especially while the expence is so considerable, and to be wholly borne by themselves." [36]

The cumulative impact of the King's College governors' decisions on student charges, the length of the B.A. program, and the proposal of Edward Antill was to accentuate the elitist and exclusive character of the college. A college education was an expensive undertaking. A King's College education was prohibitively expensive for most New Yorkers. It probably cost a father £50 to £80 a year, £200 to £320 for four years to maintain a son at King's College.[37] How many fathers could manage it? [38] Thirty-five to 40 percent of New York's adult males were slaves, indentured servants, agricultural laborers, urban workers, and mariners, none of whom could afford to send a son to King's College. The last three groups earned annual wages of £25 to £60. Farmers, who comprised about 45 percent of the colony's adult males, were in a better position. While the great majority of farms produced a small cash surplus—perhaps £25 a year for the average farm—the largest landholders could garner more than £1,000 a year from rents and the sale of agricultural products. Still, probably two-thirds of the farmers found the cost of a King's College education prohibitive, another sixth might manage it but only under the most trying circumstances, and a sixth could handle it. Roughly the same breakdown holds true for artisans, who made up about 10 percent of the adult men. A small group of manufacturers with considerable capital invested in their businesses—distilling, tanning, ropemaking, sugar refining—had high incomes, but most artisans earned less than £120 a year, with wage-earning artisans averaging £75 to £85 a year.

A final group supplied most of the students at King's College. Comprising 5 to 10 percent of the adult males, they either engaged in commerce or pursued careers as professionals, government officials, and schoolmasters. Their income varied widely. Many peddlers, schoolmasters, and country doctors earned no more than a moderately successful carpenter. But shopkeepers averaged in the neighborhood of £350 a year and established merchants about £900 a year. Lawyers, by far the best-paid professionals, often had incomes that approached those of the most prosperous merchants. While one-fifth of the men in this category could not afford the costs of a King's College education and another fifth might do so only at great sacrifice, three-fifths could afford it.

In sum, about three-quarters of all fathers (and 70 percent of nonslave fathers) could not possibly afford to educate a son at King's College. Another 11 percent (14 percent of nonslave fathers) might consider it, but the increased expense of maintaining a son at college rather than at home placed so heavy a strain on family finances as to make it an unlikely prospect. That leaves a prosperous but small group of farmers, artisans, professionals, and commercial people—14 percent of the adult males and 16.5 percent of the nonslave males—who might have reasonably considered sending a son to King's College. In fact, this estimate may be too optimistic. The most thorough study of American social structure in this period suggests that only one in ten colonial fathers could afford to send a son to any college.[39] Moreover, the extremely high costs at King's College, especially coming as they did on top of heavy expenses for preparatory education, could easily persuade families either to drop plans for college, or to withdraw a son after a year or two (almost half the students left before obtaining a degree, staying a median period of one and a half years), or to patronize one of King's College's competitors. A boy who could procure entrance into the sophomore or junior class at Princeton could obtain his B.A. for one-third to one-half the cost at King's College.

Doubtless other college founders besides Edward Antill and Reverend William Smith disagreed with the governors' approach to recruiting students, but opposition voices were relatively quiet and the differences in outlook among the founders were comparatively mild. Not that other proponents of the college failed to become agitated over questions of opportunity and mobility. The triumvirate feared that by controlling the college the Anglicans would regulate access to gentility and to political and professional preferment in the colony, just as Anglicans in England monopolized Oxford and Cambridge and required religious tests for political office. One New York dissenter lamented that in England there were "none of our Persuasion in the Direction of Affairs, either in Church or State," nor did he know of any dissenters in the nobility. "If my Son had the Wisdom of a *Socrates*, or the Genius of a *Bacon*," he could exercise his talents no "further than the Extent of the Walls of his own Closet." New York, in contrast, should keep the road to "Honors and Preferments" open to the son of the "modest Plebeian." [40] The concern of these men, however, was with religious barriers to opportunity, not economic ones. If most New Yorkers could not afford a proper education, so be it.

During the very months when Benjamin Nicoll battled with the triumvirate over the religious dimensions of a college designed for "general Use," the four men agreed to new bar association rules which, by requiring a B.A. and £200 for a clerkship, put a law career well beyond the financial reach of all but a fraction of New York's population. In 1764 the bar reduced the B.A. requirement to two years in college, but, as a father of one King's College student observed, the regulations still "greatly impede[d] the lower class of people from creeping in." [41] The same could be said of the regulations governing the college itself. The New York Bar Association and King's College were operated with something of the same mentality. It was a mentality that hailed the merits of talent and virtue over birth and wealth but never let the latter attributes lose their role as keys to success in the next generation.

The controversies and decisions explored in this and the previous five chapters had a cumulative and lasting impact on the shape of King's College. One way to measure this impact is to look at the students and contributors which the new college attracted. In 1755 the governors decided it was high time to solicit funds privately, since the lottery proceeds were tied up in a political tangle. They circulated a subscription list and in a trice received promises of over £3,000, a sum not far short of that raised by the first two lotteries. Governor Hardy of New York topped the list of contributors with a £500 pledge, Samuel Johnson and twenty-one governors added almost £1,500, and forty-three others contributed just under £1,100. [42]

What kinds of people patronized King's College despite the journalistic and political fire which had raked it since 1753? The typical contributor, whether or not he was a governor, was a New York City resident whose age fell somewhere between the early thirties and the early sixties. He had been born in the colony if not in the city, had never attended college, and had prospered as a merchant. He belonged to or was on the fringes of the upper class, and he worshiped at Trinity Church. The forty-three contributors who were not on the board tended to be a little younger than the governors and were much less likely to have held a significant political or judicial position. Also, their ranks, unlike those of the governors, included women (15 percent) and New Yorkers belonging to the middle and upper middle class (roughly 25 percent). Among both governors and nongovernors there was a minority who belonged to the Dutch church, or who had been born in other colonies or in Great Britain, or who had attended college or the Inns of Court, or who pursued careers as lawyers, provincial officials, or clerics, but only in the case of occupation did the proportion exceed one quarter.

If the great majority of contributors were urban, upper-class Anglicans, so were many of the 209 liberal arts pupils who matriculated at King's College between 1754 and 1776. But many were not. A greater diversity of backgrounds among students than among contributors makes it difficult to generalize about the students, but the attributes which predominated among them are definite. An undergraduate picked at random more than likely had grown up within thirty miles of the campus (true for over 75 percent), either on Manhattan Island, where more than half the students had spent all or most of their youth, or else in adjacent areas in Westchester County, western Long Island, or New Jersey. His father probably engaged in commerce—as a merchant, shopkeeper, ship's captain—or was an artisan-entrepreneur (over 65 percent, with the odds heavily on the side of a commercial vocation); or perhaps he was in the professions (about 20 percent). More than likely the boy was an Anglican (over 65 percent) and, if not, he was probably Dutch Reformed. The chances are strong that his family belonged either to the upper or upper middle class, with the odds favoring the latter over the former.[43]

These generalizations should not obscure the other side of the picture. King's College students also grew up in the Hudson River valley, southern Connecticut, eastern Long Island, Virginia, Great Britain, and the West Indies, with the latter possibly the source of 5 percent of the undergraduates. Their fathers were military officers, government officials, large landowners, and farmers (with remarkably few of the latter). A handful were Presbyterians,

and they were joined by boys whose fathers included a Baptist, a
Lutheran, a Moravian, and a Jew. Some students came from families who belonged neither to the upper class nor to the upper
middle class but to the "middle middle" class. (And one can re-
state the generalization in the previous paragraph on class affiliation to read that the majority of boys came from middle rather
than upper-class families.) Even families whose social status was
fairly high might live in relatively straightened circumstances.
One boy enjoyed the prestige of having a grandfather who had
been an assemblyman, a member of the provincial council, and a
Trinity vestryman, but his father was one of the most inept merchants ever to grace the shores of the Hudson River. Initially the
father tried his hands as a merchant in New York City, but according to his son, he was "uniformly unsuccessful." So he moved
up the Hudson to Peekskill, opened a store and a grist mill, and
"failed miserably." Back he went to the city, but now he was
bankrupt and spent a short period in jail. An appointment for five
years as King's Gauger provided steady employment, but the lure
of private enterprise proved irresistible. He opened a store at Sing
Sing and failed again.[44]

Despite the many exceptions, the dominant biographical patterns among the students of King's College are unmistakable, and
so is the manner in which the controversies and decisions discussed in these chapters influenced them. Take, for example, the
geographical background of the students. Is it any wonder that
rural New Yorkers, especially those who lived very far from the
city, should shun a college distinguished by its Anglican identity,
its high cost, and its location in a city that seemed to suffer the
usual moral ills of urban life. Although proponents of a rural setting for the college had lost the controversy over its location, their
misgivings about cities still were shared by many New Yorkers. A
Lake Champlain area resident who enrolled his son soon "re-
pented" his act. "[I] hoped from his Early Education that the Corruption of the Moral Characters of the Youth at [New] York
would not efect him. However I will remove him so soon as in my
power." Probably this father and undoubtedly other parents
agreed with Jean de Crèvecoeur's contention that the college

should have "been erected far from the city, in some rural retreat, where the scholars had been far removed from the tumults of business, and the dissipations and pleasures that are so numerous in large cities." [45] Whether it be their antiurban prejudices, their dissenting religious beliefs, or their modest economic standing, those rural New Yorkers who had any interest in a college at all were likely to find Princeton or Yale more attractive than King's College. Not surprisingly, King's College was comparatively popular in and around New York City, where Anglicans and families of affluence were much more numerous and suspicion of the city was less intense.

A note of caution should be sounded before concluding. First, if one thinks of King's College as an urban institution, one should recognize that even in New York City the college's drawing power was limited, in part because it was circumscribed by the same factors which undermined its appeal in the backcountry. During the two decades before the American Revolution no more than ninety-five families in the city enrolled their sons at King's College, although the number of households in the city ranged from 2,400 in the 1750s to 3,800 in the 1770s. [46] At no time did even 1 percent of the families in New York City have a son studying at the college. Second, while the King's College Controversy had a considerable impact on the shape of the college, one must be careful not to exaggerate the controversy's significance. Note, for instance, that some of William Livingston's own relatives did not pay much attention to him. At the very moment that Livingston was denouncing the college in "The Watch-Tower," his aunt and his brother joined the college contributors of 1755. The same brother and a second cousin became two of King's College's most diligent governors. And two of Livingston's brothers and three of his cousins enrolled sons at the college. While William himself and a few of his relatives educated their sons at Princeton, the Livingston family also supported King's College from the day it opened.

In 1746 the College of New Jersey was founded ostensibly to promote the "learned Education of Our Youth in New Jersey." In reality, Princeton became an intercolonial institution mainly for Presbyterian and Congregational youths, while New Jerseyites comprised a minority of the students. In 1746 the New York assembly took steps to establish a provincial college which would contribute to the "Advancement of Learning" in New York.[47] Actually a study of its benefactors and its students reveals that it was patronized primarily by upper-class and upper-middle-class families from New York City and the surrounding area, whose members worshiped at Anglican and Dutch Reformed churches and whose breadwinners pursued commercial and professional careers. Although King's College had taken root in a relatively small constituency, it would turn out to be a loyal and durable one which would see to the college's survival.

2.
PORTRAIT OF
A COLONIAL COLLEGE

INTRODUCTION

FOUNDED AMIDST one controversy, King's College soon became embroiled in a much more pervasive conflict, the American Revolution. In the interim its leaders struggled to make the college a viable institution. They succeeded in establishing a sound financial base and a respectable educational program, but only on the eve of the Revolution did the college begin to attract students in numbers large enough to suggest that it would become the influential institution envisioned by its founders. Samuel Johnson, president from 1754 to 1763, played the most vital role in fleshing out the structure of the college. Myles Cooper, Johnson's successor, modified some of Johnson's practices and presided over the founding of a medical school. But his most ambitious project, the conversion of King's College into American University, a new world Oxford which would serve as a pillar of loyalty to the British Empire and the Anglican church, was stymied by the rebel victory in the Revolution. In a college which was both so new and so small, it was relatively easy for each president to put his personal stamp on the institution, especially on its curriculum and its undergraduate life. The result was an intellectual and political legacy which sharply distinguished King's College from most other colonial colleges. However, neither Johnson nor Cooper altered the basic shape of the college which had been forged by the controversies and decisions described in Part 1.

7.

THE FIRST PRESIDENCY

SAMUEL JOHNSON once wrote of himself that "those that knew him best, knew him to be one of the most undesigning men that lived, and that he was far from being addicted to worldly views. . . ." Johnson, in other words, may have feared that men about him were losing their moral bearings, but he saw himself as one who acted only out of a virtuous "sense of duty." As a result, Johnson was headstrong, sometimes contemptuous of those who did not see an issue from his perspective, and liable to impugn their motives. James DeLancey, whose "good-for-nothing management" stirred Johnson's ire during the King's College Controversy, was not the only associate to feel the sting of Johnson's righteousness.[1] While many Anglican clerics respected his leadership, several others resented what they considered to be his meddlesomeness and his imperiousness.

There was much at stake when Johnson committed himself to the presidency of King's College in 1754. Convinced that the drift toward irreligion in the colonies must be reversed, he had a mission to fulfill. Proud of his accomplishments and his friendships, he had a reputation to uphold. Yet the college he was about to head already faced serious problems. Johnson's determination made him the kind of man who would not permit his college to fail. But his self-assurance could also make it unpleasant for those who disagreed with his remedies, especially should they decide that the college's major problem was Johnson himself.

Despite the heritage of bitterness that survived the King's College Controversy, the college did not fare badly in its first years. By the summer of 1757 thirty pupils were pursuing liberal arts degrees. William Johnson, the president's youngest son, assisted his father in 1755 and was "much loved & esteemed" by the students, but Billy left for ordination in London before the year was out.[2] Johnson replaced him with Leonard Cutting, a thirty-one-year-old Cambridge graduate who had taught at Cambridge and was an Anglican to boot. Only one thing could have pleased Johnson more than hiring a Cambridge graduate—hiring an Oxford graduate. He found Cutting a "Worthy Tutor" with an exceptional command of the classics.[3]

For more than a year Johnson and Cutting drilled their pupils in "virtuous habits" and "useful knowledge." But late in 1756 New York City was visited with smallpox, a disease so dreaded by Johnson that he had accepted the King's College presidency only after extracting a concession from the lottery trustees that he could leave town during an epidemic. In December Johnson retreated to Westchester County, then waited impatiently while the lingering threat of smallpox in the city turned his flight into a year-long retirement. It "is a great mortification to me to be so long separated from my dear young pupils," he lamented as the early months of 1757 slipped by. Cutting regretted it too, since the entire teaching burden fell on his shoulders. The college governors decided to hire an additional tutor, a move called for also by the fact that neither Johnson nor Cutting felt comfortable teaching mathematics and natural philosophy.[4] But finding a qualified candidate took time. Through the spring, summer, and fall of 1757 Cutting handled all the instruction by himself. Finally, late in 1757 Daniel Treadwell joined the faculty as professor of mathematics and natural philosophy, the college's first professor. Treadwell merited the honor. Professor John Winthrop, with whom Treadwell studied at Harvard, considered him a scholar of "uncommon proficiency in mathematical learning." The breadth of Treadwell's knowledge put John Adams to shame one day in 1759 when the two men spent several hours conversing "upon Politicks, War, Geography, Physicks, &c." But Treadwell never achieved the renown within his grasp. Consumption cut short his life in

Samuel Johnson's Sketch for the Seal of King's College
The Seal of King's College

The woman on the throne, symbolizing the college, holds an open Bible in her right hand, while just to her left are the words "God is my light" (in Hebrew), and in a semicircle above her is her motto (in Latin), "In Thy light shall we see light" (Ps. 36: 9). The Hebrew name Jehovah crowns the seal, while the rising sun in the lower right alludes to His words, "The sun of righteousness shall arise with healing in its wings" (Mal. 4: 2). The children symbolize students. They are urged to learn in the spirit of 1 Pet. 2: 1–2 (inscribed below them): to put away all malice and guile and, like newborn babes, to long for pure spiritual milk, that they might grow thereby. In 1787 Columbia College adopted virtually the same seal.
CREDIT: COLUMBIANA, COLUMBIA UNIVERSITY

1760 at the age of twenty-four. Adams later recalled him as "the greatest Schollar, of my time, whose early death . . . American science has still reason to deplore. . . ." [5]

When Samuel Johnson returned to New York City in December 1757, King's College could boast an outstanding faculty for a school of its size. Johnson instituted a course of studies that utilized the special talents of each teacher. He himself would take entering students for their first year and part of the first half of their second year, teaching them Latin, Greek, rhetoric, logic, and ethics, and striving to make them "intelligent and serious Christians." For the balance of their second year they would study the classics with Cutting, and mathematics and logic with Treadwell. Treadwell would continue to teach them mathematics for part of the third year, with the emphasis in the third and the first half of the fourth years on natural philosophy, also under Treadwell's guidance. During the students' final half-year, Johnson would explain his *Elementa Philosophica.*[6]

Johnson rejoined the college just in time to put the finishing touches on its first graduating class. The occasion called for a commencement, a public celebration in which the college could display both the scholarly proficiency of its students and the prerogatives of its cherished degree-granting privileges. Degrees were by no means confined to matriculated students. Between 1758 and 1776 King's College honored 108 of its own students and 59 other gentlemen, the latter receiving degrees for work done elsewhere, honorary degrees, or, in two-thirds of the cases, ad eundem degrees (a custom by which the holder of a degree from one college could obtain the same degree from another college if he enriched its coffers with a small fee). Indicative of the college's public standing, more than half of the 59 special recipients were prospective or ordained Anglican priests. For the initial commencement Johnson rounded up an impressive array of 21 degree candidates, only 5 of whom had studied at King's College.[7]

The commencement of 1758, the "first Solemnity of its Kind, ever celebrated here," led off with a magnificent procession to St. George's Chapel, with the degree candidates at the head, followed by President Johnson and Lieutenant Governor DeLancey (his hard feelings apparently overcome by the passage of time and the attraction of a public spectacle), then by the governors, the "Clergy of all Denominations in this City, and other Gentlemen of Distinction of this and the neighbouring Provinces." Once gathered at the chapel, the audience enjoyed a "learned and elegant *Oratio Inauguralis*" by Johnson and several orations and debates by the degree candidates. Daniel Treadwell "demonstrated the Revolution of the Earth round the Sun . . . and defended the Thesis" against two challengers, who must have had somewhat the worse of the argument. President Johnson "in a solemn Manner, conferred the Honours of the College" upon the degree recipients and closed the ceremony with a "solemn pathetick Exhortation." The procession then marched to the City-Arms tavern and had a bash, if the bill for a postcommencement affair five years later is any indication. The bill that year for fifty-nine people included charges for fifty-six bottles of madeira, eleven bottles of claret, punch, thirteen bottles of beer, fourteen bottles of cider, and, not surprisingly, a seven-shilling charge for "tumblers and glasses brock." [8]

While the college slowly gained a stable footing, its leaders made a number of decisions about its organization. Johnson occasionally talked as if he had thoughts of modeling King's College after Oxford, for which he felt "great affection." He was familiar with Oxford through his visit there in 1723, through correspondence with English ecclesiastics in touch with the university, probably through conversations with American friends who journeyed to Oxford while in England for ordination, and through the *Oxonia Illustrata* and the copy of Oxford's laws which he had in his library. He even assured Bishop Berkeley's son in 1756 that he would "make that university my pattern as far as may be. . . ." [9] What Johnson appears actually to have had in mind, however, was an institution that resembled Oxford not in the details of its organization but in the illustriousness of its academic accomplishments and in the political and religious principles for which it stood— principles such as an unswerving devotion to monarchy and episcopacy. It was soon obvious that for the more mundane aspects of its structure King's College would turn to the American collegiate tradition.

This tradition reached back to Harvard College, whose seventeenth-century founders modeled it on Cambridge and Oxford but modified it to suit their special circumstances. The American species of *genus universitas* was perpetuated and refined as Harvard graduates founded Yale in the image of their alma mater, with some modifications, and as Yale graduates behaved in the same fashion when founding Princeton. While the heritage from Cambridge and Oxford was still identifiable in mid-eighteenth-century Harvard, Princeton, and Yale, the distinctive American features of the three colleges were equally prominent. Each was academically, administratively, and geographically separate from other colleges and lacked formal "higher faculties" in law, medicine, or theology (whereas Oxford and Cambridge were universities composed of several undergraduate colleges as well as of higher faculties). American colleges were governed by nonacademic, nonresident boards of community leaders (while faculty members played a major role in governing the colleges at Oxford and Cambridge). Finally, undergraduates at American colleges were organized for instructional purposes in horizontal groupings, corresponding to the stages of academic progress—freshman, sophomore, junior, senior (while, in the main, English university students were organized for social purposes in vertical groupings, determined by financial factors and lasting throughout a student's undergraduate years, with instruction handled separately through individual relationships between tutors and students).[10]

Since both James DeLancey and his son had studied at Cambridge, the founders of King's College had firsthand insight into the operation of an English university. But an American college promised much more in the way of an institution that was feasible financially, attractive to students, and readily at the control of the laymen who headed it. In any case, American colleges were a more familiar part of the founders' landscape than English universities. The College of New Jersey was twenty miles away, not two thousand, and some of its patrons, men like William Smith, Sr., and Peter Van Brugh Livingston, were good friends with several founders of King's College. Yale was an especially common landmark. Its alumni were well represented in the inner circle which organized King's, particularly by Henry Barclay, Benjamin Nicoll, and, above all, by Samuel Johnson. When Johnson and the lottery trustees agreed on an advertisement which announced the opening of the college, it apparently did not occur to them to establish anything but the usual horizontal system of classes. The authors of the charter of 1754 even worked with a copy of Princeton's charter in hand (perhaps choosing Princeton's because no other college in the northern colonies had a royal charter). While they ignored sections of it and introduced some new wrinkles, they copied other parts practically word for word.[11] Johnson did the same thing with the "Laws and Customs of the New Jersey College" when composing the "Laws and Orders of the College of New York," following them closely on some points, making a few changes on others.[12] The cumulative impact was ironic: King's College soon looked strikingly like its denominational rival in New Jersey.

While the lottery trustees continued to meet until mid-1756, disbursing the funds appropriated by the assembly and periodically examining the students, the governors appointed by the charter began meeting regularly in 1755 and assumed most of the responsibility for running the college. Johnson and the sixteen governors who attended meetings regularly between 1755 and 1758 (another eight governors attended on occasion) settled such other organizational issues as the composition of a "Proper Collection of Prayers" for services and the design of a college seal and then focused their attention on constructing "suitable Edifices." [13] A group of New Yorkers on Princeton's board of trustees had put the matter bluntly a few years before: a college would "not in Common Reputation be Esteemed a Colledge till some publick Buildings are built. . . ." Moreover, to Johnson and several governors a residential building for students was so integral a part of collegiate education, going back beyond Yale and Harvard to earliest Oxford and Cambridge, that it hardly seemed possible to envision a college without one. How could college authorities seriously attempt to shape the minds and morals of their students without a dormitory, especially in a city filled with taverns, scoundrels, and women of "ill fame." Samuel Johnson waited impatiently for the day when the pupils would be "under our Eye." [14]

Johnson expected the college first to construct a president's house, but the governors decided instead to devote their skimpy funds entirely to a single building which would house the students as well as the president and his family.[15] The building would form one side of what eventually would be an open quadrangle, with buildings arranged along three sides of the quadrangle and the fourth side left open to admit air and sunshine more freely than was possible in a full or closed quadrangle. It was a design popular at Cambridge and adopted by Harvard, and it reflected the governors' optimism about the future growth of the college. Johnson hoped that a second side, consisting of a chapel, hall, and

Detail from the "Palm Tree Print"
The print appeared in *Scenographia Americana or a Collection of Views of North America and the West Indies* . . . , published in London in 1768.
CREDIT: COLUMBIANA, COLUMBIA UNIVERSITY

library, would be constructed in good time. Meanwhile they would omit a few partitions from the first building—its basic design called exclusively for lodgings—and use part of it for classes, meals, and religious services.[16] With great fanfare the governor of New York laid the cornerstone for King's College's first building in August 1756. Three years and nine months passed before the students finally began to "Lodge and Diet" in it. Three decades passed before the growth of the college persuaded its leaders to undertake additional construction.[17]

A single building made a rather meager quadrangle. Otherwise King's College, as the building as well as the institution was called, was an architectural success. Three stories high and crowned by a cupola, constructed of gray stone, 180 feet long and 30 feet wide, the building rested at the top of a gentle slope which extended some 150 yards to the bank of the Hudson River. Twenty windows running the length of both upper stories, front and back, provided collegians with a lovely perspective south toward the city and north toward upper Manhattan. Sixteen windows running the length of the first floor were interspersed with

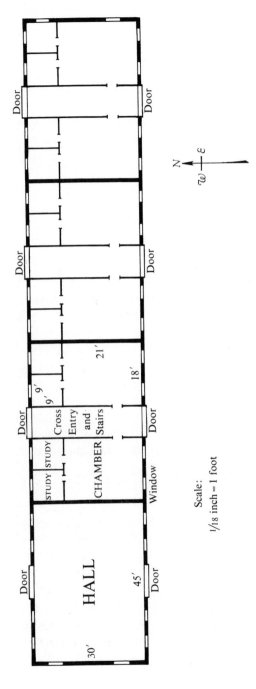

HALL

CHAMBER

STUDY STUDY

Cross
Entry
and
Stairs

Door
Door
Door
Door
Door
Door

Window

30′
45′
9′
9′
21′
18′

N
E
S
W

Scale:
1/18 inch = 1 foot

First Floor of King's College

four doors, three of them leading to cross-entries and stairs, the fourth, toward the west or Hudson River end of the building, opening into the hall. The result was a college which visitors found uniquely impressive, praising it as "beautifully built," of "fine appearance," and located "in a fine, airy situation." An Englishman traveling through the colonies thought it "the most beautifully situated of any college, I believe, in the world" and predicted that the completed quadrangle would be "exceedingly handsome." [18]

Except for a hall and a library of identical size above it, the interior of King's College consisted almost entirely of "apartments." Students ate meals, heard lectures, went to religious services, and attended various other gatherings in the hall. Probably no rooms were constructed specifically or exclusively for classes, a not uncommon feature in early American and English colleges. Harvard built its first classrooms (in the sense we understand the word) in 1766. Had the King's College building been constructed according to the original plan there would have been twenty-four apartments with two students normally sharing each apartment. As it was there were no more than twenty apartments, and the president occupied at least one of those on the east end of the building. The steward had his kitchen in the basement. Each apartment extended the width of the building, so that it would have windows on both the front and the back, a prime consideration when artificial light was inadequate. The back part of an apartment consisted of two studies, each with its own window. The front part, comprising about two-thirds of the apartment, was a roomy sleeping area with two windows.[19]

In most respects the architecture of King's College followed in a tradition that dated from the early colleges at Oxford and Cambridge: its height of three stories; the placement of the library on the second floor where it would be distant from the dampness of both the roof and the basement; the construction of apartments which reached across the building so that there would be sufficient light; the provision of a study for each student; the use of several entries with staircases giving access only to two apartments on each floor; and the absence of rooms designed specifically for classes. Yet King's College resembled most closely the old building at Yale, constructed in 1718. Perhaps it was not simply a coincidence that Samuel Johnson had been a tutor at Yale in 1718.[20]

While the governors oversaw the construction of King's College they also sought funds with which to pay £14,000 or £15,000 in expenses during the college's first seven years, about £10,000 of which were consumed by building costs. These were staggering figures for a young institution, especially since most of the costs accrued within a three-year period, 1757–1760. The college was forced to turn over most of its funds directly to creditors, making it extremely difficult to accumulate an ample endowment. By 1761 Johnson and the governors were bemoaning the college's financial plight, with some reason, since it was not clear how expenses would be covered in upcoming years. Yet, King's College surmounted the financial crunch of its initial years more easily than did most colonial colleges. If only a small part of its funds were left over for an endowment, at least the college did not confront a shortage of money with which to pay its bills. From mid-1754 through mid-1761 King's College received about £17,000, from the lottery proceeds, the seven-year appropriation from the assembly, tuition and room rents, the private subscription among New Yorkers in 1755, and several special gifts and bequests, from Edward Antill, the SPG, and two childless governors, Paul Richard and Joseph Murray. Murray, whose guiding hand had helped steer the college project through several stormy years, provided the key to financial survival. In 1757 he left the college the bulk of his estate, which eventually yielded King's about £10,000. It was the largest single gift presented to a colonial college. Without it the 1760s and 1770s would have been much more difficult years for the college than they were.[21]

By 1759 King's College had many attributes of a modern college: a charter, rules, a faculty, students, governors, alumni, honorary degree recipients, a small endowment, plans in the works for a fund-raising campaign, a campus, and a building under construction. All of this suggests the emergence of a formalized, well-defined organization that was gaining an existence and an identity apart from the particular people who ran it. Although this process was indeed underway, King's College remained an intensely personal institution. At its heart were Samuel Johnson and, in some respects, his family: his wife, Charity Nicoll, his sons, William Samuel and William, and his stepchildren, especially Benjamin and Gloriana Nicoll. They were a cohesive unit, and their letters are replete with expressions of affection, concern, advice, and eagerness to cooperate, expressions that were constantly backed by the family's actions. For instance, the Johnsons as a family had responded to the vicissitudes of the King's College Controversy. Johnson and his stepson consulted repeatedly and worked together to achieve their goals. From Stratford his sons William Samuel and William advised and consoled.

The opening of the college only enhanced the role of the Johnson family. Charity Johnson joined her husband in New York City, William Johnson became the first tutor, and Benjamin Nicoll assumed leadership of the governors. In Johnson's eyes Nicoll was the "life and soul of the whole affair, and everything depended on his activity and influence. . . ." [22] Nicoll persuaded the governors to follow his stepfather's lead and cajoled them when tensions developed. As a lawyer in Connecticut, William Samuel Johnson of necessity participated less directly in the launching of the college. But by sustaining his father's spirit through several family deaths during these years he became an increasingly important psychological support. Indeed, William Samuel's contacts with the college outlasted those of any of the Johnsons: in 1787 he became its president.

The role of the Johnson family was only one aspect of the interpenetration of family and college during Samuel Johnson's presidency. When one searches for prototypes of King's College one is impressed by the influence of Princeton and Yale. But closest of all to the spirit of King's College in the 1750s was the "school" which Johnson had conducted intermittently at his Stratford home during the 1730s and 1740s. New York families—the Rutgers, Jays, Van Cortlandts, DeLanceys, Stuyvesants, Cuylers, and others—dispatched their young sons to study with Johnson. Occasionally he sent his pupils to local schoolmasters for part of their instruction, but the primary thrust of their education came from within the Johnson family. At study, at supper, at play, they were treated as family members. "I assure you we both love him as near to our own as is possible . . . ," Johnson wrote Peter Jay in 1741 of Jay's eleven-year-old son, Augustus, a rather dull lad. "And you may still depend upon it, that no care or pains shall be wanting for his best advantage, for my Wife & I have this winter, in taking pains to teach him to read, done that for him which we never did for our own, nor could we have patience to do, but for one whom we love like our own. . . ." [23]

The same kind of personal relationships characterized the educational process at King's College. Johnson acted the role of a father educating his children, a role sustained by his genuine feelings of affection toward young people. He referred to students as "my dear sons" or "my dear children," "whom I tenderly love," and he phrased letters of recommendation to reflect his very personal conception of their education: "The bearer hereof is Mr. Epinetus Townsend . . . , whom I carried through the course of his education and graduated M. A. . . ." [24] The completion of the building—the "House" in Johnson's terms—symbolized the fulfillment of this highly personal dimension of the college, not a departure from it. Johnson, his wife, and his students were now under one roof, where they could eat, sleep, study, and pray together, almost as a family. [25] Some New York parents expected as much. Before construction of the college building, parents nagged Johnson to take their sons into his home in the city, so that, as Edward Antill wrote of his son, "his Heart may be Improved as well as his head." [26]

The small size of the college—Johnson never had more than thirty students at one time—contributed to the personal and familial character of college life. So did ties of friendship, kinship, and marriage among Johnson, the students, and their families, especially since close to three-fifths of the fifty-two matriculants during the 1750s were related, mostly as sons and nephews, to men who at some point were college governors. Johnson was related to several governors himself through his stepson, and he felt a "particular friendship for many of the principal families" to which the governors and some of the students belonged. [27]

The personal nature of the college and the pivotal role of Johnson and his family meant that students at King's College, unlike most college students today, had intimate contact with the president, who was the leading intellectual figure on the campus. However, this also meant that personal and family problems could rapidly become college problems—and it so happened that these were years of trial for Johnson and his family. In his sixties by 1757, Johnson was beginning to find his work a "constant drudgery," "the perpetual confinement to hard service requiring his daily attention without relaxation." Moreover, Johnson was plagued by occasional ill health, by the "frequent danger of the smallpox," and, above all, by a "succession of troubles one on the back of another in my family. . . ." [28]

The death of Johnson's first grandson shortly after birth early in 1756, a setback to Johnson's "hopes of seeing a male descendant of my own a little advanced in life before I go off the stage . . . ," was followed only a few months later by the shattering news that smallpox had taken his beloved son William, while in England to be ordained. "The wound is exceeding deep," Johnson wrote plaintively to his surviving son. Johnson had barely absorbed that blow when he found that God was calling him "to pass through another great revolution" in his circumstances. During the winter of 1757–58, when he and his wife ironically retired to Westchester to avoid the smallpox, his "dear wife" was "seized with an illness that made her life very uncomfortable . . ." and grew "worse and worse" until she died in June. [29]

The void left by Charity Johnson's death was filled in a limited way by Gloriana Maverick, Johnson's stepdaughter and a widow for several years. She had been living with the Johnsons since the death of her husband and now became the "stay of his family." Yet, incredibly, she soon "seemed consumptive and at length declining more and more she died June 28, 1759." The sole intimate member of his family now remaining in New York was Benjamin Nicoll, who was "very dear and very helpful" to his stepfather. "[N]o son could be more tender of a father than he was of his father-in-law [stepfather]," wrote Johnson. It was thus "a most fatal shock to the President" when Nicoll "sickened and died at 42 in April 1760." Johnson was now "stripped and solitary," his only son seventy miles away at Stratford. New York City "seemed almost a wilderness." [30]

Johnson's familial calamities and a sequence of events which accompanied them plummeted King's College into a "very suffering condition" by 1760. In October 1759 the threat of smallpox had once again forced Johnson to flee the city, this time to Stratford. Cutting and Treadwell carried on, but Treadwell soon became "consumptive." By February 1760 he had ceased teaching and "before spring was far advanced he died." According to Johnson's recollection, he "hired a man to assist Mr. Cutting, the best he could get, but he made but a poor hand of it. So that the College suffered greatly in his [Johnson's] absence." With Johnson continuing to take refuge at Stratford, the weight of leadership fell ever more heavily on the shoulders of Benjamin Nicoll, and his death in April 1760 left the college adrift. By the time Johnson returned in May, four or five students had departed, and the college was falling "much into disrepute." [31]

Even before Johnson's second flight from the smallpox there were signs of trouble. The number of matriculants dropped from an average of eleven per year from 1756 through 1758 to four in 1759. Johnson himself complained in 1759 that the college was "dragging on very heavily," and he admitted that his absence for most of 1757 might have contributed to the slide.[32] Nor could his personal capacity to meet the problems of his job have survived unimpaired the deaths of his grandson, son, wife, and stepdaughter. Johnson's second departure greatly aggravated the situation. The president was the heart and soul of the college, yet a student entering in 1756 had had no contact with him for much of his freshman year, part of his second year, and most of his senior year. The point was not lost on New York parents. The French and Indian War (1754–1763) provided an additional handicap, luring several students from the college and stimulating inflation which, especially by pushing up building costs, intensified the squeeze on funds.[33]

Johnson's return did not spark an immediate revival in college fortunes. Beset by a series of troubles, the school foundered all the more because its reputation had tumbled. Only six students matriculated in 1760, another six in 1761, and the student body stabilized at about twenty. Replacing Treadwell proved difficult, creating a competitive disadvantage for King's in an age when science was a popular feature of the college curriculum. "[W]e go on heavily . . . ," lamented Johnson fifteen months after Treadwell ceased teaching, "especially for want of a teacher in mathematics and experimental philosophy." [34] Johnson unwittingly compounded the college's difficulties through his tolerance for the "little untoward humors" of his pupils. Word spread (probably with substantial embellishment) that discipline was lax, a serious failing in the eyes of many parents. Johnson himself confessed later that there was "perhaps a little too much tenderness and lenity in discipline." [35] By 1761 fighting in the French and Indian War had ceased, but New York settled into a postwar depression at the same time that prices remained high, with food prices climbing by 1762 to a higher level than during the war. The college thus faced its crisis with dwindling financial reserves, amidst an economic environment unfavorable to the attraction either of new funds or new students. [36]

People too close to an issue often lose sight of the larger realities which shape the context in which they work. Tempers began to flare as Johnson and the governors each sought to blame the other for the hard times which had befallen their college. Even before Johnson returned from his second leave of absence, the governors had begun to wonder whether he might best serve the college by stepping down. Upon his return Johnson concluded that the responsibility for the college's continuing adversity lay with the governors, who failed to take his advice on measures to restore prosperity. "The stupidity of many of our governors," Johnson wrote his son, "is such that it looks as if they would let their college come to nothing in spite of all that I can do to save it." [37]

Relationships between Johnson and the governors had never been overly friendly. Johnson considered them "an unweildly Body," too "immersed in other Affairs," and, for the most part, "utter strangers to learning and Colleges." [38] During the 1750s Benjamin Nicoll had helped smooth out the rough spots. The gov-

ernors cooperated by usually delegating academic matters to a
special group with whom Johnson like to work, among them Nicoll and the clerics on the board. At Johnson's behest, the governors made this arrangement more permanent early in 1759 by appointing the same gentlemen to a standing committee which
would "visit the College," "see that the College Laws are put in
Execution," and "Graduate such of the Students . . . as they
shall think worthy." [39]

The subsequent crisis and Nicoll's death destroyed this harmony. The president was soon accusing the governors of caring
for "little else but their Gain and pleasures." [40] From Johnson's
point of view, his controversy with the governors revolved around
three issues. First was the establishment of a grammar school,
which Johnson had earlier touted primarily as a means of upgrad-
ing the academic quality of the college; if entrants were better
prepared Johnson could pitch the college curriculum at a higher
level. Now he argued that the "want of a good grammar school"
accounted for the small number of matriculants, "as few were
qualified for admission," an allusion to the fact that there were no
public grammar schools in the colony and few private ones. [41]
Johnson took several steps to organize a grammar school, but the
governors refused to cooperate, perhaps for fear of overtaxing the
college's small reserve of funds. Their obstinacy exasperated Johnson. He later claimed, with striking myopia, that it was due to
their failure to act on this issue that the college's "reputation much
suffered and mine with it." [42]

If the governors did in fact plead a shortage of funds, Johnson
thought it a poor excuse. He believed that they were dragging
their feet on this point, too. Johnson had visions of thousands of
pounds in English pockets only waiting for some energetic representative of King's College to collect them (as it turned out, he
was right). The governors had toyed with the idea of soliciting
funds in England since 1755, but they never found a volunteer to
undertake the mission. Johnson's hopes did not falter, but frustration almost choked him when he learned early in 1762 that the
College of Philadelphia had beaten King's College to the punch.
"And now here comes Dr. Smith of Philadelphia going home to

beg for their college," he wrote his son, "so we have lost our opportunity for that, at least for two or three years. Such are our
stupid doings!" [43]

At almost the same moment Johnson and the governors clashed
over a third issue, the appointment of the president's successor.
Johnson had no illusions about serving indefinitely, but he expected to retire at his discretion and to help choose a successor.[44]
In 1759 his burden of personal tragedy and academic responsibility had prompted him to inquire privately whether East Apthorp, an Anglican minister at Cambridge, Massachusetts, might
be interested in the job. However, the more Apthorp learned
about King's College the less enthusiastic he seemed to be. During
Johnson's second flight from the smallpox the governors took it
upon themselves, with Johnson's consent, to contact the archbishop of Canterbury. They asked him to seek out a man who
would be "qualified to succed Dr. Johnson in the presidentship in
case of his death or resignation. . . ." Johnson himself advised the
archbishop that the candidate, whom Johnson expected to serve as
vice-president until his own resignation, should be an Oxonian, a
"good and eloquent preacher," a "truly exemplary person," "well
acquainted" with the Hebrew Scriptures and "all other parts of
polite literature," and unmarried.[45]

Late in 1761 Johnson learned that the archbishop had located
one Myles Cooper, an Oxford M.A. and an Anglican cleric who
was a well-respected fellow and eager to come. He was a little
young, and his preaching and his command of Hebrew were not
up to snuff, but then not many Oxford graduates wanted to live in
New York City. Johnson was satisfied, so he called a meeting of
the governors, only to encounter vigorous opposition. "None objected against him for his youth or the doubt about his preaching," related Johnson. "But what need of so many tutors for so
few scholars? And how could they provide salaries?" Oliver De-
Lancey, brother of the former lieutenant governor, finally got
down to the nub of the problem. He "talked of his expecting I was
to resign when they sent for another." Johnson retorted that he
had no thought of resigning right away, certainly not until the
summer of 1763. Finally, DeLancey got up and left the meeting,

and the other governors let the issue drop. They voted, by a "slender majority," to hire Cooper, but Johnson was flabbergasted at the way he had been treated and undoubtedly suspicious that he had not seen the end of the matter.[46] The climax of the president's struggle with the governors was not far off, but in the meantime the gloom which had enveloped Johnson and his college since 1759 began to dissipate. In 1761, Johnson had found new personal strength in his remarriage (to Sarah Beach), a source of "unspeakable satisfaction," and in the birth of a grandson. The college also finally located a professor of natural philosophy and mathematics, Robert Harpur, an alumnus of Glasgow University and a teacher for several years before leaving his native Ireland. He "will do very well," conceded Johnson, despite the fact that he was a Presbyterian. By spring 1762 Johnson was even complimenting the governors for being "much revived," mainly because they agreed to send James Jay on a fundraising venture to England.[47] Jay, a shrewd but neurotic member of one of the colony's leading families, promptly tried to undercut Reverend William Smith of the College of Philadelphia by applying to the king for a "brief" (a royally sanctioned campaign through official channels, especially through parish churches), while Smith concentrated on lining up contributors privately. Smith got wind of Jay's scheme, and the only way they could settle the matter was to apply jointly for a brief and split the proceeds. Although one British minister suggested that it would be more appropriate to hang New Yorkers than assist them, since some New York merchants had traded with the enemy during the French and Indian War, the king approved the brief and personally contributed £400 to King's College. Johnson was ecstatic at the "glorious news." He expected a "great sum," which would eliminate the college's financial distress and permit such measures as the establishment of a grammar school.[48]

When Myles Cooper debarked at New York in October 1762, Samuel Johnson had already decided to make Cooper's first year his own last year. He would familiarize Cooper with the ins and outs of the college, Cooper would relieve him of some of the "daily Drudgery" which was so "burthensom" to his years, and, then, by the next commencement, he would return to Stratford and reassume his pulpit. The plan seemed all the more sensible when he discovered Cooper to be an "amiable [,] ingenious and accomplished young gentleman," well qualified to "take charge" of the college after a year's initiation. Their months together should be pleasurable ones.[49]

The president was thus jolted when the governors intimated that he should step down immediately, and with no compensation or pension. His son roundly condemned their "baseness, ingratitude, and barbarity" and spent four days in New York trying to smooth out "Daddy's affairs." [50] Johnson decided to stay on, and his supporters among the governors restrained the opposition. But his last year proved no kinder than earlier years. Even his bitterness about his shabby treatment by the governors faded momentarily before the tragedy which befell him in February 1763: the smallpox claimed his second wife. Within three weeks of her death Johnson retired to Stratford.

Samuel Johnson's brief term in office ended on a note that seemed to typify his years in New York. Johnson had expected his presidency to be a public triumph, the pinnacle of an illustrious career. Instead, he returned to Stratford in despair that, as his son put it, he had "seen his family ruined and experienced nothing but distress and trouble. . . ." Yet, Johnson and the governors had launched what turned out to be a durable institution, no mean feat for a college hedged in by proliferating competition and by public antagonism and indifference. Johnson had contributed to his college in many ways, from lending his prestige to a fledgling operation—even if that prestige became somewhat tarnished—to persevering in behalf of the college in the face of disappointment and obstinacy. It was Johnson, for instance, who discovered James Jay and persuaded the governors to hire him, an action which soon produced a bonanza.[51]

Johnson's feelings of paternal affection for King's College outlasted his sense of bitterness. In 1766 he visited the college—"my college" he called it—and was gratified to find it in "good condition." [52] Still, from afar one cannot help feeling sad about Johnson and his college, especially that a man of Johnson's qualities as an educator and an intellectual should reach so few young New Yorkers, and that men who had endured several years of controversy should be so blind to its impact that they would blame the problems of their college largely on each others' personal shortcomings.

8.

MYLES COOPER
TAKES THE REINS

"I KNEW HIM WELL," one governor recalled of Myles Cooper several years after the American Revolution had forced King's College's second president to flee to his native England. "He was honest, just, learned, and liberal; judicious, sensible, friendly, and convivial; he loved good company, and good company loved him; he was by no means dissipated. He loved God, honoured his King, esteemed his friends, and hated rebellion." [1] The latter sentiment led to Cooper's hasty departure from the college one May night in 1775, a howling New York mob not too many paces behind him; but for twelve years he presided over King's College with some success.

The rector of Trinity Church once quipped that Cooper knew "every Body, and every Thing that passes here" in the city.[2] Cooper's facile manner, his fondness for good food and drink, his bulky size and pudgy face, all convey the impression of an easygoing and tractable man. But Cooper was not docile. His "Witty and entertaining" qualities and his "high Taste for Amusem[en]t" were matched by his energy, ambition, and resoluteness, traits that were all the more fruitful because they were wrapped in such a pleasant package.[3] What gave rise and direction to Cooper's drive is hard to tell because little is known of his early years. He came from a well-established family in Cumberland, near the Scottish border, attended local schools, and entered Queen's College, Ox-

ford. Seven years later, in 1760, he earned his M.A. Before consenting to join the King's College faculty in 1762, at age twenty-
five, he served successively as a schoolmaster, a chaplain at
Queen's College, and a curate of a country church near Oxford.
During the nine years before he moved to New York, then, Cooper's life was immersed in two intertwined English institutions,
Oxford and the Anglican church.[4]

Cooper quickly impressed his collegiate and clerical associates
in New York—a man of excellent judgment, one governor called
him.[5] The board undoubtedly welcomed a person of his con-
viviality after fencing for several years with a troubled and sometimes cantankerous Samuel Johnson. Cooper soon gained recognition among friends and enemies alike as a "mighty advocate" of
the Anglican church. His travels in its behalf (as well as for his
own pleasure) earned him the epithet "Rambling Cooper." In 1765
Anglican clerics in the middle colonies named Cooper president of
their convention, a signal honor in light of his youth and his
recent arrival.[6]

One New Yorker joked at Cooper's death that his "Library sold
for £5, the Liquors in his cellar for £150." [7] Unquestionably the
new president was not an intellectual of Samuel Johnson's calibre.
His surviving correspondence reveals little of Johnson's scholarly
curiosity or intensity. Instead, Cooper's letters deal almost exclusively with administrative and social concerns, though these are
sometimes phrased with a wit and comic sarcasm that make them
entertaining reading. Yet Cooper was also a man who aggressively
sought new books for the college library because he believed that
nothing "but Libraries can make us learned; and nothing but
Learning can make us wiser than we are; and till we *are* made
wiser . . . we can never be happy." One contemporary judged
him, fairly it would seem, to be "a pretty neat classical Scholar,
and of a good taste for the belles Lettres" but of only "very slight
Insight" into mathematics and natural philosophy.[8] He regularly
turned his hand at poetry and in 1761 published a volume of
pleasant if not profound poems. In 1774 he published a brief text
on moral philosophy for use in American colleges, basing it
largely on Aristotelian ethics. Thus, while not a thinker of John-

son's calibre, he was capable of providing intellectual leadership within the college community.

Cooper promptly hinted in what direction his leadership would take the college. On November 16, 1762, the day that Cooper first joined the faculty, the governors decided to clean house. They failed in their effort to dump Johnson, but they did appoint a committee to "enquire into the State and circumstances of the College" and to suggest new regulations for the "better ordering and good Government thereof." Neither Johnson nor Cooper served officially on the committee, but both men influenced its deliberations, with Cooper's voice carrying the most weight. On March 1, 1763, the day that Cooper officially took charge of the college, the committee unveiled a new "Plan of Education," a new set of statutes, and proposals for a grammar school and a formal library. Cooper later confessed that "our plan of Education" was "copied, in the most material parts, from Queen's College in Oxford. . . ." Obviously this was not Samuel Johnson's doing. The official program omitted any mention of science and mathematics, to which Johnson had devoted close to two years. King's College students, like students at Oxford, were now to confine their studies largely to Latin and Greek grammar, the classics, logic, metaphysics, and ethics. Aristotle, a curricular deity at Queen's College, marched to the head of the class. Several of Johnson's cherished authors fell by the wayside.[9]

In operation, the change in the curriculum turned out to be neither so drastic nor so regressive as it might at first appear. But there was a shift in emphasis that tipped Cooper's hand. Johnson revered Oxford but patterned his college after the American collegiate tradition with which he was so familiar. Cooper revered Oxford, and it was the only university he knew. He saw no reason why an infant college in the wilderness should not bow to the traditions of England's greatest educational institution.

The revision of the statutes served mainly to tighten up the collegiate way of living. While the completion of the college building prompted the changes, they also reflected Cooper's allegiance to a vital tradition at Queen's College, and a conviction, shared by Cooper and the governors, that "pretty strict discipline" could

Myles Cooper, President of King's College 1763–1775
The portrait by John Singleton Copley hangs in the King's College Room, Columbia University.
CREDIT: COLUMBIANA, COLUMBIA UNIVERSITY

help rescue the college's failing reputation. The statutes required students to eat and sleep at the college and to wear gowns. Punishments were outlined for virtually every conceivable transgression. The president and faculty were even authorized to visit students' chambers "at whatever hour they please" and, should admission be refused, to force open the doors.[10]

Cooper and the governors followed up these measures a year later by surrounding King's College—and its students—with a "board fence eight foot high with Nails at the top." The college hired a porter to sit at the east gate with a set of rules in hand telling when to let students pass, a custom that Cooper appropriated directly from Queen's College.[11] In 1771 the president crowned his system of discipline with the introduction of the "Black Book," a book of "Misdemeanours" in which Oxford proctors traditionally recorded student transgressions. Whereas Samuel Johnson admitted that he had been too lenient with his students, Cooper was soon boasting that "with Respect to *Discipline* (which, it seems is one heavy Accusation exhibited against us,) we are far from being outdone by any College on the American Continent; and I *know* of none in Europe, to which, in this Article, we are really inferior." [12]

If reforms in the curriculum and the collegiate way of life owed much to Cooper, the decision to establish a grammar school was obviously an admission that Johnson had had a good point all along. Perhaps his departure and Jay's success in England permitted the governors to recognize it. The governors placed the grammar school under their own watchful eye, decided its students should learn Latin, Greek, and English, and hired an experienced schoolmaster in Matthew Cushing, a forty-three-year-old Harvard graduate. The school opened in August 1763. By November twenty-seven scholars were attending daily, and prospects were so encouraging that the governors arranged with a second teacher to assist Cushing and to set up his own school in writing and arithmetic.[13] Cooper was in "great hopes" that entrants to the college would increase both in number and in quality. From Stratford Samuel Johnson cheered the school and chastised the governors for not acting earlier.[14]

The governors' decision to organize a library was inspired by the acquisition of some fifteen hundred books. Joseph Murray willed the college a "considerable Number," probably several hundred. Reverend Duncombe Bristowe, an SPG member and for thirty years a London rector, left his library of "near 1500 Volumes" to the SPG and recommended that the Society give it to

King's College. About a thousand volumes reached the college in 1763, but the remaining books disappeared.[15] Several small gifts of books were added during the thirteen years before the Revolution, including a present in 1772 of all books published during the previous several years by Oxford's Clarendon Press. The library also became the repository for various "curiosities" donated to the college, including a collection of insects and a "collection of ancient alphabets on copper plate." [16]

Jean de Crèvecoeur thought the King's College library an "excellent" one. Situated on the second floor above the hall, the room was spacious and well lighted, but the library's collection of books was probably weighted heavily towards law and theology. Traditionally, college libraries serviced scholars, not undergraduates—Thomas Bradbury Chandler used the King's College library while preparing some of his publications—but this library apparently was organized with students in mind. "With such essential Helps to Learning," commented one optimistic New Yorker in 1763, "may we not flatter ourselves with the Prospect of soon seeing our youth . . . vie with our Neighbours in the knowledge and Improvement of the Liberal Arts and Sciences." [17] In 1763 that was a moot question.

While Cooper and the governors revamped the college, James Jay and William Smith accumulated in England a fund which made possible more sweeping changes. Once the king approved the brief they sought (August 1762), professional "brief-layers" took over. They distributed 11,500 copies of the brief, which sanctioned and explained the fund-raising venture, to churchwardens throughout England. Normally, appeals were read in local churches, then the churchwardens called at individual homes to solicit contributions and turned over the proceeds to the brief-layers. Smith and Jay employed a variety of schemes to drum up interest in the brief and to gain donations on their own. They printed and distributed various pieces of "campaign literature," persuaded newspapers to carry items on the collection, encouraged local ministers to preach in behalf of the colleges, and organized special groups of clerics to preach in place of regular ministers. The latter practice reached its peak one Sunday in London when thirteen clerics visited churches to advertise the brief. Smith and Jay often accompanied the churchwardens on their house-to-house solicitations and contacted numerous potential donors privately. Smith apparently had an easier time of it than Jay. The former's status as a cleric facilitated making contacts and enabled him to preach his own sermons and coach other clerics. According to Smith, Jay did "his best," but his appearance was "unpromising," his manner lacked confidence, and he stuttered and spoke too rapidly, a description that makes one wonder either about Jay's "best" or Smith's veracity.[18]

Despite these handicaps and an abortive trip to Ireland, the fund-raising drive was incredibly successful. Private solicitations by Smith and Jay brought in about £3,100 sterling, the whole campaign some £16,000 sterling. Unsolicited gifts amounted to a meager £200 sterling. King's College eventually garnered net proceeds of £6,366 sterling, more than £11,500 in New York currency.[19] The triumph was marred only by a bitter and protracted dispute between Jay and the college governors over the transfer of the funds to New York. Jay charged that the governors questioned his integrity by drawing for funds without his authorization from the London bank which handled the money. The governors became angered at Jay when he let the bank return their bills protested, even though he had received enough money to cover them. Jay's personal vanity, touchiness about his authority as the college's agent, and the excessive remuneration he expected for his services snarled the conflict. So did the governors' stubbornness— "foolish punctilio" one board member called it. The college sued Jay, Jay countersued, and the thickety muddle was not cleared up until 1773.[20]

Due to the Jay controversy part of the funds did not reach King's College until the 1770s, but the governors received more than three-quarters of the proceeds (£9,000 New York currency) by the close of 1764. The college already had accumulated a surplus in the neighborhood of £5,000. Through June 1761 the board had collected £17,000 in income and incurred only £14,000 to £15,000 in expenses. During the next three years income from gifts, the assembly grant, tuition, and rent exceeded expenses by another £2,000. Most of the £9,000 from England was probably added to these surpluses, creating by 1765 an endowment that may have been as high as £14,000. Myles Cooper expected the English funds to push the endowment up to £20,000, an estimate that seems inflated.[21] From 1765 to 1767 the endowment was augmented by additional proceeds from the Jay collection and other gifts, probably reaching a point where interest and student fees amply covered annual expenses. Despite its small number of students, King's College could now boast the largest endowment of all the colonial colleges. At the opening of the American Revolution it exceeded £17,000.[22]

The college accumulated other income-producing property, though not until 1772 did the governors discover how well they were doing. When Myles Cooper visited England in 1772 he was amazed to learn that James Jay had procured for the college a 20,000-acre tract. In 1763 the president of the Board of Trade had intimated to Jay that a grant might be in the offing. The governors instructed Jay to pursue the matter, but by the time the Privy Council gave its approval Jay and the governors were at logger-heads. Jay declined either to inform the governors or to pay a nominal charge for issuance of the king's mandamus.[23] Unaware of Jay's success, the governors decided to seek some acreage on their own from the governor of New York. In 1767 the provincial council granted the college a tract in present-day Vermont, an area claimed by both New York and New Hampshire. Three years earlier the Crown had resolved a long-standing dispute between the two colonies by confirming New York's title to all the land west of the Connecticut River and north of Massachusetts, but continuing friction delayed the grant until 1770. Lieutenant Governor Cadwallader Colden finally consented to a 24,000-acre township, appropriately named Kingsland, which was supposed to become the county seat of recently formed Gloucester County. Now known as Washington, the township was located between the Connecticut River and the Green Mountains, about twelve miles southeast of present-day Montpelier. Confident that the land was "very Good in Quality and like to be speedily settled if suitable Encouragement is given," the governors took several steps to attract tenants. But the area was sparsely settled—in 1771 there were less than eight hundred people living on Gloucester County's more than 2 million acres—and the inhabitants were reluctant to line the pockets of distant New Yorkers. King's College received little, if any, income from the land before the Revolution.[24]

The college took advantage of Jay's mandamus from the king, once Cooper stumbled upon it. In 1774 King's received title to a 20,000-acre tract thirty-five miles north of Kingsland, near the present-day town of Johnson, Vermont. The same year Governor William Tryon of New York presented the college with 10,000 acres out of his own holdings, located about twenty miles north of Kingsland, near present-day Worcester, Vermont. By 1775, then, the college owned 54,000 acres in three separate tracts, all within the borders of present-day Vermont.[25]

The accession of a vigorous, young president, the influx of funds which turned the college's financial situation around, the new measures to combat student unruliness, the establishment of a successful grammar school, and the promise of increased enrollment all helped restore some of the optimism that had languished during Johnson's last years. Friends of the college believed it to be "in a much more flourishing Condition than ever." One governor expressed his renewed conviction that it would "do well, in spight of the Devil, and many of his Imps here."[26] The resignation of Leonard Cutting in 1763 provoked a few anxious moments. A clerical friend of Cooper's from Oxford agreed to join the faculty, but he died just as he was about to leave England. When other efforts to hire a clergyman from Oxford or Cambridge failed, the college settled for a layman, and a shining light at that.[27] Samuel Clossy was a native of Ireland, the recipient of B.A. and M.D. degrees from Trinity College, Dublin, and a fellow of Ireland's College of Physicians. Dedicated to the empiricism of Bacon and Locke, he published a pioneering study on morbid anatomy in 1763. Clossy migrated to New York City that same year and promptly displayed his skills to all comers by delivering a series of lectures on anatomy, which he illustrated by dissecting two cadavers. The governors permitted Clossy to hold medical lectures at the college and appointed him a tutor and professor of natural philosophy.[28]

Cooper, Clossy, and Robert Harpur—educated respectively at Oxford, Trinity College, Dublin, and Glasgow—proved an able trio. Cooper taught classical languages and literature, ethics, rhetoric, logic, and metaphysics. Clossy and Harpur apparently helped teach some of these subjects and handled natural philosophy and mathematics themselves. Although Harpur officially resigned as professor of mathematics in 1767, the trio remained at King's College until the Revolution. They were joined in 1767 by a distinguished medical faculty, on which Clossy also served. Four years earlier the board had rejected a proposal for a medical faculty, in part for fear of overtaxing the college resources. But a hefty endowment created new options, and one of the first fruits was the King's College Medical School, the second medical school in the American colonies. For the next eight years the medical faculty offered instruction that fell little short of any in Europe.

Signs of a prosperous future seemed to abound. Yet, adversity continued to dog the college, much to the consternation of its leaders. Samuel Auchmuty, rector of Trinity Church and a governor, was no less dispirited at the decade's close than Samuel Johnson had been at its opening. The college "labors under so many external and internal Difficulties," wrote Auchmuty, "that I know not what will become of it. . . . It is very discouraging to a person who has an undertaking at heart . . . to find every thing going retrograde. It is discouraging & disheartening." [29] The controversy with James Jay annoyed Auchmuty, but other matters probably depressed him more. What looked like an upsurge in the number of students back in 1763 and 1764 quickly leveled off. Soon there were only twenty-five or so, about the number in attendance for the rest of the decade. In 1768–69, fifteen years after its founding, King's College had no more students than it did in 1756, two years after its founding.

Johnson's panacea, the grammar school, had fared no better. In 1764 there were fifty students. By 1767 there were fifteen. Since the school was costing the college £170 "and upwards" a year, the governors retrenched by firing the usher. Four years later conditions were just as bleak, so the board worked out a less formal and less expensive arrangement with the school's master, Matthew Cushing. Apparently the grammar school attracted enough students to continue in operation until the Revolution, with Alexander Leslie, the former usher, succeeding Cushing as master in 1775.[30] Just as Johnson turned on the governors in 1760, blaming much of the college's woes on their neglect, so Auchmuty and Cooper began to snipe at them. Cooper grumbled that when he called for a meeting, it was "more than an even wager" that he would not muster a quorum.[31]

It hardly seemed that King's College was about to enter upon, as the faculty and governors later described it, "the Period of its greatest Felicity." Yet, such was the case. The number of students and the attentiveness of the governors suddenly picked up with the opening of 1770s. Whereas in 1768–69 the usual twenty-four or twenty-five students enjoyed the spaciousness of a building designed for at least a dozen more, by 1773 Cooper delighted in announcing that "our numbers yearly increase, and our present Apartments overflow." In 1771–72 there were forty students. By the fall of 1772 there were forty-five liberal arts undergraduates as well as several medical students—a level which the college maintained until the outbreak of the Revolution. Perhaps it was not impressive when compared to Princeton or Yale, but to the governors it betokened the success of their institution. The College "will rise & flourish, I trust," declared one governor, "notwithstanding the Opposition & Calumnies of its Enemies. . . ."[32]

The reasons for the sudden upturn are obscure. It did not reflect a breakthrough into the ranks either of rural New Yorkers or of dissenters. If anything, the percentage of Anglicans was higher in the decade before the Revolution than earlier, perhaps 75 percent. Part of the increase can be attributed to several mid-century associates of Samuel Johnson—Samuel Auchmuty, Benjamin Nicoll, Thomas Bradbury Chandler, and others—whose college age sons now entered King's. No doubt, too, the college benefited from the rise in the number of Anglicans in the New York City area—the overall population of the city increased by 60 percent between 1756 and 1771. Most important, the college succeeded in tapping the burgeoning group of newly prosperous, commercial families in the city and surrounding area, families of middling and humble origin. Their sons more than made up for the drop in students from the interrelated upper-class network which founded and managed the college. In the 1750s close to three-fifths of the students had been related to men who at some point were governors of the college. In the 1770s that proportion dropped to below one-fifth.

The climb in number of students accompanied a virtual reorganization of the board of governors. At the opening of the 1770s the board elected nine new members (five had died, four resigned). Remarkably enough in light of past experience, eight of the nine served the college diligently during the next few years. Also, two new ex officio governors and an original governor who had neglected the college in the 1760s began to attend meetings regularly. These men joined four original governors who had labored faithfully since the 1750s—John Watts, John Livingston, Johannes Ritzema, and Leonard Lispenard—and four governors who had emerged as champions of the college in the 1760s—Samuel Auchmuty, James Duane, John Tabor Kempe, and Thomas Jones. Despite changes in personnel, members of the provincial elite still dominated the board. So did Anglicans, with four Anglican clerics now among its ranks: Cooper, Auchmuty, and two assistant ministers at Trinity Church. While Anglican clerics assumed a more prominent role, several of the laymen who had fought obstinately with Samuel Johnson had either died or stopped attending, factors which facilitated cooperation between Cooper and the governors. The committee of visitation, first organized by Johnson, handled the immediate chores of governing the college and succeeded in working smoothly with Cooper. In fact, the entire board admired the president. In 1770 they prepared a "Testimonial" to his "Good Conduct, Dilegence & Abilitys." They also praised him for remaining single, an attribute which may not have thrilled Cooper himself but which delighted the governors after the family crises of Johnson's years.[33]

Neither Cooper nor several of the governors were about to let pass the opportunity afforded by this harmony and energy. With a sizable endowment to underwrite expansion and a dramatic increase in students to encourage it, Cooper and the governors decided to act. The board that had met sixteen times between 1764 and 1769 met twenty-eight times between 1771 and 1773. For years King's College had suffered the embarrassments of a poor relative, struggling along with a handful of students while neighboring colleges seemed to flourish. Now, insisted one governor, King's was about to gain an "evident Superiority over all others on the Continent." [34]

9.

THE COMING
OF THE REVOLUTION

COLUMBIA UNIVERSITY has often honored its sons who performed so nobly in the nation's service during the American Revolution: Alexander Hamilton, John Jay, Gouverneur Morris, Robert R. Livingston, Jr., and Egbert Benson. The Bicentennial of the American Revolution is stimulating a new round of tributes. It may come as a shock, then, to realize that the men who educated these heroic figures would regard them more as symbols of failure than as sources of pride. Had the leaders of King's College in the 1760s and 1770s selected those alumni who best embodied the ideals for which the college stood, they would probably have chosen Samuel Auchmuty (Jr.) and Thomas Barclay. While Hamilton and his associates regrettably joined the rebels of 1776 and betrayed the British monarchy, Auchmuty and Barclay fought for the empire and then devoted their lives to its service. Auchmuty rose to the rank of general in the British army, fought in India, Egypt, and South America, and was knighted for his accomplishments. Barclay became a distinguished lawyer and political leader in Nova Scotia and then served thirty years in the British diplomatic corps. Barclay's continuing commitment to the values of his undergraduate education was reflected in a letter he wrote in 1799:

I find that those who were termed Royalists or Loyalists, in addition to their attachment to their king and country, preserve their principles of honor and integrity, of openness and sincerity, which marked the Americans previous to the year 1773; while those who have sold their king for a Republican Government, have adopted all the frivolity, intrigue, and insincerity of the French, and in relinquishing their allegiance, resigned at the same time, almost universally, religion and morality.[1]

Samuel Auchmuty and Thomas Barclay were not idiosyncratic products of an otherwise radical college community. Probably half or more of all the King's College students and alumni living in 1776 became loyalists. So did Myles Cooper, four of the five other men who taught liberal arts at King's between 1770 and 1777, and more than two-thirds of the governors who participated in policy making during the early 1770s. The college leaders conceived of their institution as a bulwark of the established order, not as its critic. On the very eve of the Revolution they sought to strengthen the college's ties to the Crown.

In January 1771 Cooper hinted that something was afoot when he reported to a friend that the governors had given him a "Leave of absence to take a voyage to England." By the time Cooper sailed in October he had been charged with important tasks by both the college and the Anglican clergy. Earlier, on a day in September, a committee of governors had met at Bolton's Tavern to map out plans for the college. They settled several minor points— that Cooper should try to resolve the Jay controversy and should ask the Crown to remit quit rents on Kingsland—but the conversation centered on a topic of greater consequence. Would not a "Royal Charter for the College constituting it a University" prove "beneficial" to the college and strengthen the "connection and harmony between the mother country and this colony"? Indeed it would, and at the same time the king might show his favor by founding "2 or more Professorships" at the new university and by bestowing upon it all other "useful privileges" enjoyed by Oxford, Cambridge, and Trinity College, Dublin.[2]

Cooper had kept one eye on Oxford ever since arriving in New York City. Now his provincial college was to become the first British university in the new world, giving it both a unique and superior position among the colonial colleges. In some respects this vision dated from the 1750s. Struck by New York City's central location and its prospects for becoming the "grand seat of the councills held for promoting the British interest in this part of the world," the founders of King's College expected their seminary to become an intercolonial institution which would diffuse learning throughout "his majesties plantations," much as did Oxford and Cambridge throughout England.[3] By 1770 the shape and significance of the vision had been deeply influenced by the literalness of Cooper's regard for Oxford as a model and by the reaction of Cooper and the governors to the Revolutionary crisis which had unfolded during the 1760s.

The governors divulged the official goals of their project in addresses to the king, his ministers, and leading British ecclesiastics. The keynote was timely—King's College provided imperial authorities with an "instrument" for "cementing the Union between Great Britain and the Colonies. . . ." Already the college could boast numbers of sons who were "an Honour to the province for their Loyalty, Learning & Virtue." Should the king turn the college into a thriving university, it would "diffuse a Spirit of Loyalty . . . thro' his Majesty's American Dominions." The governors plied ecclesiastical officials with special words about the "peculiar Relation which this College bears to the Safety of the American Church. . . ." A university would enable "Members of the Church of England to maintain and extend its Discipline and Doctrine . . ." and would furnish "a sufficient Number of Persons qualified to spread the glorious Gospel among the native Heathen. . . ." But these religious goals would serve no less to render American subjects "obedient and affectionate to the Constitution." [4]

The governors had rejected the draft of an address to the king which played on a more militant variation of the same theme. This draft placed the quest for the king's patronage within the historical context of denominational rivalry. At mid-century Anglicans had found themselves "surrounded with Enemies," obliged to forego the higher education of their sons or else risk the "Danger of having their principles perverted" at seminaries controlled by dissenters. So they had established King's College, where their offspring would be instructed in principles of loyalty and "Love of the Mother Country." They had lamented the "Prospect of Opposition" from dissenters, but they could not avoid it, and the "unceasing Endeavours" of their enemies since mid-century had prevented the college from attaining "those inestimable advantages of which it is capable." The implication was obvious. The king should aid his Anglican subjects. In their hands alone could he expect higher education in the colonies to serve, not undermine, his kingdom.

This particular version of the college's past probably found special favor among the clerical supporters of King's. Myles Cooper had utilized just such an explanation of the college's difficulties in 1770, the year before. There "arose an Opposition coeval with ye College itself. . . ," related Cooper to a fellow cleric, "which hath been continued, without Interruption, to this very Day, with much Resentment, Inveteracy, and Malice." "[E]very Dissenter of high principles, upon the Continent, is our Enemy—
. . . many of their Missionaries, from the northern into the southern provinces, make it their Business, nay, have it in charge from their Masters, to decry this Institution by all *possible* Means.
. . . ." Samuel Auchmuty and Charles Inglis, fellow clerics and governors, shared Cooper's viewpoint.[5] They did not contrive it for the purposes of the moment. The conception of the beleaguered Anglican church made sense to them in light of lengthy yet unsuccessful struggles to secure a colonial bishop and to establish a flourishing Anglican college.

Clerical feelings ran especially strong at that moment because the opposition had recently given new proof of its relentlessness. Six years earlier the clerics, with Cooper, Charles Inglis, Thomas Bradbury Chandler, and Samuel Seabury in the lead, had renewed their campaign for a colonial biship.[6] By 1771 they had succeeded mainly in creating new enemies and in heightening their own sense of persecution. In 1768 the triumvirate had again reared its nasty head and engaged the clerics in a press war that lasted more than a year. Animosities generated during the King's College Controversy flared anew, leaving the clerics with the impression that the intervening years had been only a lull in an insidious effort to ruin their church. Conventions of dissenting clerics seemed to confirm Anglican fears, as did the formation of a society of dissenters in New York City in 1769, an organization of laymen whose avowed purpose was to "Counteract" the Episcopalians. The clerical governors could not help but view the plans for a university in light of their struggles against the "Adversaries of the National Church." Cooper's mission to England held out promise of victory over inveterate enemies.[7]

By 1771 Anglican ministers had gained a stronger voice on the college board of governors than at any time previously. Cooper, Auchmuty, Charles Inglis, and John Ogilvie ably represented the church and found the lay governors more sympathetic to their ideas than had Johnson. But to cast the university project mainly as a means of overcoming dissenting enemies must have seemed impolitic to some governors. Dissenters in the colonies and at home had just demonstrated their political leverage by blocking the appointment of a colonial bishop. Why explicitly challenge the same forces once again? More importantly, the governors could capture better their own sense of the college's purpose as well as capitalize on the preoccupations of imperial officials by falling back on the broader goal of political loyalty. Non-Anglicans on the board and those Anglican laymen who remained wary of clerical ambitions had few reservations about backing a program which mutually strengthened the college and the empire. So the board played down a religious version of the problem and emphasized how the proposed university could become the "happy Means" of "perpetuating to the latest Ages the Union between Great Britain and her Colonies."[8] And the governors meant it, if one goes by their behavior in the American Revolution.

Of the twenty-one governors who participated regularly in the decisions of 1771–1774, fifteen became loyalists during the Revolution, nine of them leaving the United States permanently. Of the remaining six governors, one had died by 1776 and at least two adopted equivocal positions during the war. One cannot automatically read political positions of 1777 back into 1771, especially in so volatile, unique, and unpredictable a controversy. But the evidence suggests that by 1771 many of those governors who became loyalists had already moved close to the positions which they eventually took.

For the clerics there does not appear to have ever been much question. True, not until 1773 did they begin to publish loyalist political statements. During the 1760s they concentrated on the appointment of a colonial bishop. But they could hardly plead this cause without supporting the king and his government, a stance that suited their political temperament and their conception of the Anglican church's function anyway. The "Clergy have always boasted of their Attachment to the present happy Constitution," they announced during the 1768 newspaper war with the triumvirate. The year before Samuel Auchmuty warned SPG officials that should the Anglican church in America collapse, then "farewell Loyalty, Obedience, and Dependence." [9]

The economic, legal, and political interests of the lay governors precipitated more complex behavior on their part. The 1760s found lay governors protesting the Stamp Act and backing a political party in New York which was allied with the Sons of Liberty. However, in 1769 and 1770 several key controversies and the mass meetings, rioting, and effigy burning which accompanied them— over the imprisonment of Alexander McDougall of the Sons of Liberty, over the enforcement of nonimportation against the Townshend Acts, over the erection of a new liberty pole—sorted many New Yorkers into political alignments which foreshadowed their division into loyalists and patriots six years later. Men of conservative persuasion and of substantial commercial interests, of whom the King's College governors numbered not a few, broke with the Sons of Liberty and other radicals. By 1771 probably the great majority of governors, both lay and clerical, could look upon the loyalist sentiments expressed in their addresses to the king and others not simply as a tactic to gain favors from the Crown but as a genuine expression of their political concern. They well knew that in 1771 to imitate Oxford—that "loyal and right principled" university—could not help but have political implications. [10]

Myles Cooper sailed for England in October 1771, armed with addresses not only from the college governors but also from the

Charles Inglis
Inglis was interim president of King's College, 1771–1772, and a college governor, 1770–1781. An outspoken loyalist, he migrated to Nova Scotia in the 1780s and became the principal founder of King's College of Nova Scotia. The portrait is from the painting by Robert Field in the National Portrait Gallery.
CREDIT: COLUMBIANA, COLUMBIA UNIVERSITY

Anglican clergy of New York and New Jersey "on the Subject of American Bishops." During the next eight months he consulted with numerous political and ecclesiastical figures, appeared before the Board of Trade, initiated but apparently did not follow through on a fund-raising venture in Ireland, and visited with old friends.[11] Meanwhile, Charles Inglis presided over King's College in Cooper's absence and found it a "heavy Charge." How his heart must have sunk when rumors reached New York City that Cooper had died six days after arriving in England! To Inglis's "great joy," Cooper returned to New York in September 1772. The college celebrated his homecoming with speeches by the students, "affectionate" addresses by the professors, and a forensic debate on "Whether a Spirit of Conquest was salutary to the Romans?" a topic perhaps deemed relevant to the occasion.[12]

Despite the festivities, Cooper did not return the conquering hero. He had convinced the British government to remit the quit rents on Kingsland, and he brought back a collection of books donated by the Clarendon Press and the King's mandamus for 24,000 acres solicited by James Jay several years earlier. But British officials refused to take any action on the university charter, not because they opposed it but because no one presented them with a document to act upon. The governors had failed to draw one up before Cooper's departure for England, and Cooper declined to compose one himself, particularly for fear of offending the governors. Cooper did, however, sound out the appropriate officials and smooth the way. He reported that the way was "so far prepared" at the Board of Trade that a charter would encounter "no great Difficulty" if it were forwarded "with all convenient Dispatch." Cooper also considered it "not *improbable*" that the Crown would establish professorships in the new university. So the governors appointed a committee to draft a charter for their next meeting. For reasons unexplained, the committee presented the draft to the governors in August 1774, twenty-two months later.[13]

The new charter took more than twelve thousand words to describe a structure that looked like Oxford and functioned like King's College—or at least King's College with a few modifications which the governors had been contemplating for some time.[14] The charter established "the American University in the Province of New York," to consist of King's College and all other colleges founded in New York under the provisions of the charter.

Myles Cooper remained as president of King's College; the president of King's College was always to double as president of the university; and the president of each college in the university was to be an Anglican. At the same time, the charter retained the religious liberty clause for students. The university and its colleges were to be ruled by a three-level governing structure: the regents, who, like the governors of King's College, held ultimate authority in all matters; the Academical Senate, which actually ran the university; and a Minor Academical Senate in each college, which enforced "good Order and Discipline among the Students" and handled other responsibilities delegated by the regents. The governors of King's College were converted into the regents in membership as well as authority. The same elected members and holders of the same ex officio positions became regents and were empowered to chose enough additional regents to make a body of fifty colonials. To their numbers were added several "Protectors to the American University": the president of the Privy Council, the chancellor of the exchequer, the bishop of London, and others.

The governing board of King's College had proven in the past to be a cumbersome body. Quorums were hard to come by; governors residing outside the city rarely attended meetings; and a quorum of fifteen created a sizable group for the president and his closest associates to manage. Johnson and Cooper had resorted to a committee of visitation to administer the college, which had functioned with some success. The university charter codified the arrangement by providing that the regents could name twelve of their members, all residents of New York City, to be the Academical Senate, with seven a quorum. The senators could make any laws or decisions for the "better government of the University," subject to alteration or rejection by the regents. While the senate increased administrative efficiency, it also helped perpetuate control of higher education in the colony by New York City interests and probably made it easier for Cooper (an ex officio senator) and his coterie of clerics to influence decision-making. The Minor Academical Senates, composed of the president and faculty in each college, created an illusion of faculty government. Whether these senates would do anything more than execute decisions from above and handle matters too small to merit the attention of those above was left for the regents to decide.

Despite the continuity between King's College and the American University, the charter reflected in several important ways Cooper's allegiance to Oxford: the conception of a university composed of several colleges; the provision for regius professorships (the number and kind were left open); and the formation of a body, similar to the Oxford Convocation, which was made up of all the regents, faculty, and degree holders (if the latter paid their dues), and which could elect two representatives to the New York General Assembly. There was even a rough parallel between the regents, Academical Senate, and Minor Academical Senates at American University, and Convocation, the Hebdomadal Board, and the college governments at Oxford, with the crucial difference that at Oxford more power flowed up from the bottom of the structure than down from the top. In all but two of Oxford's twenty colleges and five halls formed the Hebdomadal Board, which was the main administrative organ for the university.[15] American University also borrowed a number of academic officers from Oxford: a chancellor, vice-chancellor, chamberlains, and proctors.

The charter created a legal and administrative framework which could accommodate major expansion while leaving control in the same hands. The vaguest, yet the most intriguing aspect of the plan was the provision for establishing additional colleges. What kinds of colleges did the governors have in mind—new academic-residential units on or near the King's College campus, much like Oxford, or separate campuses, perhaps scattered throughout the province, like the State University of New York today? The latter was probably the case, but the governors may not have given the point much hard thought. They were having enough trouble floating one small seminary in New York City. The university charter opened the way for new colleges in the future, but the immediate payoff came in regius professorships, the right to elect two assemblymen, the efficiencies of the Academical Senate, and the like. There was, however, a plan afoot to establish another college in

New York, the kind of college that might well have been placed under the auspices of American University.

When Myles Cooper sailed to England in 1771 he carried with him a proposal for royal funding of a "College or Seminary" in the Mohawk River valley, where Indians would be educated for the Anglican ministry. Charles Inglis drew up the "Memorial" after consulting with Cooper and Sir William Johnson, the Albany-based superintendent of Indian affairs. Earlier Cooper and Samuel Auchmuty had revived the idea (first broached by the SPG in the 1750s) of educating Indian youths for the ministry at King's College. Auchmuty even assured Sir William Johnson in 1767 that the college governors would "give" the Indians their education and would allow them to lodge in the college building. Johnson "greatly approve[d]," since he thought that conversion of the Iroquois to Anglicanism would serve his political goal of securing their allegiance to the Crown. Presbyterianism and Congregationalism seemed to render their worshippers "Enemies to all our Law & the British Consti[tu]tion," a growing concern which soured Johnson on his practice of sending Indian youths to Eleazar Wheelock, a dissenting educator in Connecticut. However, Johnson first wanted to establish one or two elementary schools among the Indians, from which candidates for King's College would be chosen. A shortage of funds and missionaries held up implementation of the project. In 1771 Inglis came up with a new plan, which called for, among other things, location of a college among the Iroquois and a contribution of £500 sterling from the Crown. However, the Crown did not cooperate, and no further steps were taken before the Revolution undermined plans for both the Indian college and American University.[16]

By the time the governors gave their approval to a draft of the university charter they had already laid some of the groundwork for securing the assent of the king. One tactic was to cultivate Governor William Tryon of New York, a friend to the Anglican church and the college and a man with connections in the British government. In March 1774, shortly before Tryon was to return to England, the governors conferred on him an LL.D., presented him with "a very long diploma," and requested his influence in favor of their university project. Tryon agreed to recommend the charter "to the Consideration and Notice of the Crown" and bestowed on the college 10,000 acres to support a professorship of municipal law.[17] Cooper could not resist the impulse to crank out one of his poems in Tryon's honor, proclaiming that

> Since Time his earliest race began,
> A truer, braver, worthier man
> Ne'er Trod on English ground.[18]

Earlier in 1774 the college had commissioned John Vardill, a member of the faculty, to promote the charter and the regius professorships in London. Vardill was a King's College graduate, a fervent Anglican, a controversialist who contributed several essays to New York newspapers, and a man of unshakeable loyalist sentiments. Due to the increase in students, Cooper had hired him in 1772 or early 1773 to assist in teaching classical languages and history. When Vardill decided late in 1773 to go to England for ordination, the governors gave him a leave of absence, arranged with him to represent the college, and named him professor of natural law and fellow of King's College, a title probably intended to impress imperial officials.[19]

By mid-1775 chances for royal approval and patronage of American University were looking good. With relationships between the Crown and the colonies deteriorating rapidly, the ministry sought to detach New York from the Continental Association by placating its citizenry. Lord Dartmouth, secretary of state for the colonies, indicated to Lieutenant Governor Cadwallader Colden at the close of 1774 that New York's conduct justly entitled "its well disposed and peaceable Inhabitants to His Majesty's particular Favor and Indulgence."[20] The king's solicitousness had already paid off three months earlier. Vardill reported to one of the governors that His Majesty had appointed him a *"Royal Professor"* in the college, "for the purpose of defending the *Christian* . . . *Religion*, by annual Lectures on those Subjects." Vardill confessed that the salary was small, but "his *Majesty* desires it may be considered only as an instance of his resolution . . . to encourage the Christian Religion, & patronise the College of New York. . . ." Vardill also was optimistic that, with Tryon's assistance, "some higher marks of attention & munificence may be obtained" for the college. Actually, as Vardill admitted, his appointment as regius professor of divinity had not yet "pass'd thro the formalities of Office"—it did not do so until 1778—but it was promptly announced in the New York press, and news of it spread to other colonies.[21]

Meanwhile, the university charter itself met with favor. In February 1775 Tryon forwarded a copy to Lord Dartmouth, enclosing a letter which expressed his full support. Dartmouth could find only one questionable point in the charter, concerning the right to elect two representatives to the New York General Assembly. This was a matter for the assembly to decide. Otherwise Dartmouth believed that the charter was not "liable to any material objection." [22]

While the college's loyalist stance won friends in London, it created enemies in New York. New Yorkers did not require much perceptiveness to detect how Cooper and his college associates stood on the issues. Cooper was not a man to hide his feelings, and his feelings on the imperial crisis were robust. As a "Specimen of his Zeal," he constantly gave toasts to the memory of Archbishop Laud, no doubt whenever he attended get-togethers of the "Church and King Club." In fact, Cooper soon became identified as the author of several loyalist pamphlets which had actually been penned by his fellow clerics.[23] Whether he took as hard a line in America as he did when he returned to England in 1775 is difficult to tell, but he told an Oxford audience in 1776 that the "Power of any Nation" had never been "better employed" than in the war to suppress the "wicked and unprovoked Rebellion." "Never was there a more worthy Object of military Exertion. . . ." [24]

John Vardill, who became a British spy during the war, first publicized his sentiments on the imperial crisis while serving on the King's College faculty in 1772 and 1773. In an anonymous newspaper essay Vardill attacked President Witherspoon of Princeton and Old Nassau's students for having "very often entered deeply into the Party Politics and Contentions of England

. . . ," a reference particularly to the commencement of 1770, where Princeton students appeared in American homespun and defended the proposition that *"The Non-Importation Agreement reflects a Glory on the American Merchants, and was a noble Exertion of Self denial and public Spirit."* Such principles, contended Vardill, were "dangerous in the highest Degree, to our happy Constitution." One only need "turn his Eyes to Boston, where he may see Men acting on those Principles, and in such a Manner as to be a Disgrace to all Order and Government," to reject them with disgust. Vardill boasted that King's College students, unlike those at Princeton, were not "taught to pace in the political Trammels, of any Sect or Party. . . ." They studied polity, not politics, and they did so through "Books of Natural Law," not through "canvassing the Proceedings and Principles of different Factions. . . ." [25]

The King's College faculty was not unanimous in its loyalism. Samuel Clossy equivocated for a while before committing himself to the British cause. Robert Harpur, the only non-Anglican on the faculty, eventually joined the rebels and served actively in the new state government.[26] Nonetheless a loyalist mood predominated on the campus. As Vardill intimated, it sometimes surfaced less in outright expressions of support for the British or of antipathy toward American radicals than in a pronounced obliviousness to the Revolutionary movement. While commencements in the 1760s had been marked on occasion by an "Oration in Praise of Liberty" or an oration which argued that *"The Well-being of the People is the supreme Law,"* in the 1770s students confined their performances to innocuous topics like "Taste" and "Cheerfulness," delivered before audiences which included royal officials, Anglican clerics, and the "principal Officers" of the British army.[27] The political tenor at King's did not dissuade Marinus Willett, an active member of the Sons of Liberty, from educating his son there in the 1770s. Nor did it stop Alexander Hamilton, an undergraduate from 1773 to 1775, from publishing a defense of the Continental Congress or from drilling with a company of American volunteers. But one finds no evidence of collective anti-British action by the students to match that of students at Princeton, who hanged a British spokesman in effigy and held their own tea party (burning the college steward's tea, while passing "many spirited resolves") in imitation of the Boston Tea Party.[28]

The drift of the colonies toward revolution finally reached into the heart of the King's College in the spring of 1775. In April Myles Cooper was one of five New Yorkers to be warned in a public letter that "Repeated insults and unparalleled oppressions have reduced the *Americans* to a state of desperation. Executions of villains in effigy will now no longer gratify their resentment. . . . The injury you have done to your country can not admit of reparation. Fly for your lives, or anticipate your doom. . . ." Cooper retreated for a few days to a British warship anchored in the New York City harbor but soon returned to his duties. About midnight on May 10 a "murderous band" of some size tried to make good the letter's promise. With an eye to seizing Cooper and, in Cadwallader Colden's judgment, to committing the "most violent abuse upon him," the mob "broke the College Gate open." Aroused by a pupil (a "heaven-directed youth," Cooper later called him), the president escaped half-dressed through a back way and sought safety in the home of a friend. The next day he boarded a British vessel. Two weeks later he sailed for England. "We hope the Non-exportation Agreement to Great-Britain will always except such traitors to the Liberties of America," commented one newspaper.[29]

King's College continued in operation for two more years, under the direction of Reverend Benjamin Moore, King's '68 and a member of the Trinity parish staff. Moore admitted a new class in 1775, but he was soon lamenting that the "turbulence and confusion" were suppressing "every literary pursuit." In April 1776 the New York Committee of Safety, noting that there were very few, if any students in the college, ordered the governors to prepare it for the reception of American troops. "In consequence of this demand," according to Moore, "the students were dispersed, the Library, apparatus, etc., were deposited in the City Hall, and the College was turned into an Hospital." [30]

Less than two months later Moore gathered his flock at the Wall Street home of one of the governors, which was "now occupied for the Purposes of a College." In 1777 Moore still was holding forth on Wall Street, while the British, who had captured the city, now inhabited the college building. Moore filed the annual call for matriculants in the *New York Mercury* during the summer of 1777, and at least two boys responded.[31] But King's College probably closed soon after. The governors met occasionally through 1781. One of their final acts was to assure Cooper that although "Science has suffered Much in this Country by the Tumult and Disorder of the Times," they expected her "to expand her Wings again with some Vigor on the first Renewal of the Blessings of Peace and Good Order." Cooper himself anticipated, at least into 1779, that a "happy termination" of the war might permit him to resume his "old situation." The American victory shattered his hopes.[32] Yorktown and the peace which followed also spelled the end of plans for the first British university in the new world. The spirit of loyalist education was transplanted to Nova Scotia, where Charles Inglis took the lead in founding another King's College in the 1780s, while New York's King's College reopened in the 1780s as part of the newly created University of the State of New York.

It is customary to note that college histories overemphasize administrative issues while ignoring educational processes, which are the raison d'être of the college in the first place. Presidents and trustees thus dominate the academic stage, while students appear extraneous to the whole operation. The point is well taken. However, it should not be forgotten that in some respects the social significance of a college does not depend on its educational program for students. This is especially obvious in twentieth-century universities, where the education of students is only one of several functions which include the creation of new knowledge, the provision of social services through consultants and the like, the employment of large numbers of adults ranging from intellectuals to gardeners, and the furnishing of public entertainment through football and other sports programs. Eighteenth-century colleges were much more single-minded about educating their pupils, but it still would be unwise to gauge the social significance of a colonial college by its impact on students alone. A few examples should suffice to make the point.

Simply by surviving, King's College influenced the shape of higher education in the colonies. By draining a good part of the resources that New Yorkers were likely to devote to higher education—in terms of money, leadership, and potential students—it consumed enough "educational space" in New York to discourage the founding of another college, even one attuned to different political or religious interests. At the same time its domination by Anglicans contributed to the emergence of a new pattern of higher education in the colonies, one in which the various denominations learned to adjust to one another by each gaining a dominant voice in at least one college. Once Johnson and his clerical associates had a college under their own wing, even if an ailing one, they soon dropped their efforts to undermine Presbyterian control of Princeton. Theodore Frelinghuysen, on the other hand, decided that the Dutch Reformed church could not compete with the Presbyterians and Anglicans unless it founded its own college. "Let every one provide for his own House . . . ," proclaimed Frelinghuysen. Everyone did, eventually. The interaction of New Side Presbyterians, Old Side Presbyterians, Anglicans, and Dutch Reformed which helped produce Princeton, the College of Philadelphia, King's College, and Queen's College foreshadowed an explosion of college founding in the nineteenth century. Spurred in part by denominational considerations, Americans by 1860 had founded some one hundred eighty colleges which survived into the twentieth century and a good many others which did not.[33]

As a final example, it seems likely that the marginal success of the educational program at King's did not deter some New Yorkers from experiencing a sense of civic pride in their college and a feeling that New York was beginning to measure up to English cultural standards. The architecture and setting of the college won plaudits from visitors. Annual commencement ceremonies and a growing body of degree holders enhanced the civility of life. A medical school added a distinctive luster, despite the fact it trained few practitioners. Had the American Revolution not intervened, the transformation of King's College into American University would have confirmed what some New Yorkers were gradually realizing. Once a Dutch trading outpost, their city was now becoming a British cultural center.

10.
THE EDUCATION OF
WISE AND GOOD MEN

But allow me to ask you, Gentlemen; is the main purpose of education to make us able and rich, or wise and good men?

DAVID FORDYCE, one of Samuel Johnson's favorite writers on education, captured in this simple question the spirit that underlay the curriculum at King's College.[1] The same spirit was reflected in the frequency with which both Johnson and Myles Cooper invoked that magical word, virtue, when discussing the goals of life and of education. The good man—the man whom educators should strive to rear—was a man of virtue, a man characterized by his reverence for God and Christian principles, by his capacity to govern his passions with his reason and thus to pursue the path of righteousness unswervingly, and by his patriotism and devotion to public service. Johnson and Cooper did not agree exactly on the nature of virtue. Johnson's conception was steeped in Christian piety and Puritan morality. Cooper did not hesitate to name piety the "queen" of virtues, but compared to Johnson, he played it down. And, Aristotelian that Cooper was, he stressed qualities like urbanity and magnanimity at the expense of humility and frugality. But regarding the significance of virtue the two presidents were one, reflecting not simply a common outlook among eighteenth-century educators but also the passionate conviction of two men who considered themselves moral philosophers as well as Anglican ministers.[2]

In 1754 Samuel Johnson spelled out for New Yorkers the goals of a King's College education as he saw them. The "chief thing that is aimed at in this college," he announced in the newspapers, "is to teach and engage the children to know God in Jesus Christ, and to love and serve Him in all sobriety, godliness, and righteousness of life. . . ." Looking back on his presidency several years later Johnson reaffirmed that his "first and chief care" had indeed been to give the students "a truly Christian education," for only then might they be "truly good men as well as knowing and learned." Contrary to what may appear to be the case, Johnson's concept of the good man was expansive, not restrictive. If the touchstone was a knowledge of and love for God and Christian principles, good men also were to be educated in "all virtuous habits and all such useful knowledge as may render them creditable to their families and friends, ornaments to their country, and useful to the public weal in their generations." From here it was not much of a step to a broadly conceived educational program. Indeed, Johnson went on to pledge to New Yorkers that, beyond insisting on a "serious, virtuous, and industrious course of life," he expected to instruct students in the "learned languages," logic, rhetoric, mathematics, geography, history, moral and natural philosophy, in fact in "everything that can contribute to their true happiness, both here and hereafter." Johnson was not above bringing a dancing master to the college to give budding gentlemen the polish and confidence that one expected of "ornaments" and public servants.[3]

Living as we do in an age in which the pursuit of knowledge is so often divorced from moral purpose, it is difficult to recapture the perspective of educators who found it hard to think of knowledge outside a moral context. There was not a subject in the curriculum at King's College that did not in one way or another serve a significant moral goal, and it was normally this function that Johnson had in mind when he described a subject as useful. Through a study of physics and astronomy, for example, students developed "a sense of the beauty, harmony, order and usefulness appearing in the whole system of nature." This not only inspired "the most grand and august apprehensions of the Deity" but also cultivated an appreciation of the beauty, harmony, and order which should prevail in the moral world. Training in logic—"the art of reasoning"—equipped students with a tool for distinguishing truth from falsehood and thus helped them determine virtuous courses of action in their personal lives and in their roles as public figures. By reading the authors of classical Greece and Rome, "who studied nature more and understood it better than any nations have ever done since . . . ," undergraduates would imbibe "those great maxims of wisdom" which had "stood the test of time." Undoubtedly Johnson believed with David Fordyce that "Times and manners" may have changed since the golden age of Greece and Rome, but not so much "as to make any considerable change in the maxims of civil and political prudence." "The essential rules of life and right conduct are invariable." The classics thus remained rich storehouses of wisdom on the most "ticklish" of matters.[4]

If the intellectual strands of the college curriculum were knit together by a concern with virtue and wisdom, so the curriculum itself was similarly intertwined with undergraduate life outside the classroom. Virtue was a matter of habit as well as of intellect. The collegiate way of living provided a supplementary means of instruction, whereby prayer, rules, and faculty surveillance took the place of lectures and recitations in teaching virtuous conduct. By their senior year, when undergraduates studied Johnson's *Elementa Philosophica*, the students should have been thoroughly familiar with the president's conception of moral duty. The good man, according to *Elementa Philosophica*, gladly fulfilled three kinds of duties: to himself—human virtue; to God—divine virtue; and to his neighbor—social virtue. Among the human virtues were prudence, humility, moderation, sobriety, chastity, patience, fortitude, frugality, and industry. To God the good man owed gratitude, love, trust, submission, and a conscientious attempt at imitation. To his fellow creatures the good man was inoffensive, charitable, generous, friendly, forgiving, just, and of proper deportment in whatever happened to be his "station" in life.[5]

Samuel Johnson envisioned a pattern of collegiate life in which undergraduates would internalize these qualities by living in ac-

cordance with them. A daily routine of prayer and worship served
to inculcate the divine virtues. Grace before and after each meal
was a minor part of a process that commenced at "Morning
Prayers" every day shortly after dawn. With the students gathered before him, the president offered several prayers. Then, either alone, in unison with the students, or alternating with them,
he recited or chanted the Ten Commandments, about thirty
verses of Psalms, the Gloria Patri, a collect, the Hundredth
Psalm, the Nicene Creed, and the Lord's Prayer—a series of devo-
tions broken only by a student's reading of a selection from the
Old Testament. The service concluded with extensive prayers,
including "A Prayer Peculiar to the College." A similar service
was held each evening after supper. Johnson also insisted that
students daily "read a portion of the Holy Scriptures" and pray in
their rooms. On Sunday they were to attend services at one of the
city's churches. Undergraduates thus were called upon several
times a day to affirm their gratitude, love, and submission to God.
At the same time worship provided a vehicle for emphasizing
human and social virtues. Students pledged that they would guard
against their "passions and youthful lusts and all temptations."
They beseeched God to engage them "to the utmost diligence" in
their studies. And they recided daily their intention to "adorn"
their professions

> by truly virtuous and exemplary lives, that we may be creditable to
> our families and friends, ornaments to our country, and useful in
> our generation to promote thy glory and the good of mankind.[6]

The balance of the students' time theoretically was regulated by a
stringent set of rules which directed undergraduates to order their
lives according to social and human virtues. Laughing, jostling,
and winking in class or in worship were verboten. So were drunk-
enness, fornication, lying, theft, cursing, cock fighting, playing
cards and dice, maiming, slandering, or "grievously abusing" anyone, and frequenting "houses of ill fame" or otherwise keeping
company with persons of "known scandalous behavior." Students
were to treat all "superiors and especially the authority of the
college with duty and respect," such as by "rising, standing, un-

Photographs of the Bachelor of Arts and Master of Arts Diplomas of
John Jay Signed by President Myles Cooper

CREDIT: COLUMBIA UNIVERSITY LIBRARIES

covering the head, preserving a proper distance and using the most respectful language." Swearing at or otherwise insulting a professor was regarded with particular disfavor.[7]

Of course, Johnson expected undergraduates to spend much of their day, other than the time reserved for meals and prayer, attending classes and studying industriously in their rooms. Classes consisted largely of lectures and recitations. While Johnson delivered lectures that were the equivalent of sermons in length and formality, he also believed that students should "be obliged to give an account of the authors they read," should be put on "frequent and repeated trials in the exertion of their rational powers," and should devote a fair proportion of their time to preparing "exercises and compositions," such as orations, poems, and theses. Otherwise the extensive reading demanded of undergraduates would load their minds "with a mass of crude and undigested notions."[8]

Normally the school year began in July and lasted until June, with a week off in the fall, two weeks at Christmas, and a week at Easter. A month's vacation followed commencement in June. Students were examined each quarter by a committee of college governors. Toward the close of their fourth year candidates for the B.A. had to pass an examination on their entire course of instruction. The president, the faculty, the governors, and any M.A.'s from the college could ask any question they thought proper. Upon receiving his B.A. a graduate could qualify for an M.A. if he waited three years, paid a fee, and did not indulge in any "gross immorality." Much the same regimen was adopted by Myles Cooper during his presidency.[9]

In turning to the heart of Johnson's educational program, the curriculum, one finds that the most reliable sources available describe its operation in 1759.[10] The discussion which follows will do the same. However, it should be remembered that for four and one-half years during Johnson's seven-year tenure there was no regular professor of natural philosophy and mathematics and that the president himself was absent for a year and a half.

Samuel Johnson, like Myles Cooper after him, believed that incoming students should have mastered the Greek and Latin languages. And each year Johnson, like Cooper, found that he could either admit students "very raw" or else have no students at all. In Johnson's case, the admission requirements included a command of Latin grammar and an ability to translate Cicero and Virgil from Latin into English and the New Testament from Greek into Latin.[11] But the boys who visited the president's chambers each summer seeking admission did "but poorly so that we go over all these again the first year. . . ." Johnson liked to take the students himself for their first year and part of their second, so that at the same time he reviewed Latin and Greek he could teach "religion and morality" and thus make his pupils "truly good men." Lectures on the New Testament, the major work read in Greek, provided students with "a plan of Christianity," while Jean Heuzet's *Selectae E Profanis*, a Latin reader, served as a basis for lectures in moral philosophy. Heuzet designed his work for just such a purpose, organizing his excerpts (from both Roman and Greek authors) in sections devoted to God, prudence, justice, fortitude, and temperance. "In a Word," explained Heuzet, "the Reader has here an Assemblage of several Strokes of Morality and History, many of which may serve as Rules and Models for the different Conditions of Life. . . ." [12]

For Latin grammar Johnson probably used John Clarke's *An Introduction to the Making of Latin*, a popular work which could double as an elementary text in classical literature and history. The rules of grammar are illustrated with selections from classical authors, and the book includes a lengthy history of Greece and Rome. Although Johnson considered Hebrew the "mother of all language and eloquence," he made its study optional, recommended it mainly for prospective ministers, and could not persuade more than three or four boys to "give any attention to it" during his presidency.[13]

While teaching languages, ethics, and religion, and familiarizing the students with the classics, Johnson carried them "thro' a Course of Rhetoric & Oratory & making Theories." "Making theories" or logic was designed to teach, in Johnson's words, "the rules of thinking regularly, and reasoning justly, whereby we learn to distinguish truth from falsehood, and proceed from things

simple to things compound, and from things precarious and con-
tingent to things necessary. . . ." Johnson relied primarily on
William Duncan's *The Elements of Logic*, a text which embraced the
"new logic." Duncan divided his work into four books, in each of
which he examined a major step in the "procedure of our own
thoughts" from perception through to the arrangement of ideas
into complex structures. Duncan patterned his book after *The
Port-Royal Logic*, a pioneering text of the 1660s which drew its inspiration from Réné Descartes's *Discourse on Method* and modified
or rejected substantial segments of the scholastic and Ramist logic
which traditionally dominated treatises in logic.[14]

Duncan did assign a large role to deductive logic. He argued,
for example, that mathematics, morality, and natural religion are
based on intuitive judgments, judgments the truth of which is
self-evident, e.g., the whole is greater than any of its parts. One
establishes additional truths in these three "sciences" by deducing
them from the intuitive judgments through syllogistic reasoning.
However, Duncan defined two other kinds of knowledge, natural
and historical, and described special methods of inquiry for each
which are independent of the Aristotelian syllogism. Judgments
about the natural world, stated Duncan, are grounded in experience, not in intuition. One moves from these judgments to truths
about the natural world through "Induction, and Experiments
made with particular Objects," not through syllogistic reasoning.
Duncan assured his readers that "while the philosophy of Aristotle prevailed in the schools," knowledge of nature was "at a
stand." Now, however, "we have returned to the way of trial and
experiment," and great advances "have already been made." In
this way Duncan attempted to answer the call of Réné Descartes
that, as historian Wilbur Samuel Howell has written, logic "accept experiment rather than disputation as the chief instrument in
the quest for truth," that it be a genuine theory of inquiry aimed
at discovering what is unknown rather than an instrument for
bringing "the old truth to bear upon the new situation." [15]

Duncan also briefly introduced students to historical knowledge. Here the "Foundation of our Belief" is testimony, not intuition or experience. Truth is established in this area not by syl-

logistic reasoning or by experiment but by *"Criticism* and *probable Conjecture,"* a process by which one evaluates the reliability of witnesses and their testimony, past and present. Like most logicians before him, Duncan put his greatest faith in the certainty of knowledge obtained through deduction from intuitive judgments. But he recognized the practical reliability of natural and historical knowledge and thus provided students with intellectual tools distinguished by their diversity and utility. Wilbur Samuel Howell has called *The Elements of Logic* "the most challenging and most up-to-date book of its time, place, and class." Samuel Johnson may well have modified Duncan's ideas as he discussed them in class, but the president obviously was less than zealous about introducing the syllogistic disputations which traditionally formed the backbone of training in logic. Five years after King's College opened, Johnson confessed that his students had yet to take them up. Apparently he gave in soon after, since the commencement of 1762 featured disputations in Latin on whether there was a vacuum in nature and whether there could be virtue and vice without free will.[16]

Rhetoric—the art of "Speaking and Writing with elegance and dignity, in order to instruct, persuade, and please"—was formally conceived by Johnson in neo-Ciceronian terms, that is, to consist of the four classical doctrines of invention, arrangement, style, and delivery. Cicero himself defined these terms nicely:

> Invention is the discovery of valid or seemingly valid arguments to render one's cause plausible. Arrangement is the distribution of arguments thus discovered in the proper order. Expression [Cicero's term for style] is the fitting of the proper language to the invented matter. . . . Delivery is the control of voice and body in a manner suitable to the dignity of the subject matter and the style.

However, Johnson's choice of texts suggests that, at least with freshmen, he followed in the path of those eighteenth-century Ciceronians who focused mainly on the third doctrine, style. For Johnson this meant teaching the traditional tropes and figures, those "most striking and beautiful expressions" used to produce stylistic effects—metaphor, irony, allegory, hyperbole, onomatopoeia, repetition, circumlocution, and dozens more.[17] John Stirling's *System of Rhetorick*, one of Johnson's texts, consists of nothing more than a list of ninety-four tropes and figures, with each term defined in a two-line rhyme and its use illustrated in a footnote. Johnson's other text, Anthony Blackwall's *Introduction to the Classics*, supplements an account of the "chief tropes and figures" with a discussion of their "Nature, Necessity, and Use," and employs numerous examples, primarily from the classics. Students used the tropes and figures both in composing their own oral and written work and in their stylistic analyses of classical writings.[18] The latter may have been part of a larger effort by Johnson to instruct students in the "art of criticism, which teaches the true force of words and phrases, the nature of style, and a true taste, so as to make a right judgment of authors. . . ." If so, then Johnson was moving in the direction of the "new rhetoric" which was just then emerging in Britain, an approach to rhetoric that added, among other things, an interest in literary taste and criticism to the older neo-Ciceronian concern with perfecting written and oral discourse.[19]

Johnson may well have touched on invention, arrangement, and delivery as well as style when he taught his pupils to make "themes and declamations." The latter were either memorized passages from the classics or brief compositions written by the students and delivered from memory. The students also prepared dissertations, i.e., scholarly treatises maintaining a particular position. In fact, Johnson testified that throughout their four years his undergraduates made "declamations and dissertations, pro and con on various subjects" in both Latin and English.

The president thus guided his pupils during their freshman year and the first half of their sophomore year through the intricacies of grammar, rhetoric, logic, ethics, and a "plan of Christianity with its evidences," while dipping here and there into classical literature and history. During the first part of their sophomore year the students also were tutored in the "higher Classics" by Leonard Cutting. Then about the middle of the year the sophomores finished up with Johnson and divided the remaining months between Cutting and Daniel Treadwell. Cutting ex-

plained successively a number of Greek and Roman works—
Homer's epic poems, *Aesop's Fables*, Xenophon's *Cyropaedia*,
Terence's comedies, Cicero's *De Officiis* and *De Oratore*, Caesar's
Commentaries, Martial's *Epigrams*, and a work on ancient geography
by Dionysius Periegetes.

In discussing these works Cutting lectured on ethics, rhetoric,
and the "principles of polity & poetry." "Principles of polity" introduced students to "wise government," not to government as it
functioned. For example, in *Cyropaedia*, which is supposedly a history of the life and career of the Persian ruler, Cyrus, Xenophon
answered questions about how one should rule and be ruled by
describing an idealized constitutional monarchy that actually re-
sembles more the governments of Sparta and Athens than that of
Persia. Cutting's pupils also read Samuel Pufendorf's *De Officio
Hominis*, which the German political philosopher and jurist published in 1673. Pufendorf acquainted students with the modern
political theory of contract, according to which the community
and the government originated not in God's commands but in
people's consent. He did not use the theory to justify popular
resistance to rulers, but he did emphasize the moral limitations on
rulers. Rulers and citizens were knit together by mutual obligations which were morally binding and which rested ultimately on
natural law. Pufendorf thus provided Cutting with an opportunity
not only to emphasize the moral duties of man but also to explore
the rational bases for these duties. An "excellent foundation to
begin the study of law upon," commented one alumnus on Pufendorf's *De Officio Hominis* and Cicero's *De Officiis* soon after leaving
King's College and embarking on a law career.[20]

While the sophomores pursued the second half of their year-
long course with Cutting they also spent part of each day with
Daniel Treadwell, studying logic, arithmetic, geometry, and trigonometry. It was probably at this point that they probed more
deeply into some of the epistemological issues raised in Duncan's
Elements of Logic by reading John Locke's *An Essay Concerning
Human Understanding*. Locke did not intend the *Essay* as a text in
logic, but his monumental effort at demolishing traditional authority as a source of truth and replacing it with empiricism "outlined

168 PORTRAIT OF A COLONIAL COLLEGE

more influentially than any previous work the modern method by which knowledge is to be sought, validated, and understood." [21]

The more mundane subject of arithmetic consisted of elementary problems that any King's College student might expect to face later, whether in buying land, lending money, or investing in an enterprise. Judging by the workbook of one of Robert Harpur's pupils, the following were typical problems:

Fellowship [Partnership]
A. B. and C, trading to Guinea, with £480, £680, and £840 in 3 years Time did gain £1010, how much is each man's Share of the Gain?

Exchange
Trading to the east Indies, my Employer there owes me £3000: 17: 2¼ sterling, how much is that in their Currency at 112½ per Cent?

Surveying
Sheweth how to exhibit a map or plan of any portion of land, and to find its area, or content in acres &c. . . .

For geometry Treadwell used *Euclid's Elements of Geometry, The First Six, the Eleventh and Twelfth Books*, edited by Edmund Stone, who believed that geometry was good for the soul. It so inured a man to truth—in his "searching after and demonstrating geometrical truths"—that he learns "constantly" to seek truth "in all sorts of subjects." [22]

During their junior and the first half of their senior years the students worked exclusively with Treadwell. They continued their study of mathematics and took up geography, but they concentrated on "Natural & Experimental Philosophy." Treadwell's text was John Rowning's *A Compendious System of Natural Philosophy*, a popular eighteenth-century work by a devoted Newtonian. Its 300 pages cover the study of mechanics, hydrostatics, pneumatics, optics, and astronomy. Rowning, like many a good natural philosopher of his era, attempted to reduce the explanation of natural phenomena to a handful of principles—in his case three. After all, an unnecessary multiplication of principles was *"not consistent with the Regard a Philosopher should have to the Uniformity of*

Nature. . . ." Rowning's effort at simplification led to some distortions, but his text was competent and up-to-date. King's College students did not learn, as did Harvard undergraduates earlier in the century, that the gelatinous algae found in wet meadows was the "nocturnall Pollution" of some "wanton Star." [23]

Rowning's text was a rich source of material for lectures, but traditional lectures could hardly convey the spirit of a science that thrived on observation and experiment. By 1759 King's College had already spent £200 sterling on an "Apparatus of Instruments for teaching Experimental Philosophy" and had ordered additional equipment costing £250 sterling. "It will I believe be at least equal to that at Cambridge," asserted Johnson (measuring up to Harvard was an academic virtue even then). The apparatus included a "Reflecting Telliscope," an air pump, and a "great number" of other instruments. In 1774 the governors decided to buy an orrery (a mechanical apparatus illustrating the movement of the planets), perhaps to keep up with Princeton, which had acquired one three years earlier.[24] An elaborate scientific apparatus, no less than a handsome building, had become a sine qua non of an American college.

About the middle of their final year the seniors resumed their studies with Johnson, dividing their time between Johnson and Treadwell. The president required them "to read in their chambers a variety of the best authors" in all their subjects, but the core of their meetings with Johnson was his *Elementa Philosophica*. He explained both parts of the work—the "Noetica" and the "Ethica"—thus providing a capstone course in metaphysics, epistemology, and moral philosophy. The theme of this final course, and in a sense the dominant theme of the undergraduate curriculum, was expressed in a quote from Bishop Berkeley which Johnson was planning to insert on the title page of a revised edition of his *Elementa Philosophica:*

Whatever the world thinks, He who has not much meditated on God, The Human Mind & the *Summum Bonum*, may possibly make a thriving Earth-worm; but will most indubitably make but a Sorry patriot & a sorry Statesman.[25]

Johnson modestly described *Elementa Philosophica* as "these short Draughts" and asked that it be "considered only as a Text on which to lecture more particularly to the pupills & to assist them in bringing their Instructions to Remembrance. . . ." [26] Johnson undoubtedly used it this way, and in so doing he probably revealed an emotional intensity about the issues that was partially disguised by the measured statements in his text. *Elementa Philosophica* was Johnson's attempt to reconcile the New Learning with the old—to harmonize Lockean empiricism and Newtonian physics with Christian revelation. How, in other words, could one reject much of scholasticism without undermining the religious world view it rationalized? How could one participate in the Enlightenment without becoming a deist?

The problem was a deeply personal one for Johnson, one that had commanded immense amounts of his time in reading, reflection, and conversation. Upon discovering the New Learning— Bacon, Descartes, Locke, Newton—while a youth just out of college, Johnson had gradually turned his back on the scholasticism of his Yale education, eventually condemning it as so many "scholastic cobwebs." But he also began to realize, and realize painfully, that the rationalism and empiricism of the Enlightenment were tools whose destructive power was greater than he had bargained for. In overturning part of the medieval intellectual heritage they challenged its whole fabric, orthodox Christianity included. And the weakening of this buttress of moral and social order was unleashing a "torrent of irreligion and vice" that threatened "to lay waste all before it." Philosophers whose writings once seemed to Johnson "like a flood of day to his low state of mind" now became suspect. He discovered, as he later recalled, that the more they "pretended to reason and deep speculation the more they dwindled in faith." [27]

In *Elementa Philosophica* Johnson demonstrated the breadth of his reading on the problem, his particularly heavy debt to British philosophers and theologians, the eclectic and often contradictory manner in which he drew on them, and the relative balance in intellectual perspective which he had so far (1752) managed to maintain in his efforts to reconcile fundamentally incompatible ideas.

The central concept in the "Noetica," which deals with metaphysics and epistemology, was provided by Bishop Berkeley's philosophy of immaterialism. As interpreted by Johnson, an object of sense was not actually a physical object which existed outside the mind. It was, in fact, an idea planted in one's mind by God at the very instant it was perceived. If one perceived a tree it was not because there was some solid matter "out there" giving off qualities which the mind perceived as a tree. One saw a tree because God put the idea of the tree in one's mind at the moment one perceived it.[28]

This is a peculiar theory of perception, and it violates common sense. But it served Johnson's purposes nicely. It permitted him to agree substantially with the fundamental Lockean premise that ideas were not innate but were rooted in perception, a premise essential to empiricism. At the same time it put God at the center of the empirical process. The deists seemingly would reduce Him to a First Cause, who created a material world and then stepped aside to let it operate by itself according to rational principles which man could discover on his own. In *Elementa Philosophica* God shone forth as the ever-active nerve center of an idealist world in which all perception depended on Him as Immediate Cause. Moreover, this concept removed a source of "inextricable scepticism" in Locke by eliminating the gap between perception and reality. Locke readily admitted that we do not necessarily perceive the world exactly as it exists; or, to put it in Johnson's terms, if the pictures in our minds are "representations of things without us," they may not be exact representations of the "originals"—in which case we can never be certain that conclusions based on perceptions deal with the real nature of things. But to make the perceptions themselves reality, with God as their direct source, resolved this problem. Of course, Johnson built a complex system of thought around this basic concept, drawing extensively on Berkeley and elaborating on Berkeley with ideas of his own and of others. Johnson even imposed on Berkeleian empiricism a Platonic-like conception of "intellectual light," an intuitive knowledge of eternal truth which was conferred on man by God and which transcended perception.[29]

172 PORTRAIT OF A COLONIAL COLLEGE

In the "Ethica," the second part of *Elementa Philosophica*, Johnson sought to harmonize traditional Christianity with natural religion. Drawing on British moralists such as David Fordyce, Samuel Clarke, and, above all, William Wollaston, Johnson synthesized Christian and secular ethics in the concept of happiness. Happiness, stated Johnson, was the "great end" of our being. And ethics was the "art of living happily, by the right knowledge of ourselves, and the practice of virtue. . . ." While Johnson's conception of happiness embraced our well being in this world, the "supreme happiness" which was our overriding goal still came in the next world. It was toward achieving that ultimate happiness that we should strive in this life by perfecting ourselves in knowledge and virtue, confident that our efforts would bring happiness "in some good degree" even here. The pursuit of knowledge and virtue meant, above all, that we should learn to know and love God. But we should also endeavor to know the spiritual and natural world that God has created, and we should strive not just to love God but to live a thoroughly virtuous life. This, of course, is exactly what Johnson sought to teach his students at King's College throughout their four years. Even at commencement he could not resist the opportunity to remind the seniors a final time that knowledge and virtue should

> still be the great pursuit of your lives. You must not therefore now lay aside your books, but still, as far as the business of life will permit, be continually building upon the foundation already laid. And that you may be virtuous as well as knowing, devote yourselves to a steady course of diligence, and renounce all idle companions, and vicious company, and be perpetually upon your guard against all temptations. . . .[30]

The clash of new learning with old, of science and reason with traditional Christianity that Johnson had tried so hard to resolve in *Elementa Philosophica* continued to challenge the president well after the publication of his text. In his later years, however, Johnson showed an increasing willingness to subordinate science to the dictates of religious orthodoxy. Shortly before his death in 1772 he wrote in his autobiography of his conviction that "the Holy

Scriptures teach the only true system of natural philosophy as well as the only true religion . . . ," a belief that put him squarely in opposition to the Newtonianism that he had greeted so enthusiastically as a youth. Even by the time Johnson taught his first seniors at King's College he had retreated from the intellectual positions taken in his text. The major influence on his rethinking was John Hutchinson, an Englishman whose *Moses Principia*, published in 1724, enjoyed some popularity among those who did not take him immediately for the humbug he was. Hutchinson contended that all knowledge could be found in the original Hebrew version of the Old Testament. Hutchinson's own grammatical innovations made it possible for him to interpret the Old Testament in a way that no one had before. Modern science was dispatched to the intellectual refuse heap. Biblical literalism took its place. Gravitation, for example, was to be attributed to the cherubim.[31]

By 1756 Johnson was convinced that the cause of Hutchinson and his followers was the "cause of God." What it was that gradually drove Johnson down this intellectual dead end is hard to say. His affinity for Berkeley suggested the lengths to which he was willing to go to preserve religious orthodoxy. The troubles with his college and the series of deaths which was decimating his family must have deepened the feelings of despair about the future that were so much a part of his religious conservatism. Whatever the case, one suspects that Johnson's Hutchinsonianism affected his pedagogy in other ways besides his persistent but largely futile efforts to persuade undergraduates to study Hebrew.[32]

Yet, if there was ever proof that Johnson retained much of his intellectual perspective and balance in the 1750s, it can be found in the overall nature of the King's College curriculum itself. Despite his growing apprehension that the new science would undermine religion, he instituted an educational program that fell little short of the curricula at other American colleges in its fidelity to the New Learning. Indeed, during Treadwell's brief tenure it probably exceeded all of them in the amount of time devoted to science and mathematics—close to two years. True, Johnson realized that science appealed to undergraduates and that without an emphasis on natural philosophy his college could never compete for students. But even this attitude bespeaks a flexibility which clashes with any notion that Johnson's thinking in 1759 can be described in the same terms that historian Theodore Hornberger uses to assess Johnson's mind a decade later, as "sadly lacking in perspective and warped by a determination that science must be subservient to orthodoxy, whatever the cost." [33]

If Johnson did not turn his back on Newton in designing the King's College curriculum, neither did he reject several other progressive currents which he had encountered since his days at Yale. Of course, by instructing freshmen and sophomores in Latin grammar, rhetoric, and logic, Johnson made plain the medieval roots of his curriculum, in this case the medieval trivium. And his devotion to the classics reflected his debt to the ideal of gentlemanly education—"polite learning"—which the Renaissance had added to the medieval curriculum. But the shape and content of the educational program also had more recent origins, as one can see in Johnson's course on the new logic, or in the way he encouraged students to read belles lettres and modern history in their "spare time"; or in his use of moral philosophy, not theology, to synthesize and rationalize for seniors the intellectual experience of the previous three and a half years; or in his emphasis on the English language—apparent in his choice of texts, in the written and oral exercises which he assigned, and in his use of English as a medium of instruction. [34]

In formulating the curriculum Johnson drew not only on his wide reading in philosophy, theology, and literature but also on a number of works which dealt specifically with education. During the very years that the college was being planned, 1747 to 1753, he read innovative works on education by David Fordyce, John Locke, Benjamin Franklin, Robert Dodsley, and Reverend William Smith. Fordyce's *Dialogues Concerning Education* so impressed Johnson that he read it twice and recommended it to Cadwallader Colden as the "prettiest thing in its kind, and the best system both in physical, metaphysical, and moral philosophy, I have ever seen." These five authors varied in the degree to which they quarrelled with traditional curricula, making it difficult to generalize about their ideas. Among the more common of their suggestions for reforming curricula were, first, to include modern languages, especially English, and modern history, politics, and belles lettres, while retaining a strong but not excessive emphasis on those founts of virtue and wisdom, the classics; second, to teach geography and chronology, indispensable handmaidens to the study of history; third, to integrate the New Learning into the curriculum at the expense of traditional courses in metaphysics and logic; and, fourth, to offer courses in the "practical arts"—drawing, the history of commerce, merchants accounts, agriculture, gardening, and the like—which served both to accommodate newer types of students, such as prospective merchants, and to provide the broad education that was essential if one wished to produce gentlemen, not pedants. The value of any subject was to be judged against the overriding goals of the curriculum—to train youths in virtue and wisdom and to qualify them for public service.[35]

Measured against these recommendations, Johnson did moderately well. Yet, he clearly agreed with them more fully in his rhetoric than in practice. For example, when he announced the opening of the college in 1754 he included husbandry and commerce among the prospective courses, but they were never taught. This was partly a matter of priorities. Johnson never doubted that at some point in their education students should peruse the classics and should do so in the original tongues. On this issue he could never see his way to agreeing with Locke, who saw no reason for gentlemen to study Greek, or with Franklin, who believed that most students could survive just beautifully by reading the classics in translation. Unless students immersed themselves in the classics, insisted the president, they would "always be of but small account in the eyes of the learned and polite world. . . ." Johnson expected entering students already to have mastered Latin and Greek grammar and to have made significant headway in reading classical orators, poets, historians, and moralists. But in most cases they had not, so that it was "unavoidable that our 2 first years be chiefly taken up in classical Learning." Had King's College attracted the older, better-prepared students for whom Johnson hoped, his curriculum might have been more progressive than it was. For instance, rather than having undergraduates read English belles lettres just in their spare time, he might have given systematic attention in the classroom to Shakespeare, Milton, Pope, Addison, and Swift, whose works he considered "the best English classics." [36]

When Myles Cooper succeeded Samuel Johnson in 1763 he promptly revamped the King's College curriculum to suit his own intellectual tastes. Cooper was only twenty-five at the time. Unlike Johnson, he had never undergone an intellectual awakening which called into question the substance of his formal education. Indeed, he had spent the previous nine years at or nearby Oxford and had neither read nor experienced much beyond what Oxford offered him. Thus he modeled the curriculum at King's College, at least "in the most material parts," on that at Queen's College; and he felt no need to justify his "Plan of Education" other than by pointing to its source. Cooper's plan, as approved by the governors in 1763, called for the study of grammar, rhetoric, logic, ethics, metaphysics, and the classics. Indeed, Cooper prescribed an almost overwhelming dose of the classics—poetry, drama, history, and philosophy—dividing among the four years no less than forty-three titles plus Terence's comedies and the tragedies of Sophocles, Euripides, and Aeschylus. The official program ignored natural philosophy and mathematics.[37] However, several sources indicate that in operation the curriculum varied in several respects from the plan approved in 1763. The account that follows attempts to sketch the typical curriculum which students actually followed during Cooper's tenure, but at many points it is very hard to determine exactly what was studied and for how long.[38] Cooper apparently handled much of the instruction himself. Robert Harpur taught mathematics, while Samuel Clossy took over natural philosophy from Harpur in 1765 and taught it until 1776. Harpur and Clossy may have also assisted Cooper in teaching Latin, Greek, rhetoric, and logic. Charles Inglis served in Cooper's place from the fall of 1771 to the fall of 1772, while John Vardill shared with Cooper the tutoring duties in Latin, Greek, and classical history during 1773.

Like Johnson, Cooper devoted much of the first two years of

the curriculum to Latin and Greek grammar and to a selection of classical authors. Cooper used some of his predecessor's standbys, such as the New Testament and *Aesop's Fables* for Greek, and he tutored the freshman in such works of Latin poetry and history as Sallust's *History of the Jurgurthine War*, Caesar's *Commentaries*, Ovid's *Metamorphoses*, and Virgil's *Eclogues*. The sophomores undertook a program of classical studies much like Cutting's: Terence's comedies; Latin poetry, such as Martial's *Epigrams*, Virgil's *Aeneid* and *Georgics*, and Ovid's *Epistles*; works on or oriented toward ethics, like Cicero's *De Officiis*, Xenophon's *Cyropaedia*, and Epictetus's *Enchiridion*; and possibly a volume or two of classical history, like Xenophon's *Anabasis*. These works provided a basis for frequent excursions into rhetoric and ethics. The balance of the program for freshmen and sophomores included an introduction to logic and indeterminable amounts of mathematics and natural philosophy, the former probably embracing arithmetic, geometry, and algebra, and the latter possibly drawn in part from James Ferguson's *Lectures on Select Subjects in Mechanics, hydrostatics, hydraulics, pneumatics, and optics*, a reputable and up-to-date text.[39]

Cooper and Johnson differed in their organization of the curriculum for the first two years, but the variations seem slight when compared to the divergence in their handling of the last two years. Where Johnson's upperclassmen turned their attention primarily to science and mathematics, Cooper's juniors and seniors renewed their studies in the classics, ethics, rhetoric, and logic, while adding metaphysics, and possibly again devoting some portion of their time to natural philosophy and mathematics. Juniors now found that the steady diet of classics included Lucian and a host of poets, such as Homer, Catullus, Tibullus, and Horace, while seniors concentrated on classical historians, like Thucydides, Herodotus, Livy, Tacitus, and Lucan. During both years Cicero, Demosthenes, and Isocrates were used to study oratory. Upperclassmen may have also been introduced to the moral and political ideas of two outstanding seventeenth-century figures who wrote in Latin, Hugo Grotius and Samuel Pufendorf.

Thus, Cooper's curriculum, particularly that segment of it

178 PORTRAIT OF A COLONIAL COLLEGE

taught by the president himself, indicates an admiration for Greek
and Roman learning that exceeded even Johnson's. Moreover,
Cooper designed the curriculum to suit not only his esteem for the
classical authors noted above but also his scholastic Aristotelianism. Where Johnson introduced his students to the new
logic, Cooper insisted that Aristotle had so perfected logic that
"for nearly two thousand years, the art has undergone nothing
more than minor additions. . . ." He used neo-Aristotelian texts
in logic (Robert Sanderson's *Logicae Artis Compendium* and John
Wallis's *Institutio Logicae*), appended a section on "The Aristotelian
Method of Argumentation" to his own *Ethices Compendium*, and
compelled his students to engage frequently in syllogistic disputations. Cooper's courses in logic thus focused on deductive analysis. The test of a statement's truth was not its factual accuracy but
its consistency with a proposition already recognized as true. The
sentiments of some King's College pupils may well have been
echoed by a Queen's College, Oxford student of the 1770s who
lamented that "Sanderson is the great oracle next to Aristotle, to
whose bust the wranglers in the hall seem to pay a more profound
reverence than to common sense." [40]

Ethics as taught by Myles Cooper showed a similar regard for the
Greek master. *Ethices Compendium, in Usum Collegiorum Americanorum*, which Cooper published in 1774 and which doubtless reflected his lectures during previous years, was an elementary dis-
tillation of Aristotelian ethics, with some scholastic modifications.
Cooper no doubt was inspired by Daniel Whitby's *Ethices Compendium in Usum Juventutis Academicae*, a text which was used at
Queen's College and upon which Cooper apparently relied at
King's College until publishing his own work. [41] In his text Cooper argued that the "*Ultimate End of Ethics* is the highest happiness
which may be obtained in this life." Then, after quickly disposing
of the Epicurians, the Platonists, and the Stoics, Cooper agreed
with Aristotle that "the essence of human happiness consists in
acting according to the best and most perfect virtue." Chapters
follow on the will, the intellect, external and internal norms of actions, the nature of good action, and the passions.

Cooper then launched into an extended discussion of moral vir-

ETHICES

COMPENDIUM,

IN USUM

COLLEGIORUM AMERICANORUM,

EMENDATIUS EDITUM

A M. COOPER LL. D.

COLLEGII REGALIS PRÆSIDE.

CUI ACCEDIT

METHODUS ARGUMENTANDI

ARISTOTELICA.

[*New-York*]

NOVI-EBORACI,

Impensis JACOBI RIVINGTON, Bibliopolæ
M.DCC.LXXIV.

Title Page of the Ethices Compendium *by Myles Cooper*

CREDIT: COURTESY OF THE NEW-YORK HISTORICAL SOCIETY, NEW YORK CITY tue, which he, like Aristotle, defined as a mean between extremes. Although Cooper dipped into theology for his "queen of virtues," piety, his list of moral virtues is Aristotelian: prudence, fortitude, temperance, justice, liberality, magnificence, magnanimity, modesty, kindness, truthfulness, mildness, and urbanity. Cooper concluded with Aristotelian treatments of the semivirtues (like tolerance and continence), of friendship (which Cooper called a "relative of the moral virtues"), and of the intellectual virtues, which are mentioned only in so far as they lead an individual to right reason, the directing force of the moral virtues. Like Johnson in *Elementa Philosophica*, Cooper did not discuss economics ("the management of household affairs") and politics, although he classified them along with ethics as branches of moral philosophy.

Aristotle did not rule the King's College curriculum unchallenged by the New Learning and by seventeenth- and eighteenth-century moralists. Samuel Clossy and Robert Harpur educated students in inductive and experimental approaches to truth. Clossy believed that "all human knowledge" was "derived at first from sensation, and improved and enlarged by the operations of reason and reflection. . . ." So to expand our knowledge of the natural world we must "commence with observations and experiments, and draw general conclusions therefrom by the method of induction. . . ." True to his word, Clossy performed experiments during his lectures and must have made frequent use of the college's scientific apparatus. When John Adams visited the college in 1774 he found Clossy "exhibiting a Course of Experiments to his Pupils to prove the Elasticity of the Air." [42]

Moreover, Myles Cooper's official plan called for undergraduates to read not only Grotius and Pufendorf but also Johnson's *Elementa Philosophica* (although Cooper may have listed it simply as a courtesy) and texts in metaphysics and moral philosophy by Francis Hutcheson, the Scottish philosopher. In fact, undergraduates were to study Hutcheson during both their junior and senior years. One wonders whether they did so, particularly whether they examined not just Hutcheson's theory of moral sense—that the perception and approval of virtue was an emotional not a rational process—but his progressive political concepts as well—natural rights, the contract theory of government, popular sovereignty, the right of resistance—concepts which were at variance with Cooper's own political ideas. Apparently Cooper also introduced freshmen and sophomores to modern history and English poetry. Indeed, among the prizes awarded to outstanding students were copies of Milton's *Paradise Lost* and Oliver Goldsmith's *History of England*. Nor did Cooper's preoccupation with the Latin and Greek languages, keys to the classics and to the Aristotelian texts he used, preclude frequent exercises in the use of English. In the 1770s Cooper even permitted undergraduates to study French and Italian with a local teacher, who boasted that the "principal students" at the college were "under his tuition." King's College students during Cooper's presidency were by no means left ignorant of the philosophical, scientific, and literary achievements of seventeenth- and eighteenth-century Europe.[43]

One would like to know, however, just what the seniors said at the commencement of 1772 when they entertained the audience with "a judicious *Comparison of modern and ancient Learning*, and an accurate Estimate of the peculiar Excellencies of each. . . ." Cooper's Aristotelianism on top of his regard for classical poets, playwrights, historians, rhetoricians, and philosophers makes one suspect that the ancients gained the lion's share of the praise. Perhaps one hears a bit of Cooper speaking in the words of a former pupil who, a few years after graduating from King's College, visited the ancient ruins of Rome, by which he was duly impressed:

> Is it surprising that a People capable of such undertakings should become Masters of the World? such Giant Minds found no Task too difficult: How insignificant is the Character of the Moderns when put in competition with Them—how little & despicable are their Works.

Appropriately, the young man dispatched to New York "a Case containing seven folio Volumes of the Antiquities of Rome & other Works," which he asked his brother to "present to the College."[44]

Cooper predictably expected King's College students to endure countless lectures and recitations, but he probably outdistanced

Johnson in requiring his pupils to engage in formal written and oral exercises. Throughout their four years, in both Latin and English, they wrote poetry, themes, and philosophical essays, and practiced disputations, declamations, orations, repetitions, and dissertations. As a poet, Cooper emphasized the writing of verses. In fact, he seems to have turned out an army of amateur poets. The letters and writings of former Cooper students like Gulian Verplanck, Peter Van Schaack, John Vardill, Gouverneur Morris, and Robert R. Livingston are sprinkled with verses. The students probably appreciated Cooper's own light and occasional verse. His poetry ranged from tales, epitaphs, elegies, and epigrams to political verses and odes to women, with many of the poems in rather thumping, well-rhymed, four-line stanzas. Alexander Hamilton "now and then paid his court to the muses" while under Cooper's tutelage, according to a college chum, while Robert R. Livingston composed a "College Exercise" which doubled as a commentary on the cook, as these stanzas indicate:

> When good roast beef & rich ragouts
>   Delight the happy soldiers eyes
> For them he quits his savage foes
>   And courts the joyous prize
>
> We students too would quit our book
>   When e'er we heard the dinner bell
> Could we believe our frugal cook
>   For once had cater'd well [45]

King's students not only wrote poetry. They delivered orations on it. One commencement featured "two English Dissertations *on the Advantages and Disadvantages of Poetry,*" while another included "an English Oration on the *Beauties of Poetry.*" Cooper's concern with oratory is ironic, since he disliked to preach and confessed that "not one of ye small Talents I possess, is any way related to *Oratory.*" Friends discovered little reason to disagree with him.[46] Yet King's students undoubtedly were asked to give the subject frequent and close attention. Almost half the prizes awarded to undergraduates were for oratorical excellence.

Myles Cooper instituted a curriculum which differed from

Samuel Johnson's in several respects—in its extraordinary emphasis on the classics, in its Aristotelianism and the accompanying use of texts in Latin for logic and ethics, in its comparatively modest attention to the New Learning, and in its secularism. On the last point, several sources indicate that the education of a Christian gentleman under Cooper was less a matter of piety and more a matter of refinement. Ironically, Cooper's curriculum, when compared to that at other colonial colleges, turns out to be decidedly more distinctive than Johnson's—but not in a way that has won Cooper many plaudits for his enlightenment. Cooper's educational program also was distinctive in its political message. However, before exploring that crucial dimension of the curriculum, let us broaden our examination by bringing the students into the picture. One can talk at length about, say, the intellectual subtleties of Samuel Johnson's senior year course on his *Elementa Philosophica*. It is well not to lose sight of the fact that less than twenty-five people ever took it.

11.
THE UNDERGRADUATE EXPERIENCE

"WHILE A LAD AT COLLEGE," recalled one King's College alumnus, "my friends . . . and myself went on a fishing and shooting party down the Sound. The wind heading us, and we too lazy to row, [we] determined to land on an island in the Sound, where we found a flock of fine fat sheep belonging to old Chris. DeLancey. This determined us to sup upon mutton. We shot one of the sheep and roasted it for supper." Old Chris DeLancey took the incident with good humor, but it was hardly the kind of behavior which the leaders of King's College had in mind when they envisioned virtuous young gentlemen. Myles Cooper believed that youngsters of promise were, among other things, "very sober," "regular in their behaviour," and "diligent & attentive to Business." Moreover, it was imperative that these qualities be acquired during the college years if they had not been achieved earlier. The teens constituted a "critical Period," one King's College alumnus advised his nephew, "when you must lay a Foundation for the Character you are to sustain in your manhood." [1] How, then, did the faculty and trustees go about making the curricular program and the collegiate way of living work? And to what extent did their efforts result in an orderly and uniform educational experience?

Obviously it was one thing to lay out an elaborate program of studies and parietal rules but another thing to expect students to follow it. Why should sixteen-year-old boys exert themselves studying Latin or Greek, or physics for that matter? Why should they diligently rise at dawn every morning, wear gowns on campus or off, refrain from drinking or swearing, and return to their chambers by 10:00 P.M. on summer evenings? The answers are complex, but the governors and faculty of King's College had some interesting thoughts on these matters, and they took various measures to get students to behave the way they wanted them to.

College authorities put some faith in the power of example. Indeed, Samuel Johnson warned parents of prospective students not to expect much from King's College if they themselves had been poor models for their children, since examples had such a "very powerful influence over young minds." John Vardill, a graduate of King's College and a tutor there in the 1770s, emphasized the crucial role of emulation, by which he meant a blend of imitation and ambition, a zeal to equal or outstrip an adult who had impressed a student. Students had constantly before them "Examples of Men who have risen to Grandeur by their Abilities," a reference to the governors and other city grandees like them. Their achievements, and the hope of matching them, would inspire undergraduates to master the virtuous habits and the useful knowledge which the college authorities sought to instill. The same process could work with historical as well as contemporary figures, especially the more the students immersed themselves in the classics. One former student urged his younger brother to study history and "observe the Actions of the greatest Men that ever existed . . ."; it will inspire "you with a noble Emulation, to make your self remarkable in your Profession, & to raise [yourself] above the common herd of Mankind. . . ." [2]

The role of emulation, as conceived by John Vardill, shaded into a second means of shaping student behavior, through reward and punishment. The New Yorkers of "Eminence and Influence" who set examples and could inspire emulation also held the keys that unlocked doors to political, professional, and mercantile careers. On their "Opinion" would depend the reputation of a youth. Should a student incur a disgrace, it would "quickly circulate," and "impress a Stigma on his Name" (a process facilitated by the fact that governors sat on disciplinary and examining committees). On the other hand, if a student "attracted the Notice of

those around him" because of his "Excellencies," he would "have
the superior Benefit of entering on Business with the good Opinion of his Fellow Citizens. . . ." Students would thus fear to of-
fend and seek to please prominent people outside the college
through their behavior inside the college. It was this very issue
which George Rapalje raised when he pleaded for reinstatement
because his expulsion would "be an almost insuperable Obstacle
to my being received into any Employment." Another student,
who was forced to drop out before earning a degree, made sure he
procured a testimonial from the president that he had not been
dismissed for any "misdemeanor" but was leaving with the reputation of a good scholar and of one whose deportment was satisfac-
tory to the college authorities.[3]

Long-term consequences, affecting employment and community reputation, added a great deal of weight to the elaborate system of rewards and punishments which college leaders developed
to manipulate student behavior. Let them "always feel the com-
fort, the pleasure and advantage of an orderly, regular and obedient behavior," advised Samuel Johnson on the education of
young children, "and let pain, shame and disgrace ever attend the
contrary." Similar principles were implemented at King's College,
except on the question of pain. There is no indication that the faculty or the governors resorted to corporal punishment. However,
the threat of shame and disgrace was heavily relied upon to deter
wayward behavior. While corporal punishment was "improper,"
Vardill noted, disgrace was the "principal Sanction of the [college]
Laws." [4] When a student was expelled, groups outside the college—family, neighbors, potential masters or employers—helped
generate feelings of shame. But the college community itself could
serve as a forum for the same purpose. "Degradation"—demotion
to a lower class, usually temporary—might stigmatize a student,
especially since a keen sense of social hierarchy was common
among those associated with the college. More dramatic were the
periodic reprimands and confessions staged in the college hall.
One student who had been expelled gained readmittance only
after he made a "Publick confession of his fault" in the hall before
a committee of governors, President Cooper, the faculty, and the

students. Another undergraduate, who had stolen "8 Sheets of Paper & a Pen-Knife," was

> reprimanded in the College Hall before all the Students. & after having his Gown stripped off by the Porter, he was ordered to kneel down & read a Paper containing an Acknowledgement of his Crime, expressing much Sorrow for it, & promising Amendment for the future—He was then forbidden to wear his Gown or Cap for one Week.[5]

Any penalty might carry a stigma, and ultimately there was always the threat of incurring a "disgraceful" reputation, but many punishments were expected to operate by means other than shame. Obviously, confinement to the college grounds or to one's chambers had special qualities as sanctions. So did fines and academic exercises. Both were common. The exercises usually involved translating Latin passages into English or *The Spectator* or *The Guardian* into Latin. Expulsion could bring more than disgrace if it closed off the path to a degree. One student "left" college in his senior year after committing a "great fault" toward a professor. Several years later he decided to seek ordination but could not get the support he needed from the clergy because he had no degree. In this case Samuel Johnson, then retired, persuaded the governors to overlook the youth's earlier "faults & follies" and award him a degree.[6]

These sanctions were used to punish or deter a wide variety of behaviors: failing to prepare written assignments or to attend an examination, breaking windows or lying to the governors, sneaking over the college fence or simply disappearing for several days, or, to cite the kind of behavior that brought expulsion, "abusing" a faculty member, such as the case where a student challenged President Cooper to a duel with pistols in the middle of recitation. During Cooper's regime discipline was undoubtedly more systematic than during Johnson's. During the 1770s a committee of governors heard cases regularly and meted out the punishments deemed necessary "so that *peace* and *good order*" might be preserved. But even Samuel Johnson was vehement, in words if not always in action, that parents and others responsible for shaping the conduct of young people should utilize every means to discourage "hateful vices, idleness, gaming, intemperance and lewdness, as being the most fatal banes of virtue and public good. . . ." [7]

The governors and faculty also used rewards to mold student behavior, particularly to encourage academic excellence. If students could be degraded for missing "*two* Recitations in Succession," they could in rare instances be promoted ahead of time for making "extraordinary progress" in their studies. If degrees could be denied for poor performance at the final examination and "general irregularity in attendance," they could be conferred for academic diligence. Outstanding students could be singled out as valedictorians and salutatorians and displayed at public commencements. If fines could be assessed for misbehavior, the proceeds could be used to purchase books which would be awarded to pupils who excelled in their studies and their conduct. The most elaborate effort to affect behavior through rewards was the organization in 1766 of a "Literary Society," composed of about twenty-five city gentlemen, among them the faculty and a number of governors. Their goal was to encourage learning by conferring medals and books on deserving students. The members contributed about £100, spent most of it on specially engraved silver medals, and presented them to students on several occasions during the next few years, usually at commencement and usually for excellence in oratory. Just as the Greeks contended with the "greatest ardour" at the Olympic Games for the prize of an olive branch, so the students were expected to strive for "a reward of literary merit." [8]

A third means relied on by the governors and faculty to influence student behavior was to anchor their messages in the authority of religion and tradition and to dignify them with pomp and ritual. Charles Inglis, a governor and interim president during Cooper's trip to England in 1772, could give almost cosmic significance to obeying the college laws. As he told the students, the "sacred law of Order" was "Heaven's first law." To spurn it was to bring on "confusion and ruin." During Samuel Johnson's presidency the students prayed methodically that they would "abhor all mischief, and quarrelling, lying, and stealing, evil speaking and filthiness and all sorts of wickedness . . . ," especially since God "seest me wherever I am." In 1763 the new plan of education and the new set of college laws were proclaimed with "becoming solemnity" in the hall before the governors, professors, and students, so as to "give them the greater Weight and Sanction." Thus, from translating Caesar at the entrance examination to pronouncing orations at commencement, the collegiate experience was clothed in tradition and elaborated in ritual: wearing gowns, studying Latin and Greek, attending morning and evening prayers, abjuring dice and cards, uncovering one's head before "the authority of the college," copying the laws and appending one's signature to them at matriculation, and so on.[9]

A related way of impressing students was exhortation. Commencement was regarded as a prime opportunity to fire up the seniors, but by then they had undoubtedly heard it all dozens of times. A good example of the kind of rhetoric used to inspire students is the address given the undergraduates by Charles Inglis upon his becoming interim president. Inglis urged the students to obey the statutes and to be diligent in their studies. He reminded them that if they wished to "act a distinguished part in life hereafter," to "rise above the common herd," they must now cheerfully submit to "virtuous discipline" and make advances in useful knowledge. "Surely you must be ambitious to excel," he exhorted them. Let it be the "ambition of each to outstrip the other in the career of literary fame. Esteem it a disgrace to be ignorant of any thing. . . ." What could be more contemptible than a student to whom "science opened all its treasures," yet who remained "buried in his native ignorance and barbarity"? [10]

The discussion so far suggests that college authorities viewed education almost as an adversary relationship, in which students had constantly to be threatened, exhorted, rewarded, and otherwise motivated by their elders in order to behave properly and to master the liberal arts and sciences. Yet, the governors and faculty often saw their role less as creating a kind of disciplinary cocoon within which students were to operate than as helping them down a road on which they were already headed, but from which they sometimes strayed or the point of which they did not understand. And college authorities counted on the students to go part of the way on their own, because they had internalized parental values, or had learned the lesson of obedience, or could perceive by themselves that virtuous behavior suited their self-interest, or even because they liked what they were doing.

The procedures described above were used to mold undergraduates into the kinds of people deemed desirable by the college authorities. In describing these procedures and in sketching the formal structure of the curriculum and the collegiate way, one can easily convey a sense of orderliness and uniformity about education at King's College that would be staggeringly misleading. For instance, the curriculum seems rather systematic when examined from the point of view of how the faculty organized it; but when one turns around and tries to understand how it operated in terms of student behavior, it becomes something of a shambles. Professors go to classes. Students miss them. Professors assign readings. Some students ignore them; others read more than they were asked. The curriculum covers four years. Students often leave after two. And so on. For similar reasons it can be deceptive to describe the "typical day" in a student's life. And the typical student has never existed.

Of course, compared to students at today's universities, the King's College undergraduates seem homogeneous and their experiences relatively uniform. They were all male, white, English-speaking, and (except for one Jew) Protestant and northern European in extraction. In most cases their families were prosperous. They were all pursuing the same curriculum and the same degree in a single college under the watchful eye of a tiny faculty. But it is important not to let this comparative uniformity mask the diversity and disorderliness which lay underneath. Undergraduate experiences are typically more varied and less systematic than histories of higher education suggest. Moreover, King's College students were attending a fledgling college in a bustling city, in a period first of war, then of pre-Revolutionary turbulence. Also, despite their homogeneity, they did not share some of the attributes, such as age and manner of preparatory education, that college students usually share today. And they were going through a process that was customary neither within their families (the fathers of less than 10 percent of the boys had attended college) nor within their community (degrees opened doors, but most doors opened without them).

One can grasp something of the character and variety of undergraduate education at King's College by comparing the experiences of several students. Note, for instance, the remarkably different responses to the curriculum and to the collegiate way exhibited by two of Myles Cooper's students, Benjamin Moore and James Davan. Moore was born and raised on his father's farm at Newtown, Long Island and entered King's College in 1764, at age 15. He was a studious lad and relished the opportunity to spend four years at college. "*Then* I was lost to the Wo[rld and] all it's [sic] perplexing Cares," he recalled fondly three years after graduating. "Then 'from morn to eve; from eve to dewy morn' Cheerfulness & Peace were my constant Companions." Moore dutifully obeyed the college rules and enthusiastically "followed science thro' her flowering paths." At the end of his junior year the members of the literary society were so struck by his "diligent Attendance, good Behavior and general improvement since his Entrance into College" that they bestowed on him £5 worth of books. Nor did Moore's exertions slacken during his senior year. He graduated at the head of his class, and the literary society awarded him a silver medal at commencement. Afterward Moore tutored boys in Latin and Greek while he studied theology. He subsequently became "the finished and the well furnished divine" and served as the Episcopal bishop of New York and as president of Columbia, though some might feel that his most important accomplishment was fathering Clement Moore, who wrote " 'Twas the night before Christmas. . . ." [11]

James Davan, son of a leather dresser and breeches maker, lived in Elizabethown, New Jersey and New York City before commencing a dismal career as an undergraduate at King's College in 1772, at age thirteen.[12] Right away his behavior earned him confinement to the college grounds. He then made several attempts to sneak out, denied that he had done so, and was suspended.

Within a month he was restored, but the situation degenerated in the summer of 1773. President Cooper accused him of being "notoriously guilty" of missing classes and prayers. Cooper prescribed written exercises to be read in the hall, but Davan "absented himself" instead of doing the exercises. The governors suspended him again and declared him "deserving of the highest Censure." When Davan persevered in ignoring Cooper and the governors, they confined him to his chambers for four weeks. In the summer of 1774 Davan somehow made it into the junior class, but his relationship with Cooper was strained. First, on one occasion he refused repeatedly to admit Cooper to his room, eventually "causing four Doors to be broke open before he could be laid hold of." Then he joined three other students in stealing thirteen bottles of wine from Cooper's closet and failed to turn in a class exercise, a translation from Lucian. The latter exploit brought him confinement to the college grounds until the assignment was completed. The very next morning he skipped out after prayers. He was then ordered to translate a selection from Virgil's *Aeneid* as well as the assignment from Lucian. When he ignored both, the discipline committee added yet another translation to the list, this time an issue of *The Guardian* from English into Latin. By April 1775 Davan had not done "one word." In fact, he had fled "into the Country" for a week without leave. So the governors degraded him until he had "completed *Double*" the exercises he owed, and then tacked on two more issues of *The Guardian*. But before this decision could be read to him he missed prayers, so he was given another half issue of *The Guardian*. When he still balked, the discipline committee threatened to bring his case before the entire board of governors. Apparently this moved him to action. In June 1775 he entered his senior year. But in August he was again hauled before the committee for failing to do his assignments and for frequently missing classes. He was confined within the college walls and given more exercises. At some point during his senior year he dropped out and moved on to a comparatively anonymous life as an adult.[13]

Obviously Benjamin Moore and James Davan had radically different kinds of intellectual and social experiences at King's Col-

Benjamin Moore (B.A., King's College, 1768)
Moore was president pro tempore of King's College, 1775–1777, and president of
Columbia College, 1801–1811.
CREDIT: COLUMBIANA, COLUMBIA UNIVERSITY

lege. One cannot help but feel that statements about the impact of
the college on Moore would not apply to Davan, at least not
without some modifications. Yet, the differences between them—
in age, maturity, motivation, demeanor, length of stay, perhaps in

intelligence and educational preparation for college—were common variations among all King's College undergraduates. For one thing, there was little system in the admission of students. This was normal at eighteenth-century colleges; and the process operated all the more loosely at a college short on students in a colony short on schools. The median age for entering students was about fourteen and a half, but some were twelve, others nineteen, and the rest fell at all ages in between. The governors finally ruled that students should be at least fourteen at the time of matriculation, but they did so only after the number of undergraduates had begun to climb in the 1770s, and they continued to waive the point for students of "extraordinary qualification." [14]

If the undergraduates did not march through college in chronological lockstep, neither did they prepare for college in any uniform way. There were no public schools, few long-lived private schools, and obviously no ladder of grades that students climbed on their way from the three R's to the freshman class. John Jay left home at age seven to board and study with a cleric nearby his home. At ten he returned home and was tutored privately before entering King's College at fourteen. Peter Van Schaack studied at Kinderhook Academy, in his home town near Albany, then at age fourteen was sent to a cleric on Staten Island, where he was tutored for two winters before enrolling at King's. At least eight matriculants studied with Reverend Samuel Seabury on Long Island, while a goodly number of boys must have prepared at the King's College grammar school. The entrance examination supposedly set standards by which poorly prepared or dull students could be screened out. But translating Latin and Greek had little bearing on some of the skills needed to excel at oratory, logic, mathematics, or natural philosophy. In any case, students were admitted even if they did poorly on the exam. So, variations in age and maturity were compounded by variations in preparation and intelligence. [15]

Once a student matriculated at King's College, the chances were barely even that he would graduate. Only 108 of the 209 students earned B.A. degrees. James Davan lasted until his senior year before departing, but the median period of stay for those not graduating was about one and a half years. The high "dropout" rate not only adds another important variable to the undergraduate experience but raises an interesting question about why so many students failed to stay through graduation. The explanation for about a quarter of them is clear-cut. Sometime between 1775 and 1777 their studies were disrupted by the American Revolution and by the closing of King's College. The ostensible reasons for most of the thirty early leavers during Samuel Johnson's presidency also are known, since he made notations in the Matricula. A third went "to merchandize" or "business." Five "went to Physic" or to "study Physic," one left to study law, and four transferred to the College of Philadelphia. Three went into the army or "to Privateering," one fled the smallpox, one died, one "went to nothing," and four simply "left," possibly for disciplinary reasons.[16]

Behind these notations lay a variety of factors: cost, student and parental dissatisfaction, impatience to pursue professional or technical education, and the shallow roots of collegiate education among New York's upper and middle classes. The rate of attrition was highest during Johnson's presidency, when discontent with Johnson, his college, and his absences provoked some parents to transfer their sons to the College of Philadelphia and persuaded others that they might as well get their sons moving along in mercantile careers. One suspects that a major factor during both presidencies was the college's urban location, which would help explain why the College of Philadelphia also suffered an unusually high attrition rate. Perhaps the proximity of the college attracted local families who did not necessarily expect their sons to spend four years there, while the proximity of the city distracted students from their academic endeavors. This would apply especially to boys headed for mercantile careers, who both attended and dropped out of King's College in unusually high numbers. Those boys who found the most practical value in a degree—prospective ministers and lawyers—were the most likely to graduate, but King's College did not educate many of the former.

If the manner of admitting students and the practice of leaving early accentuated the variability of the undergraduate experience at King's College, so did certain social factors which can best be illuminated by comparing two additional students, John Watts and Epenetus Townsend. When John Watts entered King's College in 1762, he must have found it the most natural thing in the world to do. To be sure, New York had had a college for only eight years, but John himself was just a few weeks short of thirteen. Almost as far back as he could remember King's College had been an intimate part of his world. As a young boy he had undoubtedly watched the construction of the college building, which was located only a few blocks from his father's town house on Broadway. During the same period his older brother had attended the college, graduating in 1760. First and second cousins of John's abounded among the students, two of them attending briefly in 1757, a third graduating in 1761, a fourth in 1762, and a fifth enrolling in the same class with John. Kinship and friendship connections between family and college extended to the governors as well. The first time that John had to "recite" before a committee of governors he encountered his cousin and the rector of his church. Two second cousins who had been board members died before John matriculated, but he still could count on the patronage of two of the college's most eminent governors, his uncle and his father. As for the faculty, Samuel Johnson was a family friend.[17]

John Watts was privileged to grow up in one of New York's leading families. His father was a wealthy merchant and a member of the New York Council. His mother was a DeLancey. Samuel Johnson was not blind to such realities. Johnson had a habit of entering the names of the members of each class in the matriculation book roughly in the order of their social status, much like the practice of ranking students at Yale. Johnson placed Watts's name at the head of his class. There is nothing to indicate that students at King's College, like students at Yale, followed this order when it was time to "Declame" or "Stand at Prayers and Recitations."[18] But John's social standing undoubtedly brought him ready acceptance by boys of other prominent families whom he knew at college: John Jay, Gouverneur Morris, Robert R. Livingston, John Stevens, Gulian Verplanck, Daniel Ludlow, Richard Harison. Thus John Watts probably belonged to those "few Select One's" who gathered regularly for conversations in John Jay's room. And John Watts and all the boys mentioned above plus a number of other young New Yorkers met weekly at a "Social Club" several years later. Watts's social situation at college enhanced lasting friendships, since most of the boys lived in the building and since only one student dropped out of his class. John did well academically, was named salutatorian, and delivered an oration at his commencement to "General Gage, and General Burton, His Majesty's Council, and the Clergy of the City and neighbouring Governments, and an exceeding[ly] numerous and splendid Audience." [19]

John Watts's world naturally broadened as he matured, but his activities still ran along comfortable, familiar paths. He clerked in the law office of a King's College governor, trod the path to London and the Inns of Court which his cousin had taken a few years earlier, returned to New York City to practice law, married his cousin, lived on Broadway, became a wealthy man, and, like his father and grandfather before him, served in public life—as speaker of the New York assembly, a representative in the United States Congress, a county judge, and a trustee of Columbia. At his death he was buried in Trinity Churchyard, and a statue of him was erected there.[20]

Epenetus Townsend entered college at about the same age as John Watts and attended just a few years before him, but the character of their social experiences differed markedly. When Epenetus enrolled in the college's second class in 1755 he embarked on a venture in a world largely unfamiliar to him. He had grown up on his father's farm at Oyster Bay, Long Island and had few, if any, friends and relatives in New York City to smooth the way for him. He knew no one among the students, governors, or faculty of the college. His father, Micajah, had chosen King's College mainly out of a sense of provincial loyalty, being "Desirous of the Prosperity of our infant College" but hardly expecting that his son would "be under so good advantages as at the older ones in the Neighbouring Provinces." Micajah Townsend was a prosperous farmer and a figure of some prominence in his

198   PORTRAIT OF A COLONIAL COLLEGE

community. But this hardly made Epenetus Townsend the social
equal of John Watts. Even Micajah referred to himself as a "yeo-
man." Samuel Johnson placed Epenetus fifth in his tiny class of
six, below such boys as John Johnston, whose father was an East
Jersey Proprietor and whose mother was a Heathcote, and Tele-
mon Cruger, son of a wealthy New York assemblyman who had
sponsored much of the legislation organizing King's College.[21]

It was not easy for a boy of thirteen to adjust to life in the city
among strangers, particularly when he had to live in town because
the college as yet had no building. Samuel Johnson later recalled
Epenetus as an "amiable and virtuous" youth, but the boy soon
began to incur college fines for "Neglect of Duty." After all,
explained his father, he had "no parents to forwarn him." In fact,
the situation proved so hard for him—one suspects a touch of
homesickness—that his father brought him home and "Kept him
the greatest part of the first year at a grammar school. . . ." By
1756 Epenetus was back at King's, only to catch the smallpox in
December. He soon recovered, but it left such a "weakness in his
Eys" that he could not study until April of 1757. Then, when he
resumed full time he found himself restricted to working with
Leonard Cutting, the tutor in classics, since the smallpox had
driven Samuel Johnson into a year-long retreat in Westchester
County. Meanwhile, the problems at the college and the opportunities opened up by the French and Indian War had begun to
shrink Epenetus's class. By the end of his sophomore year it was
down to four. Epenetus plugged along through his junior year.
Johnson returned and Daniel Treadwell joined the faculty, but
Epenetus's three remaining classmates departed. In his senior year
Epenetus carried on alone, living in town, perhaps enjoying the
attention he must have received from the faculty. However, when
the time for commencement arrived, a single graduate hardly
seemed to justify a public celebration, so the governors presented
him with his degree at one of their meetings. Epenetus went on to
become an Anglican cleric on the New York frontier, but his
loyalist sympathies soon got him into trouble. He abandoned his
pulpit, was taken prisoner by the rebels at one point, then finally
headed for Nova Scotia with his family. They never arrived. The

vessel on which they were traveling foundered, and everyone on board drowned.[22]

A number of factors accounted for the substantial differences in the social experiences of John Watts and Epenetus Townsend at King's College, none more so then the contrasts in their families. Few students could match the web of social relationships that linked John Watts to the college community. But at least two-fifths of the undergraduates enjoyed ties of blood and marriage to that network of families which dominated the social, political, and economic hierarchies of New York City and the surrounding area. These relationships tended to clusters, such as the one Watts belonged to. These clusters, in turn, were linked by family ties that had developed over three or four generations, so that technically some eighty-five or ninety of all the King's College students were not too distantly related. Over seventy of them had close familial ties to one or more of the governors. Not all of them belonged to the upper class, but most of them found that in attending King's they were moving within familiar circles.

The remaining three-fifths or so of the undergraduates had, like Epenetus Townsend, almost no direct or important family ties to the dominant family network. Nor did they have relatives among the governors or (expect for brothers and, infrequently, a cousin) among the students. A few had the advantage of upper-class membership. The families of a number enjoyed occupational, political, religious, and other kinds of associations with one another or with the dominant social group. But by and large the texture and meaning of their social experiences at King's College were significantly different from that of John Watts. A student of *"real gentility,"* noted Myles Cooper, "will chuse the best for his Associates." [23]

There were other variables that added different dimensions to the undergraduate experience. George Washington's stepson, John Parke Custis, for example, enjoyed the attentions of his slave while at King's and somehow managed to spend almost £300 New York currency in four months. In contrast, William Lamson was forced to drop out for lack of funds. Some students could not keep up with the regular assignments. Others went well beyond them.

Both John Jay and Alexander Hamilton prepared for future law careers by perusing such works as Hugo Grotius's *Law of War and Peace* and Giles Jacob's *New Law Dictionary*. Hamilton and four other students met weekly on their own to improve themselves in composition, debating, and public speaking.[24]

But let us turn to another kind of issue, one that suggests more about disorderliness than about diversity in the undergraduate experience. The issue is pointed up nicely in the tribulations of Robert Harpur (for whom, incidentally, Harpur College in Binghamton, New York was named). No one was welcomed more enthusiastically by the King's College community than was Harpur in 1761. Students and leaders alike were delighted to have a teacher in mathematics and science after a hiatus of a year and a half. Harpur himself was equally satisfied. "When I consider my collegiate life alone," he wrote in 1765, "I envy not the greatest or happiest on earth. . . ." But there was something about Robert Harpur that soon antagonized the students. Perhaps it was his Presbyterian religion or his Irish heritage. Perhaps he was an incompetent teacher, as an anonymous letter alleged in 1765. More than likely it was his role as a strict disciplinarian, which provoked the restless adolescents already chafing at a patrolled life. Harpur was raised in the kind of family that believed there was nothing healthier than a lively fear of God. "On the Sabbath, when a child," Harpur recalled, his mother "would not permit me scarcely to speak or go to the door, nor even to smile, but would rebuke me at once." Harpur grew into a puritanical fellow who could not abide such "sinful practices" as horse racing, attending stage plays, and walking on the Sabbath.[25]

By 1765 someone—it may not have been a student—had decided that Robert Harpur must go. The challenge, an anonymous letter to a governor from "A:B," was either a clever "poison pen" letter or else a serious indictment of Harpur's teaching. The author supposedly had heard in a recent conversation that Robert Harpur was an abysmal instructor whose ineptness was discouraging New Yorkers from enrolling their sons at the college. His knowledge was "insufficient," he had "no method," and he lacked

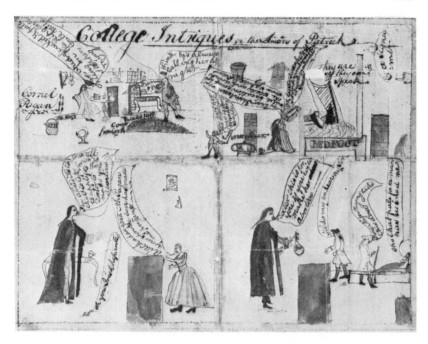

Cartoon Depicting the Adventures of "Patrick Pagan"
Directed against Robert Harpur, the cartoon was devised by John Vardill, then a
senior at King's College. Six and a half years later Vardill joined Harpur on the
college faculty.
CREDIT: COLUMBIA UNIVERSITY LIBRARIES

"a proper way of communicating his Ideas." As long as Harpur
remained, "he would reflect nothing but disgrace upon the Institution." [26]

The next year the attack shifted in focus from incompetence to
fornication. One day a spicy cartoon was "affixed up in the College Hall." In several scenes it depicted Harpur (Patrick Pagan in
the cartoon) deciding he was "tired of euclid" and in need of the
company of Miss Myng, plying Miss Myng with spruce beer
("you need not fear Misstress, the Juce is verry weak & simple"),
and the two of them so absorbed with each other in bed that "they
can't speak." Then follows Harpur learning from Miss Myng that
"your spruce beer has made me pregnant," Harpur, in his aca-

demic robe, arranging for an abortion, and the doctor administering a dose of medicine to Miss Myng, the latter moaning that "that pale face man has ruined me." [27]

Such a "Scandalous and Defamatory Libel" angered the college governors, as did rumors about Harpur, to the same effect as the cartoon, which were propagated by several students. The governors apprehended the culprits, demanded that they produce evidence to substantiate their claims, which they could not, and handed out appropriate punishments. Just how Robert Harpur took it all we do not know, but nine months later he resigned. However, he stayed on as a private tutor. The students now resorted largely to abusing him with bad language. In 1773 seven boys were punished for "ill-using Mr Harpur, by *calling Names* in the Dark. . . ." The next year a boy was expelled for insulting Harpur "with the most indecent language, repeatedly." [28] But Harpur stuck it out. After the Revolution he declined to reassume a teaching position, but he served assiduously as a regent and a trustee of Columbia.

Every undergraduate who participated in the various assaults on Robert Harpur had pledged at his matriculation that he would not "molest" the professors and that he would pay them "such respect" as they should direct. Obviously it did not work out that way. And that was only one facet of the collegiate way that looked a lot more orderly on paper than in operation. The "Black Book" is testimony to the fact that undergraduates of all ages and classes violated college rules—by playing cards, getting drunk, shooting guns, defying the president, stealing tea cups, spitting in the cook's face, creating "Noise and Confusion," and, of course, missing prayers and classes. During the 1770s the governors indicated in a number of general statements their concern over the widespread failure of students to attend church on Sundays, to wear caps and gowns, to attend recitations faithfully, and, above all, to complete the academic exercises which were assigned them. [29]

Yet, disorderliness of this character is at once the most obvious and the most deceptive of any. If each student committed one serious offense each year he was at the college, the "Black Book" would run for pages and the governors would be at their wits' end, but students could be obeying most of the rules most of the time. It is difficult both to measure the volume of deviant behavior and to judge its significance. Even the "Black Book" has serious drawbacks. It was kept only for a little more than four years. It includes mainly those offenses considered important enough to be dealt with by the governors, though Cooper occasionally entered actions that he took on his own. Both kinds of violations were defined, pursued, and recorded erratically. Still, the "Black Book" does provide some perspective on the extent of this kind of disorderliness.

Seven undergraduates spent four full academic years at the college during the period the "Black Book" was in use. Two of them do not appear in it at all. One student is listed for one offense, one student for two, one for three, one for four, and one for five. John Livingston (3 offenses) was punished in his junior year, along with several friends, for creating such a commotion in the college building that a professor had to interrupt his lecture. In his senior year he was listed for owing two exercises and for going into the country for a week without leave. Jacob Remsen (4 offenses) was punished in his sophomore year for beating another student and for "absenting himself from College under Pretence of Sickness, for several Days, tho it was proved he had been fishing on some of those Days. . . ." In his junior year he was listed for repeatedly playing cards. During his last year he went into the country without permission. Most students committed offenses worthy of the "Black Book" at least once during their undergraduate stay, the majority two or more times. Between 1772 and 1775 anywhere from one-third to three-quarters of the students were disciplined in a single academic year. With regard to age, the largest number of students disciplined were around seventeen, but by and large the ages of students noted in the "Black Book" were fairly well distributed.[30]

In 1771 a committee of governors reported that a "Spirit of Contumacy" prevailed among the undergraduates and that "effectual Methods" were needed to "put a stop to this *growing evil*." From the evidence in the "Black Book" it is obvious that the perception of a college crime wave by the governors does not mean that students were running rampant. Some undergraduates were remarkably rule-abiding during the 1770s. One finds nothing in the college records to contradict the father of a student in the class of 1774, who claimed that he did not "know a Boy in the City freer from vice, or more careful of his behavior" than his son.[31] Yet, at the same time, the incidences of disorderliness were frequent enough to suggest that, at best, official values like obedience, submissiveness, diligence, and order penetrated the student culture irregularly.

Undergraduate life was disorderly in another, less obvious way. The term "collegiate way" connotes a relatively self-contained community. Yet, King's College was located in a city, and the boundary between the city and the college was thinner and more readily traversed than one might think. The issue had been discussed as early as the 1740s, when some New Yorkers applauded the opportunity which students would have to observe city gentlemen of taste and learning, while others lamented that undergraduate morals would crumble before an onslaught of prostitutes, taverns, and other temptations to vice and idleness. The college building was expected to provide a way of regulating the interplay between the college community and the urban community. But for two-thirds of Samuel Johnson's presidency there was no building. Students like Epenetus Townsend lived in town. Others resided at home. None was supervised very thoroughly by college authorities. Once the building was completed, Johnson does not appear to have demanded that students move in, despite earlier statements about having them under his eye. For instance, John Jay, who matriculated in 1760, lived in town his first two years and usually ate meals in town until March 1763. At that point the governors, prodded by Cooper and possibly by financial considerations, issued new statutes requiring every student to lodge and board at the college. But even Cooper relented on the matter. And in the 1770s there was not enough space in the building for all the students anyway. Cooper was by then pleased to have the apartments "overflow," but he found it especially difficult to discipline "Such [students] as do not lodge in the College." [32] After all, it was hard to confine a boy to his chambers when he lived in town.

It is quite possible that no more than thirty-five boys could be housed at the college. And from the fall of 1772 until the outbreak of the Revolution about forty-five were enrolled. Overall at least one-third and perhaps two-fifths of the King's College students lived at home or lodged in town for part or all of their undergraduate years.

Even those boys who lived at college did not lose touch with the social life of the city. The majority of students had grown up in New York City and had developed friendships and contacts which carried over into college days. Friends came to the college for chats, once in a while even for a meal in a student's room. In turn, students visited the city daily. Sometimes it was illicit, as in the case where a student was punished for "having come thro' a Hole in the College-fence, at 12 o'Clock at Night." [33] Most of the time it was legal. One boy's usual schedule in the summer was to "get up about Six or a Little after, dress myself & go to chappel," have breakfast, then "go to my Studys, with which I am employ'd till twelve [;] than I take a walk & return about one," dine, "& after dinner study till Six at which time, the Bell always [rings] for Prayers [;] they being over College is broak up, & then we take what Amusement we please." Bed time in the summer was 10:00 P.M. Like this youth, students normally were free for an hour and a half at noon and from prayers to bed time each evening.[34]

We have no record as to how King's College students used their free time on school days and weekends. Undoubtedly they went to their barbers, shopped for clothes, bought newspapers and supplies, and stopped at "Spring-Gardens, Near the College," where "Pyes and Tarts" and the "best of Madeira, Mead, Cakes, &C." were served from 7:00 to 9:00 P.M. Once Long Islander lamented that he could not fly, for if he could he would visit his family and relatives once or twice a week. The families of many undergraduates did live nearby, and apparently students went home regularly. If we can judge by the experience of one post-Revolutionary undergraduate who kept a diary, they also attended plays, dances, and political functions, called on young ladies, and engaged in a variety of other delights. Robert R. Livingston must have done something to earn a reputation while at King's College as a "very Proteus of Love," a youth "devoted to all the gay amusements that the favor of the Ladies & an agreeable set of companions afford." [35]

Sometimes students went into the country rather than the city. Owning a horse was thus handy. One undergraduate observed grumpily that there was "no other exercise to be us'd here," so that he either had "to keep a Horse or hire a poor miserable hack to take an Airing twice or thrice a Week. . . ." Students who lingered near the campus found life less healthy but more exciting. The section of town around the college grew progressively seedier during the 1760s and 1770s. It was noted for its "mean" buildings, numerous taverns, rowdy incidents, and, above all, its lively trade in prostitution. By the mid-1760s "infamous houses" were catering to soldiers of the king quartered nearby. Several years later a visitor to the city claimed that some five hundred "ladies of pleasure" kept their lodgings between the college and St. Paul's Chapel a few blocks away. In fact, he recorded that the entrance to the college was "thro' one of the streets where the most noted prostitutes live," a circumstance which he characterized as "a little unlucky." [36] The sensitivity of college authorities to problems like these had played a role in their decisions to construct a fence around the college and to make the students wear gowns. When worn off campus academic gowns gave students a conspicuousness that, it was hoped, would dissuade them from indulging in forbidden behavior. Students, not being fools, were undoubtedly aware of their conspicuousness, which may be one reason why in 1774 the governors had to threaten dismissal for any undergraduate caught "going without his *Academical Habit*, by *Day* or by *Night*; in *public* or in *private*." [37]

If the collegiate way was hardly as embracing as it might appear, it should also be remembered that one group of students escaped its clutches entirely. These were the private students. They neither matriculated nor followed the B.A. program, nor are they included in the list of 209 liberal arts pupils. But they appeared on campus regularly—to consult with Samuel Johnson about readings in theology, to be tutored by Robert Harpur in mathematics, to attend Samuel Clossy's lectures in natural philosophy, or to study Latin and Greek with Leonard Cutting. Private students paid fees directly to their professors rather than tuition, which made them attractive to the faculty. The governors condoned the practice as long as private instruction did not interfere with a professor's "College Business." In at least one instance a private pupil resided at the college. Otherwise they were not regular members of the college and were not subject to its "Laws and Orders." The number of private pupils who studied at King's is impossible to determine, but there is evidence that between 1770 and 1776 Robert Harpur taught navigation, surveying, and mathematics to fourteen boys who were not matriculants in the college.[38]

Private pupils, students living in town, undergraduates frequenting the city daily, early leavers, open disregard for the rules, and flagrant abuse of a faculty member—all these detract from a neat, orderly picture of the collegiate way. The last two phenomena listed above—what one historian calls "Rowdies, Riots, and Rebellions"—have gained the most attention in studies of higher education in early America.[39] But the others were equally significant. In examining them we begin to understand something of the character of an urban colonial college, for the numbers of private pupils and early leavers as well as the interaction of the college community with the city community were all part of being an urban institution. Ironically, one suspects that these, in turn, may have served to keep rowdyism from being less explosive than it might have been (or than it was at Yale, where recalcitrant students drove President Clap into retirement). The "excessive restraints" of the collegiate way were diluted by living in town or by going there daily. Dropping out was a way of voting against the college with one's feet rather than with one's sense of prankishness. Private pupils could gain some of the benefits of collegiate instruction without enduring its "extra–curricular" life. The collegiate way of a small town college remained an ideal in the minds of Samuel Johnson and Myles Cooper, but the students did not experience it in the same way as did undergraduates at Princeton and Yale. After the Revolution, the college leaders would abandon the ideal.[40]

12.
THE INTELLECTUAL AND POLITICAL LEGACY

DURING THE TWO DECADES on each side of 1800 alumni of King's College contributed in various ways to the welfare of Columbia. One served as president, several as professors, and twelve as trustees. Apparently for some students the experience of attending King's College created a strong sense of institutional loyalty. And that loyalty helped sustain the college in later years. One only wishes that it was as easy to suggest other ways that King's College influenced the social and intellectual lives of its students. The issue is elusive to begin with; and the undercurrent of diversity and disorderliness in the undergraduate experience makes it all the more slippery.

Even where the college had an explicit message for the students, as it did in much of the formal curriculum, it is exasperating to gauge its influence. For example, it seems undeniable that some students developed rhetorical skills, both oral and written, that served them in good stead as clerics and lawyers and as local, state, national, and imperial leaders. But what does one make of courses in metaphysics and ethics, apart from noting that one finds few Berkeleians or Aristotelians pontificating in late eighteenth-century New York?

The social significance of the undergraduate experience seems fairly clear-cut in some instances. Friendships were developed at college that had an important bearing on adult relationships. John Jay recommended a college friend for a military post in 1776, despite the latter's often "reprehensible" behavior, because an "early acquaintance with him at College" along with "an opinion of his abilities" and a respect for the memory of his father persuaded Jay to "promote his welfare." [1] Jay formed a friendship at King's College with Robert R. Livingston that led not only to a law partnership but to an association which affected state and national politics. But how does one pin down the impact of less tangible facets of the social and intellectual experience, such as a value like social hierarchy? Students encountered it in many forms, whether it was Johnson's habit of ranking students in the Matricula, or the college statutes which required the junior classes to "pay such respect to the senior classes" as the president and faculty might direct, the rare privilege given to George Washington's stepson of eating with the faculty (like a fellow commoner at Oxford), the circles of friendship that in many cases followed ties of family and social class, or the expressions of a faculty member who believed that one's "Virtues and Vices" were determined to "a considerable Degree" by one's "Birth, Station, and Companions," and therefore parents should send their boys to King's College, where they would mingle with virtuous blue bloods, instead of to Princeton, where they would suffer exposure to the lower moral standards of farmers' sons.[2]

Rather than make an overall appraisal of the impact of the curriculum and the collegiate way on the students' thinking, which the evidence does not justify, this chapter attacks the problem by examining a single but crucial thread: was there a connection between a King's College education and an alumnus's political views in the Revolutionary and post-Revolutionary periods? The chapter concludes by surveying the occupations of the alumni.

King's College alumni, like other Americans, responded to the Revolutionary crisis in diverse ways. Reverend John Rutgers Marshall defended every British measure from the Stamp Act to the Boston Port Bill and declared in 1775 that if the British would only take five or six members of the Continental Congress and hang them, the rest would submit. For his efforts Marshall was beaten twice by the rebels and once left for dead. Edward Antill, son of the college benefactor, joined the American expedition to

Canada in 1775, fought with the rebels at Trenton, Princeton, and Yorktown, survived a period of imprisonment, and "[r]etired from the din of arms and a military life clothed in laurels. . . ." Somewhere in between Marshall and Antill was Anthony Lispenard, who sat out the war quietly in New York City, doing his best to disguise his sentiments. And what can one say of Rudolph Ritzema, who initially fought with the Americans and contended that Tories should be banished from the country since such "miscreants ought not to breathe the same air with men resolved to be free," then turned around, became a British officer, and condemned the American "rabble" for their intolerance.[3]

However, there were patterns in the Revolutionary sentiments of the King's College alumni. Probably half or more of those living in 1776 became loyalists during the war. No other college in the northern colonies educated anywhere near as high a percentage of loyalists. Sixteen percent of Harvard's alumni living in 1776 became loyalists. Among Princeton's alumni the percentage was undoubtedly lower than sixteen.[4] To be sure, patriots are fairly easy to find among the alumni of King's College. Several played spectacular roles in the Revolution and in the formation of the new nation. And some, such as Henry Rutgers, even became radical revolutionaries. Rutgers was so zealous a Son of Liberty that the British confiscated his house and branded it with a "G.R." for George Rex. However, one can save time by looking for alumni revolutionaries in the conservative camp. Certainly that is where almost all of them carved out distinguished roles for themselves, if they made a political splash at all. And as conservatives, they adhered to political views which overlapped with those of the loyalist alumni in important ways.

The historian Alfred Young has labeled the conservative patriots who came to the fore in New York politics in 1776 the "conservative Whigs," distinguishing them from the more radical "popular Whigs" in New York and from the loyalists. "Without exception," writes Young, "the conservative Whig leaders of the 1770's became the nationalist leaders of the 1780's and the Federalist leaders of 1788." Most of the popular Whigs, in turn, became antifederalists. Who led the conservative Whigs in New

John Jay (B.A., King's College, 1764)
Jay was president of the Continental Congress, secretary of foreign affairs under the Confederation, first chief justice of the United States Supreme Court, and governor of New York.
CREDIT: COLUMBIANA, COLUMBIA UNIVERSITY

York? Five of their eight primary leaders, including all but one of the younger men, were King's College alumni: John Jay, Robert R. Livingston, Gouverneur Morris, Egbert Benson, and Alexander Hamilton. Later, as these men became the Federalists of 1788 and, except for Livingston, distinguished Federalists in the 1790s, they were allied politically with more than half a dozen other

King's College alumni, men like Robert Troup, Gulian Verplanck, and John W. Watkins.[5]

In looking both at the alumni who became conservative Whigs
and at those who became loyalists, one notes two significant
strains of political thinking which might be traced back to the intellectual and social character of their education at King's College.
Not that their education *produced* those views. Obviously their
outlooks were rooted in a number of factors, extending from their
early family upbringing to their immediate economic interests.
And each strain shows up in different individuals in different
ways and to different degrees. But remember that these men had
been exposed for several years, at a fairly early age, to the political
and social climate at King's College, and then, within a matter of a
few years, had been called upon to make crucial political decisions
to which the outlooks fostered at King's were indubitably relevant. They could easily have perceived and responded to the
issues through a frame of reference influenced by their college education.

The first strain was a profound commitment to hierarchical politics. Among revolutionaries no group voiced this outlook more
persistently than the conservative Whigs from King's College.
When expressed by Gouverneur Morris it could become a strident
mocking of tradesmen-turned-politicians as "Poor reptiles . . .
struggling to cast off their winter's slough," or an invocation of the
iron fist, as in Morris's comment to Jay that

> You and I, my friend, know by Experience, that when a few Men
> of Sense and Spirit get together, and declare that they are the Au-
> thority, such few as are of a different Opinion may easily be con-
> vinced of their mistake by that powerful Argument the Halter.

Behind Morris's haughtiness lay deep misgivings about popular
rule, a "fear and Trembling" that the future might bring forth
"the worst of all possible dominions"—"the domination of a riotous mob." [6] Morris's conservative Whig friends shared his apprehensions about popular rule, and they also shared a sense that political salvation lay in the continuing ascendancy of a ruling elite.
They believed, to quote historian Gordon Wood, in "a hierar-

Gouverneur Morris (B.A., King's College, 1768)
Morris was a member of the Continental Congress, assistant superintendent of
finance under the Confederation, delegate to the Constitutional Convention of 1787,
and United States' minister to France. The portrait is by Thomas Sully after Ezra
Ames.
CREDIT: COLUMBIANA, COLUMBIA UNIVERSITY

chical society of different gradations and a unitary authority to
which deference from the lower to higher should be paid"; and
those at the top should have first acquired the "attributes of social
superiority—wealth, education, experience, and connections"—
before assuming political command. "Can it be thought," asked

Robert R. Livingston, "that an enlightened people believe that the science of government level to the meanest Capacity?" Disturbed by the emergence of "new men" during the Revolution, John Jay complained that "Effrontery and arrogance" were "giving rank and Importance to men whom Wisdom would have left in obscurity." If the conservative Whigs from King's College believed in preserving aristocratic politics in a republic, they regarded aristocrats as men like themselves. They had, to quote Wood again, an "elitist social consciousness," a "sense of being socially established, of possessing attributes—family, education, and refinements—that others lacked, above all, of being accepted by and being able to move easily among those who considered themselves to be the respectable and cultivated." [7]

Among alumni who became loyalists the commitment to hierarchical politics and the misgivings about popular rule were, if anything, more intense. Since their writings are slim and their opinions varied from the heady Whiggism of Peter Van Schaack to the High Church Toryism of a few Anglican clerics, it is difficult to generalize about them. For many the hierarchical pattern of politics was undoubtedly layered with the obligations due a king from his subjects and the "deference" due an "august Mother" from her colonies. [8] But if that attitude survived the Revolution for the more than two dozen alumni who fled to Nova Scotia, New Brunswick, Quebec, and England, it was extinguished in a greater number who made their peace with republicanism. What remained was a devotion to aristocratic politics much like that of the conservative Whigs, which was one reason why loyalists like Van Schaack and Richard Harison and a figure like John Watts, who was "at best neutral" during the Revolution, could easily find common political ground with Hamilton, Jay, Benson, and other King's College Federalists during the 1780s and 1790s. [9]

A second strain which one detects in the thinking of some alumni is a comparatively dispassionate attitude toward the power of imperial and national rulers. Like most Americans, these alumni were aware of the dangers of power and they feared its misuse, but they did not readily share the "paranoiac mistrust of power" that characterized the radical Whigs. To the latter, writes Gordon Wood, "[e]very accumulation of political power, however tiny and piecemeal, was seen as frighteningly tyrannical, viewed as some sinister plot to upset the delicately maintained relationships of power and esteem." Thus the radical Whigs suffered paroxysms of anxiety in the 1770s over the impending enslavement of the Americans by the British. Peter Van Schaack appears to have typified better the outlook of King's College alumni when he wrote that

> taking the whole of the Acts complained of together, they do not I think manifest a System of Slavery, but may fairly be imputed to human frailty and the Difficulty of the Subject. Most of them seem to have sprung out of particular Occasions & are unconnected with each other.

Isaac Wilkins, class of 1760, advised Americans not to believe "such men as tell you that Great Britain would enslave you; Great Britain wishes to see us free and happy. . . ." [10] As one moves to the political right of Van Schaack one finds an increasing confidence in British power, even a sense of its benevolence, rather than anxiety at its arbitrariness. Of course, the staunchest Tories among the alumni, like other Tories, may have suffered their own form of paranoia—a belief that the Revolutionary movement was a conspiracy of New Englanders—but that reflected their heightened sensitivity to the dangers of popular power running amuck in a society where the "Marks of Subordination" were "totally confounded." "No man loves Liberty more than I do," asserted John Vardill, "but of all Tyranny I most dread that of the Multitude." [11]

Even to the political left of Peter Van Schaack—at least among those alumni who became conservative patriots—there is a muted quality in some cases to their radical Whiggism. True, Alexander Hamilton could be as pointed as any American about the threat of enslavement, calling it "the offspring of mature deliberation. It has been fostered by time, and strengthened by every artifice human subtilty is capable of." But conservative Whigs could also use the rhetoric without feeling the full force of its emotional

power, as in the case of John Jay's "Address to the People of
Great Britain," which, writes historian Richard B. Morris,
"survives as proof of the fact that if you associate with radicals
long enough some of the radical rhetoric is bound to rub off on
you."[12]

A belief in hierarchical politics and a comparatively dispassionate attitude toward the power of rulers contributed to the ease
with which King's College alumni transcended political localism
and developed strong imperial or national political allegiances.
Those who rejected imperial union, the conservative Whigs, soon
became a nationalist phalanx, confident that power in central
hands—as long as they were elitist hands—could be properly
checked. If some of the most persistent defenders of imperial leadership were former students of Myles Cooper, so were two of the
three authors of the *Federalist Papers*. Both loyalists and Federalists
spoke a different political language from the antifederalists of
1787–1788, who not only were localists, but whose localism was
rooted in a radical Whiggish distrust of "distant governmental,
even representational, authority" and in a democratic concern
with keeping power close to ordinary people.[13] It should come as
no surprise that one is hard put to find King's College men in their
ranks.

When one turns from the outlooks of the alumni to their education at college, one confronts a difficult problem documenting the
intellectual and social experiences that contributed to those outlooks, particularly in the absence of almost any undergraduate
writings—lecture notes, essays, letters, or diaries. Yet, Presidents
Samuel Johnson and Myles Cooper, tutors Leonard Cutting
(1755–1763) and John Vardill (1772–1773), interim President
Charles Inglis (1771–1772) and President pro tempore Benjamin
Moore (1775–1777) shared a set of political and social attitudes
that could easily have nurtured the strains of thinking described
above. Undoubtedly such faculty attitudes penetrated classroom
lectures and comments—especially in courses on moral philosophy, the "principles of polity," and classical and modern history—
as well as conversations with students outside of class. The same
attitudes also were reflected in what the faculty chose to omit or

Alexander Hamilton
Hamilton attended King's College between 1773 and 1775 but did not graduate. He
was George Washington's aide-de-camp during the Revolutionary war, principal
author of the *Federalist Papers*, and first secretary of the treasury of the United States.
The engraving is by Frederick Girsch from John Trumbull's portrait.
CREDIT: COLUMBIANA, COLUMBIA UNIVERSITY

not to emphasize. At the College of Philadelphia, Professor
Francis Alison spoke strongly in support of revolution when "publick liberty & safety" could not be "otherwise secured," while
Provost William Smith encouraged students to read *Disquisitions
on Government* by Algernon Sidney, a hero to the radical Whigs.[14]

As we shall see, one can hardly imagine Myles Cooper doing likewise. Moreover, some of the distinguished and energetic governors of the college, men like Samuel Auchmuty, John Watts,
Johannes Ritzema, even James Duane, could have reinforced the
faculty's views through their public actions and expressions during the imperial crisis of the 1760s and 1770s. Not only were relationships between the faculty and students much closer than those
today, but the governors were familiar and visible figures. Students encountered them in a variety of settings, from examinations and disciplinary hearings on campus to pulpits and private
homes in the city. Finally, the students themselves probably influenced one anothers' attitudes in the directions outlined above,
since many of them came from families which predisposed them
that way.

A moment's reflection should suggest why King's College did
not become a prolific nursery of radical Whigs. Radical
Whiggism, the dominant strain in colonial political thinking,
stemmed from the opposition view of English politics which
developed in eighteenth-century England. Emanating from a
"cluster of malcontents drawn from every segment of the [En-
glish] political spectrum—from the far left, the inheritors of
seventeenth-century libertarianism, as well as from the far right
. . .—" the "shrill, persistent, penetrating" voice of opposition
filled English newspapers, periodicals, and pamphlets with viru-
lent attacks on the king's government. "On major points of doctrine," writes historian Bernard Bailyn, "their views were not
different from those generally expressed in Georgian England: the
difference lay in emphasis."

> Writers in the mainstream and in the opposition counter-current
> wrote from the same basic set of beliefs, but where the one group
> stressed the benefits of the balance of England's mixed constitution,
> the other pointed to the difficulties of maintaining it in the face of
> ministerial encroachments. Where the standard stress was on the
> history of English liberty and the tradition of political integrity, the
> opposition pointed to the sudden appearance of what they believed
> to be the systematic effort of "The Robinarch" to corrupt the elec-
> torate, and the uncontrollable machinations of a newly-risen money

interest, unknown to the constitution, that battened on the poor and helpless and bought favors wholesale of the government.[15]

Americans responded mainly to the left wing of the opposition press, absorbing word by acrimonious word the fulminations of writers like John Trenchard and Thomas Gordon. "For these cof- feehouse radicals and pamphleteers," writes Bailyn, "the political world was a struggle between power and liberty. . . ." Power was ever the insatiable aggressor, liberty ever its "natural prey." Power destroyed like fire, breaking through its "Bounds" unless checked by constant vigilance and moral stamina. "Almost all Men desire Power," warned Trenchard and Gordon, "and few lose any Opportunity to get it. . . ." So in all governments noth- ing could "be left to Chance, or the Humours of Men in Author- ity." When citizens relaxed their vigilance, they soon found them- selves in chains. Trenchard and Gordon spelled out the various stratagems used by potential tyrants to expand their power—the creation of standing armies, intrusions on the freedom of the press, the subversion of the judiciary's independence, and so on—so that the citizenry could recognize its danger before it was too late. The message permeated the colonies, creating by mid- century a fear that "threats to free government . . . lurked every- where." Nowhere was the danger perceived as greater than from the king's ministers.[16]

Few Americans escaped a healthy dose of radical rhetoric dur- ing the three decades before the Revolution—certainly not those Americans located in New York City. During the King's College Controversy the triumvirate bombarded New Yorkers with warn- ings about the depradations certain to be wrought on the liberty of the citizenry if power hungry ecclesiastics were not checked then and there. But the triumvirate, Trenchard's and Gordon's most vociferous disciples in mid-century New York, failed to gain an effective voice at King's College. And the faculty there (always ex- cepting Robert Harpur) shielded its charges as best it could from the rhetoric of radical Whigs when the latter turned their fire on imperial officials. As for its own message, the faculty talked the language of England's political and religious "establishment," not that of the opposition. The governors did likewise in their official pronouncements. From the 1750s to the 1770s they dispatched address after address to the king, his ministers, ecclesiastical officials, and the universities, each address pledging the college's dedication to inspiring youths with "firm and steady principles of Loyalty, and an Ardent affection for our happy Constitution." [17] The growing separation of the colonies from the mother country in the 1760s and 1770s only heightened the protestations of loyalty and affection. If the leaders of Princeton identified no less with the ideology of England's political dissidents than with the theology of its religious dissidents, the faculty and some of the governors at King's College looked to the king of England as well as the Church of England to give the college support and a distinctive identity. Their college was in this sense truly the king's college, and the king's college did not readily take to the opposition view of English politics.

Myles Cooper once claimed that he was not a "quarrelsome Animal: for I never desire to differ with any one but Whigs and Republicans—till I am married." Just how sweepingly the faculty rebuked such hallowed Whig principles as natural rights and the contract theory of government is hard to say. During the King's College Controversy the Anglican clerics who dueled with the triumvirate turned their backs on John Locke and resurrected Tory defenders of Church and Crown like William Oldisworth and William Hume. Thus the clerics argued that God himself had put men under government and had "made it their Duty to be obedient to Rule and Order." More than two decades later, in a sermon at Oxford in 1776, Myles Cooper berated those people whose heads were "filled with ideas of Original Compacts which never existed" and who believed that certain powers were "derived solely from the People" when they were actually " 'ordained of God.' " But the views expressed in the classroom may have been less reactionary than these pronouncements suggest. For one thing, Samuel Johnson, unlike Cooper, believed that civil governments were founded in compacts, either "tacit or explicit," while such a staunch defender of Church and Crown as John Vardill went so far as to declare that should British politicians clearly trespass on the common good and should all attempts at "petition and remonstrance" prove "ineffectual," then "recourse must be had to those *latent* powers in society, which no precedents, no social compact, can destroy." The *"inalienable rights* of humanity" would justify such a response.[18] For another thing, both Johnson and Cooper apparently included in the college curriculum the works of moral and political philosophers of progressive outlooks, such as Samuel Pufendorf (though Pufendorf did not sanction the right of revolution) and possibly even Francis Hutcheson (who did). Finally, the many centrist Whigs among the governors may have had a moderating effect on the faculty.

In any case, what separated the faculty of King's College from the radical Whigs was not necessarily a matter of fundamental doctrine. It was a matter of emphasis, attitude, and mood, the kinds of differences which Bernard Bailyn touches on in the passage quoted earlier. While the radical Whigs in the colonies cried out a warning against insidious machinations by British ministers, John Vardill and Myles Cooper sang the praises of the "Constitutional Liberty" enjoyed by all Britons. Constitutional liberty was what King's College students valued, insisted Vardill in 1772; and the governors would "spurn with Indignation" any attempt "to diminish a due Sense of that Liberty." In the same breath Vardill denounced the "unbridled Licentiousness" of religious and political dissenters, especially the trustees and faculty of Princeton, who disseminated factious principles "injurious to our happy Constitution." [19]

While President John Witherspoon of Princeton publicly condemned the "cunning and cruelty of oppressive and corrupt ministers," Myles Cooper proclaimed that "no subjects of any government are so free from arbitrary controll, or enjoy such constitutional Rights, as the subjects of Britain." In Cooper's eyes the theory that "a regular System was formed, 'by a corrupt and abandoned Administration,' for oppressing and enslaving the colonies . . ." was a myth foisted on the Americans by clever radicals. It triumphed when the "voice of Reason" was "drowned in the din of licentious Tumult." During his own presidency Samuel Johnson, no less than Myles Cooper, probably displayed a profound sense of confidence in the wisdom and integrity of British leadership. Until the events of the mid-1760s altered his views, Johnson's "attitude toward English political leaders was courteous and deferential," writes historian Joseph Ellis. He

> seemed to believe that English officials were immune to the corruptive influences of the world. . . . He had unbounded faith in the crown's capacity to restore order in the American colonies. In fact, Johnson's vision of English institutions and officials was the vision of a provincial colonist who stood in awe of the mother country.[20]

The minds of many Americans in the 1760s can be compared to an intellectual switchboard. The basic ideological wiring was provided by the opposition view of English politics. Nurtured on the rhetoric of radical libertarianism, the colonists were predisposed to respond to certain danger signals which indicated that a more general threat to their liberty might exist. When confronted with a succession of danger signals in the 1760s and 1770s—arbitrary legislation, a proliferation of royal officials, a standing army in Boston—the colonists "saw about them, with increasing clarity, not merely mistaken, or even evil, policies violating the principles upon which freedom rested, but what appeared to be evidence of nothing less than a deliberate conspiracy launched surreptitiously by plotters against liberty both in England and in America." It was this vision "above all else that in the end propelled them into Revolution." [21] King's College students, however, were wired differently, if the faculty had any influence on them. They were not predisposed by their college education to read and respond to the same signals in the same manner. And thus they were not as likely to perceive the same underlying patterns. While conspiracy was not alien to their political thinking, some of them undoubtedly were attuned to looking for conspirators not among the king's ministers but among the radical Whigs themselves.

A belief in hierarchical politics was even more deeply ingrained in the ideology of the college leaders than an "establishment" view of power. It embraced virtually all the governors and faculty, with Robert Harpur perhaps again an exception. Indeed, it underlay the rationale for having a college in the first place. Men of such diverse views as Samuel Johnson and William Smith, Jr., expected the college to train a ruling elite, by cultivating a "genteel Distinction" in its students, broadening their knowledge, instilling the appropriate values, and developing their elite identity. Those founders and governors who did not spell out a systematic view of the college's function at the least believed it would provide advantages to the children of the gentry, advantages which would serve them in good stead as they gravitated toward the positions of leadership they were expected to assume.[22] In other words, the college would enhance the "attributes of social superiority" of boys of high birth and wealth and would confer some degree of social legitimacy on those boys from lesser families.

An elitist theory of politics, buttressed by an elitist theory of education, was not uncommon in eighteenth-century America. But it was hardly pervasive, even among the elite. Moreover, in stark contrast to the New Side Presbyterian founders of Princeton, the hierarchic and antidemocratic side of elitist political thinking was a matter of unusually intense conviction for Samuel Johnson, Myles Cooper, and their Anglican associates at King's College. After all, a "Reverence for Governors" was "essentially necessary, to the Preservation of Order." [23] And "Order," as they understood it, seemed a terribly fragile phenomenon by the 1760s.

A belief in hierarchical politics suffuses the writings of the King's College faculty. Myles Cooper insisted that the "Health of a State requires a regular and due subordination of its Members to the governing power. . . . Let every man then be contented with his Station, and faithfully discharge its attendant duties." The citizenry should eschew "wild, visionary, enthusiastic Notions," for instance that "they may set up their pretended Natural Rights in Opposition to the positive Laws of the State. . . ." Samuel Johnson, like Cooper, argued that the "peace, order and prosperity of every political system, depends on the steady and inflexible obedience of every subject to the wise and wholesome political laws and constitutions of the community. . . ." While favoring representative government, Johnson lamented that annual elections in Connecticut force leaders into a "servile compliance" with the populace and "all their humors and schemes." The "greatest part of the multitude are generally the most unthinking. . . ." The welfare of the community depends on the skill and integrity of its lawgivers, and "there are comparatively but few that are duly qualified" to lead. John Vardill reminded Americans that the mother country and the colonies have a reciprocal relationship in which each has its duties to the other. "The *authority* of the one should be the *beneficial* authority of a parent; and the *obedience* of the other, the *liberal* obedience of a *child*." [24]

If views such as these and the ones detailed before were incorporated into the rhetoric and the message of the faculty at college—and it seems that they must have been—then the faculty could well have predisposed many students toward a loyalist stance in the Revolution. Perhaps this is what one alumnus meant when he testified that while a student of John Vardill's at college, Vardill "always instilled Notions of Loyalty" in him.[25] Just as intriguing is the distinct possibility that patriot and loyalist alike absorbed these views in some fashion at college and then carried them into post-Revolutionary New York. Obviously the process would be a complex one, in which ideas were selectively accepted, then modified and reformed with changing circumstances. But it is not fanciful to think that there could have been a direct connection between the outlooks cultivated by Samuel Johnson and Myles Cooper and those voiced by their former students as Federalist politicians and sympathizers in the 1780s and 1790s. In this way Samuel Johnson and Myles Cooper, despite the repudiation of some of their views in the American Revolution, contributed to the perpetuation of political conservatism in the new republic.

In turning from the intellectual legacy of King's College to the occupations of its alumni, one is struck by the fact that the primary carriers of that legacy were lawyers. During the King's College Controversy Samuel Johnson and his clerical collaborators assailed the trio of upstart lawyers who challenged not simply their ideology but their role as intellectuals. Much to the clerics' dismay, the triumvirate seemingly propounded a view of society in which ministers were superfluous—in some ways detrimental—to the political, educational, even the religious life of the community. Ironically, King's College advanced the very process against which the clerics had struggled, the displacement of ministers by lawyers as the primary intellectuals in America.[26] Johnson and Cooper educated a corps of lawyers whose ideas had a much more profound impact and commanded a far greater audience than those of the clerical alumni.

Not that the college failed to train any ministers of note. The Reverends Benjamin Moore and Samuel Provoost filled the position of bishop of New York from 1786 to 1811. The former also served as president of Columbia, the latter as chairman of the trustees. But the clerical alumni, no more than two of them non–Anglicans, numbered less than twenty; and the majority of them lived out their lives in relatively insignificant pulpits scattered among a number of small towns in the northern United States and Canada.[27]

In the 1760s Provost William Smith of the College of Philadelphia lamented that his pupils were running madly after careers in law and commerce. Johnson knew what Smith meant. Johnson's own son disappointed him by rejecting the ministry for the law, explaining to his father that he could never stomach the confining and sedentary character of a cleric's life. Many a Harvard and Yale student in the 1750s and 1760s and several King's College students similarly forsook the ministry for the law. Overall more than forty students, at least a fifth of the matriculants, became lawyers. Thirty-eight alumni were admitted to the bar of New York, twenty-nine of them graduates. Princeton graduated thirteen future members of the bar of New York during the same period (1758–1776), Yale three.[28] Sons from upper-class families, who virtually ignored the ministry and medicine, composed at least two-fifths of the lawyers from King's College. Moreover, the bar attracted the college's most precocious pupils, including a majority of the valedictorians and salutatorians.

The King's College lawyers not only became the intellectuals of the new republic; it was they, among all the alumni, who gained far and away the greatest stature as national, state, and local leaders. Several of them have figured prominently in this chapter: Alexander Hamilton, John Jay, Gouverneur Morris, Robert R. Livingston, and Egbert Benson. To their ranks should be added the names of other lawyers who, although they could not match the national standing of the above, played significant roles in the political, legal, and civic life of New York: Richard Harison, John Watts, Peter Van Schaack, Anthony Hoffman, Robert Troup, Philip Pell, and Stephen Lush. In New York City King's College alumni predominated among the group of lawyers in 1800 whom one historian has called "an array of names never since surpassed in the juridical history of the city. . . . Brilliant in their chosen profession, influential in politics and in business and interested in promoting the economic and cultural welfare of the young metropolis, they stood at the very top of New York's citizenry." [29] Even in Nova Scotia and New Brunswick, it was lawyers like Thomas Barclay and William Hubbard who most distinguished themselves among the alumni who migrated there.

In all, at least two-fifths of the King's College students pursued one of the three major professions. Roughly half that number took up law, while a few more students became doctors than ministers. In sharp contrast to the lawyers, most of the doctors had unexceptional careers. However, Samuel Bard cut a memorable figure in New York medical circles from the 1760s to the early nineteenth century, and Benjamin Kissam was one of the city's more eminent practitioners. Add to their number the alumni of the medical school at King's and one is talking about several of the leading medical men in post-Revolutionary New York City. Another 15 percent to 20 percent of the students form a miscellaneous group of military officers (about 5 percent, mostly in the British army), estate owners and farmers, minor public officials, teachers, and other individuals who do not fit in the professional and mercantile categories, such as inventor John Stevens, who built the first seagoing steamboat in America and the first American steam locomotive.

The balance of the students, in the neighborhood of two-fifths, chose commercial, manufacturing, and financial occupations, with most of them emphasizing the first. Here, as with the statements on other occupations, precision is marred not only by the incompleteness of the data but also by the difficulty categorizing students who shifted occupations or whose occupational pursuits cut across the categories. It appears that the King's College alumni who became merchants were usually following in the footsteps of successful fathers, while most of those who chose one of the professions were selecting a vocation different from that of their fathers. Although the merchants as a whole could not touch the lawyers if one judges them by their accomplishments as statesmen, community leaders, and intellectuals, their ranks did include several sparkling figures. Henry Cruger, for example, sat in Parliament in the 1770s and 1780s and was mayor of Bristol, England, then returned to New York and served a term in the state senate. Gulian Verplanck was president of the Bank of New York and represented New York City in the state assembly, twice serving as speaker. Henry Rutgers also sat in the state assembly, was a leader of the Clintonians in New York City, and patronized education in New York and New Jersey by promoting schools for poor children and by serving as a regent of the University of the State of New York and a trustee of both Princeton and Queen's College. The latter honored him by taking his name.[30]

In checking through the more than two hundred alumni of King's College, one has no trouble finding a sizable group of distinguished individuals. Yet, one is equally impressed by the large number, certainly a healthy majority, whose careers were rather modest and who exerted little leadership that is visible to the historian. In other words, for such an advantaged group, the record is a little meager. Moreover, if King's College alumni held important positions in the professional, political, and commercial elites of post-Revolutionary New York, they shared the stage with a great many others. Note, for example, the make-up of some of the elective political bodies between 1783 and 1800. Only one alumnus sat on the New York City Common Council, the power center in the city government. Alumni composed only about 10 percent of the state assemblymen who were elected from the city.[31] And alumni composed less than 5 percent of the state senators from all parts of the state. This is a far cry from what some founders had envisioned at mid-century. Of course, the intervening years had been jolting ones for the college. At its outset the King's College Controversy dissuaded many parents from enrolling their sons, thus contributing to the small number of students. At its closing the Revolution helped disperse some of those New Yorkers who had attended. And all along the weight of time and events took its toll in lives lost. By 1790 at least a fifth of the alumni were dead. At least a fifth of those still living resided in Canada, England, and the West Indies. By 1790 the number of alumni in New York City was less than fifty, the number in the entire state probably less than ninety. Meanwhile, the population of the city had jumped from some 13,000 at mid-century to 33,000, that of the state from 75,000 to 340,000. Of course, by then Columbia was replenishing the ranks of the alumni. But that is another story.

3.
THE KING'S COLLEGE
MEDICAL SCHOOL

INTRODUCTION

ONE DAY in October 1775 the "famous Dr. Dubuke" breezed into New York City from Boston and announced that he was prepared to cure anything from green wounds and black jaundice to the bloody flux, harelips, and venereal disease. Five months later Dr. Dubuke boarded the stage for New Jersey, sporting a brand he had received for stealing indigo.[1] Despite his ignominious punishment, Dr. Dubuke symbolized the sorry state of medicine in eighteenth-century New York. A charlatan of the most obvious kind, he had lasted in New York for five months and been convicted not of fraud, malpractice, or of failing to procure a medical license, but of stealing.

Viewed from the perspective of Myles Cooper, the founding of the King's College Medical School in 1767 broadened the college's educational impact and foreshadowed an attempt to transform King's College into American University. Viewed from the perspective of several New York doctors, the medical school reflected an attempt to professionalize the practice of medicine in New York, so that men of Dr. Dubuke's ilk would no longer find New York City a haven for their quackery. At mid-century the city had no system for licensing physicians and surgeons, no provision for medical education outside of apprenticeship, no professional society of doctors, and no hospital. Typically, of the thirteen city doctors who jointly announced in 1745 the end of a recent yellow fever epidemic, only one had studied at a medical school. Even the city's most respected doctors failed to display much professional esprit. Cadwallader Colden complained in 1745 that they refused to communicate their observations to one another because each feared a "design to supplant" him in his "trade." [2]

By 1775, however, only Philadelphia rivaled New York City as a colonial medical center. New York boasted one of the two medical schools in England's new world colonies, the first colonial law which licensed physicians and surgeons, a vigorous and competent medical community, an informal medical society, and a hospital nearing completion. New York had reached only the periphery of modern medical practice, however, as suggested by the ease with which a man like Dubuke managed to survive.

13.

EDUCATION AND
THE PROFESSIONALIZATION
OF MEDICINE

THE CAMPAIGN to upgrade medicine in New York City, which
eventuated in the founding of the King's College Medical School,
grew out of the city's success in attracting talented and well-
trained physicians during the two decades after 1745. Their skill,
their vision, their thirst for social prestige, and their belief in the
superiority of European modes of medical education and practice
made it impossible for these doctors to tolerate the medical "free-
for-all" they witnessed about them.[1] Three men, John Bard, Peter
Middleton, and John Jones, provided the nucleus of a reputable
medical profession in the city. When John Bard migrated to New
York from Philadelphia in 1745, Benjamin Franklin recommended
him as "an ingenious Physician and Surgeon, and a discreet,
worthy and honest Man." Peter Middleton, a young Scot with an
M.D. from the University of St. Andrews, settled in New York
shortly after 1750, as did John Jones, a Long Islander who had
studied with the leading anatomists and surgeons in London and
Paris.[2] The three men soon developed a warm personal and professional camaraderie that lasted until Middleton's death in 1781.[3]

The quality and professional character of their medical practice
quickly set Bard, Middleton, and Jones apart from most of the
forty or so doctors in New York City in the 1750s.[4] Both Bard
and Jones won public esteem for their surgical achievements, particularly for their success at "extracting the Stone from the human

Bladder." Moreover, Bard's report of his 1759 operation on a woman for an extrauterine pregnancy earned a reading before a society of London physicians and publication in London's *Medical Observations and Inquiries*. By 1761 reports on two of Peter Middleton's cases had been communicated to a society of physicians in Edinburgh. Professor Robert Whytt of the University of Edinburgh described one of Middleton's reports as "the Clearest proof of the Sensibility of the *Pleura* in a man, that I have any where met with. . . ." [5] The Europeanization of medical practice in New York gained additional impetus when Samuel Clossy and John Bard's son, Samuel, established practices there in the 1760s. Clossy's M.D. degree from Trinity College, Dublin, his pioneering study on morbid anatomy, and his successful anatomy lectures in New York City put his reputation beyond question. Samuel Bard began practicing in New York City in 1766, upon completing two years at King's College and four years of medical studies in London and Edinburgh. As a student at Edinburgh, where he received an M.D. in 1765, Bard had repeatedly demonstrated the talent, the enthusiasm for medical science, and the capacity for work which would make him a dominant figure in New York medicine from 1766 until his death in 1821.[6]

John and Samuel Bard, Peter Middleton, John Jones, and Samuel Clossy—let us call them the "professionals" for convenience sake—soon formed an alliance that reflected their fundamental agreement about the nature of medical practice. Influenced by European professional ideals, each regarded himself as a scientific and an ethical practitioner.[7] Together they believed that these attributes distinguished them from most of the doctors in eighteenth-century New York. By 1766 there were, indeed, perhaps seven or eight other city doctors whom they recognized as colleagues, men like William Farquhar, John Charlton, James Smith, and John Van Brugh Tennent.[8] Yet, if all these men shared similar attitudes toward medicine, the professionals took the lead in implementing and disseminating them. In fact, the King's College Medical School would turn out to be largely the creation of Middleton, Jones, Clossy, and Samuel Bard.

The professionals' scientific and ethical conceptions of medicine led them to condemn the majority of New York City's physicians as "empirics." The term "empiric" embraced on one hand charlatans like Dr. Dubuke, deliberately dishonest doctors who masked their medical ignorance with bombastic publicity about their curative skills. But other empirics, probably a majority, lacked the charlatan's penchant for blatant deception. The professionals considered these men damaging to the prestige of the profession and the lives of New York's citizenry primarily because their practice was, literally, empirical.[9]

To men who equated responsible medicine with rational science, the empirics' method seemed sloppy, superficial, and dangerous. Relying largely on his past experience, the empiric discounted the value of exploring the causes of disease or the reasons why a particular cure succeeded or failed. When he treated a patient, the empiric asked instead whether he had encountered a similar case before. If so, he prescribed what had worked previously. If he did not know a successful cure or he was unfamiliar with the case, the empiric resorted to trial and error—or so the professionals believed; for "being unacquainted with the Nature of the Distemper, or any certain Method of Cure, they *range* thro' the whole Materia Medica, in Hopes they may fortunately *hit* upon a Remedy at last." [10] Dr. Roelof Kierstede exemplified a successful empiric in mid-century New York City. His 1745 obituary noted that he was "eminent in his Profession, altho' not skill'd in the technical Terms thereof, which often drew on him the Contempt of his Brethren; yet his great Knowledge of Simples [medicines], his extensive Charity and successful Cures to poor People, has made . . . his death a real public loss." Outside New York City empiricism was even more widespread. A Maryland physician commented upon visiting Albany in 1744 that the town's doctors were "all empyricks, having no knowledge or learning but what they have acquired by bare experience." [11]

The professionals reserved their admiration for the "rational Physician." In contrast to the empiric, the rational physician organized his medical knowledge into theories which explained the functioning of the body and the cause and treatment of disease. Should he encounter an unusual illness, he did not rely on trial and error; instead, claimed Peter Middleton, he "applies the Ideas he had already formed in his Mind, about the Nature of Diseases in general, to this particular Case; by which he easily discerns the Genius of the Disease; whence it arises; the true Indications of Cure; and what Method ought chiefly to be pursued. . . ." Experience, in the form of observations and experiments, remained the fundamental source of medical data for the rationalist. But, as Samuel Clossy announced in his first lecture at the King's College Medical School, he and his associates hoped "to prove in a while" that there was "something more than mere Empiricism" among them.[12] Experience provided the empiric with isolated bits of information, a kind of medical grab bag through which one rummaged when seeking the cure for a disease. Experience provided the rationalist with the building blocks of generalization and theory, which in turn explained with increasing comprehensiveness the nature of disease and the means of its treatment.[13]

In practice the distinction between the empiric and the rationalist lacked the crispness suggested by these ideal types, but the professionals considered the differences to be crucial. Moreover, the conception of the physician as a rational scientist implied other assumptions about his training, intellectual outlooks, and professional behavior. The professionals believed that the physician needed first of all to master the several dimensions of knowledge that comprised medical science. For instance, how could one understand human physiology without studying anatomy and natural philosophy? While anatomy introduced the physician to the intricate structure of the human body, natural philosophy acquainted him with the principles of pneumatics, optics, hydraulics, and mechanics, which supposedly helped explain such bodily processes as breathing, seeing, the circulation of the blood, and the operation of the bones and muscles.[14] Chemistry and botany were, in similar fashion, prerequisites to understanding the nature of drugs. When the physician matched his grasp of these subjects with studies which focused directly on the theory and practice of medicine, he gained a coherent perspective on medical science which he could not achieve through fragmentary learning.

The professionals did not think of this process as the mastery of a fixed body of knowledge. They saw themselves as the inheritors of a rich intellectual legacy that reached back to the Greeks. But they also believed that William Harvey's discovery of the circulation of the blood had ushered in the "most memorable *AEra* in the History of Physic." Experiment and observation had uncovered so much new physiological and pathological data during the past century and a half that a mere "*Catalogue*" of it would "fill a Volume." Nor had the "moderns" exhausted the possibilities for medical discovery. None "but very superficial minds can imagine, that the limits of our present knowledge are the limits of the art," John Jones told his surgery students. This conception of medical science shaped in several ways the professionals' image of the "judicious and rational Physician." First, he should be thoroughly familiar with the standard medical authorities of his own and previous ages—men like Hippocrates, Hermann Boerhaave, John Huxham, Thomas Sydenham, Giovanni Battista Morgagni, and Percival Pott—"without whose assistance, the greatest genius, wou'd be nothing more, than an ignorant, & presumptuous practitioner." Moreover, living in an age of medical discovery, he should recognize that "Continual study" was essential. Those physicians and surgeons who neglected to "inform themselves, of the new discoveries made in different parts of the world" became "only servile imitators"; after "twenty years labour," they were "little wiser than their first masters." [15] Finally, the rational physician should himself participate in the process of discovery, evaluating his own observations in light of established medical opinion and communicating his insights to professional colleagues.

The professionals believed so strongly that medical competence reflected rational science that their discussions of medical ethics served in part simply to confer moral legitimacy on scientific medicine: the doctor had a moral obligation to practice medicine in the ways outlined above. Samuel Bard did caution prospective physicians that they should never "despise a Man for the want of a regular Education" and should "treat even harmless Ignorance, with Delicacy and Compassion." But Bard also declared that should doctors encounter ignorance "joined with foolhardiness and Presumption," they must "give it no quarter." [16] For the professionals, whose dedication to scientific medicine often bordered on arrogance, it was not difficult to identify the empiric's practice as foolhardy.

However, the five men did emphasize other ethical considerations. A doctor should visit his patients frequently, listen to them attentively, be particularly solicitous to those suffering both poverty and disease at once, and, above all, unquestioningly place the "Welfare of his *Patient*" before "every Consideration which Pride and Avarice can suggest. . . ." Toward his fellow practitioners the doctor should be open, honest, and willing to join in consultations. He should never "pretend to Secrets," nor "practice those little Arts of Cunning and Dissimulation," nor "attempt to raise . . . [his] Fame on the Ruins of another's reputation. . . ." In all his professional relationships the doctor should ever be the gentleman: "decent in his Appearance," "discreet in his Manners," "humane," and "compassionate." [17]

Judged by this set of scientific and ethical criteria, the majority of New York City doctors in the 1760s impressed Middleton, Clossy, Jones, and the two Bards as inferior practitioners. The state of medical practice in New York seemed all the more barbaric when the professionals compared it to their inflated image of medicine in Europe. How "wide is the Distance," lamented Middleton in 1769, between the "unequalled Lustre" of British medicine and the "present obscure and illiterate Scenes before us" in New York. How "unequal" and "absurd" was a comparison of Europe's "towering and enlightened Geniuses of ancient and modern Days" with the "*favourite* Wonder-working *Doctors* of this Place." [18] What Middleton was really talking about was the practice of Europe's medical elite in urban and educational centers like London, Paris, Edinburgh, Leyden, and Dublin. New York City's medical profession, he hoped, would someday take its place among them.

If Middleton's picture of European medicine boldly overlooked the "empirical" practice of most European doctors, his characterization of medicine in New York underplayed the signs of progress. For one thing, between 1745 and 1766 the strength of the medical community had been bolstered by a steady accession of competent practitioners. Among them were not only the Bards, Middleton, Jones, and Clossy, but also such reputable doctors as John Charlton, Beekman Van Beuren, and three young recipients of M.D.'s from Leyden who established practices in the mid-1760s: John Van Brugh Tennent, Benjamin Prime, and James Smith. By the mid-1760s most of these men were meeting regularly in a medical society. Although historians usually claim that the society dated from 1749, the evidence suggests that it more than likely had its beginnings after 1760. Here the professionals and their associates planned the King's College Medical School and the city's first hospital.[19]

Also, by 1766 Samuel Clossy had dramatically upgraded the quality of medical education in New York by instituting lectures in anatomy. He began them shortly after his arrival at New York in 1763. The "young gentlemen of the Profession" responded so enthusiastically that Clossy decided to lecture on a regular basis. The King's College governors declined his suggestion that they appoint him a professor of anatomy, but they did permit him to offer his courses at the college. Under this arrangement, Clossy lectured on anatomy during the winters of 1764–65 and 1765–66 and on materia medica (the source, composition, preparation, and use of medicines) during the summer of 1765.[20] Another indication of progress in the practice of medicine in New York was the law, passed by the legislature in 1760, which established procedures for licensing physicians and surgeons. The first such colonial law, it stipulated that no one could practice as a physician or surgeon in New York City without first passing an examination in "Physick or Surgery," administered by a committee of prominent political figures. Violators were subject to a five-pound fine for each offense. However, the law exempted anyone already practicing in the city.[21]

Despite these accomplishments, Peter Middleton could marshal a variety of evidence to substantiate his harsh words about medical practice in New York. The 1760 licensing law itself was a case in point. Just who pressed for passage of the law is difficult to tell. Between 1749 and 1754 New York City's newspaper readers were treated to occasional essays which condemned the city's *"vile Quacks* and *base Pretenders"* and proposed licensing procedures. Dr. Henry Van Beuren complained, for example, that "Every pitiful Fellow now a-Days . . . assumes to himself, with no small Arrogance, the Appellation of *Doctor*. . . ." William Smith, Jr., used the *Independent Reflector* to attack the "greatest Part" of the city's doctors as "meer Pretenders to a Profession, of which they are entirely ignorant." Both Van Beuren and Smith argued that "proper Regulation" by the legislature was essential, and Smith suggested in some detail the contents of a licensing law.[22] A third author went so far as to describe a particularly gruesome obstetrical procedure which, he claimed, two city surgeons had recently used with fatal consequences for three infants and two mothers.[23] Despite indications of both a need for legal regulation and of backing for it within and outside the medical community, no law was immediately forthcoming, and the issue largely disappeared from the press for the next several years. No doubt the hiatus reflected public engrossment in the French and Indian War, which began in 1754. But the delay also hinted that proponents of the legislation were neither effectively organized nor widely supported. Finally, late in 1759 the New York General Assembly responded to an "Application . . . made to them" and passed a licensing act. Six months later the governor signed it into law.[24]

During the fifteen years between the passage of the law and the outbreak of the Revolution, quacks frequented New York City as regularly as ever. "Doctor Stork" claimed that he was "surgeon and occulist to her royal highness the Princess of Wales." Ibrahim Mustapha, master of "Turkish Inoculation," ballyhooed his position as "Inoculator to his Sublime Highness and the Janissaries." No one advertised that he had been licensed by the colony of New York.[25] Nor is there a record of any convictions for not procuring a license.[26] In 1770 and again in 1773 New York City was even blessed with visits by James Graham, the "Emperor of Quacks," who soon after opened his enormously successful "Temple of Health" in London. Among its attractions was the "Grand Celestial Bed"; Graham assured childless couples that copulation on the bed would bring immediate conception.[27]

Although "well meant, and truly commendable so far as it operates," commented Peter Middleton in 1769, the licensing law passed in 1760 was "evidently inadequate to remedy all the Mischiefs then complain'd of. . . ." Apparently the law met much the same fate that, during the next century, would befall most New York laws which regulated medical practice. By and large, public authorities failed to enforce them, and the citizenry ignored them.[28] In the 1760s enforcement proved a futile task for a city with no police force and with a populace unsympathetic to the law. Even many of those New Yorkers who resented dishonest charlatans had no quarrel with conscientious empirics. The empiric, like any good artisan, relied on a down-to-earth approach that was familiar, comprehensible, and geared to results.[29]

The professionals, however, viewed the quacks and empirics with defiance. Middleton and his associates blamed them for, among other things, perpetuating medicine's inferior status.[30] Signs abounded that most members of the city's upper class continued to hold medicine in low esteem, even though they might recognize the worth of a John Jones or a Peter Middleton. How else to explain the private jokes about the "Black Art" and the "Profession that does more Mischief than them all," or the public denunciations of doctors as "merciless Butchers of Human Kind," or the enthusiasm for performances of such satirical attacks on doctors as *The Mock Doctor; or, The Dumb Lady Cured* and *The Anatomist or Sham Doctor*, or, finally, the consistency with which the city's elite directed its sons toward mercantile and law careers and away from medicine.[31]

Even more galling to the professionals and their associates was the failure of many New Yorkers, including some who were "otherwise valuable for their Penetration and Good Sense," to distinguish carefully between reputable doctors and "the most obscure and superficial *Traders* in Physic." [32] New Yorkers regularly patronized the city's better-known empirics.[33] Charlatans, also found the city a profitable marketplace—or so their frequent visits suggest. As a result, claimed Middleton, the doctor "of Modesty and real Merit" occasionally lost some of his business or never attracted what he deserved in the first place. Even a man of Clossy's stature had a difficult time establishing a practice.[34] The city's better-trained doctors thus looked upon empirics and quacks with an antipathy nurtured not only by professional scorn and social resentment but also, in some cases, by economic rivalry.[35]

In the mid-1760s New York's medical leaders finally agreed that a medical school offered a feasible solution to the city's medical jumble. A school had been an "Object of Speculation" before then, according to Peter Middleton. Samuel Bard had been mulling it over since 1762, when he learned that John Morgan, a fellow student at Edinburgh, intended to establish the colonies' first medical school at Philadelphia. Bard shared with Morgan and several other American students at Edinburgh not only a concern for professional standards but also an awakened sense of cultural nationalism, a desire to promote the cultural stature and independence of the young colonies by building an American "Edinburgh."[36] Samuel Clossy took a more concrete step toward founding a school in New York when he launched his anatomy lectures in 1763. But the turning point came in 1765. Just at the time when the New York medical community, through the addition of new members like Clossy, Samuel Bard, and James Smith, reached a stage where it could sustain a school, Morgan showed the way by organizing a school in conjunction with the College of Philadelphia. By following Philadelphia's "laudable Example," the New Yorkers would be able to train systematically a corps of young doctors in the scientific and ethical conceptions which they regarded as the bedrock of professional practice.[37] Moreover, by doing so they would eliminate the contradiction inherent in their contention that the city should bar from practice those doctors considered incompetent by the professionals even though there was little provision for educating competent ones.

While implementation of the 1760 licensing law depended on the cooperation of public officials and others outside the profession, New York's medical leaders expected to organize and conduct a medical school largely by drawing on their own resources. They did, however, need to persuade King's College to take the school under its wing and grant degrees to its graduates. The degree would serve, first of all, as a "licence to practise," without

Samuel Bard
An alumnus of King's College, Bard was professor of the practice of medicine at the
King's College Medical School, 1767–1776, and dean of the Columbia College
medical faculty, 1792–1804. The portrait is from an engraving by W. Main taken
from McClelland's copy of John Vanderlyn's portrait. Columbia College is shown
in the background.
CREDIT: COLUMBIANA, COLUMBIA UNIVERSITY

further examination by a licensing agency, just as an Oxford or
Cambridge medical degree legally and professionally entitled its
holder to practice. Second, the degree would testify to a doctor's
merit and provide the public with an easy and reliable means of
distinguishing competent from incompetent practitioners. As

Peter Middleton explained, the "Uncertainty of forming an adequate Opinion, of the Abilities and Judgment of such as shall henceforth practise the Healing Art among us, and which has been so frequently and justly complained of . . . , [would] be effectually removed." Third, by conferring a badge of distinction that reflected the achievement of minimum professional standards and that qualified its recipient "to enter legally upon the Practice of Physic," the professionals probably expected that more rigorous enforcement of the 1760 licensing law would eventually become feasible. As the public learned to identify the professionally trained doctor and to think of him as exclusively qualified to heal, doctors who failed to obtain medical degrees from King's College or some other reputable school or who failed to demonstrate competence when examined under the procedures established in 1760 might be barred from practice.[38]

By educating "such as intend the Practice of Physic, especially in this City and Colony," a medical school thus was expected to improve the quality of medical practice in New York, "place the whole Profession above the Contempt and Jest of Mankind" (in other words, make it socially respectable in the eyes of New York's upper class), and give professional practice a stability that was unattainable as long as medical empirics and imposters successfully diverted public attention away from "responsible" doctors.[39] In their quest for professionalization through an alliance with King's College, New York medical leaders set out on a path similar to that followed earlier in the century by Scottish physicians and surgeons in Edinburgh and Glasgow. In the 1720s, for instance, Edinburgh practitioners moved to upgrade the standards of medical practice by working through the University of Edinburgh. On recommendation of the Edinburgh Royal College of Physicians, the town council established a regular medical faculty at the university in 1726. Where Edinburgh formerly had awarded M.D.'s on an honorary basis, now the physicians and surgeons on the medical faculty set up stringent criteria that gradually transformed the M.D. degree into a symbol of excellence. The College of Physicians and Surgeons in mid-century Glasgow also strengthened its ties to the town's university, supporting the development of a medical faculty and urging high standards. By the 1770s an M.D. from Glasgow was gaining the stature previously precluded by the university's habit of granting M.D.'s in absentia and without examination.[40]

However, proponents of the King's College Medical School did not anticipate achieving their goals by using the medical school to reproduce British guild distinctions among physicians, surgeons, and apothecaries, whereas the Edinburgh Royal College of Physicians took several steps during the 1750s to increase the separation among the three groups. It was John Morgan who insisted that American physicians, like physicians in "great Britain and all polished countries," should leave surgery to the surgeons and the preparation and dispensing of drugs to apothecaries. Morgan thus hoped that most graduates of Philadelphia's medical school would become physicians in the sense that the Royal College of Physicians used the term, with perhaps a few students turning to surgery.[41] However, even among British doctors such specialization was rare outside of cities like London, Dublin, and Edinburgh. The typical colonial doctor combined all three functions. Advocates of a medical school in New York expected its graduates to concentrate on a career either as a physician or a surgeon, but not one to the exclusion of the other and not without following the colonial practice of serving as one's own pharmacist.[42]

Indeed, the comprehensive practice of the colonial doctor furnished supporters of a medical school with an additional argument against relying solely on apprenticeship, the usual means of education for those doctors who had had any medical education at all. As one newspaper essayist complained in 1766:

> The mechanic, to acquire the lowest Trade, serves a much longer Time than most of the Students of Physic do to learn . . . to be DOCTORS. Can any [but] the most ignorant imagine that an Apprenticeship of a few Years, with an intruding Empirick, who knows nothing, comparatively, himself, can . . . [educate] the most sanguine Genius in those three Branches that are here center'd in one: viz. Physick, Surgery, and Pharmacy![43]

The duration of a medical apprenticeship varied, but three or four years was common. If the length of an apprentice's term struck some observers as brief, the greater deficiency lay in the narrow character of the preparation. Obviously an empiric devoted minor attention to the scientific and ethical dimensions of medicine. But even a professional was hard put to provide by himself the broad theoretical and practical exposure to medicine which a medical faculty of several professors could offer. A master found his efforts circumscribed by the limitations on his time, his library, and the range of his knowledge and experience, as well as by his lack of the equipment that facilitated the teaching of anatomy and natural philosophy. Moreover, since masters charged fees—£80 to £100 per annum for room, board, and education was not an unusual fee for a well-established doctor—the inspiration to teach was often overshadowed by the desire for an extra source of income and for cheap labor to perform rudimentary tasks. As a result, apprenticeship education was notoriously uneven. Variables like the length of the term, the competence of the master, and the degree of his interest in educating his apprentices all contributed to the difficulty in judging the quality of an apprentice-trained practitioner.[44]

A medical school, however, would "rescue this beneficent Branch of Learning from the Obscurity which still continues to veil it in this place . . . ," wrote John Jones, Peter Middleton, Samuel Clossy, Samuel Bard, and James Smith to the governors of King's College on August 4, 1767. The five men urged that they be appointed professors in the school, with "every honorary Mark of Respect" which the governors could bestow. The next day Dr. John Van Brugh Tennent asked that he be included on the medical faculty.[45] The governors did not hesitate to grant both requests, despite the fact that four years earlier they had rejected a proposal for a medical school tendered by Sir James Jay, the first New Yorker to earn an M.D. from Edinburgh.

While raising funds for King's College in England, Jay had learned of plans for a medical school in Philadelphia. He modestly suggested that King's College counter Philadelphia's move by appointing a medical faculty to consist of himself and two or three physicians whom he could "introduce" to New York, each to receive an annual salary of £100 sterling.[46] The scheme charmed neither the city's medical community, who no doubt resented Jay's attempt to bypass them, nor the college governors, who offered the same objection to Jay that they used in 1764 to deny Samuel Clossy a professorship in anatomy: the college funds were "so overcharged." [47] But the tripling of the endowment between 1763 and 1767 eliminated that objection. Moreover, the petitioners of 1767 apparently agreed to forego salaries and rely on student fees for income, so that the founding of a medical school required little financial commitment on the governors' part. Also, Myles Cooper was by now firmly entrenched as college president after four years in office. Doubtless he already looked forward to turning his provincial college into a university. The founding of a medical school in Philadelphia provided all the more incentive to get on with it, while the bitter dispute with Jay over the handling of the English funds ruled out his participation in the undertaking.

The college governors thus responded promptly to the August 1767 proposals by appointing a committee of three governors to work out the details of the school with the six professors.[48] The professors had already suggested a set of courses—anatomy, surgery, the theory and practice of medicine, chemistry, materia medica, and midwifery—which reflected their familiarity with the curricula at Edinburgh and Leyden. However, the professors and the governors' committee settled on degree requirements which selectively combined features common at Edinburgh and Leyden with those at Oxford, resulting in a program that closely resembled the one established earlier that year by the College of Philadelphia. Students could earn a Bachelor of Medicine degree three years after matriculating if they attended "at least, one complete Course of Lectures under each Professor," passed a general examination upon finishing their course work, and, for those who did not have a B.A., demonstrated a "competent Knowledge" of Latin and natural philosophy. A student who had apprenticed for three years to a reputable practitioner became eligible for the M.B. degree two years after matriculation. While the M.B. degree served as a "licence to practise, and a Certificate of . . . having attended the College," the college reserved its "heighest Honor" for the M.D. degree. Requirements for an M.D. included at least a year's interval after earning an M.B., a second round of courses, a second examination, a minimum age of twenty-two, and the publication and public defense of a "Treatise upon some *Medical Subject.*" [49]

On November 2, 1767, New Yorkers celebrated the opening of the colony's first medical school. The governors and faculty of King's College, the governor of New York, the "Judges of the Supreme Court in their Robes, and the Gentlemen of the Law in their Gowns . . . walked in Procession to the College-Hall; where they were entertained with a very elegant and learned Discourse, by Doctor Middleton. . . ." The *New-York Mercury* noted confidently that the "Satisfaction of the learned and splendid Audience on this Occasion, was universal. . . ." The *Mercury* also expressed a hope that the widespread enthusiasm for the school would "recommend it to the attention" of prospective doctors, especially those who planned to practice in the city and colony of New York. The *Mercury* had put its finger on the crucial issue that lay ahead.[50]

The organization of a medical school signaled a new phase in the professionalization of New York doctors. It also suggested that King's College was beginning to transcend the boundaries inherited from the decisions and controversies at the time of its founding. For instance, the coalition of doctors which proposed the medical school and served as its faculty included two Presbyterians, one of them no less a figure than the brother of William Smith, Jr. Initially Samuel Bard had worried that the affiliation of the medical school with King's College would "make the Presbeterian partie our Enimys. . . ." However, Bard and his colleagues studiously avoided any signs of religious partiality, sharing John Bard's view that "an attachment to parties both in Church and State" did not "become" the professional physician and would always be "Inconsistent" with his "Interest" anyway.[51] Undoubtedly the medical school and the liberal arts college together gained a broader overall appeal than King's College had enjoyed by itself before 1767, if only by attracting prospective and practicing doctors. Whether the medical school reached those groups which had previously shunned the college, such as Presbyterians and residents in the Hudson River valley, is another matter. Judging by the matriculants in the M.B. and M.D. programs, it did not. And there is no evidence to indicate that the nondenominational character of the medical school altered the public image of the liberal arts college. The religious neutrality of the professionals could not overshadow the partisanship of a man like Myles Cooper.

14.
THE LIMITS OF
ACADEMIC MEDICAL TRAINING

THE ESTABLISHMENT of a medical school in twentieth-century America requires a vast commitment of social resources. Staffing alone poses a major task. Building and equipment costs rapidly reach astronomical figures. For instance, by 1970 estimates of the total cost for establishing New York City's Mount Sinai School of Medicine, which admitted its first class in 1968, had exceeded $150,000,000. Only two-thirds of that sum had been raised by 1970, despite grants from the federal and state governments and from numerous private donors.[1] Obviously it is impossible to establish a medical school without widespread support. On the other hand, once a school opens there is no difficulty attracting students. In 1971 Mount Sinai admitted forty-three first-year students. About eighteen hundred applied, even though minimum yearly expenses for tuition, room, board, and books were estimated at $4,700.[2]

Against this background, the founding of the King's College Medical School looks like the contemporary world turned upside down. Once the medical faculty and the college governors reached an agreement on the project, starting the school was easy. The problem was attracting students. Indeed, the King's College Medical School opened in 1767 with no new capital investment and virtually no start-up expenses. The professors lectured in the college hall, while the college and the professors already owned most of the necessary equipment. Faculty remuneration came from student fees. In other words, since the founders of the medical school did not have to seek outside support, they were able to launch their school despite widespread public indifference and despite some hostility toward the school among a few city doctors. Nor did the building of a city hospital, which would permit clinical instruction for medical students, reflect public enthusiasm for the professors' educational reforms. Samuel Bard, Peter Middleton, and John Jones did, it is true, initiate the campaign for the hospital in 1769 with clinical instruction in mind. And construction of the building between 1773 and 1775 did depend heavily on public funds. But the hospital was touted and supported primarily as a way to provide care for New York's sick poor.[3]

Students and their families, unlike the professors, could not regard so lightly public apathy toward the school. The time and funds required to earn a King's College medical degree forced them to question whether it was worth it. Some prospective doctors decided it was not. During the first three years, 1767–1769, thirteen students matriculated in the M.B. program; eleven completed it. However, the college could not sustain this creditable record. During the six years from 1770 to 1775 only five students matriculated in the M.B. program; one completed it. Not surprisingly, throughout the nine years that the school operated only two M.B.'s proceeded to take their M.D.'s.[4] However, the eighteen matriculants by no means composed the entire audience at medical lectures, or there would have been little point to offering courses after 1772. Courses were open to matriculants and nonmatriculants alike. In each case the students paid a fee directly to the professor instead of tuition to the school. Samuel Clossy earned more than £100 in student fees each winter for teaching anatomy, so he attracted in the neighborhood of ten pupils a year.[5] Undoubtedly nonmatriculants attended the lectures of other medical professors, but it is impossible to determine the number of students involved. Liberal arts pupils at King's College, especially those who planned careers in medicine, provided one source of nonmatriculated students. A friend of Alexander Hamilton testified that Hamilton, who "originally destined himself to the Science of Physic," attended Clossy's lectures while an undergraduate at King's College.[6] At least twelve liberal arts pupils at King's College between 1767 and 1776 became doctors without officially enrolling in the medical school.

The medical faculty thus found that the number of students justified regular course offerings. But the professors intended to provide a comprehensive medical education, not incidental instruction in a course or two; and they expected students to work for a degree which would serve both as a license to practice and as a means by which the public could distinguish the competent from the incompetent doctor. The steep drop-off in the number of matriculants after 1769 thus represented a real failure, even though students continued to attend the lectures.

As prospective students and their families weighed the costs of a medical education at King's College against its potential benefits, they confronted several discouraging factors. First was the size of the financial investment. An M.B. candidate spent a total of £25 to £30 New York currency just in fees for his courses (King's College liberal arts students paid the highest liberal arts tuition in the colonies: £20 for four years). Other expenses might include a diploma fee, charges for tutoring in Latin, the cost of clothes, books, and paper, and, for those whose families did not live in New York City, substantial sums for room, board, and such items as firewood, candles, washing, and mending. Although medical students lived in town, not in the college building, college rates provide some perspective on living costs. Charges for room and board for seven months (the usual length of medical courses) amounted to about £19.[7]

The irony of the situation lay in the fact that, if most New York families found the expense of medical education extremely burdensome, sons of New York's wealthiest families rarely chose the medical profession as a career. The medical school thus was likely to draw its students from families where the fathers were shopkeepers, lesser merchants, doctors, ministers, and prosperous artisans and farmers. Such families, though they fell in the upper 20 percent of New York's socioeconomic hierarchy, did not belong to the elite who dominated the colony's economic, social, and political life.

Costs did not bar these families from patronizing the King's College Medical School. But other factors might make them wonder whether the onerous financial undertaking was worth it, particularly if they regarded a medical school education as supplementary to apprenticeship. Apprenticeship, after all, retained its public standing as a legitimate means of medical education. Even the College of Philadelphia obliged each M.B. candidate to serve a "sufficient apprenticeship." [8] In contrast, the College of New York officially ignored apprenticeship, neither requiring it for a degree nor giving much credit to those students who apprenticed (they could earn an M.B. in two instead of three years after matriculation if they met all other requirements). On the surface this seemed to ease the demands on the medical student, but King's College provided no equivalent experience whether in preparing drugs, in observing a doctor while he practiced, or in interacting occasionally with patients. King's College, unlike the College of Philadelphia, could not even offer clinical instruction, since the city lacked a hospital. The hopes that had mounted with the laying of a cornerstone in 1773 evaporated in 1775 when fire gutted the unfinished hospital.

Thus the King's College medical faculty could no more claim to provide a rounded medical education than could proponents of apprenticeship. And to combine an apprenticeship with an M.B. program would consume large amounts of time and money. New Jersey's professional physicians responded to the establishment of medical schools in the colonies by tightening apprenticeship practices in New Jersey. Members of the recently founded (1766) New Jersey Medical Society agreed in 1767 not to accept an apprentice for less than four years, only one of which could be spent at a medical school. They settled on an annual apprentice fee of £100 New Jersey currency.[9] Such an arrangement hardly encouraged the pursuit of a medical degree on top of an apprenticeship. The more attractive compromise—for those who wished to attend medical school at all—was to take two or three courses during one winter.

Prospective physicians in New York found little more encouragement to matriculate in the medical school. No public statute or

professional agreement spurred them to earn a degree. Nor did a
degree have much market value outside New York City, where
scattered settlements and extensive reliance on lay medicine and
self-medication made it difficult to recoup a hefty financial investment in education.[10] Moreover, students who ignored the degree
program could take two or three courses without diverting their
attention to passing the rigorous Latin examination, which was
conducted in the college hall before the student body. In 1774 the
medical faculty insisted that it was "absolutely necessary" to shift
the Latin examination to the president's chambers and allow some
leeway to students who "should not appear so well informed in
this respect. . . ." The governors ignored the request.[11]

All these considerations might have slipped into the background
if the medical school graduates could have demonstrated a decisive
superiority over untrained and apprentice-trained doctors.
Chances are that M.B. recipients performed more competently
than young doctors who chose not to attend the medical school.
But this was not necessarily so, and the differences were not dramatic enough to catch and hold the public eye. The problem
proved especially hard to overcome because the school prided itself on what would turn out to be its weakest point: its emphasis
on medical theory.

The medical professors, like most eighteenth-century medical
scientists, were caught in a stream of thinking that often flowed
away from their goal. The striking breakthroughs in physical
science during the previous century spurred them to seek a similar
grand synthesis which would bring order out of their chaotic data
on human physiology and pathology, just as Newton's *Principia*
had dramatically clarified the world of mechanics and astronomy.
But the penchant to streamline their limited knowledge resulted in
overarching theories with skimpy empirical foundations.[12] The
medical faculty thus yearned to arm its students with medical
theories which missed the mark so widely that their value to the
prospective physician depended less on scientific validity than on
social legitimacy: some patients believed in them and expected
their physicians to know and use them. Peter Middleton, for instance, proposed to counter "empiricism" with what was little

more than an updated version of age-old humoral pathology. When confronted with a patient's fever, declared Middleton, the rational physician examines the state of the patient's "circulating Fluids." Is the patient's blood excessive, or thin, or viscous, or suffering from "a *putrid Dissolution*"? [13] If excessive, bleed him. If thin, prescribe a diet and drugs which will thicken it, and so on. Humoral pathologists were capable of ascribing most any disease to a condition of the bodily fluids. Fortunately, the limitations on the value of the King's College medical curriculum were not defined exclusively by the limits of eighteenth-century medical theory, but the handicap was hard to surmount.

The King's College Medical School offered courses each year until the Revolution closed the school in April 1776. The professors normally lectured from November to May, but on at least two occasions a course was presented during the summer months. Neither James Smith nor John Van Brugh Tennent played an important role in the school's operation. Both men may have lectured during the first two years, but by early 1770 Tennent had died and Smith had left New York. The annual mainstays of the curriculum were Samuel Clossy in anatomy, John Jones in surgery, Peter Middleton in the theory of medicine, and Samuel Bard in the practice of medicine. With less frequency the medical school offered courses in materia medica, taught by Clossy and Middleton, and in chemistry, taught first by Smith, then by Bard. Tennent may have lectured on midwifery before his death.[14]

Surviving sources permit an exploration of four of the medical school courses. Samuel Bard's lectures in chemistry and the practice of medicine demonstrate as well as any both the roots and the limitations of the King's College medical curriculum. Bard was not a chemist. When the college named him professor of chemistry in 1770 he simply turned to the lecture notes he had taken in William Cullen's chemistry courses at Edinburgh, just as John Morgan did for his chemistry course at the College of Philadelphia.[15] Although Cullen himself could not claim any significant chemical discoveries and had published little in the area, his students found him an inspiring teacher who organized his material effectively and utilized the better writings on chemistry, particularly *Elementa Chemiae* published in 1724 by Hermann Boerhaave. Cullen impressed Bard so much that the New Yorker took chemistry courses with him for three years running.[16]

Bard followed Cullen and most eighteenth-century professors of chemistry by focusing on the "application of chemistry to the theory of physick, and the art of pharmacy." The heart of Bard's course was a Linnaean-like classification and analysis of all "chemical bodies," which Bard borrowed from Cullen. The taxonomy started with six classes (saline, inflammable, metallic, earthy, watery, and aerial), then progressively subdivided each class (saline bodies into simple and compound, simple salts into acids and alkalis, alkalis into fixed and volatile, fixed alkalis into vegetable and fossil, and so on). Bard first presented an overview of the scheme, so that students would learn a systematic way of defining chemical terms and not use them "in the loose vague Sence of the generallity of Chemists." Then he explored the "particular history" of each substance. Is it "native" or "artificial"? If native, how is it found in its natural state? If artificial, what are the different methods of its production? And so on.[17]

Just how valuable Bard's students found this introduction to chemistry is not readily ascertainable, but the utility of the course was narrowly circumscribed by the premodern state of chemical science. Bard paid homage to the four Aristotelian elements: fire, earth, air, and water; and he taught his pupils the then popular theories of phlogiston and elective attraction. Unaware of the existence of oxygen, Bard could not explain such an essential physiological process as respiration.[18]

Samuel Bard exercised more initiative in organizing his course on the practice of medicine, since he could draw on both his wide reading and his personal experience. The course consisted of a survey of human diseases, such as smallpox, quinsy, "putrid malignant fevers," measles, palsy, and pleuropneumonia. For each disease, Bard outlined the symptoms, causes, and methods of cure, in a manner similar to that in Hermann Boerhaave's *Aphorisms*. However, Bard felt severely handicapped by the absence of a hospital, which, he claimed, "affords the best and only means of properly instructing Pupils in the Practice of Medicine. . . ." [19]

During the years when Bard composed his lectures on the practice of medicine, Hermann Boerhaave's physiological and pathological theories still dominated the thinking of many European and American physicians. Boerhaave developed an elaborate and rather sophisticated theory that traced most diseases to the faulty interaction of the bodily fluids (blood, bodily secretions, etc.) with the bodily solids (body fibers, especially those comprising the blood vessels and lymphatic vessels). Thus one's solids might become too stiff or too lax and disrupt the proper circulation of the fluids, or the fluids themselves might become too thin or too salty. Stiff blood vessels, for instance, exerted excessive action on the blood and thickened it, rendering it susceptible to clotting. This problem could be remedied by bloodletting, which thinned the blood, and by a watery diet and oily medicines, which softened the fibers of the blood vessels. Bard confronted Boerhaave's ideas throughout his medical education. Typically, Bard's professor in the practice of medicine at Edinburgh lectured on Boerhaave's *Aphorisms*.[20] However, through courses, reading, and discussion, Bard learned to admire also the work of such British physicians as Thomas Sydenham, John Huxham, John Pringle, John Fothergill, Robert Whytt, and, in particular, William Cullen. Bard's lectures drew on their thinking and research as well as Boerhaave's.[21]

The influence of Cullen on Bard foreshadowed the popularity that the Edinburgh professor's medical ideas would gain among American physicians after the Revolution. Cullen emphasized much more than Boerhaave the role of nervous and vascular tensions in causing illness. Thus, while Professor John Jones taught the Boerhaavian doctrine that an inflammation might result primarily from an obstruction in the arteries, Bard denied it and argued in his lectures that an inflammation resulted from an increased oscillatory motion of the capillary vessels. In turn, Bard followed Cullen in urging treatment which relaxed the patient. Bard particularly recommended opium, with which he had experimented at Edinburgh. He advised his students that he expected opium to gain wide use in the treatment of inflammatory disorders.[22]

Bard's eclectic approach to the practice of medicine called for only piecemeal use of Cullen's ideas. More often Bard drew on the work of Boerhaave and his followers. In any case, despite variations in theories of pathology, Boerhaave, Cullen, and proponents of other theories prescribed many of the same cures. The King's College students learned from Bard the "Methodus Medendi" that many another eighteenth-century doctor relied upon: bleeding, cupping, purging, the use of emetics, dietetics, medicinal concoctions containing "the Bark" and "snake Root," access to dry cool air, and so on—cures that were effective at times but that were often of dubious value.[23] The problem lay, however, not so much in eighteenth-century therapeutics, but in the defective theories of physiology and pathology they reflected.

Unlike Samuel Bard's two courses, Samuel Clossy's lectures on anatomy utilized a body of knowledge that had reached a modern stage. By the opening of the eighteenth century anatomists had recorded the gross features of the human body. Clossy himself had spent four years at British hospitals probing the causes of disease by dissecting bodies. His lectures reflected this experience as well as his studies in Dublin and London with the likes of George Cleghorn and William Hunter, and his extensive reading in the works of Galen, Andreas Vesalius, Giovanni Battista Morgagni, and numerous other European anatomists.[24]

Clossy organized his lectures in a manner that generally followed the structure of De Humani Corporis Fabrica by Andreas Vesalius, whom Clossy regarded as the most distinguished of modern anatomists. Clossy first considered the "Dry" and "Fresh" bones, with their "Cartilages, Ligaments, and Membranes," then discussed the muscles, the arteries and veins, and the nerves, and concluded by examining "all the Viscera of the three Cavities." The last included the cranial cavity—where he examined the brain and the eye—and the thoracic and abdominal cavities. Throughout the lectures Clossy supplemented his discussion of structure with observations on the physiology and pathology of the various parts of the body.[25]

The spirit of Clossy's course can be grasped by surveying the demonstrations that accompanied his lectures. Among his exhibits were skeletons, individual bones, and numerous anatomical preparations, such as "injected Preparations" showing "the Capillary Vessels of every Muscle," and a "Heart & Lung injected & finely prepared." Clossy confirmed "the Blood's Motion from Arteries to Veins" by having his students examine the membranes of frogs through a double reflecting microscope. When possible, Clossy illustrated his lectures by dissecting an "Adult Subject." [26]

Although Clossy remained largely unaware of little-explored dimensions of anatomy like histology, he managed to present reasonably accurate data in an empirical framework, thus providing the student with a foundation on which to build his medical knowledge. The stumbling block lay in making effective use of anatomical data. The physician might know the gross structure of the body, but his inadequate understanding of physiology and pathology made it difficult for him to exploit fully his anatomical information in the day-to-day treatment of disease.[27]

Should the doctor turn his hand at surgery, he would make greater use of his anatomical knowledge. When prospective surgeons combined their work under Clossy with study under John Jones, professor of surgery, they received the soundest preparation available in England's new world colonies. Jones was an intelligent, skillful, and successful surgeon who contributed to the improvement of surgical practice throughout the colonies by publishing his *Plain Concise Practical Remarks on the Treatment of Wounds and Fractures.*[28]

Jones lectured to his students on a variety of pathological conditions, from inflammatory tumors, cancers, encysted tumors, and hernias, to ulcers, burns, general wounds, and gunshot wounds. He explained the cause of each disorder and indicated the means of treatment. Jones approached surgery not as a "low mechanic art," but as a science in which an operation was but "a single point, in the cure of diseases." Thus he discussed medicinal and dietetic therapy, much of it based on Boerhaavian thinking, as well as surgical therapy, and suggested how to integrate all three. Jones based his surgical advice on his own experience and on his familiarity with the work of a large number of European surgeons, among them Percival Pott, Henri Le Dran, Samuel Sharp, and William Hewson.[29]

During the concluding section of his course, Jones used cadavers to demonstrate "those methods of operating which are recommended by the best modern Surgeons. . . ." Over the years students watched him demonstrate amputations, castrations, trephinings, tonsillectomies, lithotomies, the removal of various kinds of tumors, and the surgical treatment of inflammations, hernias, emphysema, and hydrocele. Students did not, however, perform operations themselves, although Jones "earnestly" recommended that they practice frequently on dead bodies before starting on "living ones." [30]

Jones's course provided prospective surgeons and physicians with a reasonably comprehensive and up-to-date introduction to surgery and with exposure to the technique of a skilled practitioner. Jones also conveyed a sense that surgery was just as legitimate an area of professional medical practice as internal medicine, contrary to the attitudes which predominated in England and which John Morgan voiced in Philadelphia. However, in spite of Jones's efforts to transform surgery into a respectable science, the surgeon remained on the fringes of eighteenth-century medicine. The dangers of infection and the lack of anesthesia severely hampered him and restricted much of his work to surface disorders. Moreover, current pathological theories furnished little justification for the use of surgery in the treatment of most diseases. As historian Richard Shryock writes: "Of what avail was surgery if illness resided in the humors: where was the man who could operate on the blood?" [31]

Ideally, the value of the medical curriculum should be explored by examining not what was taught but what students learned and how they used it. Unfortunately, the identity of virtually all the nonmatriculants is not known, and data on the matriculants is meager. The American Revolution not only closed the medical school, it disrupted the professional lives of its alumni and contributed to their dispersal. Two students did, however, distinguish themselves in post-Revolutionary New York. Samuel Nicoll, M.B. '74 and a recipient of an M.D. from Edinburgh in 1776, served on the Columbia medical faculty in the 1790s; and Nicholas Romayne, who matriculated in 1774 but later switched to Edinburgh for his M.D., became a dominant and controversial medical figure after the Revolution, serving at various times as president of the New York County Medical Society, president of the College of Physicians and Surgeons of New York, and a professor at several medical schools. But other alumni turned up in such scattered locations as Ulster County, New York: West Suffield, Connecticut; London; and several islands in the West Indies. Unquestionably, the students failed to have the kind of impact on medical practice in New York that the founders of the school had anticipated in 1767.

During the mid-1760s the practice of medicine throughout the middle colonies seemed to turn the corner toward professionalism. John Morgan and his colleagues established the College of Philadelphia Medical School and Philadelphia's first medical society. Fourteen New Jersey physicians organized the first colony-wide medical society. In unprecedented fashion for colonial doctors, the New Jerseyites agreed to a "Table of Fees and Rates" and rules for apprenticeships, and launched a plan to gain control over entry into medical practice throughout New Jersey.[32] New York City's professional physicians founded a medical society and the colonies' second medical school.

Yet, beneath these surface reforms medical practice continued to look much the same to most colonists. In the 1770s, just as in the 1750s, New Yorkers patronized the city's quacks and empirics. And professionals once again warned New Yorkers "of the deadly Effects, that arise from the Application of the Sick, to illiterate, ignorant, boasting Pretenders." A handful of New York physicians now pointed to their King's College M.B.'s as proof of competence, but other doctors still staked their reputations on outlandish claims, such as being "A Seventh Son of A Seventh Son," while shopkeepers dispensed wonder drugs like "Doctor Hill's Newly Improved Great Stomachick Tincture," "The Golden Medical Cephalic Snuff," and "Dr. Ryan's Incomparable

Worm-Destroying Sugar Plumbs." [33] In the 1770s, in other words, the professionalization of medicine still depended largely on the efforts of a small group of Europe-oriented physicians and surgeons, because they had not yet succeeded in convincing many New Yorkers that their goals reflected urgent public needs.

The breakup of the professionals during the Revolution thus posed a problem because it eliminated the only source of coherence in the movement to normalize professional medical education in New York. In 1785 Columbia reestablished its medical school, but only Samuel Bard remained from the pre-Revolutionary faculty. Clossy had returned to Ireland, Jones had moved to Philadelphia, and Middleton had died. Proponents of professional medical education now found their efforts hindered not only by the reluctance of students to pursue medical degrees—Columbia's medical school averaged eighteen entrants and two degree recipients annually from 1793 through 1802—but also by infighting among the professionals themselves. A chaotic era ensued, dominated by personal and professional rivalries, and by proliferating medical schools which competed for a limited audience. The combination proved fatal for the Columbia Medical School. Thirty years of medical factionalism and intrigue culminated in 1814 in its dissolution and the absorption of its faculty by the College of Physicians and Surgeons of New York. [34]

Ironically, the College of Physicians and Surgeons, now united with Columbia University, dates its origin from 1767. The logic may be skewed, but the dating at least provides some compensation for the tendency of historians to equate pre-Revolutionary professional medical education with the achievements of John Morgan, William Shippen, and Benjamin Rush at the College of Philadelphia. [35] There is little point, however, in reviving the civic rivalry that spurred New York's professionals to found a medical school in 1767 and which surfaced during the 1960s in a claim that King's College, not the College of Philadelphia, merits recognition as the first fully established medical school in America since it was "the first to offer *all* the then generally accepted medical courses. . . ." One is much more impressed by the similarities—not the differences—in the pre-Revolutionary histories of the two schools.

If the medical curriculum at King's College incorporated much misleading information, so did the curriculum at the College of Philadelphia. If King's College could not sustain the initial enthusiasm for its M.B. program, the College of Philadelphia faced a similar decline in enrollment, graduating twenty-six M.B.'s between 1768 and 1771, then just three more before the Revolution.[36] Proponents of professional education in both cities confronted public indifference and a flourishing community of quacks and empirics. Above all, physicians in Philadelphia and New York were hampered by the rudimentary state of their medical knowledge. The fulfillment of their plans for professionalization awaited the scientific breakthroughs of the nineteenth century.

4.
KING'S COLLEGE
BECOMES COLUMBIA

INTRODUCTION

THE "TRANSFORMING HAND" of the American Revolution reshaped "many aspects" of colonial society, suggested historian J. Franklin Jameson half a century ago. "The stream of revolution, once started, could not be confined within narrow banks, but spread abroad upon the land." Yet Jameson found it difficult to generalize about the impact of the Revolution on education; and of collegiate education he could only point to a rapid increase in the number of colleges during the post-Revolutionary years. What of King's College? How did the Revolution affect a college whose leaders had supported the British? One can sense that the question merits exploration by imagining how Myles Cooper might have reacted had he visited Columbia in 1789. How shocked he would have been to learn that Episcopalians no longer composed a majority of either the students, the faculty, or the active trustees; or that the president was a layman; or that, by some Revolutionary magic, the treasurer of the college was the son of William Livingston.[1] Nor would Cooper have been pleased to discover that most of the students lived in town and that the collegiate way had disintegrated to the point where the porter devoted his energies to keeping neighbors off the college grounds, not students on them. And what to make of the pronouncements among students and faculty about the virtues of republicanism, or of the serious challenges to the study of Greek which were soon to convince some trustees that Greek should be dispensed with?[2]

In 1775 Myles Cooper had prided himself on his success at

tightening up the collegiate way, at strengthening the classicism of the curriculum, and, above all, at enhancing the college's role as defender of monarchical and Episcopal principles. By 1789 his achievements were gravely threatened where they were not already overturned. Clearly the Revolution had profoundly affected his college. Or so, at least, it seemed.

15.

RESHAPING KING'S COLLEGE

SEPTEMBER 1777, Bridge Head, New York, a month short of Burgoyne's disastrous surrender at Saratoga—Reverend Charles Inglis, rector of Trinity Church and a devoted governor of King's College, solemnly assured a group of British soldiers that their cause was just and honorable, "the Cause of Truth against Falsehood, of Loyalty against Rebellion, of legal Government against Usurpation, of Constitutional Freedom against Tyranny—in short it is the cause of human happiness of millions against Outrage and Oppression." Six years later, in September 1783, Inglis sadly prepared to leave New York before the last of the British army embarked for home. The year before Inglis had still held out hope that the "Face of Affairs" might change, but now, "stripped" of his estate and "compelled to abandon" his rectorate, he saw no alternative but to join the "prodigious" migration of loyalists to Nova Scotia. Inglis helped draw up plans for an episcopate in Nova Scotia and, on the eve of his departure, turned his attention to founding a college there. Joined by Reverend Benjamin Moore, president pro tempore of King's College after Cooper's flight, and by three other Anglican clerics, Inglis petitioned British authorities to establish a college which would "diffuse religious literature, loyalty and good morals among His Majesty's subjects. . . ." [1]

Four years passed before Charles Inglis reached his new home—he sailed first to England and was named bishop of Nova Scotia. But by 1790 King's College of Nova Scotia had opened its doors, its president always to be an Anglican clergyman and its purpose to be the inculcation of knowledge, loyalty, and virtue. "[O]ne of my principal motives for pushing it forward," Inglis revealed to a friend, "was to prevent the importation of American Divines and American politics into the province. Unless we have a seminary here, the youth of Nova Scotia will be sent for their education to the Revolted Colonies—the inevitable consequence would be, a corruption of their religious and political principles." [2]

Thus the spirit of loyalist education that had flourished at King's College, New York in the 1770s was, in a sense, transplanted to Nova Scotia. Moreover, the men who had engendered that spirit at King's College had, like Charles Inglis, moved on. Of the twenty-one governors who actually ran the college in the early 1770s, only five remained in New York City by 1784, most of the others having emigrated, retired to the countryside, or died. True, in 1784 a group identifying itself as the governors of King's College petitioned the New York legislature to reopen the college and to "render it the Mother of an University to be established within this State . . . ," language reminiscent of that used in the proposed charter of 1774. But if the vision of a university had survived the Revolution, the character of the vision had changed. Not only had most of the petitioners supported the Revolution. Not only did their ranks include ex officio governors who would never have associated themselves with the pre-Revolutionary college—men like John Rodgers, pastor of the New York City Presbyterian church, John Morin Scott, one of William Livingston's triumvirate, and George Clinton, the Presbyterian governor of New York. But the petitioners explicitly called for a revision of the college charter to suit "that Liberality and that civil and religious Freedom" which the Revolution had secured. [3]

The British army had barely left New York when Governor Clinton first raised the issue of education in the young republic, calling on the state legislature to give its attention to the "Revival and Encouragement of Seminaries of Learning." The senate and the assembly each appointed a committee to pursue the matter, the senate's chaired by James Duane. Duane was a sturdy and long-standing friend of both King's College and Trinity Church and had been a strong proponent of American University before he cast his lot with the revolutionaries. Duane's committee soon produced a bill "for establishing a University within this State." Then, while the senate was considering the bill, Duane joined with a group of prestigious New Yorkers in the aforementioned petition, requesting the legislature to reorganize King's College and make it the "Mother" of the proposed university. Despite the petitioners' identification as governors of King's College, the majority of them had not served as governors before the Revolution but now qualified ex officio—Governor Clinton, the chief justice, treasurer, attorney general, and secretary of New York State, and the ministers of New York City's Presbyterian, Episcopal, and Dutch Reformed churches.[4]

Their petition and the modifications of Duane's bill which it inspired have led Sydney Sherwood, author of the most exhaustive study of the subject, to claim that "guardians" of the "old college" had "captured" the movement to found a state university and had deflected it toward fulfilling their parochial ambitions of expanding the educational influence of King's College. His argument falters on several counts, not the least of which is the fact that no one knows exactly what was initially proposed in Duane's bill. Certainly if one examines the petitioners and their message it is misleading to call them "guardians" of King's College. While they were concerned for the future of the college, the import of their petition was to clear the way for reforming King's College and integrating it into the new university. Indeed, the act finally passed by the legislature suggests that if anything was captured in 1784 it was King's College itself.[5] In 1779 Pennsylvania legislators, reacting to the loyalist sympathies of some leaders of the College of Philadelphia, moved quickly upon the departure of British troops to restructure control of the institution. In 1784 the New York legislature followed their example.

The title of the 1784 act tells part of the story—"*An Act for granting certain Privileges to the College heretofore called King's College, for altering the Name and Charter thereof, and erecting an University within this State.*" The name of King's College was changed to Columbia College, symbolizing both the rejection of England and the glorification of America. Mercifully the legislature rejected the name "State College." [6] The key feature in the legislation was the establishment of a board of regents, the governing body of the newly created University of the State of New York. The regents could found "Schools and Colleges" in the state; and they controlled all the institutions belonging to the university, which included Columbia College, any colleges or schools which the regents founded, and any colleges or schools founded separately which joined the university. The regents had "full Power" to make "Ordinances and By-Laws" for each institution in the university, to appoint its president and faculty, and to manage its estate, with the stipulation that the estate of King's College and of any institution which joined the university could be used only for that particular school or college.

The 1784 act elaborated on these various points and included some minor qualifications, but the above description in essence defines the regents' purview. Who, then, served as regents? It was a large, diverse, geographically dispersed group, composed of six state political figures ex officio, the mayors of New York City and Albany ex officio, two residents from each of New York's twelve counties, one representative from any religious denomination in the state whose clergy should decide to name one, and the president and one representative from each institution founded separately which joined the university. [7] Faculty members were regents ex officio but could vote only on matters affecting exclusively their respective institutions.

Reflecting the ideals embodied in New York's constitution of 1777, which guaranteed the "free exercise and enjoyment of religious profession and worship," the legislature refused to give a "preference" to any religious group. [8] Nor could religious tests be required of professors, from whom, incidentally, the presidents of the various colleges were to be chosen. The act did not, however, exclude denominational influences from the university. Each denomination could select a regent, and any "religious Body or Society of Men" could endow a professorship for the "Promotion" of its "particular religious Tenets."

In one fundamental way the new university harked back to the proposed charter of 1774, which may bespeak the role of James Duane, a coauthor of both the 1774 charter and the 1784 legislation.[9] Building on an unusual concept implied in the charter of American University, the University of the State of New York theoretically consisted of a group of dispersed institutions knit together by a single governing body, the regents. In contrast, when the Pennsylvania legislature converted the College of Philadelphia into the University of the State of Pennsylvania, they simply created a new group of trustees without altering fundamentally the organization or the scope of the institution.

In most respects, however, the University of the State of New York differed markedly from American University. Think of the implications of each for King's College. The charter of 1774 enhanced the urban, Anglican, imperial dimensions of King's and assured it the dominant voice in the university by converting its governors into regents and by making its president automatically president of the university. The act of 1784 gave King's College no special privileges in the University of the State of New York and turned control of the college over to a predominantly rural and non-Episcopal group of revolutionaries who had comparatively little sympathy for the old college. Only one man who had served as a governor of King's College before the Revolution qualified as a regent in 1784: James Duane. Control of the college had been restructured to the point that even William Livingston could have lived with it.

It soon turned out, however, that the issue of control had not been resolved satisfactorily. The regents immediately set about to reopen Columbia, the only college in the university, but they had a devil of a time getting a quorum (a majority of all regents). Few regents lived in or even near New York City, and apparently a number were decidedly unenthusiastic about their new positions. The regents had one regular meeting in May 1784, then operated through a committee for several months. Students were admitted, professors hired, and plans made to raise funds, with a handful of regents from New York City doing the lion's share of the work.[10] Finally, Governor Clinton called on the state legislature for help. James Duane introduced a bill into the senate which added twenty

New York City residents to the regents. Apparently some legislators balked, so another thirteen regents from Albany and rural
New York were added to the list. The bill also reduced the
quorum to nine. "They were all good Columbia men," writes
Sherwood of the twenty city residents; and their nomination combined with the lowered quorum gave Columbia "autocratic control" over the "whole State system" of education.[11] Actually what
had happened was that the legislature had made it possible for
New York City's professional elite to dominate both Columbia
and the university, if the other regents let them. They did.

From 1784 through the spring of 1787, when the university was
reorganized, over sixty different men attended meetings of the
regents.[12] But nineteen predominated, two-thirds of whom had
been named in the second piece of legislation. To a man the "nineteen" lived in New York City. A few had close ties to King's
College, mostly as alumni. But there were still striking differences
between the regents of Columbia and the governors of King's
College. Two-thirds of the "nineteen" were not Episcopalians. Of
the seven clergymen, only one was an Episcopalian. Of the twelve
laymen, only two ever served as a warden or vestryman of Trinity
Church, each for a year. Indeed, the largest number were Presbyterians, including the chancellor, secretary, and treasurer of the
university. Moreover, most of the "nineteen" were hearty revolutionaries. And none was a merchant. Clergymen, lawyers, politicians, doctors, and educators composed the group, with doctors
and college professors assuming an importance denied them at
King's College. In fact, members of the liberal arts faculty not
only sat as regents but throughout the 1780s and 1790s were delegated much more responsibility for running the college than had
been the case before the Revolution. Finally, while a majority of
the "nineteen" were "well-to-do" or "wealthy" or belonged to
"prominent old families," the group could hardly match the
King's College governors either in wealth or social status.[13]

In 1784 the regents announced proudly that a university had
been founded "on the most liberal and comprehensive principles,
extending its privileges to every denomination of mankind, unfet-
tered by tests, preference, or discrimination." Nothing conveyed

better both the eclipse of the Episcopal establishment and the vision of the new leaders than the recommendation of a committee of regents for president of the university. They proposed as candidates three distinguished Englishmen: Joseph Priestly, the renowned chemist, Richard Price, noted writer on politics, morals, and economics and an opponent of the war against the American revolutionaries, and John Jebb, an educational and political reformer. While Jebb was an Anglican cleric, Priestly and Price were dissenting ministers and had been tutors at England's dissenting academies. All three men were especially well known for their liberal religious beliefs, which were unitarian in nature.[14]

Plans for hiring a president were tabled, officially due to financial stringency, but the regents' vision and ambitions surfaced again in a blueprint for establishing professorships. The scheme provided for four faculties—arts, law, divinity, and medicine—and a group of "extra professorships," in the French, German, low Dutch, and Oriental languages, civil history, architecture, commerce, agriculture, music, and painting. The arts faculty of seven professors and the medical faculty of eight would teach courses much like those at King's College, while a law faculty of three would lecture on the "law of Nature and Nations," Roman civil law, and municipal law. The faculty of divinity was to be formed of those professorships endowed by the "different Religious Societies within the State," pursuant to the act creating the university. It was a bold plan, one against which the college's progress was measured during the next several years. While it incorporated the four faculties which had traditionally composed European universities, some of the professorships, especially most of the extra professorships, reflected innovative currents in eighteenth-century higher education. Moreover, the divinity faculty was organized in a novel manner, although no religious group took advantage of the opportunity to endow a professorship before the university was reorganized in 1787. Brimming with enthusiasm for America's wartime ally and surmising that France might become a lucrative source of contributions, the regents had appointed a professor of the French language at their very first meeting. Now they rapidly filled most of the professorships in the arts and medicine and two of the extra professorships (Oriental and German languages). In several cases professors "doubled up." [15]

At the same time the regents sought funds with which to pay the professors, to repair the college building, which had suffered badly in the hands of the British army, and to replace the library collection and the scientific equipment, which had largely disappeared.[16] A surprisingly large portion of the college's pre-Revolutionary estate survived the social and financial dislocations of the war, but it took quite a while to straighten it out. In the meantime, wonder of wonders, the regents succeeded in persuading the state legislature to grant Columbia £2,552, the first public funds voted the college since 1753. On top of that, both the state legislature and the Continental Congress (which was meeting in New York) suspended "public business" on the day of Columbia's first commencement (1786), so that they could "support the important interests of Education by their countenance. . . ." The governor of New York and the state legislators even marched in the commencement procession. Columbia, it appeared, had finally gained the public stature that had eluded it for so long.[17]

But there was a snag. The regents discovered that some New Yorkers were less than charmed with the direction of events. Uneasiness about the regency dated from 1784, when a few rural legislators resisted the grant of funds for rebuilding Columbia and the revisions which reduced the quorum and vastly increased the number of regents from New York City. Little happened during the intervening years to allay their apprehensions. On only one occasion did the regents give formal attention to meeting the educational needs of the state other than by strengthening Columbia's educational program; in 1785 they appointed a committee to examine "Ways and Means of promoting literature throughout the State," from which nothing was ever heard. Moreover, the regents appear to have interpreted their responsibility to include higher education only. This attitude distressed parents and educators who considered the founding of schools and academies more pertinent to their own aspirations. Finally, even the regents admitted that the domination of the regency by a rather small group of urbanites "excited jealousy and dissatisfaction," which was hardly conducive to the "interest of literature." [18]

In 1787 a committee of regents, headed by the ever present James Duane, proposed that control of higher education in the state be decentralized. Each college should be "entrusted to a distinct Corporation with competent powers and privileges, under such subordination to the Regents as shall be thought wise and Salutary." A single body of regents was simply not up to the task of managing several colleges scattered about the state. The committee also recommended that provision be made for encouraging the founding of academies and for "erecting Public Schools." Duane's committee drafted a bill which Alexander Hamilton, a committee member, presented to the assembly. Several days later a second bill, also aimed at reforming the regency, was introduced into the senate by Ezra L'Hommedieu, a regent but a Long Islander who was not among the "nineteen." [19]

The bills differed in several respects, the most consequential of which was L'Hommedieu's stipulation that the trustees of each college be appointed by the state legislature. [20] William Livingston had proposed much the same arrangement thirty-five years earlier. Its implications for shifting control of Columbia displeased the New York City interests who dominated the college no less in 1787 than at mid-century. The regents were willing to forego responsibility for overseeing secondary and higher education throughout the state so that they could concentrate on the plum in the educational pie, but to surrender control of Columbia at the same time defeated their purpose. The regents put Duane, Hamilton, L'Hommedieu, and three others on a committee and asked them to seek a compromise. [21]

The intricacies of the negotiations which followed are not known to us, but the resulting act satisfied the New York City men who dominated the regency. In effect, they gave up any influence in the state university in return for strengthening their control of Columbia College. A new group of men (which included only two of the "nineteen") became regents, two of them ex officio, the rest to be replaced by legislative appointment. It was not an especially different kind of group from the "nineteen," except for two factors: college professors were excluded by law from becoming regents, apparently reflecting some resentment toward the influence exercised by Columbia professors in running their own college; and only a handful of the regents lived in New York City. The regents were empowered to incorporate (but not found) new academies and colleges in the state, to confer doctoral degrees, and to inspect and report yearly to the legislature on all colleges, academies, and schools in the state. They would not, however, actually run the various colleges and academies. This power was turned over to private groups of self-perpetuating trustees at each institution, just as the "nineteen" had hoped for.[22]

In the short run, the significance of the act for Columbia College was to limit the responsibilities of the men who managed the institution, not to alter its character or control. Now they could do what they had been doing for the past three years without opening themselves up to criticism for maintaining an urban cliquishness or for neglecting their other duties. The act revived the charter of 1754 and converted seventeen of the "nineteen" into trustees of Columbia. While twelve trustees were added to their ranks, all but one of the men who dominated the trustees meetings for the next three years (1787–1789) had been among the "nineteen." Even the treasurer and secretary of the regents, both Presbyterians, continued as treasurer and clerk under the trustees. In the latter 1780s, as in the middle 1780s, Columbia was managed by an urban, interdenominational, professional elite, among whom Episcopalians formed a minority.

In the longer run, two consequences of the 1787 act stand out. First, the act confirmed Columbia's status as an urban, not a state-wide institution, under private, not public control. At mid-century King's College had been conceived as a provincial institution, a goal symbolized by the name given its governing board: "The Governors of the College of the Province of New York." Although the triumvirate failed in its bid to put the college under legislative domination, twenty ex officio members were placed on its board, the majority of them state judicial and political officials. In 1784 the college had been reestablished as the "Mother" of the

University of the State of New York, under the direction of state-appointed regents from all counties in New York. And in 1787 Ezra L'Hommedieu had proposed to make its trustees legislative appointees. Yet, all along it had functioned mainly as an urban institution, located in New York City, managed by city leaders, even attended primarily by residents of the city and surrounding area. Now that fact was recognized legally. The act dropped all ex officio positions on the board, put only city residents on it, renamed them "*The Trustees of* Columbia College, *in the City of* New-York," and specified that meetings be held in the city. Columbia's ties to the state were not severed. The regents inspected the college yearly, and the legislature responded on more than one occasion to Columbia's pleas for financial assistance. It was, after all, an age in which the distinctions between public and private institutions remained fuzzy.[23] But in 1787 the college looked toward a future where it could never be thought of as "State College," but only as one of several privately controlled colleges in the state, one whose fortunes were intimately linked with the fortunes of New York City.

A second outgrowth of the 1787 legislation was a modest drift back toward Episcopalianism. Through a process of selective attendance and co-optation, Episcopalians soon composed a majority of the active trustees. In 1800 an Episcopal clergyman took over the reins of Columbia for the first time since the Revolution. In the early nineteenth century Columbia once again found itself the target of accusations that it was a sectarian college.[24] But the shift during the 1790s was neither dramatic nor subject to contention. Non-Episcopalians continued to attend trustees meetings in significant numbers and play important roles. Indeed, of the three clerics named to the board during the 1790s, two were Presbyterians, one Dutch Reformed. Nor did the composition of the faculty change radically. In 1797 the liberal arts faculty of eight included a Presbyterian clergyman, a Lutheran clergyman, a prominent Dutch Reformed layman, and a Presbyterian layman. Moreover, Presbyterians and Dutch churchmen remained conspicuous figures in the operation of the college in the early nineteenth century. A trustees committee of six which overhauled the educational program in 1810 included three Presbyterian ministers and one Dutch Reformed minister. From 1811 to 1816 a Presbyterian minister even exercised most of the powers of the presidency, serving as provost. After Bishop Samuel Provoost's resignation as chairman of the board of trustees in 1801, two Dutch churchmen and a Presbyterian filled the post successively during the next twenty-two years.[25]

The blend of old and new in the post-Revolutionary years was symbolized by the man named president of Columbia in 1787, William Samuel Johnson. What more testimony could one want of Columbia's continuity with King's College than to have Samuel Johnson's son become the first president of Columbia. It was a kind of "hereditary succession," remarked Charles Inglis, who always thought of things in traditional terms. An Episcopalian and a Johnson once again ruled over New York's college after the aberrations of the mid-1780s. When William Samuel Johnson reminded graduating seniors that they must never forget their duty to God, to their neighbors, and to themselves, he conveyed a message that many a King's College student had heard almost word for word from his father three decades earlier.[26]

Yet William Samuel Johnson represented much that was different as well as much that was familiar about Columbia. If he was an Episcopalian, he was a layman. His father would have been appalled at the loss of religious perspective implied in the appointment of a lawyer to head a college. Moreover, while Samuel Johnson was a monarchist who deplored popular rule, William Samuel Johnson was a republican who supported the Revolution (albeit reluctantly at first), sat in the Continental Congress, and represented Connecticut at the Constitutional Convention of 1787. Finally, while Samuel Johnson was a partisan, his son was a conciliator. Samuel Johnson fought doggedly to advance the "right" causes, among which nothing surpassed the Episcopal church in importance. In so doing he incited much enmity toward himself and his college. William Samuel Johnson's whole life, writes his biographer, "was a quest for harmony and peace. Between Old Light and New Light, between England and America, between Connecticut and Pennsylvania, between North and South, be-

William Samuel Johnson, President of Columbia College 1787–1800
The painting is by S. L. Waldo after Gilbert Stuart
CREDIT: COLUMBIANA, COLUMBIA UNIVERSITY

tween the past as represented by the old Confederation, and the future as forecast in the new Constitution, he helped to bring about a new order, understanding and good will." [27]

By simply accepting the presidency Johnson participated in a conciliatory measure. The presidency posed a ticklish issue for

Columbia's leaders. The act of 1787, which revived the original charter, specifically repudiated the clauses in the charter which required that the president be an Episcopalian and that the college prayers be drawn from the Episcopal liturgy. Now the trustees could appoint whomever they wished. However, the original bargain with Trinity Church stipulated that if anyone other than an Episcopalian was named president, the college would have to return Trinity's gift of land.[28] The trustees resolved the problem by appointing an Episcopalian, but a layman whose reputation was based on his political and legal accomplishments.

A devoted Episcopalian William Samuel Johnson may have been, but he rarely let his denominational loyalties intrude upon his academic responsibilities. The same was true of his political views. He was a Federalist, or, as Alexander Hamilton put it when listing the qualifications for a successor to Johnson in 1800, his politics were of the "right sort." But Johnson kept his politics largely out of his presidency. In fact, his thirteen-year presidency was remarkably free of public contention. Johnson's biographer examined 3,500 issues of New York newspapers published between 1787 and 1800 and failed to turn up a single instance where Columbia was criticized for favoring class or political interests. Princeton, Yale, and Union, in contrast, were all attacked in the Republican press for Federalist partisanship.[29] Under Johnson's leadership Columbia enjoyed a degree of public acceptance which it had never known under his father.

In 1784 King's College had, in a sense, been revolutionized. But the college quickly was restored to urban hands. In other, more gradual ways it recaptured parts of the past from which it had been cut off by act of legislature. But Columbia was also separated from King's College by a decade of political and social turbulence, whose impact could not be escaped. If the old charter was revived, the old college was not resurrected. William Samuel Johnson enjoyed presiding over Columbia in 1790. Myles Cooper would not have. One can understand that fact better after looking at the Columbia students and the nature of their educational experience.

16.

THE FLOWERING OF AN
URBAN INSTITUTION

WEDNESDAY, MAY 2, 1792, was a day that John Barent Johnson had anticipated for weeks. A few days earlier he had passed his examination—"our last examination at College," he took care to note in his diary. Now it was commencement day. He had labored over his valedictory address for two months, though he had hardly let this responsibility interfere with either his studies or the round of social events that marked his senior year: attending balls, going to the theater, innumerable conversations with the several young ladies he found especially appealing. Commencement day, in fact, was not terribly different from any other day. He delivered his address, received his degree, dined with President Johnson, visited Miss Lefferts (an amiable lady of "great worth," though on the "pious" side), and supped with "some Gentlemen" in town.[1]

One wonders what stood out in John Barent Johnson's mind when he looked back on his college days. What impresses one who has studied King's College is the personal freedom he enjoyed and the manner in which he used it. There is a vitality and richness about his undergraduate experience that makes the early 1790s seem like the most attractive time of any to have attended King's College or Columbia in the eighteenth century.

The changes described so far in the control of King's College and Columbia after the Revolution could not help but have an effect on the kinds and numbers of students attracted by the college. New Yorkers could plainly see that it was now supported by a much greater variety of people than previously: Presbyterians as well as Episcopalians, elected legislators as well as executive appointees, Revolutionary heroes (even George Washington paid his respects, attending the commencement in 1787) as well as church bishops.

Moreover, the new men who ran Columbia in the 1780s brought to the task an aggressive competitiveness that formerly had characterized the leaders of Princeton, not King's College. They admitted students into advanced classes, rushed out the first graduating class two years after the college reopened, and charged competitive fees. In fact, in 1784 the regents established a policy that fees for tuition and room rent should not exceed those at Princeton. Their successors were still implementing the policy in the 1790s, much to the chagrin of the faculty. The latter complained that Columbia's tuition was "disreputably cheap," meaning, of course, that they thought their own incomes were disreputably low.[2] Charges for board presented the most serious problem. They were easily the biggest item in a student's budget. Since the cost of food was higher in the city than the country, especially "during the extreme seasons," the regents feared that the "extraordinary Expence" of board would prevent Columbia from ever attracting many students. One response was to lower the cost (and thus the quality) of the board to just above the point that would produce a "riotous disposition" among the students. Before the Revolution King's College had charged the highest total fees for tuition, room, and board of any colonial college. In 1785 the college was able to advertise that the regents had rendered "the course of education as cheap in this College as it is in any other." [3]

Broader support and lower costs resulted in a striking increase in the number of students. By 1787 there were about forty liberal arts pupils. By 1791 there were over ninety, about twice as many as at any point before the Revolution. Between 1791 and 1796 more liberal arts students graduated from Columbia than had ever graduated from King's College. The regents informed the legislature in 1793 that Columbia was in "a flourishing condition" and that its number of undergraduates was "very respectable." [4]

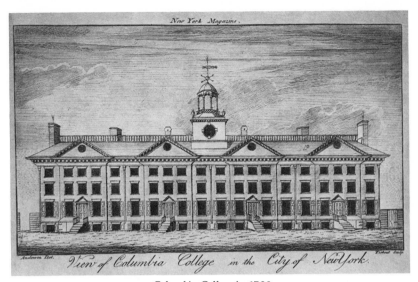

Columbia College in 1790
The picture was drawn by A. Anderson and engraved by Cornelius Tiebout.
CREDIT: COLUMBIANA, COLUMBIA UNIVERSITY

A moderate climb in numbers was matched by a modest shift in makeup. A little over forty liberal arts pupils matriculated under the regency (1784–1786), then just over forty entered during the first two years under the trustees (1787–1788).[5] Apparently the legislation of 1787 had no more immediate impact on the students than on the trustees, since there were few differences between the matriculants of 1784–1786 and those of 1787–1788. Overall the eighty-three students differed from the King's College pupils in several ways. Over 65 percent of the King's College students were Episcopalians, while the rest belonged mainly to the Dutch church. In the 1780s Episcopalians and Dutch Reformed continued to form the largest groups, but neither group comprised a majority, and Presbyterians formed a significant minority. Before the Revolution no more than two of the students who became ministers served in non–Episcopal churches. After the Revolution at least twelve of the fifteen students who joined the clergy belonged to non–Episcopal churches, half of them the Dutch church, a quarter the Presbyterian church, the rest the Baptist,

German Reformed, and Associate Reformed churches. What happened to the religious complexion of the students in the 1790s has not been researched. Chances are that the percentage of Episcopalian students increased. But it is interesting to note that Episcopalians composed only a handful of the seventeen students in the class of 1792, the last class studied. None of the four students in the class of 1792 who became ministers was Episcopalian. An examination of the students thus sustains the impression one gets by looking at the regents and the trustees. During the 1780s and early 1790s Columbia was much less an Episcopalian institution than King's College, especially when compared to King's College in the 1770s. After the Revolution Dutch churchmen continued to participate in the life of the institution, while Presbyterians, who had spurned King's College, helped manage Columbia and sent their sons there.

The profile of students in the classes of 1786 through 1792 also mirrors, though much less decisively, the diminished role of merchants and the expanded role of professionals in managing the college. Among fathers of undergraduates, there was probably a slight shift toward professionals and away from men who were in commerce or were artisan-entrepreneurs. Among students, the professions attracted a majority after the Revolution, compared to about two-fifths at King's College (law again easily outdrawing medicine or the ministry). Conversely, fewer alumni pursued vocations in commerce, manufacturing, or finance, or became artisans. Overall Columbia had closer ties than King's College to the professions and weaker ties to the mercantile community.

Columbia students also were older and more likely to graduate than pupils at King's College. The median age of King's College students was fourteen and one-half at entry and eighteen and one-half at graduation. At Columbia the median ages were sixteen and twenty, respectively. Just over half the King's College matriculants graduated. At Columbia the figure was 80 percent, and it remained high (about 75 percent) during the 1790s. The higher rate of graduation reflected both the absence of a serious disruption like the Revolution and the fact that boys heading for the ministry and law were more likely to stay through graduation than prospective merchants.

On other counts the Columbia students do not seem especially different from their counterparts at King's College. Their social class backgrounds were similar. So were their areas of residence at the time they matriculated.[6] Like the King's College undergraduates, a majority (60 percent) of the Columbia students lived in New York City or on Manhattan Island to the north of the city. Almost another fifth (18 percent) resided in other parts of the state. However, the latter did not come from Westchester and the other southern counties which had supplied a number of undergraduates at King's College, but from the northern counties: Orange, Dutchess, Columbia, Albany, Washington. Although Columbia still was neither well known nor well patronized outside New York City, it easily surpassed King's College in its appeal to non-Episcopalians who populated the more remote parts of the state.[7] The balance of students, about a fifth, came from outside the state. Virginia furnished the largest number (6 percent), while the remaining handful lived in New Jersey, South Carolina, the West Indies, and Pennsylvania. Thus, Columbia in the 1780s, like King's College, attracted a small number of students from distant areas, who provided a cosmopolitan touch to a predominantly local student body. However, in the 1790s this trickle of students gradually dried up. In 1800 seventy-eight of the eighty-two Columbia undergraduates resided in New York State, while three came from New Jersey, and one from St. Croix in the West Indies.[8]

The interplay of continuity and change in the control of the post-Revolutionary college and in the kinds of undergraduates it attracted also extended to the nature of the students' educational experience. The most decisive break with the past was the expiration of the collegiate way of living. It had never functioned as effectively as Samuel Johnson and Myles Cooper would have wished. After the Revolution it broke down altogether, and no one seems to have cared. In 1784 the college building was too dilapidated even for students to live in. According to DeWitt Clinton, Columbia's first matriculant, "apartments in the old City Hall were provided for the temporary accommodation of the College, until it was rendered fit for our reception." However, as the building underwent repair, it was the faculty who moved in, not the students. In 1787 thirty-four of the thirty-nine students were sleeping and eating "in the City." The bell in the cupola continued to toll morning prayers, but most students could no longer hear it.[9] In the 1790s visitors recorded that no students lived in the college building, although some retained studies there. If students did live at the college, their numbers were small. There were accommodations for only a fraction of the undergraduates. Thus Columbia entered the nineteenth century as a school for day students, who lived at home or lodged in the city. Three decades later the situation had not changed.[10]

The statutes of 1785 and 1788 reflected the breakdown of traditional living patterns. Unlike Myles Cooper's statutes, the statutes of 1785 did not require that students live or eat at the college. Nor did they have to wear gowns. But all students did have to attend a general roll call early each morning and remain at the college throughout the day, supposedly in their rooms when they were not at classes or meals. Boarders were to be present for an evening roll call every other night at 10:00 P.M., at which time the gates were locked. Even these requirements were dropped when the statutes were revised in 1788. Students now found that much of the day as well as the evenings and the nights were theirs to do as they pleased.[11]

What remained were bits and pieces of the collegiate way. The wearing of gowns was revived in 1787, first among the president and faculty, then among the students. The undergraduates themselves asked to wear gowns, so as "to be distinguished in their dress from the rest of their fellow citizens. . . ." It is not clear how regular a practice this became. There is no evidence that penalties were imposed for not donning one's gown. Attendance at morning and evening prayers was mandatory, unless one was officially excused by his parents. In 1791 a committee of trustees recommended that attendance at prayers be dispensed with, since many students lived "at a considerable distance," but the board

DeWitt Clinton (B.A., Columbia College, 1786)
Clinton was governor of New York State, mayor of New York City, and a leading
proponent of the construction of the Erie Canal.
CREDIT: COLUMBIANA, COLUMBIA UNIVERSITY

stood pat on the issue. Professors of required courses were supposed to take roll at each class. Small fines were assessed with
some regularity for missing prayers and classes or for failing to do
assigned exercises. President Johnson collected an average of five

hundred fines a year during the 1790s, or five to ten fines per student each year.[12]

In these and other ways the faculty sought to maintain discipline. John Kemp, professor of mathematics and natural philosophy, earned a reputation as the "chief prop" of discipline at the college. His "tyrannical Government over the Students" made quite an impression on one student during the relatively strict days of the mid-1780s. But Myles Cooper's brand of discipline—comprehensive, occasionally harsh, and heavily reliant on tactics such as disgrace and confinement—seems not to have survived his departure. The president should "be of a disposition to maintain discipline without *undue austerity* . . . ," noted trustee Alexander Hamilton, who knew from his King's College days what austere discipline could be like.[13] In any case, the students were older, and the faculty was no longer responsible for overseeing their every move. For their part, the students no longer felt cramped by the small social and psychological space afforded by the college building. Prankishness seems to have declined noticeably.

It is difficult to ascertain just why the character of undergraduate life changed so dramatically after the Revolution. Practical matters played a big part. At first the building was in disrepair. Then the growth of both the faculty and the student body placed such a demand on space that the perpetuation of the collegiate way of living would have required much new construction. It was also a matter of priorities. In 1784 the regents may have contemplated bedding and boarding all the students at the college. But they much preferred spending their limited funds on faculty, equipment, and rooms for classes, laboratories, and public exercises. In 1792 the trustees estimated that they needed £16,000 to improve the physical plant and to upgrade the quality and expand the range of the educational program. Not a pound was designated for dormitory space. By the early nineteenth century if the trustees talked at all about improving the accommodations for students, what they meant were studies where undergraduates could work during the day.[14]

Priorities reflect the attitudes and values of the decision-makers and the options that are open to them. Situated in a city where lodgings were available and where the parents and relatives of many students resided, Columbia could operate rather easily as a day school. Some students undoubtedly preferred it that way, for reasons of personal freedom, cost, and the quality of food and accommodations. On the other hand, no one among the post-Revolutionary regents, trustees, and faculty stood up in defense of the collegiate way. Despite the continuing commitment to training virtuous men, the academic stage was not dominated by a religious figure—such as Samuel Johnson or Myles Cooper—who was deeply attached to the vision of faculty and students as a tightly knit social, moral, and religious community. Indeed, the professors who took turns presiding over the college in the mid-1780s had been trained at German and Scottish universities which had no tradition of collegiate living. As for fears that the students would give in to idleness and to the immoral temptations of the city, these were probably diminished by the high percentage of undergraduates living with parents or relatives and by the fact that the students were older.

The breakdown of the collegiate way was accompanied by the flowering of an important undergraduate institution: the literary society. While students at Harvard, Yale, and Princeton had organized formal societies for literary and debating purposes before the Revolution, nothing comparable had developed at King's College. Columbia students, along with several city residents, organized a "Society for the purpose of improving themselves in Polite Literature" barely three months after the first undergraduate matriculated in 1784. The regents gave their approval and permitted the society to deposit its collection of books in the college library (after all, it was empty).[15]

The Columbia College Society quickly became a thriving institution. Its ranks included those undergraduates admitted to membership as well as an indeterminable number of recent alumni and other young men living in the city.[16] John Barent Johnson belonged to the society throughout his four years at college. During his first two years he labored over many a composition, address, or dispute which he presented at the weekly Thursday evening meetings. By his senior year he was attending sporadically.

Whether the society had slowed its pace or whether Johnson simply preferred to spend his evenings listening to Miss Salter play
the harpsichord or chatting with Miss Lefferts or Miss Fowler
about novels is hard to say. The society offered a good opportunity to sharpen one's skills at writing, orating, and debating.
"Nothing can be more incumbent on and more beneficial to a person in a country like ours than an incessant study and exercise of
Eloquence," commented one undergraduate. However, the same
student decided that his fellow students made *"carping* and not
judicious critics" when he submitted a composition which had
been previously corrected by President Johnson and was then
faulted by society members for "those very corrections." [17]

The Columbia College Society died out in the mid-1790s, but a
"great number" of other short-lived societies materialized during
Columbia's first decade. Apparently most were based in the city
rather than at the college, but students frequently participated in
their deliberations. While an undergraduate, John Barent Johnson
belonged to a theological society and was vice-president of the
Belles Lettres Association. Several undergraduates and a good
many recent alumni belonged to the Uranian Society, which was
formed about 1788. Members assembled each Tuesday evening in
the city to debate various topics, mostly political in nature:
"Would the election of the great judicial officers of this State by
the people be adviseable?" "Was it good policy in the National Assembly of France to abolish all titles of Nobility?" "Has the
American Revolution tended to improve the minds of the people?"
Members also presented and criticized literary compositions. True
to form, the Uranian Society soon expired, but the society phenomenon itself endured. In 1802 Columbia students organized the
college's first permanent literary society for undergraduates, the
Philolexian Society.[18]

The emergence of literary societies which embraced both undergraduates and townspeople reflected the increasing integration
of the college community with the urban community. Students
now moved freely and frequently back and forth between the two
communities and drew heavily on each for the ingredients that
composed their undergraduate lives. It was not an especially un-

usual day for John Barent Johnson to arise at 7:00 A.M., study, attend a medical lecture, read a Latin assignment, take the ferry to Long Island in the afternoon, ride horseback and visit friends, recross to Manhattan, attend the theater, arrive home past 10:00 P.M., and go to bed at 11:00 P.M. This particular day was not a Saturday but a Wednesday in November during the regular school session. On a typical Wednesday in the summer he arose at 5:00 A.M., attended lectures in rhetoric and in the classical languages, watched several people get baptized in the Hudson River, went to St. Paul's Chapel where he listened to a sermon addressed to the Masons, studied in the afternoon, took a walk, spent much of the evening working on an address for the Columbia College Society, and went to bed at 11:00 P.M. During his four years at Columbia, he attended dancing school, sessions of the United States Congress, innumerable plays, a book auction, dozens of sermons, the city library, various parties and dances, meetings of the several societies to which he belonged, a fire, and his barber. He frequently took walks in the city, purchased clothes, books, newspapers, and various supplies, called on friends, dined and supped with many acquaintances of his own and his parents' generation, escorted ladies here and there, and spent afternoons or evenings at their homes. With the distinction between college life and city life so thin, it is hardly surprising that some students felt the need of gowns to distinguish themselves from their fellow citizens.[19]

It is symbolic of the new order of things that the faculty now taught and lived in quarters that previously had housed the students. In 1784 the regents had set their sights on turning Columbia into a European-like university. This meant creating new professorships and new faculties and attracting men of stature to the posts, not constructing apartments for undergraduates. These were ambitious plans for such a fledgling institution. When the trustees took over Columbia in 1787 they surveyed the academic landscape and found that the educational program fell well short of the regents' goals. While just one of the liberal arts professorships was "unsupplied," the other six positions were held by three men. There was only one "extra" professor (not ten), only three medical professors (not seven), and there were no professors in law or divinity.[20] Medical instruction was languishing. Not a single medical student graduated from Columbia during the 1780s.

By 1795 Columbia was beginning to look like the university envisioned by the regents a decade earlier. Working in conjunction with the regents and the Medical Society of New York, the trustees refounded the medical school, established eight medical professorships, recruited a faculty, set up a degree program, and, by 1795, had conferred eleven M.D.'s. The board also revamped and expanded the faculty of arts, aided handsomely by a five-year grant of £750 per annum from the state legislature to support new professorships. In 1795 the faculty of arts comprised eight professors who held eleven professorships, in moral philosophy and logic, rhetoric and belles lettres, Greek and Latin, Grecian and Roman antiquities, French, Oriental languages, law, geography, mathematics, natural philosophy and astronomy, and natural history, chemistry, and agriculture.[21] The professorships in law and in natural history, chemistry, and agriculture were the newest and most distinctive. James Kent, later a renowned jurist and chief justice of the New York Supreme Court, lectured on the political history of the United States, the Constitution and the three branches of government, the state constitutions, the municipal laws of New York, and the rights of property. Only by studying the United States' own history and constitutions, asserted Kent, could prospective lawyers and statesmen "imbibe the principles of Republican Government from pure fountains. . . ." Samuel Latham Mitchill, a versatile, progressive, and widely respected scientist, ranged over such topics as earthquakes, lightning, mineral springs, limestone, manure, and milk as he lectured on geology, meteorology, hydrography, mineralogy, botany, and zoology. Columbia received a state grant of $500 to provide Mitchill with a proper "Chemical apparatus." [22]

However, a review of professorships may tell more about professorial aspirations and public image making than about what undergraduates actually were studying. For instance, three of the professorships instituted in 1792 were not exactly academic drawing cards. The professor of French complained that his class was "not only thin but very irregularly attended . . . ," since it was not a required course. The professor of Oriental languages taught Hebrew to small numbers of divinity students, few of them undergraduates at Columbia. In its first year James Kent's imaginative and challenging course on law attracted seven Columbia students and thirty-six private gentlemen, the latter chiefly lawyers and law students. The next year enrollment was down to two Columbia students and a few law clerks. The third year no one appeared for the course. Kent resigned in 1798. All three professorships were discontinued when state funds ran out at the close of the decade.[23]

How different, then, was the curriculum during Columbia's first decade from that at King's College? [24] The Revolution did not dethrone the classics. Columbia students devoted more time to Greek and Latin language and literature than to any other subject. Freshmen attended Greek and Latin class twice a day, studied grammar, perused such works as Xenophon's *Cyropaedia* and Livy's *History of Rome*, and prepared written exercises in Latin almost daily. The written exercises continued apace during the sophomore year, but the class met just once a day. Sallust, Demosthenes, Homer, and Virgil gained most of the sophomores' attention. Ideally the undergraduates had mastered Latin and Greek grammar by the beginning of their junior year. If so, the juniors read various classical works and the professor lectured twice a week on their "peculiar beauties." Seniors met once a week to go over *Longinus on the Sublime*, Cicero's *Orations*, and other works chosen to fit in with their studies in moral philosophy and rhetoric.[25]

The study of the classics did not proceed without resistance and controversy. As always, professors complained that entering students were ill prepared, especially those who were accepted into advanced classes during the 1780s. But foot dragging on the part of the students seems to have increased after the Revolution. For one thing, it was difficult to compel a close attention to Latin and Greek grammar when students spent so little of their time under faculty supervision.[26] For another, resistance to studying classical languages was encouraged by support from outside the college. "The less time we consume in acquiring those languages the better," asserted one Columbia undergraduate. In so doing, he echoed a point of view that had been expressed on several occasions in the press. "Some argued seriously against it ["classical learning"] as altogether useless," lamented the professor of Greek and Latin, "whilst others more petulantly scoffed at it, even in the public papers, as a prejudice derived from our effete and doating mother country or one of her trammels which still remain to be broken." [27] Hugh Williamson, a political, scientific, and literary figure of some repute, openly questioned President Johnson in the *New York Packet* about why, at the very time that Americans were "shaking off the chains of political prejudice and making improvements in useful knowledge . . . ," students should "continue to be deceived and led astray by the mystic charm of ancient opinion." Columbia should replace Latin and Greek with a course in "Practical Philosophy," whereby students would learn, among other things, the chemical principles involved in farming and in such mechanical arts as brewing and tanning.[28] Other critics assailed the languages without demeaning classical literature, which could be read in English translation.

  Despite the attacks, there was strong support for the classical languages at Columbia. But the issue troubled some members of the Columbia community. In 1791 a committee of trustees considered whether students might be admitted without previous knowledge of Greek and whether, indeed, they might graduate without studying Greek. The committee was unable to resolve its "variance in Opinion." A year later the trustees instituted a professorship in natural history, chemistry, and agriculture which distinctly resembled the one proposed by Williamson, particularly in Samuel Latham Mitchill's discussions on the chemistry of agriculture and on the arts of brewing, distilling, dyeing, bleaching, tanning leather, and making potash, bread, glass, and sugar.[29] Obviously, undergraduates continued to study Latin and Greek. With what intensity and success it is difficult to tell. Some students relished it.[30] Others undoubtedly despised it. Probably a good many would simply agree with one Columbia alumnus who observed that he learned "so much of the ancient languages as to be able to understand their authors in the original, without, however, preferring them to a good English translation. . . ." [31]

Studies in mathematics and in English grammar, rhetoric, and belles lettres took the most student time after classical languages and literature. While freshmen tussled with Latin and Greek grammar twice a day, they met twice a week to study English and rhetoric. Still, Columbia pupils devoted a refreshingly large amount of time to mastering the English language, under no less a figure than the college president from 1787 to 1795. Generally, undergraduates studied English grammar, rhetoric, and belles lettres for two years, while the other two years they periodically wrote compositions in English or Latin or repeated "some proper piece of English or Latin" in the college hall before the students and the faculty. Quite a few students also worked on their rhetorical skills at weekly meetings of the Columbia College Society. Freshmen started the regular program with English grammar, using Noah Webster's text, among others. Then Hugh Blair's *Lectures on Rhetoric and Belles Lettres* formed the backbone of lengthy studies in the historical development of language (especially English), in the art of writing and speaking English "with propriety, elegance, and force," and in the "principles of true taste and the rules of just criticism." The latter equipped students to "judge properly of each species of composition in every branch of elegant literature. . . ." Johnson's pupils also read belles lettres by the likes of Oliver Goldsmith, Laurence Sterne, and the English Samuel Johnson, if we can judge by John Barent Johnson's experience. During the same period the students frequently prepared English compositions or practiced translating Latin passages into English without losing the spirit and elegance of the original. William Samuel Johnson used neo-Ciceronian texts in rhetoric by John Holmes and John Stirling, but his concern with literary taste and criticism reflected the influence of the new rhetoric which had emerged in eighteenth-century Britain. Indeed, Hugh Blair, whose text was pored over by Columbia students, was one of its leading spokesmen. [32]

Mathematics was initially a two-year program, then was extended to three years in 1789. Freshmen studied arithmetic and algebra. Sophomores learned geometry, plane trigonometry, navigation, and surveying. Juniors completed the mathematics sequence with conic sections, spherical trigonometry, advanced algebra, and differential calculus. While not an unusual program, it was undoubtedly more demanding than that pursued by King's College students. John Kemp, professor of mathematics and natural philosophy, was an able mathematician and well deserved the praise of one former student for being "indefatigable in his duties." [33]

The balance of the required curriculum included natural philosophy, geography, moral philosophy, and logic. The first three courses met three times a week for a year, while the once majestic subject of logic now met weekly for a year. In natural philosophy John Kemp followed the pattern of his King's College predecessors, lecturing on mechanics, hydrostatics, hydraulics, pneumatics, optics, and astronomy. He concluded the course by investigating a subject which particularly intrigued many Americans, electricity and magnetism. Columbia purchased expensive and elaborate scientific equipment during the 1780s, so that Kemp had at his disposal a reflecting achromatic telescope, a compound microscope, a camera obscura, a "complete apparatus of mechanical powers," an "electrical machine," a special compass, and several other instruments. Kemp made the most of them. He reportedly conducted six hundred experiments each year.[34] Geography, moral philosophy, and logic were all taught by John Daniel Gros, a German Reformed clergyman from the Bavarian Palatinate who had studied at the universities of Marburg and Heidelberg and had migrated to the colonies in 1764. Gros's geography course was actually a blend of geography, chronology, history, and politics. He described the globe in "all general matters" and surveyed the "Rise, extent, and fall of Ancient Empires," ancient and modern chronology, the "present state of the World," and the "origin of the present States and Kingdoms, their extent, power, commerce, religion and customs." [35]

Moral philosophy was a broad ranging course of the kind that John Witherspoon had taught at Princeton for more than a decade. Unlike Samuel Johnson and Myles Cooper, who evince little civic concern in their texts on moral philosophy, Gros treated a great variety of political and social issues in his book, *Natural Principles of Rectitude*. He did not publish the work until 1795, the year he retired from the faculty, but it followed closely the course which he taught to one hundred thirty or so students during the previous decade. Gros was an unstinting rationalist who believed in an immutable law of right and wrong which it was man's duty to discover through his reason and to follow through his moral will. The founding of the United States he held up as an example of political rationalism in practice, a society constructed on principles of "natural justice." He hoped his book would become a means "to inflame the American youth with a true love for their country, with a spirit of patriotism worthy their great rights and privileges, as the free-born sons of the free and independent states of North-America." [36]

Gros divided moral philosophy into three parts. First he introduced the "natural and invariable principles of justice and equity" which should regulate all human conduct. Then he examined at great length "how those principles are to be applied to the various states of man." His text concludes with a brief section on the application of his principles to relationships among nations. For the latter, Gros drew on work of the Swiss jurist, Emerich de Vattel, and considered the natural rights of nations, such as public security and defense, the duties nations owe to themselves and to other nations, war, the rights of victors, diplomacy, and treaties.[37] Two-thirds of Gros's text (and undoubtedly much of his course) dealt with the second part of moral philosophy, which he divided into ethics, natural jurisprudence, general economy, and politics.

Gros treated ethics much as Samuel Johnson did. He examined man's duties to God, himself, and humanity. But Gros's discussions of jurisprudence, economy, and politics go well beyond Johnson's as he explored peoples' "rights in things," especially property rights, the principles governing interpersonal relationships, particularly those within the family, and the origin, nature, and organization of "civil society." Gros upheld the rights of property holders against any "levelling system," the right of husbands to "chief government" in the family, and the parental rights of teachers over students, though the latter should be exercised "with that sincerity, gentleness, assiduity, faithfulness, moderation and watchfulness, requisite in fathers who truly love their children." [38] Gros apparently was true to his own precepts, for one graduate characterized him as a "worthy and kind Father," while another recalled how Gros was "almost idolized by his pupils." Both slavery and capital punishment were criticized by Gros, perhaps sparking commencement addresses in 1793 by seniors "On the Inhumanity of the Slave Trade" and "On the Impropriety of Capital Punishments." In stark contrast to Johnson and Cooper, Gros lamented that "religious establishments have ever taken place." [39]

Gros spoke no less favorably of revolutionary France than of revolutionary America as a worthy example of a society founded on the "principles of nature." Yet, his republicanism is not as far removed as it might seem from the monarchism of Samuel Johnson and Myles Cooper. The key concept in his political philosophy, argues historian Wilson Smith, is duty.

> At the very center of Gros's concept of government is the governor, not the governed. . . . He does admit that the actual source of all power in the state is the people, but . . . the right to direct the moral action of the people lies in the government. Sovereignty resides in "the moral or public person of the state"; it is "the right of the public rulers."

Smith finds, appropriately so, a "thread of stern moral obligation to the state" running throughout Gros's text. If Gros, unlike Cooper, envisioned a point where violent resistance to established authority can be justified, what mattered to him in the post-Revolutionary years was "that Americans should perceive their political obligations and carry them out with integrity." [40]

There is no direct evidence about Gros's third course, logic, but his discussion of "logical truth" in *Natural Principles of Rectitude* sheds some light on his approach. Following in the footsteps of William Duncan, a proponent of the new logic and the author of the text used by Samuel Johnson, Gros delineated three different ways of determining truth. The first is experimental, by relying on the senses. The second is rational, by engaging in a proper mode of argumentation from first principles. The third is historical, by depending on the testimony of others. Gros explored the criteria for using each process. Experimental truth requires, among other things, that the mind be attentive, the sensory organs sound, and the object of sensation within a proper distance. Rational truth depends on first principles which are indubitable. The key to historical truth lies in reputable eye witnesses. Undoubtedly Gros, like most adherents of the new logic, emphasized inductive rather than deductive logic. Meanwhile, Robert Sanderson and the other Peripatetics whom Myles Cooper had esteemed were dropped from the Columbia curriculum. Neither Gros's text, nor the plan of education, nor the commencement programs, nor anything else, for that matter, indicates that the students engaged in syllogistic disputations.[41]

Just how frequently undergraduates supplemented this basic liberal arts program with "elective" courses is difficult to tell. The offering varied from year to year. At one time or another between 1784 and 1794 students might have selected courses in French, Hebrew, German, law, natural history and chemistry, and, in the medical school, botany, anatomy, plus several other subjects. Probably students could attend any course for which they were willing to pay the usual £2 or $5 fee. We know that some undergraduates studied French, law, and medicine. Several students, in fact, enrolled in the medical program while still undergraduates and attended medical lectures regularly. Undoubtedly a number of students elected Samuel Latham Mitchill's course in natural history, chemistry, and agriculture. The trustees thought well enough of the course to make it part of the required curriculum in the late 1790s, about the same time that Princeton instituted a professorship in chemistry and Yale made plans for a professorship in chemistry and natural history.[42]

Overall the curriculum during Columbia's first decade varied significantly from Myles Cooper's educational program without being notably innovative. Cooper's expulsion spelled the end of his Oxonian regime, especially his Aristotelianism, his boundless veneration for the classics, and his relative disdain for mathematics and science. Columbia's leaders restored some of the progressive strains that Samuel Johnson had introduced (but which had been eliminated or toned down by Cooper) and updated other parts of the educational program, particularly the study of rhetoric and moral philosophy. The result was not very different from the curriculum presided over by John Witherspoon at Princeton in the 1770s and 1780s, except for the absence of instruction in divinity.[43] Typically, some of the more unusual features of the curriculum, such as the courses in law and French, were not included in the required program and were the first to expire when funds ran short.

Yet the curriculum was still appreciably more progressive than during Myles Cooper's presidency. So, too, was the political message which permeated the educational program. "Study carefully the fundamental principles of civil government, especially of Republican Government," President William Samuel Johnson advised graduating seniors. An undergraduate concluded pointedly in one of his weekly essays that a review of ancient history indicated that as "mankind increased in civilization and knowledge, Monarchy was thrown off and a republican form of government established in its stead." [44] The *New York Daily Advertiser* reported in August 1788 that Columbia's "president and professors in their academical habits, followed by the students bearing different kinds of mathematical and astronomical instruments" marched in a procession celebrating the adoption of the new Constitution. They were preceded by a flag emblazoned with the motto: *"Science and liberty mutually support and adorn each other."* For Columbia people, as for many other Americans, a heightened sensitivity to personal liberty spilled over into antislavery sentiment. One might have expected it of the moral philosophy professor, John Daniel Gros. But the professor of Greek and Latin was even more vehement in his antipathy to human bondage. He attacked slavery in the newspapers and later reflected that "nothing seemed to him so inconsistent and revolting as to read in our declaration of independence and declaration of rights, that 'All men are born free and independent' and yet see numbers of men set up to auction in our streets; and sold exactly like horses or oxen." "Savage Barbarity," one undergraduate called slavery.[45]

However, John Daniel Gros was not the only Columbia man to view republicanism and liberty through relatively conservative lenses. "See whether true Liberty," President Johnson advised the senior class, "does not consist in an exact obedience to law, a submission to the public will, a surrender of all individual, inferior, partial, subordinate interests, emoluments, and objects to general, public, and universal welfare." [46] John Vardill had made exactly the same point to discredit the Sons of Liberty in 1772. Despite the flowering of republican sentiment, subordination to political authority remained a crucial value in the moral code inculcated by the Columbia College faculty.

From the perspective of the students, the curriculum meant the usual rhythmical pattern of academic exercises, punctuated by examinations and climaxed by commencement. At the beginning of each quarter the undergraduates met in the college hall to learn the plan of study for the session. For the next several weeks they attended two or three class meetings each morning, five mornings a week (Saturday morning classes were instituted in 1791). Afternoons were given over primarily to studying. As usual, schedules were attuned to the sun. On summer mornings John Barent Johnson arose about 5:00 A.M. to make his first lecture at 6:00 A.M. In the winter he slept until 7:00 or 8:00 A.M., then headed for his first class. Sometimes he went to bed about 10:30 P.M. in the summer, but most of the time, year around, he went to bed about 11:00 P.M. In the summer he just got along on less sleep.[47]

The pattern was not terribly different from that at King's College, but Columbia students did enjoy one post-Revolutionary innovation, quarterly review periods. In fact, they enjoyed them a little too much. Classes were suspended a week before each quarterly examination, so that students had an opportunity to go over the session's work. John Barent Johnson used the days effectively, but even a pupil of his diligence found it a good time to get in some handball. In 1791 the trustees decided that the free time encouraged "Habits Of Idleness." They did not drop the "Term of

Revision," as it was called, but they did require the students to "attend their respective professors daily" for guidance in reviewing. Examinations were conducted orally in the hall by the faculty and trustees. Students attended the three or four days that exams lasted, waiting their turn to be queried. Twice a year, in the spring and fall, examinations were followed by a vacation of four to six weeks. John Barent Johnson took "jaunts" to New England, Albany, and elsewhere, and he sometimes went "a gunning," but he also studied a good deal and read for pleasure. To qualify for a degree seniors had to pass an oral examination on the "whole course of their studies." They were given a month without classes to prepare for it.[48]

All in all, the pace of academic life seems to have been reasonable: measured but not regimented, demanding but not frenzied. One student protested the fact that all students must undergo the same "mechanical rotine of study." "If a student has a taste, genius or inclination for any particular science . . . ," he should be permitted "to pursue that science in preference to the rest. . . ."[49] Obviously the point has merit. But when one recalls the success of the Columbia College Society, or the extra courses which undergraduates elected, or John Barent Johnson's extensive outside reading in divinity and other subjects, one is impressed by the way that some students found both the time and the opportunity to explore beyond the required program.

The passage of time inevitably brings changes in an institution. But in the case of the transition from King's College to Columbia the changes pivoted on a critical event, the American Revolution. Columbia, like a good many American institutions of the time, reflected both the radicalism and the conservatism of the Revolution. In the 1770s King's College was strengthening its ties to the Anglican church and the English Crown and was seeking to become an imperial university. The Revolution sharply deflected the college from that path and decimated the leadership that was taking it there. The institution which reappeared in the 1780s, even after the failure at radical reorganization in 1784, reflected the transforming thrust of the Revolution, particularly in the political ideology and the denominational makeup of its leaders and students and in the new sensitivity to attracting students through minimizing costs. Yet, the institution itself survived the Revolution, eventually under its old charter. It was still managed by an urban elite primarily to suit its own needs and outlooks, and the urbanism of its students and its undergraduate life was more decisive than ever. Even a bias toward Episcopalianism and political conservatism continued as a part of its distinctive character. A comparison of Columbia with King's College thus reveals an institution that was unquestionably different from its colonial predecessor yet was also clearly identifiable as its descendant.

RETROSPECT: CROSSCURRENTS IN EIGHTEENTH-CENTURY AMERICA

WHAT CENTRAL THEMES in American life during the eighteenth century does one see mirrored in the history of King's College and Columbia? The development of a distinctive American culture? Perhaps. Or is it a contrary theme, the Anglicization of colonial culture? In truth, one sees both of these, and the dual reflection goes to the heart of the issue.

Historians are gradually realizing that the colonial New England experience may not have been as prototypically American as had previously been thought. Indeed, Jack Greene suggests that for much of the colonial period New England was "atypical, peculiar, even anachronistic." Greene points out

> how powerful [were] the restraints imposed by Puritan culture upon all aspects of rural New England life and how long it took for New England to assimilate to a pattern of behavior that, to one degree or another, had long since come to dominate the societies of the rest of the colonies.

Moreover, writes Greene, the "vantage point" provided by New England helps us to

> see vividly just how weak the corporate impulse was in other British colonies, how unimposing were their figures of traditional authority,

how great were the possibilities for material gain and how rapid and pervasive was the development of highly autonomous behavior.[1]

While New England falls historiographically rearward in the parade of colonies toward an American (and modern) mentality and society, the middle colonies are moving to the front. Milton Klein has nominated New York as drum major. The "homogeneous English communities of New England and the South" may appeal to those searching for an Arcadian past, writes Klein, but it was colonies like New York, characterized by a "disordered, complex, heterogeneous population," which represented, "in germinal form," the nation that emerged in the nineteenth century.[2] The heterogeneity of the colony's ethnic and religious makeup, along with the diversity of its economy, its geographic sectionalism, and its social structure produced a complex and dynamic political process that cannot be reduced to clashes "between democrats and aristocrats, conservatives and radicals," but can be partially captured in a series of dualisms:

> If there was deference, there was also democracy. If there was aristocracy, there was also public accountability. If there were family rivalries, there were also popular issues. If there were local concerns, there were also Anglo-American interests. If there was social stratification and monopoly of office-holding, there was also mobility and considerable rotation in office. If there was Whig ideology imported from England, there was also the uniquely American idiom in which it was couched by provincial politicians to suit the colony's special political dynamic. If the articulate were spokesmen of conservatism and status, there were also inarticulate believers in liberty and equality.[3]

No one has ever accused the colony of New York of being the "land of steady habits." And in New York City features such as ethnic and religious heterogeneity, the complexity of social and economic patterns, and the emerging modernity of outlook provided the warp and woof of urban life. In this setting a coalition of diverse and incompatible groups sought to found a college. Their creation reflected the tensions and contradictions they brought to the task.

The most anomalous group in the mix were the Anglican clerics. Most of those who participated in the founding of the college were, in one way or another, New Englanders, by heritage and upbringing for several, by education and professional associations for most. None had grown up in New York City. To be sure, they spurned the Puritan churches of New England. But their High Church Anglicanism did not cut them off from the traditionalism of New England so much as it provided reinforcement for the traditional conceptions of religion, society, and politics which were so integral a part of their outlooks and which many of their Puritan brethren in New England were now forsaking. James Wetmore probably embodied this spirit the fullest of any, as seen in the unquestioning manner in which he expected to transplant Yale, a sectarian institution suited to the corporate, homogeneous, rural society of Connecticut in 1700, to the radically different environment of mid-eighteenth century New York. Of course, he hoped to locate the college in the country, not the city, but his defeat on this issue did not compel him to alter his basic vision.

One must be careful, however, in casting these men simply as guardians of traditionalism in pluralistic and rapidly modernizing New York City, since this both distorts the complexity of Anglicanism's appeal and misses altogether the personal dilemma of Samuel Johnson, the dominant figure in the early history of the college. Johnson himself was a man of contradictions. Indeed, it was his recognition of them and his attempt to reconcile them that proved so agonizing. How, for instance, could one follow the logical dictates of Locke and Newton without undermining traditional Christianity and the social order it rationalized? In the end, despite his profoundly conservative instincts, Johnson injected his contradictions into his college, fostering both its Anglicanism and its interdenominationalism; pressing for the re-creation of the collegiate way in an urban setting, then not enforcing it; insisting on the intellectual and moral authority of the Christian and classical traditions but also emphasizing courses in logic and science that taught ways to find new truths at the expense of old truths; carefully ordering his students' names in hierarchical fashion in the matricula but dropping much of the precedence that permeated undergraduate life at Harvard and Yale; organizing the curriculum to provide a "truly Christian education" but omitting theology, and so on. If Johnson represented in some ways a projection of New England traditionalism into New York, he also reflected the ambivalence that many New Englanders felt about the modernizing currents that were reshaping their region.

In New York Johnson and his fellow clerics found themselves hedged in by a veritable potpourri of overlapping religious, ethnic, regional, occupational, and socioeconomic groups, each with its own peculiar contradictions and together creating not a symphony but a cacophony. The juxtaposition of differing perspectives, interests, and cultures and the discontinuities between old and new ways of acting and thinking in a changing society produced tensions that were too much for a college to contain—at least a college as most eighteenth-century New Yorkers conceived of it. Could a college bridge the expansive gap between High Church Anglicans and radical Whigs? Could it help preserve a Dutch identity at the same time that it accelerated the Anglicization of life in New York? Could it serve distinctive religious viewpoints—Presbyterian, Anglican, Dutch Reformed—yet satisfy them all? Could it help sort out youths of talent and virtue at the same time that it protected the advantages of birth and wealth? Could it enhance professional orderliness in law and medicine in a colony where disorderliness went hand in hand with opportunity? Could it make a curriculum legitimized by religion and tradition meaningful to a clientele whose lives were characterized by secularism and innovation? Could it be both a provincial institution and an urban institution?

Some of the contradictions and ambiguities surfaced in the King's College Controversy, engendered bitter feelings, and produced some hard thinking on fundamental questions. What is a sectarian college? Is it a matter of who controls a college, or of who can attend without prejudice to his religious principles? Is it a question of exclusive control or of majority control? Can one construct a nonsectarian college without foregoing religious goals? Can a minister head a college without making it, ipso facto, a sectarian enterprise? What is a provincial college? Can it serve public needs if placed in private hands? Should it receive public funds? The clash of answers to questions like these gave shape to King's College, but the most imaginative thinking, that of the triumvirate, had the least impact. And some of the most basic issues, such as those involving social mobility, were given almost no thought at all. If the college emerged from the controversies over its founding seemingly free of some of the contradictions that underlay the friction, it was because many New Yorkers simply turned their backs on the college, much as some of the college leaders had turned their backs on substantial segments of the colony. What consensus was achieved within King's College thus came at a high price. There were sharp discontinuities between the college and the colony that belied its standing as a provincial institution.

At the heart of the new college was an alliance between Anglican clerics and New York City's mercantile and legal elite. The former were represented by the college president, the latter by the college governors. The alliance seems natural enough, and when Myles Cooper was president relationships were positively chummy. Cooper's views blended nicely with the class interests of the governors. Indeed, he and many of the governors shared a profound regard for English models of political authority, social hierarchy, gentlemanly decorum, and professional control, and, of course, for England's established religion. For a number of upper-middle and upper-class families in New York these attitudes made King's College all the more attractive a place to educate a son.

Yet, the governors' fondness for Cooper is in some ways paradoxical, and it certainly contributed to the discontinuity between the development of the college and the development of the colony. After all, Cooper was a man who implicitly accepted a host of traditional beliefs that many New Yorkers had at least questioned, if they did not reject them out of hand. While the colony edged toward Revolution, Cooper propounded a view of society that gave no quarter to liberal concepts such as natural rights and the contract theory of government. He argued instead that men should bow submissively before the divinely constituted order of things. Many of the governors, on the other hand, not only were Whigs but were aggressive, profit-oriented entrepreneurs whose

economic endeavors were speedily undermining the world that
had sustained Cooper's traditional outlooks. By 1775 Cooper was
both a characteristic figure and an absurd figure in New York.
One can see him clearly playing the role of the cosmopolitan and
sophisticated Englishman before an admiring audience of upper
and middle-class New Yorkers, but when one imagines him raising his arm in toast to Archbishop Laud during the very year that
Americans fought at Lexington and Concord, the picture suddenly jumps out of focus. If Cooper symbolized the Anglicization
of New York, he also represented a traditional fragment of England that was even more anachronistic in New York City than it
was at home.

Colleges and universities, like other social institutions, normally
have been embedded in paradox. "In practice, universities have
nearly always performed two directly contradictory functions,"
writes Lawrence Stone. Socially a "block and a sieve," they
"channel the children of the elite into elite positions," while they
also provide avenues "by which talented children of relatively
humble origins . . . may enter the ranks of the elite." Intellectually a "buttress and a land-mine," they transmit the "inherited
traditional culture of the past to each new generation," while they
generate "new ideas and new facts which challenge both the existing social system and the existing set of values." But the character
and intensity of the paradoxes which enmesh a college vary with
time and place. Michael Kammen, who has explored the role of
paradox in American life so brilliantly, suggests that colonial societies are peculiarly susceptible to contradictions and inconsisten-
cies. Multiple origins, tensions between inherited ideas and envi-
ronmental realities, and the ambivalent feelings that naturally
creep into the relationships between mother country and colony
are only some of the factors which invite paradox in a colonial setting. Societies undergoing rapid change also are liable to polarities
because of the greater likelihood of conflicts between older and
newer ways of thinking and acting.[4] Obviously in colonial, heterogeneous, urbanized, fast-paced, modernizing New York City the
possibilities for contradictions were rife.

However, if King's College was a victim of this volatile situation, it was not an innocent victim. The attempt by its leaders to impose on New Yorkers some of the traditionalism of New England and old England exacerbated tensions as the contrasts in the colony became more extreme. King's College thus contributed to the pattern of paradox in New York and through its alumni added to the political frictions of the Revolutionary and post-Revolutionary years.

Many of the ambiguities and contradictions which beset King's College survived the American Revolution, as one would expect, yet the Revolution also altered the dynamics of the situation in some ways. New York politicans first tried to create a new academic structure more suitable to the social realities of republican New York, but it proved politically and technologically infeasible. However, the reversion to the King's College charter did not betoken the restoration of King's College. For one thing, the Revolution eliminated most of the traditionalists who had led King's College and liberalized the rest, thus diminishing the gap in political ideology between the college and colony. The reorganization of the college also loosened its ties to the Anglican church and legitimized it for Presbyterians, thus moderating the inconsistency between the denominationalism of the college and the religious heterogeneity of the colony. Columbia soon enjoyed some thriving days. Ironically, Columbia lost what remained of its provincial standing just at the moment when it began to deserve it. New Yorkers started founding other colleges. This was a healthy and perhaps inevitable development for a heterogeneous, geographically sizable state. Yet it also had potentially deleterious consequences for Columbia. In losing its hegemony Columbia enhanced its chances of becoming a local and relatively insignificant institution. In the nineteenth century, when the college was plagued with unimaginative leadership, this is just what happened. Eventually, of course, Columbia not only regained the stature which it had lost but far surpassed in quality and in reputation the achievements of its eighteenth-century founders.

NOTES

1. The Shaping of King's College

INTRODUCTION

1. "Will of James Alexander," *New York Genealogical and Biographical Record* 18 (Oct. 1887): 177; William Livingston to Noah Welles, Dec. 9, 1745, Livingston-Welles Correspondence, Johnson Family Papers, Yale University Library.

1. THE CONTROVERSY OVER LOCATION

1. *New-York Gazette Revived in the Weekly Post-Boy*, Feb. 4, 1750/51; [Archibald Kennedy], *A Speech Said to have been Delivered Some Time Before the Close of the Last Sessions* . . . ([New York], 1755), p. 17; Milton M. Klein, ed., *The Independent Reflector* . . . (Cambridge: Harvard University Press, 1963), p. 171 (March 22, 1753); *New York Mercury*, Nov. 10, 1755; [William Smith], *Some Thoughts on Education: with Reasons for Erecting a College in this Province, and fixing the same at the City of New-York* . . . (New York, 1752), p. 3.

2. Cadwallader Colden to Benjamin Franklin, [Nov. 1749], Leonard W. Labaree et al., eds., *The Papers of Benjamin Franklin* (New Haven: Yale University Press, 1959–), 3: 431–32; *Independent Reflector*, pp. 171–83 (March 22, 29, 1753); Edward Antill to S. Johnson, Dec. 14, 1758 and Jan. 16, 1759, College Papers, Special Collections, Columbia University Library (cited hereafter as College Papers); [William Smith], *A General Idea of the College of Mirania* . . . (New York, 1753), pp. 9–10, 13–14, 53–59, 76–77; William Smith, "Editor's Preface to the 3rd edition of *Elementa Philosophica*," Herbert and Carol Schneider, eds., *Samuel Johnson, President of King's College: His Career and Writings* (New York: Columbia University Press, 1929), 2: 346–47; Stow Persons, "The Cyclical Theory of History in Eighteenth Century America," *American Quarterly* 6 (Summer 1954): 149–58.

3. *N. Y. Gazette Revived in the Weekly Post-Boy*, Feb. 4, 1750/51; Colden to Franklin, [Nov. 1749], *Franklin Papers*, 3: 431.

316

555 NOTES FOR PAGES 6–9

4. Colden to Franklin, [Nov. 1749], *Franklin Papers*, 3: 431. Colden's comments on higher education in this letter were not addressed specifically to the projected College of New York. Rather, Colden offered Franklin his thoughts on collegiate education after reading Franklin's recently published *Proposals Relating to the Education of Youth in Pennsylvania*. At the very same time, of course, Colden was promoting the establishment of New York's college at rural Newburgh.

5. Smith, *Some Thoughts on Education*, p. 6; Colden to Franklin, [Nov. 1749], *Franklin Papers*, 3: 431.

6. S. Johnson to [SPG], Sept. 29, 1744, #100, SPG Letters, series B, vol. 13, transcripts, Library of Congress (cited hereafter as SPG Transcripts); S. Johnson to Colden, April 18, 1744, *Samuel Johnson*, 2: 288.

7. SPG Journals, 9: 309–11, meeting of Sept. 21, 1744, photostats, Library of Congress; Philip Bearcroft to George Clinton, Oct. 4, 1744, #60, copy, SPG Transcripts, B, 13. Watkins was officially appointed to New Windsor, but he soon began to preach regularly at Newburgh, about two miles north of New Windsor. Alexander Colden and Richard Albertson to [SPG], June 4, 1752, #82, SPG Transcripts, B, 20; Watkins to SPG, March 26, 1746, #139, SPG Transcripts, B, 14.

8. Cadwallader Colden to Hezekiah Watkins, Dec. 12, 1748, George H. Moore, *Collegium Regale Novi Eboraci: The Origin and Early History of Columbia College* (New York, 1890), pp. 37–43; Watkins to SPG, Dec. 14, 1748, #64, SPG Transcripts, B, 16.

9. "Petition of Proprietors and Inhabitants of Newburgh Patent to Governor George Clinton," #103, copy, SPG Transcripts, B, 15; Lutheran Petitions of May 12 and Oct. 5, 1749, Edmund B. O'Callaghan, ed., *The Documentary History of the State of New-York* (Albany, 1849–51), 3: 583–94; Nicholas Varga, "New York Government and Politics During the Mid-Eighteenth Century" (Ph.D. diss., Fordham University, 1960), p. 154. Colden's retirement proved a temporary one. From 1761 to 1776 he served as lieutenant governor of New York.

10. "Petition of the Proprietors and Inhabitants of Newburgh Patent to Governor George Clinton," Sept. 6, 1751, *Documentary History of N. Y.*, 3: 594–98. The 1751 petition named Colden's son, Alexander, and Richard Albertson as trustees of the 500-acre tract.

11. Governor George Clinton to Attorney General William Smith, March 3, 1752, *ibid.*, 3: 598–600; "Minutes of the Board of Trinity Church," March 5, 1752, quoted in Morgan Dix et al., *A History of the Parish of Trinity Church in the City of New York* (New York: Putnam, 1898–1962), 1: 258.

12. *N. Y. Gazette Revived in the Weekly Post-Boy*, Feb. 4, 1750/51.

13. *New-York Evening Post*, May 18, 1747. Wetmore may well have written more than one of the newspaper articles supporting a Post Road location. The wording and substance of the May 18, 1747 article certainly suggest Wetmore's authorship, especially the recommendation of Rye as a location and the proposal that the rectors of the established parishes be trustees. Wetmore indicated in a

NOTES FOR PAGES 10–17

1747 letter to the bishop of London (March 26, 1747, #78, SPG Transcripts, B, 15) that he expected the assembly bill which established the college to contain clauses "making the Rectors of ye established Parishes part of the Corporation."

14. *N. Y. Evening Post*, May 18, Aug, 17, 1747, Jan. 9, 1748/49; *N. Y. Gazette Revived in the Weekly Post-Boy*, Jan. 14, 1750/51.

15. *N. Y. Gazette Revived in the Weekly Post-Boy*, Jan. 14, 1750/51; *N. Y. Evening Post*, May 18, 1747, Jan. 9, 1748/49.

16. *N. Y. Evening Post*, Jan. 9, 1748/49, Nov. 28, 1748; *N. Y. Gazette Revived in the Weekly Post-Boy*, Jan. 14, 1750/51.

17. *N. Y. Evening Post*, May 18, Aug. 17, 1747, Nov. 28, 1748, Jan. 9, 1748/49.

18. Franklin to Colden, Feb, 13, 1749/50, *Franklin Papers*, 3: 462; *Independent Reflector*, p. 171 (March 22, 1753).

19. *Journal of the Votes and Proceedings of the General Assembly Of the Colony of New-York . . . [1691–1765]* (New York, 1764–66), 2: 128, 161, 171, 226–27, 242, 321, 396–402; *The Colonial Laws of New York from the Year 1664 to the Revolution* (Albany, 1894), 3: 842–44, 908–10. A King's County representative was asked to join Henry Cruger of New York City in preparing one of the lottery bills.

20. *Independent Reflector*, p. 171 (March 22, 1753).

21. *N. Y. Evening Post*, Jan. 9, 1748/49. The Society of Friends also met in nearby Purchase.

22. Smith, *Some Thoughts on Education*, pp. 8–11. Smith was not ordained until 1753. The title "Reverend" has been used to differentiate him from two New York City lawyers who participated in the college project: William Smith and his son, William Smith, Jr.

23. *Ibid.*, pp. 4, 6, 12–13.

24. Colden to Franklin, [Nov. 1749], *Franklin Papers*, 3: 431; S. Johnson, "Autobiography," *Samuel Johnson*, 1: 32.

25. "Minutes of the Board of Trinity Church," Feb. 19, 1703, March 5, 1752, quoted in Dix, *Trinity Church Parish*, 1: 145, 258; Lewis Morris to the Secretary of the Society, SPG Archives, series A, vol. 1 (1702–04), transcript, College Papers. Financial figures are in New York currency.

26. Charity Moore to Lady Affleck, Nov. 29, 1825, Charity Clarke and Clement Moore Papers, Special Collections, Columbia University Library; *Journal of the N. Y. General Assembly [1691–1765]*, 2: 396–402; [Benjamin Nicoll], *A Brief Vindication of the Proceedings of the Trustees . . .* (New York, 1754), extracted in *Samuel Johnson*, 4: 193. Trinity Church's gift also included enough land for a street ninety feet long between Church St. and Broadway, which today forms one block of Park Place.

27. The issue was not completely dead, however. See Kennedy, *A Speech Said to have been Delivered*, p. 17; William Smith, Jr., to Silas Leonard, Jan. 20, 1755, draft, #189 (4), Box 1, William Smith Papers, New York Public Library; and *N. Y. Mercury*, Nov. 10, 1755.

2. THE KING'S COLLEGE CONTROVERSY:
THE ANGLICAN BID FOR CONTROL

1. S. Johnson to Benjamin Nicoll, Oct. 25, 1754, College Papers, Special Collections, Columbia University Library (cited hereafter as College Papers).

2. William Livingston to Noah Welles, Oct. 18, 1754, Livingston-Welles Correspondence, Johnson Family Papers, Yale University Library (cited hereafter as JFP, Yale).

3. S. Johnson to George Berkeley, Sept. 10, 1750, Herbert and Carol Schneider, eds., *Samuel Johnson, President of King's College: His Career and Writings* (New York: Columbia University Press, 1929), 1: 136–37.

4. Richard L. Bushman, *From Puritan to Yankee: Character and the Social Order in Connecticut, 1690–1765* (Cambridge: Harvard University Press, 1967), p. 166; Edwin S. Gaustad, *Historical Atlas of Religion in America* (New York and Evanston: Harper & Row, 1962), p. 167; Hector G. Kinloch, "Anglican Clergy in Connecticut, 1701–1785" (Ph.D. diss., Yale University, 1959), pp. 52–114.

5. Thomas Bradbury Chandler, *The Life of Samuel Johnson, D.D., The first President of King's College, in New-York* . . . (New York, 1805), pp. 126, 134, 146; Franklin B. Dexter, ed., *The Literary Diary of Ezra Stiles* . . . (New York: Scribners, 1901), 1: 206; S. Johnson to William Samuel Johnson, June 23, 1747, *Samuel Johnson*, 1: 125.

6. S. Johnson, "Autobiography," *Samuel Johnson*, 1: 20, 22; S. Johnson, "A Catalogue of Books," *ibid.*, 1: 497–526.

7. Theodore Hornberger, "Samuel Johnson of Yale and King's College: A Note on the Relation of Science and Religion in Provincial America," *New England Quarterly* 8 (Sept. 1935): 378–97.

8. S. Johnson, "Autobiography," *Samuel Johnson*, 1: 28; S. Johnson to Archbishop of Canterbury, July 12, 1760, *ibid.*, 1: 295; Chandler, *Life of Samuel Johnson*, p. 127.

9. Biographical and other data on Anglican clerics in this chapter have been drawn from a wide variety of sources. Especially useful were: Nelson R. Burr, *The Anglican Church in New Jersey* (Philadelphia: Church Historical Society, 1954); Franklin B. Dexter, *Biographical Sketches of the Graduates of Yale College* . . . (New York: Henry Holt & Co., 1885–1911), vols. 1–3; Kinloch, "Anglican Clergy in Connecticut, 1701–1785;" Clifford K. Shipton, *Sibley's Harvard Graduates* . . . (Boston, Cambridge: Massachusetts Historical Society, Harvard University Press, 1933–), vols. 4–15; John Clement, "Anglican Clergymen Licensed to the American Colonies, 1710–1744," *Historical Magazine of the Protestant Episcopal Church* 17 (Sept. 1948): 207–50; and George W. Lamb, "Clergymen Licensed to the American Colonies by the Bishops of London: 1745–1781," *Historical Magazine of the Protestant Episcopal Church* 13 (June 1944): 128–43.

10. Shipton, *Sibley's Harvard Graduates*, 5: 56–63; Gerald Goodwin, "The Anglican Middle Way in Early Eighteenth-Century America: Anglican Religious

Thought in the American Colonies, 1702–1750" (Ph.D. diss., University of Wisconsin, 1965), pp. 130–34; Joseph J. Ellis, "Anglicans in Connecticut, 1725–1750: The Conversion of the Missionaries," *New England Quarterly* 44 (March 1971): 74–79.

11. Timothy Cutler to Zachery Grey, April 2, 1725 and April 7, 1728, John Nichols, *Illustrations of the Literary History of the Eighteenth Century* . . . (London, 1817–58), 4: 269, 286; S. Johnson to Bishop of London, April 2, 1728, abstracted in William W. Manross, *The Fulham Papers in the Lambeth Palace Library; American Colonial Section, Calendar and Indexes* (Oxford: Clarendon Press, 1965), p. 12; Clergy of New England to SPG, July 20, 1727, William S. Perry, ed., *Historical Collections Relating to the American Colonial Church* (Hartford, 1870–73), 3: 226.

12. See, for instance, S. Johnson to the SPG, Feb. 10, 1727, April 28, 1727, Oct. 25, 1730, and Johnson to Bishop of London, April 2, 1728, all in Francis L. Hawks and William S. Perry, eds., *Documentary History of The Protestant Episcopal Church in the United States of America* . . . *Connecticut* (New York, 1863–64), 1: 113, 114, 127, 145 (cited hereafter as *Doc. Hist. Conn.*); Philip Bearcroft to S. Johnson, April 23, 1743, #191, copy, SPG Letters, series B, vol. 10, transcripts, Library of Congress (cited hereafter as SPG Transcripts).

13. S. Johnson to Benjamin Franklin, Jan. 1752, *Samuel Johnson*, 1: 155. The data on Harvard and Yale students in this and the following paragraph are based primarily on the biographies in Dexter and Shipton (see n. 9). Shipton includes all students who attended Harvard, while Dexter includes only those who graduated from Yale. See also David C. Humphrey, "Anglican 'Infiltration' of Eighteenth Century Harvard and Yale," *Historical Magazine of the Protestant Episcopal Church* 43 (Sept. 1974): 247–51.

14. S. Johnson to SPG, March 30, 1745, *Doc. Hist. Conn.*, 1: 213; James Wetmore to SPG, Oct. 1, 1745, #266, SPG Transcripts, B, 13. The College of New Jersey was not officially renamed Princeton until 1896, but the terms will be used interchangeably.

15. James Wetmore to Bishop of London, March 26, 1747, #78, SPG Transcripts, B, 15; Samuel Johnson to Bishop of London, April 28, 1747, #51, SPG Transcripts, B, 15.

16. Alan Heimert, *Religion and the American Mind: From the Great Awakening to the Revolution* (Cambridge: Harvard University Press, 1966), p. 38; Goodwin, "Anglican Middle Way in Early Eighteenth-Century America," pp. 207, 321–22. The two pamphlets were Wetmore's *A Letter Occasioned by Mr. Dickinson's Remarks* . . . (New York, 1744) and Johnson's *A Letter to Mr. Jonathan Dickinson, In Defence of Aristocles to Authades* . . . (Boston, 1747).

17. S. Johnson to Cadwallader Colden, April 15, 1747, *Collections of the New-York Historical Society*, 52 (1919): 375 (cited hereafter as *NYHS Colls.*); Thomas B. Chandler to S. Johnson, Feb. 26, 1753, *Samuel Johnson*, 1: 166.

18. James Wetmore to Bishop of London, March 26, 1747, #78, SPG Transcripts, B, 15; William Skinner to [SPG], Jan. 9, 1748/49, #91, SPG Transcripts, B, 16; Address of S. Johnson et al. to Archbishop of Canterbury, en-

closed in letter of S. Johnson et al. to [SPG ?], Jan. 29, 1755, SPG Letters, series B, vol. 3, microfilm, Library of Congress (cited hereafter as LC).

19. Henry Barclay to SPG, Oct. 3, 1752, #54, SPG Transcripts, B, 20; John Charlton et al. to SPG, Feb. 6, 1759, extracted in SPG Journals, 14: 191–92, meeting of June 15, 1759, photostats, LC; S. Johnson to Cadwallader Colden, April 15, 1747, *NYHS Colls.*, 52 (1919): 375.

20. *New York Mercury*, Dec. 3, 1753. Chandler served as a lay reader and catechist at Elizabethtown from 1748 to 1751, sailed to England in 1751 for ordination, and returned that year as SPG missionary to Elizabethtown. Samuel Seabury, Jr., served as catechist and lay reader at Huntington, Long Island from 1749 to 1752, received ordination in 1753, and in 1754 became SPG missionary to New Brunswick.

21. William Skinner to [SPG], Jan. 9, 1748/49, #91, SPG Transcripts, B, 16; Samuel Seabury et al. to Bishop of London, enclosed in letter of S. Johnson to Bishop of London, June 25, 1753, #63, Lambeth Palace Library, 1123, vol. 1, transcript, LC; S. Johnson to William Samuel Johnson, end of June, 1754, *Samuel Johnson*, 1: 191.

22. Gaustad, *Historical Atlas of Religion*, p. 167; S. Johnson to Archbishop of Canterbury, July 25, 1759, *Samuel Johnson*, 1: 291; S. Johnson to Bishop of Oxford, Oct. 25, 1754, *ibid.*, 2: 334; James Wetmore to Bishop of London, Aug. 11, 1752, *Doc. Hist. Conn.*, 1: 293–95.

23. Isaac Browne to [SPG], March 25, 1748, #74, SPG Transcripts, B, 16; S. Johnson to Archbishop of Canterbury, July 12, 1760, *Samuel Johnson*, 1: 295; S. Johnson to William Samuel Johnson, Jan. 20, 1755, *ibid.*, 1: 209.

24. *New-York Evening Post*, May 18, 1747; Wetmore to Bishop of London, March 26, 1747, #78, SPG Transcripts, B, 15.

25. John W. Pratt, *Religion, Politics, and Diversity: The Church-State Theme in New York History* (Ithaca, N.Y.: Cornell University Press, 1967), pp. 52, 58–64; Nicholas Varga, "New York Government and Politics During the Mid-Eighteenth Century" (Ph.D. diss., Fordham University, 1960), pp. 384, 387, 406, 412; David C. Humphrey, "King's College in the City of New York, 1754–1776" (Ph.D. diss., Northwestern University, 1968), pp. 24–26.

26. Aaron Burr to Philip Doddridge, April, 1748, Doddridge Correspondence, vol. 4, #154, Library of New College, London, transcript in Aaron Burr Collection (1716–1757), Princeton University Library.

27. See David C. Humphrey, "The Struggle for Sectarian Control of Princeton, 1745–1760," *New Jersey History* 91 (Summer 1973): 77–90. The charter of 1748 named four New Jersey councillors as trustees, but only by name, not ex officio.

28. Milton M. Klein, ed., *The Independent Reflector* . . . (Cambridge: Harvard University Press, 1963), p. 209 (April 26, 1753); William Smith, Jr., *The History of the Province of New-York*, ed. Michael Kammen (Cambridge: Harvard University Press, 1972), 1: 204.

29. Johnson to George Berkeley, Sept. 10, 1750, *Samuel Johnson*, 1: 136.

30. Smith, Jr., *History of New-York*, 1: 359; Cadwallader Colden to Lords of Trade, Aug. 30, 1760, E. B. O'Callaghan and B. Fernow, eds., *Documents Relative to the Colonial History of the State of New-York* . . . (Albany, 1853–87), 7: 445; E. B. O'Callaghan, "John Chambers," *New York Genealogical and Biographical Record* 3. (April 1872): 57–62; *Dictionary of American Biography*, s.v. "Joseph Murray."

31. "Subscription List," March 25, 1745, AM #13140, College Papers, Princeton University Archives; William Livingston to Noah Welles, Sept. 19, 1747, JFP, Yale; Alison B. Olson, "The Founding of Princeton University: Religion and Politics in Eighteenth-Century New Jersey," *New Jersey History* 87 (Autumn 1969): 134–38; Humphrey, "Struggle for Control of Princeton," pp. 79–80.

32. [Benjamin Nicoll], *A Brief Vindication of the Proceedings of the Trustees* . . . (New York, 1754), extracted in *Samuel Johnson*, 4: 202; "Draft Address of the Governors of the College to the Public," College Papers, Box 1. See pp. 90–91, 117.

33. In writing about the Anglican church in the northern colonies, some historians have tended to see it as a monolithic, coherent organization, despite much evidence to the contrary. The most obvious example is Carl Bridenbaugh's *Mitre and Sceptre: Transatlantic Faiths, Ideas, Personalities, and Politics, 1689–1775* (New York: Oxford University Press, 1962), but the misconception slips more subtly into other works. For instance, in his excellent introduction to the *Independent Reflector* (pp. 34–35), Milton Klein ties Anglican plans for a college in the 1740s to an incident forty-five years earlier when several New York Anglicans gave some thought to founding a college. "The Anglican proposal [at mid-century] represented the fulfillment of a *scheme* [italics mine] that had been at least a half-century in the making," writes Klein, and the Anglicans "never changed their opinion" about controlling the college. This, despite the fact that almost half a century separated the two events, that during the intervening years there is no record of any mention of a college, and that none of the Anglicans who participated in the mid-century movement had any part in the earlier incident (the oldest was under ten). Throughout this study I have found that the only way to make sense of much of the data is to recognize the disjointed, sometimes discordant manner in which the Anglican church operated. Differences in outlook between lay and clerical Anglicans is one facet of this disunity. See pp. 72–76, 329.

34. Goldsbrow Banyar to George Clarke, Nov. 23, 1754, Goldsbrow Banyar Papers, Box 1, New-York Historical Society; Rev. William Smith, "Editor's Preface to the 3d edition of *Elementa Philosophica*," *Samuel Johnson*, 2: 347.

35. Margaret W. Masson, "The Premises and Purposes of Higher Education in American Society, 1745–1770" (Ph.D. diss., University of Washington, 1971), pp. 262–67. Recently historians like Masson and Jack Greene ("Search for Identity: An Interpretation of the Meaning of Selected Patterns of Social Response in Eighteenth-Century America," *Journal of Social History* 3 [Spring 1970]: 213) have begun to explain college founding in the mid-eighteenth century by seeing it in a

social context of pervasive anxiety bordering on pessimism. Kenneth Lockridge, Gordon Wood, and others are doing the same thing with the American Revolution. Naturally historians writing in the 1960s and 1970s have been struck much more forcefully with this side of psychic life in the mid-eighteenth century than were historians writing in the 1950s, who tended to see college founding and the American Revolution within a social context of growing optimism and self-confidence. The newer emphasis has proved a fruitful one in understanding the eighteenth century, but a new wave of historical thinking often catches in its crest events that do not belong there. The case for seeing the founding of King's College within this context rests on the writings of Samuel Johnson and Reverend William Smith, who, with their fellow clerics, were a bearish lot, and on the writings of William Livingston, William Smith, Jr., and Cadwallader Colden. Obviously the writings of the former are relevant, as has been suggested above, but there is little indication that the clerics, in this instance as in so many others, spoke for the laymen. Nor should the latter be taken as spokesmen for the main body of laymen who dominated the college movement. In fact, it was some of these very men whom Livingston, Smith, Jr., and Colden were attacking in their tirades against selfishness, money grubbing, and cultural vacuity. The Anglican laymen discussed above were attuned to these issues and undoubtedly concerned about them, but there is little to indicate that they were profoundly anxious about them or that they saw the college mainly as a means of waging war on luxury or economic acquisitiveness. I have elaborated on my thoughts about their social attitudes in chapter 6.

36. Henry Barclay to S. Johnson, Dec. 24, 1753 and Jan. 5, 1754 [misdated as July 5, 1754], *Samuel Johnson*, 4: 6, 19; S. Johnson to William Samuel Johnson, Jan. 20, 1755, *ibid.*, 1: 209; Smith, Jr., *History of New-York*, 2: 168; Beverly McAnear, "American Imprints Concerning King's College," *Papers of the Bibliographical Society of America* 44 (4th Quarter 1950): 317, 325; Nicoll, *Brief Vindication, Samuel Johnson*, 4: 201–05; Receipt book of Joseph Murray's estate, Museum of the City of New York; Thomas Jones, *History of New York during the Revolutionary War . . .* , ed. Edward F. De Lancey (New York, 1879), 1: 10–11.

37. Suggestive in this regard are Frederick V. Mills, "Anglican Resistance to an American Episcopate, 1761–1789" (Ph.D. diss., University of Pennsylvania, 1967) and Borden Painter, "The Anglican Vestry in Colonial America" (Ph.D. diss., Yale University, 1965).

38. Benjamin Franklin to S. Johnson, Aug. 9, 1750, and S. Johnson to Franklin, [Jan. 1752 ?], Leonard W. Labaree et al., eds., *The Papers of Benjamin Franklin* (New Haven: Yale University Press, 1959–), 4: 37–38, 37n, 260–61.

39. Trinity Church Vestry and Episcopal Clergy of N.Y. to SPG, Nov. 3, 1755, *Samuel Johnson*, 4: 39; Johnson to George Berkeley, Aug. 12, 1752, *ibid.*, 2: 329; Johnson to Francis Astry, Oct. 30, 1752, *ibid.*, 1: 161.

40. *N.Y. Mercury*, Nov. 6, 1752; *Journal of the Votes and Proceedings of the General Assembly Of the Colony of New-York . . . [1691–1765]* (New York, 1764–66), 2: 336.

41. *The Preface* to *The Independent Reflector* (New York, 1754), extracted in *Samuel Johnson*, 4: 162; [William Livingston], *An Address to His Excellency Sir Charles Hardy* . . . (New York, 1755), p. ix.

42. William Livingston to Noah Welles, Feb. 1753, JFP, Yale; *N.Y. Mercury*, April 30, 1753.

3. THE KING'S COLLEGE CONTROVERSY:
THE CHALLENGE OF THE "REFLECTORS"

1. William Smith, Jr., to William Samuel Johnson, March 2, 1747, William Samuel Johnson Papers, Connecticut Historical Society (cited hereafter as WSJ Papers, Conn. Hist. Soc.); William Livingston to Noah Welles, Sept. 19, 1747, Livingston-Welles Correspondence, Johnson Family Papers, Yale University Library (cited hereafter as JFP, Yale).

2. L. F. S. Upton, *The Loyal Whig: William Smith of New York & Quebec* (Toronto: University of Toronto Press, 1969), p. 19; Milton M. Klein, ed., *The Independent Reflector* . . . (Cambridge: Harvard University Press, 1963), 1, 7–10.

3. Douglass C. North and Robert Paul Thomas, eds., *The Growth of the American Economy to 1860* (New York: Harper & Row, 1968), pp. 79–81; Beverly McAnear, "Politics in Provincial New York, 1689–1761" (Ph.D. diss., Stanford University, 1935), pp. 520–21, 529; *Independent Reflector*, p. 104 (Jan. 18, 1753).

4. *New-York Weekly Journal*, Feb. 13, 1748/49; William Smith, Jr., to William Samuel Johnson, 1748/49, WSJ Papers, Conn. Hist. Soc.; Livingston to Noah Welles, Jan. 13, 1745/46, JFP, Yale.

5. James Alexander to Cadwallader Colden, Nov. 12, 1744, *Collections of the New-York Historical Society*, 52 (1919): 82–83 (cited hereafter as *NYHS Colls.*); Livingston to Noah Welles, Jan. 5, 1749/50, JFP, Yale; *N.Y. Weekly Journal*, Feb. 13, 1748/49.

6. Franklin B. Dexter, *Biographical Sketches of the Graduates of Yale College* . . . (New York: Henry Holt & Co., 1885–1911), vols. 1, 2, passim; Clifford K. Shipton, *Sibley's Harvard Graduates* . . . (Boston, Cambridge: Massachusetts Historical Society, Harvard University Press, 1933–), vols. 4–12, passim.

7. Edward Antill to S. Johnson, Dec. 14, 1758 and Jan. 16, 1759, College Papers, Special Collections, Columbia University Library (cited hereafter as College Papers).

8. [Livingston], *Some Serious Thoughts on The Design of erecting a College in the Province of New-York* . . . (New York, 1749), pp. 2–3.

9. Livingston, *Some Serious Thoughts*, "Dedication," pp. 7–9; Nicholas Varga, "New York Government and Politics During the Mid-Eighteenth Century" (Ph.D. diss., Fordham University, 1960), p. 156n; William Livingston to Noah Welles, Feb. 1753, JFP, Yale; *New-York Evening Post*, May 18, 1747; *New-York Gazette Revived in the Weekly Post-Boy*, Feb. 4, 1750/51.

10. S. Johnson to Archbishop of Canterbury, June 25, 1753, quoted in William W. Kemp, *The Support of Schools in Colonial New York by the Society for the Propagation of the Gospel in Foreign Parts* (New York: Teachers College, Columbia

University, 1913), pp. 41–42. Especially helpful on the King's College Controversy are the writings of Milton Klein, Beverly McAnear, and L. F. S. Upton. Klein: "William Livingston: The *American Whig*" (Ph.D. diss., Columbia University, 1954), chs. 9 and 10; "Church, State, and Education: Testing the Issue in Colonial New York," *New York History* 45 (Oct. 1964): 291–303; *Independent Reflector*, pp. 1–50. McAnear: "Politics in Provincial New York," ch. 18; "American Imprints Concerning King's College," *Papers of the Bibliographical Society of America* 44 (4th Quarter 1950): 301–34. Upton: *The Loyal Whig*, ch. 3.

11. *Independent Reflector*, pp. 171–214 (March 22–April 26, 1753).

12. *Ibid.*, pp. 199–205 (April 19, 1753).

13. *Ibid.*, p. 90 (Jan. 4, 1753); Varga, "New York Government and Politics," p. 402.

14. *Independent Reflector*, pp. 93 (Jan. 4, 1753), 129 (Feb. 8, 1753); Livingston to Noah Welles, Jan. 17, 1753, JFP, Yale; Thomas B. Chandler to S. Johnson, Feb. 26, 1753, Herbert and Carol Schneider, eds., *Samuel Johnson, President of King's College: His Career and Writings* (New York: Columbia University Press, 1929), 1: 166.

15. *New York Mercury*, April 30, June 4, 1753; S. Johnson to Archbishop of Canterbury, June 25, 1753, *Samuel Johnson*, 4: 4; S. Johnson, "Autobiography," *ibid.*, 1: 33.

16. Samuel Seabury et al. to Bishop of London, enclosed in letter of S. Johnson to Bishop of London, June 25, 1753, #63, Lambeth Palace Library, 1123, vol. 1, transcript, Library of Congress.

17. *N.Y. Mercury*, June 18, 1753; [Rev. William Smith], *A General Idea of the College of Mirania* . . . (New York, 1753), p. 85; *Independent Reflector*, pp. 180–82 (March 29, 1753); S. Johnson, "A Paper to be Read at My Decease or Dismission," [1759?], *Samuel Johnson*, 4: 115.

18. The Anglican clerics relied especially on Oldisworth's *A Dialogue between Timothy and Philatheus* . . . (1709–11) and Hume's *The Sacred Succession* . . . (London, 1710). On Oldisworth, see Robert J. Allen, "William Oldisworth: 'the Author of *The Examiner*,' " *Philological Quarterly* 26 (April 1947): 159–80.

19. *The Craftsmen* . . . , 5th ed. ([New York, 1753]), p. vi.

20. *Independent Reflector*, p. 307 (Aug. 2, 1753); *N.Y. Mercury*, Aug. 27, Sept. 17, Sept. 24, 1753. Not all the Anglican clerics agreed personally on each of these points. See, for instance, Smith, *General Idea of the College of Mirania*, p. 28.

21. *N.Y. Mercury*, July 9, 1753.

22. *Occasional Reverberator*, Oct. 5, 1753.

23. McAnear, "Imprints Concerning King's College," pp. 313–14; *Independent Reflector*, p. 54 (title page).

24. Chauncey Graham to William Smith, Jr., July 11, 1755, #189 (6), Box 1, William Smith Papers, New York Public Library (cited hereafter as NYPL).

25. S. Johnson to Bishop of London, July 6, 1754, *Samuel Johnson*, 4: 20; Cadwallader Colden to Mrs. Colden, Oct. 14, 1753, *NYHS Colls.*, 53 (1920): 408.

26. Henry Barclay to S. Johnson, Dec. 24, 1753, and Jan. 5, 1754 (misdated July 5, 1754), *Samuel Johnson*, 4: 6, 19; *Journal* of the New York General Assembly, Nov. 1, 1754, extracted in *ibid.*, 4: 180–81.

27. S. Johnson to George Berkeley, May 14, 1739, *ibid.*, 1: 98; Klein, "William Livingston," pp. 52–53; McAnear, "Imprints Concerning King's College," p. 316.

28. Henry Barclay to S. Johnson, Dec. 24, 1753, Jan. 5, 1754 (misdated July 5, 1754), *Samuel Johnson*, 4: 5–6, 19; S. Johnson to William Samuel Johnson, May 27, 1754, *ibid.*, 4: 12; S. Johnson, "Autobiography," *ibid.*, 1: 33; *Journal* of the New York General Assembly, Nov. 1, 1754, extracted in *ibid.*, 4: 181–82.

29. *Journal* of the New York General Assembly, Nov. 1, 1754, extracted in *ibid.*, 4: 182–83; S. Johnson, "Autobiography," *ibid.*, 1: 33; S. Johnson to William Samuel Johnson, May 6, 1754, *ibid.*, 1: 184.

30. *N.Y. Gazette; or the Weekly Post-Boy*, June 3, 1754, in *ibid.*, 4: 223; S. Johnson to Thomas Clap, Feb. 5 and 19, 1754, *ibid.*, 1: 176–82.

31. S. Johnson to William Samuel Johnson, May 6, 1754, *ibid.*, 1: 184; "Minutes of the Board of Trinity Church," May 14, 1754, quoted in Morgan Dix et al., *A History of the Parish of Trinity Church in the City of New York* (New York: Putnam, 1898–1962), 1: 271; *Journal* of the New York General Assembly, Nov. 1, 1754, extracted in *Samuel Johnson*, 4: 182–83.

32. Edwin S. Gaustad, *Historical Atlas of Religion in America* (New York and Evanston: Harper & Row, 1962), p. 167.

33. *Independent Reflector*, pp. 210–11 (April 26, 1753); William Livingston to Henry Livingston, [June–July 1755], quoted in Klein, "William Livingston," p. 428; *N.Y. Mercury*, Dec. 2, 1754.

34. [Benjamin Nicoll], *A Brief Vindication of the Proceedings of the Trustees . . .* (New York, 1754), extracted in *Samuel Johnson*, 4: 195; S. Johnson to William Samuel Johnson, May 6, 1754, *ibid.*, 1: 184; Klein, "William Livingston," p. 389.

35. William Samuel Johnson to S. Johnson, May 25, 1754, Letterbook #9, WSJ Papers, Conn. Hist. Soc.; S. Johnson to William Samuel Johnson, May 27, 1754, *Samuel Johnson*, 4: 12.

36. William Smith, Jr., "Draft Account of the College," #189 (12), Box 1, William Smith Papers, NYPL (cited hereafter as "Draft Account of the College"); Klein, "William Livingston," pp. 392–95.

37. Klein, "William Livingston," pp. 397–98; "Draft Account of the College"; William Livingston to Chauncey Whittelsey, Aug. 22, 1754, *Samuel Johnson*, 4: 22.

38. *N.Y. Mercury*, Dec. 2, 23, 1754.

39. William Livingston to Chauncey Whittelsey, Aug. 22, 1754, *Samuel Johnson*, 4: 21–22; S. Johnson to William Johnson, Aug. 5, 1754, *ibid.*, 1: 195; William Johnson to S. Johnson, Aug. 23, 1754, *ibid.*, 1: 200; S. Johnson, "Autobiography," *ibid.*, 1: 34.

40. Klein, "William Livingston," pp. 405–06, 410–13; Benjamin Nicoll to

William Kempe, Oct. 14, 1754, Sedgwick Papers II, Box 1, Massachusetts Historical Society (cited hereafter as MHS); William Livingston to David Thompson, Jan. 12, 1756, William Livingston Papers, Letterbook 1754–1769, MHS.

41. Henry Barclay to S. Johnson, Nov. 4, 1754, *Samuel Johnson*, 4: 24; S. Johnson, "Autobiography," *ibid.*, 1: 34; S. Johnson to SPG, Dec. 3, 1754, *ibid.*, 4: 28–29.

42. Klein, "William Livingston," pp. 409, 413–15; Henry Barclay to S. Johnson, Nov. 4, 1754, *Samuel Johnson*, 4: 24; *Journal* of the New York General Assembly, Nov. 1, 1754, extracted in *ibid.*, 4: 189.

43. William Smith, Jr., to Eleazar Miller, Sept. 20, 1754, draft, #189 (2), Box 1, William Smith Papers, NYPL; William Livingston to David Thompson, Oct. 28, 1754, William Livingston Papers, Letterbook 1754–1769, MHS. By 1757 the lottery funds (including interest collected or due on money lent out) totaled more than £6,500.

44. *N.Y. Mercury*, Nov. 18, 1754; William Livingston to Noah Welles, Dec. 7, 1754, JFP, Yale; Klein, "William Livingston," pp. 415, 418.

45. *N.Y. Mercury*, Nov. 25, Dec. 2, 1754; William Johnson to William Samuel Johnson, Jan. 3, 1755, WSJ Papers, Conn. Hist. Soc.

46. *John Englishman's true Notion of Sister-Churches*, [April 9, 1755]; *N.Y. Mercury*, Dec. 23, 1754, May 5, 1755.

4. THE KING'S COLLEGE CONTROVERSY:
THE DUTCH AND THE DENOUEMENT

1. *Collections of the New-York Historical Society*, 24 (1896): 145; S. Johnson to William Samuel Johnson, Nov. 8, 1756, Herbert and Carol Schneider, eds., *Samuel Johnson, President of King's College: His Career and Writings* (New York: Columbia University Press, 1929), 1: 268.

2. Figures are based on records of attendance in the *Early Minutes of the Trustees: Vol. I, 1755–1770* (New York, 1932) (cited hereafter as *Governors Minutes*) and the "Minutes of the Governors of King's College, 1770–1781," photostats, both at Columbiana, Columbia University. There were actually two Dutch churches in New York City, but both were ruled by the same group of ministers, elders, deacons, and churchmasters.

3. By the term "managed" I mean attendance with some regularity at the governors meetings.

4. Henry Barclay to S. Johnson, Nov. 4, 1754, *Samuel Johnson*, 4: 25.

5. The percentage tailed off during the second decade, with Dutch Reformed students comprising probably less than one-fifth of the matriculants from 1764 through 1775.

6. Milton M. Klein, "William Livingston: The *American Whig*" (Ph.D. diss., Columbia University, 1954), p. 402.

7. Henry Barclay to S. Johnson, April 16, 1753, Hawks Papers, Church Historical Society (cited hereafter as CHS); *New-York Mercury*, April 30, 1753.

8. *Occasional Reverberator*, Sept. 21, 1753.

9. "Petition of 87 Members of the New York City Reformed Dutch Church," Feb. 1754, New York City Churches, Box 30, New-York Historical Society (cited hereafter as NYHS); Milton M. Klein, ed., *The Independent Reflector* . . . (Cambridge: Harvard University Press, 1963), p. 24n.

10. William Livingston to Aaron Burr, May 29, 1754, William Livingston Papers, Letterbook 1754–1769, Massachusetts Historical Society (cited hereafter as MHS); William Smith, Jr., "Draft Account of the College," #189 (12), Box 1, William Smith Papers, New York Public Library (cited hereafter as "Draft Account of the College").

11. "Petition of 87 Members of the New York City Reformed Dutch Church," Feb. 1754, New York City Churches, Box 30, NYHS; William Livingston to Aaron Burr, May 29, 1754, William Livingston Papers, Letterbook 1754–1769, MHS; Alexander J. Wall, "The Controversy in the Dutch Church in New York Concerning Preaching in English, 1754–1768," *New York Historical Society Quarterly Bulletin* 12 (July 1928): 49. Dutch Reformed allies of the Anglicans split on the issue.

12. S. Johnson to his sons, June 10, 1754, *Samuel Johnson*, 4: 16; William Livingston to Aaron Burr, May 29, 1754, William Livingston Papers, Letterbook 1754–1769, MHS.

13. William Smith, Jr. to Chauncey Graham, Sept. 11, 1754, draft, #189 (4), Box 1, William Smith Papers, New York Public Library (cited hereafter as NYPL).

14. Circular Letter of Coetus, Sept. 19, 1754, E. T. Corwin, ed., *Ecclesiastical Records, State of New York* (Albany: James B. Lyon, 1901–16), 5: 3493 (cited hereafter as *ERSNY*).

15. "Report on Consistory meeting," Oct. 1, 1754, *ERSNY*, 5: 3495; Consistory to Classis of Amsterdam, Oct. 17, 1754, *ERSNY*, 5: 3499–3500; "Petition of Collegiate Church to New York Assembly," Oct. 25, 1754, *ERSNY*, 5: 3505–06; Ritzema, Curtenius, et al. to Classis of Amsterdam, Sept. 3, 1755, *ERSNY*, 5: 3582–85; Ritzema to Classis of Amsterdam, March 21, 1769, *ERSNY*, 6: 4140–45; Beverly McAnear, "American Imprints Concerning King's College," *Papers of the Bibliographical Society of America* 44 (4th Quarter 1950): 328–29.

16. William Smith, Jr., "Draft Account of the College"; William Livingston to Noah Welles, Oct. 18, 1754, Livingston-Welles Correspondence, Johnson Family Papers, Yale University Library; William Livingston to David Thompson, Oct. 28, 1754, William Livingston Papers, Letterbook 1754–1769, MHS.

17. William Smith, Jr., "Draft Account of the College."

18. Henry Barclay to S. Johnson, Nov. 4, 1754, *Samuel Johnson*, 4: 25; S. Johnson to his sons, Nov. 25, 1754, *ibid.*, 4: 26; S. Johnson to his sons, Dec. 2, 1754, *ibid.*, 4: 27.

19. S. Johnson to William Samuel Johnson, May 14, 1755, *ibid.*, 4: 35; *Governors Minutes*, May 7, May 13, June 3, 1755; "Petition of King's College Governors to Assembly," June 12, 1755, *ERSNY*, 5: 3557–58.

20. William Johnson to William Samuel Johnson, June 19, 1755, William

328 NOTES FOR PAGES 63–67

Samuel Johnson Papers, Correspondence, Connecticut Historical Society; William Smith, Jr. to Chauncey Graham, June 28, 1755, draft, #189 (5), Box 1, William Smith Papers, NYPL.

21. [Theodore Frelinghuysen], *A Remark on the Disputes and Contentions in This Province* (New York, 1755), pp. 3–12; McAnear, "American Imprints Concerning King's College," pp. 327n–28n.

22. "Circular Letter of Rev. Theodore Frelinghuysen," April 17, 1755, *ERSNY*, 5: 3541; "Commission of Rev. Theodore Frelinghuysen," May 30, 1755, *ERSNY*, 5: 3551.

23. Coetus to Classis of Amsterdam, Oct. 14, 1755, *ERSNY*, 5: 3608; Curtenius, Ritzema, et al. to Classis of Amsterdam, Sept. 3, 1755, *ERSNY*, 5: 3584; Conferentie to Classis of Amsterdam, Sept. 30, 1755, *ERSNY*, 5: 3589–90.

24. "Consistory's Censure of Ritzema," Aug. 11, 1755 and "Ritzema's Reply," Aug. 12, 1755, *ERSNY*, 5: 3574–77; Coetus to Classis of Amsterdam, Oct. 14, 1755, *ERSNY*, 5: 3610; William Smith, Jr. to Dominie Van Bright, July 26, 1755, draft, #189 (3), Box 1, William Smith Papers, NYPL.

25. William Smith, Jr. to Chauncey Graham, June 28, 1755, draft, #189 (5), Box 1, William Smith Papers, NYPL; S. Johnson to William Johnson, Dec. 16, 1755, *Samuel Johnson*, 1: 230; Klein, "William Livingston," pp. 427, 429.

26. S. Johnson to William Samuel Johnson, Dec. 21, 1755, *Samuel Johnson*, 4: 39; William Livingston to David Thompson, Jan. 12, 1756, William Livingston Papers, Letterbook 1754–1769, MHS; *The Watch-Tower, Numb. LIII*, Jan. 16, 1756, NYHS.

27. S. Johnson to William Samuel Johnson, Nov. 8, 1756, *Samuel Johnson*, 1: 268; William Smith, Jr., *The History of the Province of New-York*, ed. Michael Kammen (Cambridge: Harvard University Press, 1972), 2: 207–08.

28. Classis of Amsterdam to Coetus, April 5, 1756, *ERSNY*, 5: 3658; Conferentie to Classis of Amsterdam, Oct. 12, 1758, *ERSNY*, 5: 3723; Ritzema to Classis of Amsterdam, March 21, 1769, *ERSNY*, 6: 4143–44; Classis of Amsterdam to Consistory of New York, Jan. 8, 1771, *ERSNY*, 6: 4195; Consistory of New York to Classis of Amsterdam, May 11, 1769, 6: 4160.

29. "Articles of Union," Oct. 1771, *ERSNY*, 6: 4216.

5. "CHURCH COLLEGE" OR PROVINCIAL COLLEGE?

1. William Livingston to Noah Welles, Aug. 8, 1757, Livingston-Welles Correspondence, Johnson Family Papers, Yale University Library; S. Johnson to George Berkeley, Jr., Dec. 10, 1756, Herbert and Carol Schneider, eds., *Samuel Johnson, President of King's College: His Career and Writings* (New York: Columbia University Press, 1929), 2: 338; S. Johnson to Francis Astry, Dec. 5, 1757, draft, Samuel Johnson Papers, vol. 2, Special Collections, Columbia University Library.

2. William Livingston to William Livingston, Jr., July 15, [1768?], quoted in Milton M. Klein, "William Livingston: The *American Whig*" (Ph.D. diss., Columbia University, 1954), p. 437; S. Johnson to East Apthorp, Dec. 1, 1759, *Samuel Johnson*, 4: 55.

3. *New-York Mercury*, Dec. 23, 1754.

4. [Benjamin Nicoll], *A Brief Vindication of the Proceedings of the Trustees* . . . (New York, 1754), extracted in *Samuel Johnson*, 4: 203.

5. Data on attendance drawn from the "King's College Governors Minutes" and the "Minutes of the Trustees of the College of New Jersey," transcripts, Princeton University Archives. For additional data on sectarian control at Princeton, see David C. Humphrey, "The Struggle for Sectarian Control of Princeton, 1745–1760," *New Jersey History* 91 (Summer 1973): 77–90.

6. *New-York Gazette; or the Weekly Post-Boy*, June 3, 1754, extracted in *Samuel Johnson*, 4: 223.

7. *N.Y. Mercury*, April 30, 1753, Jan. 27, 1755.

8. *Preface* to the *Independent Reflector* (New York, 1754), extracted in *Samuel Johnson*, 4: 175.

9. *Ibid.*, 4: 161.

10. S. Johnson to SPG, Jan. 10, 1743/44, Francis L. Hawks and William S. Perry, eds., *Documentary History of The Protestant Episcopal Church in the United States of America* . . . *Connecticut* (New York, 1863–64), 1: 204.

11. William Livingston to William Livingston, Jr., July 15, [1768?], quoted in Klein, "William Livingston," p. 437, but with *fatale* as *betale*.

12. "Draft Address of the College Governors to the Public," College Papers, Box 1, Special Collections, Columbia University Library.

13. Comments in this and the following paragraphs on the Anglican church are based on my reading of numerous primary and secondary sources. See David C. Humphrey, "British Influences on Eighteenth Century American Education," *History of Education Quarterly* 13 (Spring 1973): 66–67, 71 n.4, 72 n.9; David C. Humphrey, "Anglican 'Infiltration' of Eighteenth Century Harvard and Yale," *Historical Magazine of the Protestant Episcopal Church* 43 (Sept. 1974): 247–51. I can find little evidence to support Carl Bridenbaugh's contention that SPG missionaries in New England and the middle colonies operated like a well-trained and carefully coordinated military unit. Bridenbaugh, for instance, contends that SPG missionaries devoted "much time and thought" to "figuring out ways to gain control of education in the colonial colleges . . . ," a point that makes sense only if one equates the activities of a handful—Johnson, Wetmore, Timothy Cutler—with the activities of all the missionaries. There seems to be no reason for doing so. See Carl Bridenbaugh, *Mitre and Sceptre: Transatlantic Faiths, Ideas, Personalities, and Politics, 1689–1775* (New York: Oxford University Press, 1962), p. 121.

14. James Macsparran to SPG, May 19, 1744, #75, SPG Letters, series B, vol. 13, transcript, Library of Congress (cited hereafter as LC); James Macsparran, *America Dissected* . . . , included in Wilkins Updike, *History of the Episcopal Church in Narragansett, Rhode Island* . . . (New York, 1847), p. 500.

15. William Johnson to S. Johnson, Aug. 9 and Aug. 23, 1754, *Samuel Johnson*, 1: 195–96, 199.

16. S. Johnson to Archbishop of Canterbury, April 10, 1762, *ibid.*, 1: 319; S. Johnson to Francis Astry, Oct. 30, 1752, *ibid.*, 1: 161; Samuel Auchmuty to

S. Johnson, May 25, 1767, Hawks Papers, Church Historical Society; Samuel Auchmuty to S. Johnson, April 30, 1766, *ibid.* A useful summary of the problems posed by the trip to England can be found in William L. Sachse, *The Colonial American in Britain* (Madison, Wis.: University of Wisconsin Press, 1956), pp. 71–74.

17. Myles Cooper to SPG, Sept. 26, 1767, SPG Letters, series B, vol. 3, microfilm, LC. Statistics on Princeton students are based primarily on data contained in Varnum L. Collins, ed., *General Catalogue of Princeton University, 1746–1906* (Princeton, N.J.: John C. Winston Co., 1908), Frederick L. Weis's five studies on the colonial clergy, Samuel D. Alexander, *Princeton College during the Eighteenth Century* (New York, 1872), and the *Dictionary of American Biography.*

18. See, for example, George W. Pilcher, *Samuel Davies: Apostle of Dissent in Colonial Virginia* (Knoxville, Tenn.: University of Tennessee Press, 1971), pp. 106–07.

19. *Records of the Presbyterian Church in the United States of America* (Philadelphia, 1841), pp. 265–66, 271, 293, 335, 386, 399, 408, 416–17, 426, and passim.

20. One exception was Reverend Jonathan Boucher of Maryland, who recruited George Washington's stepson (John Parke Custis) for King's College.

21. Bishop of London to S. Johnson, Oct. 20, 1754, *Samuel Johnson,* 4: 23; Archbishop of Canterbury to William Smith, Jan. 19, 1755, Horace W. Smith, *Life and Correspondence of the Rev. William Smith, D.D.* (Philadelphia, 1879–80), 1: 100. It is possible that the archbishop's letter was actually written to Johnson but has been identified incorrectly by Horace Smith.

22. SPG Journals, 13: 116–17, meeting of Feb. 20, 1756, photostats, LC; Archbishop of Canterbury to S. Johnson, Sept. 27, 1758, *Samuel Johnson,* 3: 257.

23. S. Johnson to SPG, Dec. 21, 1757, *Samuel Johnson,* 4: 44–45; Henry Barclay to William Johnson, Oct. 5, 1763, James Sullivan et al., eds., *The Papers of Sir William Johnson* (Albany: University of the State of New York, 1921–1965), 13: 300.

24. S. Johnson to William Samuel Johnson, Jan. 20, March 31, 1755, *Samuel Johnson,* 1: 209, 216; William Smith, Jr., *The History of the Province of New York,* ed. Michael Kammen (Cambridge: Harvard University Press, 1972), 2: 208.

25. William Smith to SPG, Nov. 1, 1756, Horace Smith, *Life and Correspondence of William Smith,* 1: 143.

26. *Records of the Presbyterian Church,* p. 206.

6. HIGHER EDUCATION FROM AN ELITIST PERSPECTIVE

1. Ann Cock to John Tabor Kempe, June 13, June 14, 1769, John Tabor Kempe Papers, Box 1, New-York Historical Society (cited hereafter as NYHS). In writing this chapter I have found especially suggestive Ralph H. Turner, "Sponsored and Contest Mobility and the School System," *American Sociological Review* 25 (Dec. 1960): 855–67.

2. Anton-Hermann Chroust, *The Rise of the Legal Profession in America* (Norman, Okla.: University of Oklahoma Press, 1965), 1: 173, 189–90.

3. Ann Cock to John Tabor Kempe, June 13, June 14, 1769, April 2, 1773, John Tabor Kempe Papers, Box 1, NYHS; Abraham Cock to John Tabor Kempe, July 30, 1771, *ibid.*; Will of Abraham Cock, *Collections of the New-York Historical Society*, 32 (1899): 144–45 (cited hereafter as *NYHS Colls.*).

4. Will of Abraham Cock, *NYHS Colls.*, 32 (1899): 144–45; Ann Cock to John Tabor Kempe, Oct. 20, Dec. 12, 1773, John Tabor Kempe Papers, Box 1, NYHS; *New York Mercury*, Oct. 3, 1774, supplement.

5. Milton M. Klein, ed., *The Independent Reflector* . . . (Cambridge: Harvard University Press, 1963), p. 181 (March 29, 1753); "Draft Address of the Governors of the College to the Public," College Papers, Box 1, Special Collections, Columbia University Library (cited hereafter as College Papers).

6. William Lamson to SPG, Oct. 9, 1773, SPG Letters, Misc. Unbound MSS, Connecticut, Part 1, photostats, Library of Congress.

7. Cadwallader Colden to Hezekiah Watkins, Dec. 12, 1748, George H. Moore, *Collegium Regale Novi Eboraci: The Origin and Early History of Columbia College* (New York, 1890), p. 39; Ann Cock to John Tabor Kempe, June 13, 1769, John Tabor Kempe Papers, Box 1, NYHS.

8. M. Halsey Thomas, ed., "The Black Book of King's College," *Columbia University Quarterly* 23 (March 1931): 6; George Rapalje to the Governors of King's College, [July 21], 1774, College Papers.

9. John Ogilvie and Samuel Seabury to SPG, May 19, 1769, copy, SPG Letters, series B, vol. 3, microfilm, Library of Congress.

10. Ann Cock to John Tabor Kempe, June 14, 1769, John Tabor Kempe Papers, Box 1, NYHS.

11. *New-York Evening Post*, Nov. 28, 1748; [William Livingston], *Some Serious Thoughts on The Design of erecting a College in the Province of New-York* . . . (New York, 1749), p. 5; Paul M. Hamlin, *Legal Education in Colonial New York* (New York: New York University Press, 1939), p. 197.

12. Francis Harison to the Common Council of New York, Aug. 31, 1732, Moore, *Collegium Regale Novi Eboraci*, p. 36; [William Smith], *A General Idea of the College of Mirania* . . . (New York, 1753), p. 25; S. Johnson, "Advertisement," Herbert and Carol Schneider, eds., *Samuel Johnson, President of King's College: His Career and Writings* (New York: Columbia University Press, 1929), 2: 314; [William Smith], *Some Thoughts on Education: with Reasons for Erecting a College in this Province, and fixing the same at the City of New-York* . . . (New York, 1752), pp. 9–12.

13. *N.Y. Mercury*, Dec. 30, 1754.

14. *New-York Gazette Revived in the Weekly Post-Boy*, Feb. 18, 1750/51.

15. Hamlin, *Legal Education in Colonial New York*, pp. 197–200; Milton M. Klein, "The Rise of the New York Bar: The Legal Career of William Livingston," *William and Mary Quarterly*, 3d series, 15 (July 1958): 356–57.

16. *Dictionary of American Biography*, s.v. "Joseph Murray"; "Catalogue of John Chambers's Library," MS #9885–269, New York State Library; Chroust, *Rise of the Legal Profession*, 1: 187n–90n.

17. *N.Y. Gazette Revived in the Weekly Post-Boy*, Feb. 18, 1750/51; *Independent Reflector*, pp. 135–41 (Feb. 15, 1753).

18. Peter Middleton, *A Medical Discourse, or an Historical Inquiry Into the Ancient and Present State of Medicine* . . . (New York, 1769), pp. 53–55, 65; W. B. McDaniel II, ed., "John Jones' Introductory Lecture to His Course in Surgery (1769), King's College, Printed from the Author's Manuscript," *Transactions & Studies of the College of Physicians of Philadelphia*, 4th series, 8 (1940–41): 180–90.

19. Alfred W. Newcombe, "The Appointment and Instruction of S.P.G. Missionaries," *Church History* 5 (Dec. 1936): 347–48; S. Johnson, "Raphael, or The Genius of the English America: A Rhapsody," *Samuel Johnson*, 2: 567.

20. Edward Antill to S. Johnson, Dec. 14, 1758, Jan. 16, 1759, College Papers; S. Johnson, "Raphael," *Samuel Johnson*, 2: 569–79; S. Johnson, "An Exhortation to the Graduates," *ibid.*, 4: 278–80; Cadwallader Colden to S. Johnson, Dec. 20, 1752, *ibid.*, 2: 300–01; Smith, *Some Thoughts on Education*, pp. vii, 18; Smith, *General Idea of the College of Mirania*, pp. 10–12, 23–61, 75–78; Livingston, *Some Serious Thoughts*, p. 3.

21. S. Johnson, "An Exhortation to the Graduates," *Samuel Johnson*, 4: 279; Edward Antill to S. Johnson, Dec. 14, 1758, College Papers; Smith, *General Idea of the College of Mirania*, p. 14.

22. *N.Y. Gazette Revived in the Weekly Post-Boy*, Jan. 14, 1750/51.

23. Edward Antill to College Governors, Nov. 7, 1757, New York State Library; Edward Antill to Anthony Lispenard, Feb. 19, 1761 and Edward Antill to S. Johnson, Dec. 14, 1758, College Papers. The college probably received the £800 fairly promptly, but the governors had a great deal of difficulty collecting on the mortgage. The discussion in the next two paragraphs is based on Edward Antill to S. Johnson, Dec. 14, 1758, College Papers.

24. Edward Antill to S. Johnson, Jan. 16, 1759, College Papers; Smith, *General Idea of the College of Mirania*, passim; S. Johnson, "Raphael," *Samuel Johnson*, 2: 555–75; *Independent Reflector*, p. 180 (March 29, 1753); *N.Y. Gazette Revived in the Weekly Post-Boy*, Dec. 11, 1752. Smith offered some thoughts on grammar schools in the *Gazette* essay, then modified them in an essay in the *Independent Reflector*, pp. 419–25 (Nov. 8, 1753). Statements in this paragraph draw on the first essay.

25. Smith, *General Idea of the College of Mirania*, pp. 13–16, 66–68, 70–72.

26. "Draft Address of the Governors of the College to the Public," College Papers, Box 1; S. Johnson to Edward Antill, drafted on letter of Antill to Johnson, Jan. 16, 1759, College Papers.

27. Will of Andrew Barclay, *NYHS Colls.*, 32 (1899): 346; James Duane to Daniel Horsmanden, Oct. 23, 1770, John Watts Papers, vol. 3, NYHS.

28. Frederick Rudolph, *The American College and University: A History* (New York: Knopf, 1962) pp. 197–200.

29. *N.Y. Mercury*, Dec. 7, 1772.

30. Beverly McAnear, "The Selection of an Alma Mater by Pre-Revolutionary Students," *Pennsylvania Magazine of History and Biography* 73 (Oct. 1949):

433, 438; Virginia D. Harrington, *The New York Merchant on the Eve of the Revolution* (New York: Columbia University Press, 1935), pp. 312–18.

31. Micajah Townsend to the Governors of King's College, n.d., College Papers, Box 1.

32. The King's College endowment was probably about £15,000, Princeton's about £2,500. Thomas J. Wertenbaker, *Princeton, 1746–1896* (Princeton, N.J.: Princeton University Press, 1946), p. 53. However, William and Mary's annual income from sources other than tuition and room rent was higher than was King's College's, due to revenues voted the college by the Virginia provincial legislature.

33. S. Johnson to Edward Antill, drafted on letter of Antill to Johnson, Jan. 16, 1759, College Papers; S. Johnson to John Watts, June 1, 1764, *Samuel Johnson*, 4: 109–10; S. Johnson to William Samuel Johnson, Jan. 20, 1755, *ibid.*, 1: 209.

34. George Berkeley to S. Johnson, Aug. 23, 1749, *Samuel Johnson*, 1: 135.

35. "Minutes of the Trustees of the College of New Jersey," Sept. 26, 1750, Sept. 30, 1762, Dec. 9, 1767, April 5, 1769, transcripts, Princeton University Archives; McAnear, "Selection of an Alma Mater," pp. 434–35.

36. William Smith, *Discourses on Public Occasions in America*, 2d ed. (London, 1762), p. 106.

37. Estimating the cost of a college education is a difficult task. The discussions and sources of Beverly McAnear ("Selection of an Alma Mater," pp. 431–34) and Jackson Turner Main (*The Social Structure of Revolutionary America* [Princeton, N.J.: Princeton University Press, 1965], pp. 246–47) provide a helpful starting point. Suggestive sources on costs at King's College include: Ledger of Peter Jay, 1724–1768, NYHS; Myles Cooper to Jonathan Boucher, March 22, 1773 (misdated 1770), Herbert B. Howe, "Colonel George Washington and King's College," *Columbia University Quarterly* 24 (June 1932): 141; Micajah Townsend to Corporation of King's College, plus enclosures, n.d., College Papers, Box 1; letters of Andrew P. Skene, Oct. 5, 1770 and March 2, 1771, Skene Papers, New York State Library.

38. The estimates that follow are very rough and are based on occupational and income data contained in Main, *Social Structure of Revolutionary America*, chs. 1, 3, 4.

39. *Ibid.*, p. 247.

40. [Archibald Kennedy], *A Speech Said to have been Delivered Some Time Before the Close of the Last Sessions* . . . ([New York], 1755), pp. 14–15; Alan Heimert, *Religion and the American Mind: From the Great Awakening to the Revolution* (Cambridge: Harvard University Press, 1966), p. 186.

41. Chroust, *Rise of the Legal Profession*, 1: 187n–89n; Herbert Johnson, "When John Jay Was Jack," *Columbia College Today* 10 (Spring/Summer 1963): 51.

42. "Subscriptions for the College," College Papers, Box 1. The data which are summarized below both on contributors and on students have been drawn from a wide variety of primary and secondary sources. Statements on occupation

and class utilize categories outlined and defined by Main, *Social Structure of Revolutionary America*, especially pp. 41–43, 76–90, 112–13, 272–77.

43. Two hundred nine represents the number of liberal arts students who actually attended King's College between 1754 and 1776 in a degree program. My list of students is the same as that in M. Halsey Thomas, *Columbia University Officers and Alumni, 1754–1857* (New York: Columbia University Press, 1936), pp. 97–105, except that I have dropped Isaac Ogden, '58, Joseph Reade, '58, William Hanna, '59, and Richard Clarke, '62, since none of them ever actually studied at King's College, despite receiving degrees. Also, I have not included James DeLancey Walton and William Walton, since they matriculated in 1777, at a time when the college was all but closed. My data on the two hundred nine liberal arts students are incomplete, because I could not identify one-sixth of the students and because some information on those I identified was unavailable. Thus the figures I used are not as precise as they might be. I have stated some of the percentages as minimal figures ("over . . ."). I believe these are reliable, but the actual figures could be a few percentage points higher. Figures refer to the percentage of students with a certain attribute (such as those with fathers in the professions), not to the percentage of fathers or families. Not every father fits exclusively into one occupational category. If possible, I have classified each man according to his main occupation. Artisan-entrepreneurs, who were small in number, included distillers, brewers, a cooper, tailor, carpenter/lumberyard owner, builder/architect, printer/bookseller, and leather dresser/breeches maker. Professionals included ministers, lawyers, and doctors, with the latter term used as colonials used it, loosely.

44. "Autobiography of John Moore," pp. 10–15, 34–35, transcript, NYHS.

45. Philip Skene to Capt. Gamble, Dec. 19, 1770, Skene Papers, Fort Ticonderoga Library, transcript in Philip Andrew Skene Folder, Columbiana, Columbia University; J. Hector St. John Crèvecoeur, *Letters from an American Farmer* (New York: Fox, Duffield & Co., 1904), p. 351.

46. Lawrence A. Cremin, *American Education: The Colonial Experience, 1607–1783* (New York: Harper & Row, 1970), p. 539.

47. Princeton's charter of 1746, Wertenbaker, *Princeton*, p. 396; *The Colonial Laws of New York from the Year 1664 to the Revolution* . . . (Albany, 1894), 3: 607.

2. *Portrait of a Colonial College*

7. THE FIRST PRESIDENCY

1. S. Johnson, "Autobiography," Herbert and Carol Schneider, eds., *Samuel Johnson, President of King's College: His Career and Writings* (New York: Columbia University Press, 1929), 1: 20; S. Johnson to William Samuel Johnson, March 31, 1755, *ibid.*, 1: 216.

2. S. Johnson, "Autobiography," *ibid.*, 1: 37; "Matricula of King's College,"

ibid., 4: 243–45; S. Johnson to William Samuel Johnson, Feb. 3, 1755, Samuel Johnson Correspondence, vol. 1, Special Collections, Columbia University Library (cited hereafter as SCCU).

3. S. Johnson et al. to SPG, Sept. 22, 1763, SPG Letters, series B, vol. 24, microfilm, Library of Congress (cited hereafter as LC); S. Johnson to SPG, July 15, 1765, SPG Letters, series B, vol. 23, transcript, LC.

4. "State of the Case between Dr. Johnson and the Governors," [Jan. 31, 1763?], *Samuel Johnson*, 4: 94; S. Johnson, "Autobiography," *ibid.*, 1: 37; S. Johnson to A. Watts, Feb. 24, 1757, *ibid.*, 1: 273. In his autobiography Johnson mistakenly dates his departure for Westchester as during November.

5. John Winthrop to Samuel Auchmuty, April 19, 1757, College Papers, SCCU (cited hereafter as College Papers); L. H. Butterfield, ed., *Diary and Autobiography of John Adams* (Cambridge: Harvard University Press, 1962), 1: 107, 3: 261.

6. S. Johnson to East Apthorp, Dec. 1, 1759, *Samuel Johnson*, 4: 56–57; S. Johnson to Edward Antill, drafted on letter of Antill to Johnson, Jan. 16, 1759, College Papers.

7. M. Halsey Thomas, *Columbia University Officers and Alumni, 1754–1857* (New York: Columbia University Press, 1936), pp. 279–82; "Matricula of King's College," *Samuel Johnson*, 4: 246–59.

8. M. Halsey Thomas, ed., "King's College Commencement in the Newspapers," *Columbia University Quarterly* 22 (June 1930): 226–27; "Account of John Jones for Commencement Dinner," 1763, College Papers.

9. S. Johnson to Archbishop of Canterbury, Sept. 20, 1764, *Samuel Johnson*, 1: 347; S. Johnson, "Autobiography," *ibid.*, 1: 18; S. Johnson to Thomas Clap, Feb. 19, 1754, *ibid.*, 1: 181; William Johnson to S. Johnson, Aug. 2, 1754, *ibid.*, 1: 194; S. Johnson to George Berkeley, Jr., Dec. 10, 1756, *ibid.*, 2: 338.

10. Two especially helpful discussions on the development of the early American college are Samuel E. Morison, *The Founding of Harvard College* (Cambridge: Harvard University Press, 1935), and Richard Hofstadter and Walter P. Metzger, *The Development of Academic Freedom in the United States* (New York: Columbia University Press, 1955), Part One, especially ch. 3.

11. Thomas Bartow to John Chambers, Jan. 10, 1754, College Papers. Compare the King's College charter, printed in E. T. Corwin, ed., *Ecclesiastical Records, State of New York* (Albany: James B. Lyon, 1901–16), 5: 3506–14, with the Princeton charter of 1748, printed in Thomas J. Wertenbaker, *Princeton, 1746–1896* (Princeton, N.J.: Princeton University Press, 1946), pp. 396–404.

12. Compare the King's College statutes of 1755, printed in *Samuel Johnson*, 4: 225–29, with the College of New Jersey laws of 1748, included in the "Minutes of the Trustees of the College of New Jersey," Nov. 9, 1748, transcripts, Princeton University Archives.

13. *Early Minutes of the Trustees: Vol. I, 1755–1770* (New York, 1932), May 13, June 3, 1755 (cited hereafter as *Governors Minutes*).

14. "Petition of the College of New Jersey Trustees living in New York," AM (PH) 543, Princeton University Archives; S. Johnson to Edward Antill, drafted on letter of Antill to Johnson, Jan. 16, 1759, College Papers.

15. S. Johnson to William Livingston and the Trustees, Jan. 17, 1754, *Samuel Johnson*, 4: 9n; S. Johnson to William Samuel Johnson, July 21, 1755, *ibid.*, 1: 219.

16. S. Johnson to SPG, Dec. 21, 1757, *ibid.*, 4: 44; Rufus R. Wilson, ed., *Burnaby's Travels Through North America* (New York: A. Wessels Co., 1904), p. 112; Hugh Gaine, *Gaine's Universal Register, or, American and British Kalendar For the Year 1775* (New York, n.d.), p. 102; Morison, *Founding of Harvard*, pp. 275–76; Samuel E. Morison, *Three Centuries of Harvard, 1636–1936* (Cambridge: Harvard University Press, 1965), p. 59.

17. M. Halsey Thomas, "The King's College Building: with some notes on its later tenants," *New-York Historical Society Quarterly* 39 (Jan. 1955): 24, 32, 48.

18. *Ibid.*, 23–24, 30–36, 44, 47–48; J. Hector St. John Crèvecoeur, *Letters from an American Farmer* (New York: Fox, Duffield & Co., 1904), p. 351; Wilson, *Burnaby's Travels*, p. 112.

19. Wilson, *Burnaby's Travels*, p. 112; Thomas, "King's College Building," pp. 30–35, 44, 47; "Photostats: 1763–64," College Papers, Box 1; Morison, *Three Centuries of Harvard*, p. 97; Morison, *Founding of Harvard*, p. 81.

20. Morison, *Founding of Harvard*, p. 81; Edwin Oviatt, *The Beginnings of Yale (1701–1726)* (New Haven: Yale University Press, 1916), pp. 353–56.

21. For a detailed discussion of finances and information on sources, see David C. Humphrey, "King's College in the City of New York, 1754–1776" (Ph.D. diss., Northwestern University, 1968), pp. 123–31.

22. S. Johnson, "Autobiography," *Samuel Johnson*, 1: 39.

23. "Samuel Johnson's Household," *ibid.*, 1: 58; S. Johnson to Peter Jay, April 13, 1741, Frank Monaghan, "Dr. Samuel Johnson's Letters to Peter Jay," *Columbia University Quarterly* 25 (March 1933): 92–93.

24. S. Johnson, "An Exhortation to the Graduates," [1762], *Samuel Johnson*, 4: 278–80; S. Johnson to Archbishop of Canterbury, Sept. 25, 1767, *ibid.*, 1: 419.

25. S. Johnson to Edward Antill, drafted on letter of Antill to Johnson, Jan. 16, 1759, College Papers; S. Johnson to William Samuel Johnson, Dec. 19, 1756, Samuel Johnson Correspondence, vol. 2, SCCU.

26. Edward Antill to S. Johnson, Oct. 29, 1755, College Papers; Mrs. Peter DeLancey to Mrs. Cadwallader Colden, June 7, 1756, *Collections of the New-York Historical Society*, 68 (1935): 155; Henry Lloyd II to Henry Lloyd I, Feb. 21, 1759, *ibid.*, 60 (1927): 565.

27. S. Johnson to William Livingston and the Trustees, Jan. 17, 1754, *Samuel Johnson*, 4: 8.

28. S. Johnson, "Autobiography," *ibid.*, 1: 38; S. Johnson, "State of the Case between Dr. Johnson and the Governors," [Jan. 31, 1763?], *ibid.*, 4: 95; S. Johnson to J. Berriman, Dec. 24, 1761, *ibid.*, 1: 316.

29. S. Johnson to William Samuel Johnson, Feb. 6, Sept. 13, 1756, May 29, 1758, *ibid.*, 1: 235, 257, 277; S. Johnson, "Autobiography," *ibid.*, 1: 37.

30. *Ibid.*, 1: 38, 39; S. Johnson to J. Berriman, Dec. 24, 1761, *ibid.*, 1: 316.

31. S. Johnson to Archbishop of Canterbury, Feb. 15, 1760, *ibid.*, 4: 59; S. Johnson, "Autobiography," *ibid.*, 1: 38; S. Johnson to Archbishop of Canterbury, July 12, 1760, *ibid.*, 1: 296–97; S. Johnson, "State of the Case between Dr. Johnson and the Governors," [Jan. 31, 1763?], *ibid.*, 4: 94.

32. "Matricula of King's College," *ibid.*, 4: 244–47; S. Johnson to Edward Antill, drafted on letter of Antill to Johnson, Jan. 16, 1759, College Papers.

33. Micajah Townsend to Governors of King's College, n.d., College Papers, Box 1; Governors of King's College to SPG, May 14, 1762, *Governors Minutes*, Nov. 16, 1762.

34. "Matricula of King's College," *Samuel Johnson*, 4: 247–49; S. Johnson to Archbishop of Canterbury, May 20, 1761, *ibid.*, 1: 308.

35. S. Johnson to A. Watts, Sept. 1757, *ibid.*, 1: 275; S. Johnson, "State of the Case between Dr. Johnson and the Governors," [Jan. 31, 1763?], *ibid.*, 4: 95; Myles Cooper to Jonathan Boucher, March 22, 1773 (misdated 1770), Herbert B. Howe, "Colonel George Washington and King's College," *Columbia University Quarterly* 24 (June 1932): 141.

36. Virginia D. Harrington, *The New York Merchant on the Eve of the Revolution* (New York: Columbia University Press, 1935), pp. 312–15.

37. Henry Barclay, in behalf of the Governors, to Archbishop of Canterbury, Feb. 16, 1760, *Samuel Johnson*, 4: 61–62; S. Johnson to William Samuel Johnson, Feb. 1, 1762, *ibid.*, 4: 77.

38. S. Johnson to Edward Antill, drafted on letter of Antill to Johnson, Jan. 16, 1759, College Papers; S. Johnson to Archbishop of Canterbury, Aug. 10, 1763, E. B. O'Callaghan and B. Fernow, eds., *Documents Relative to the Colonial History of the State of New-York . . .* (Albany, 1853–87), 7: 538.

39. *Governors Minutes*, May 13, 1755, Dec. 16, 1756, March 20, 21, 1759.

40. S. Johnson to Archbishop of Canterbury, Aug. 10, 1763, O'Callaghan, *Documents Relative to N.Y.*, 7: 538.

41. S. Johnson to Edward Antill, drafted on letter of Antill to Johnson, Jan. 16, 1759, College Papers; S. Johnson, "Autobiography," *Samuel Johnson*, 1: 40.

42. S. Johnson to East Apthorp, June 1760, *Samuel Johnson*, 4: 69; S. Johnson to William Samuel Johnson, Oct. 12, 1761, *ibid.*, 1: 314; S. Johnson to John Watts, June 1, 1764, *ibid.*, 4: 109–10.

43. S. Johnson to William Samuel Johnson, Feb. 1, 1762, *ibid.*, 4: 78; Humphrey, "King's College," pp. 126–27, 164–66.

44. S. Johnson to William Samuel Johnson, Feb. 1, 1762, *Samuel Johnson*, 4: 78; S. Johnson, "State of the Case between Dr. Johnson and the Governors," [Jan. 31, 1763?], *ibid.*, 4: 93–94.

45. Correspondence of S. Johnson and East Apthorp, *ibid.*, 4: 52–59, 63–70; Henry Barclay, in behalf of the Governors, to Archbishop of Canterbury, Feb.

16, 1760, *ibid.*, 4: 62; S. Johnson to Archbishop of Canterbury, Feb. 15, 1760, *ibid.*, 4: 59–60.

46. [Joseph Reade, Jr. to Joseph Reade], [1761?], copy, College Papers; S. Johnson to William Samuel Johnson, Feb. 1, 1762, *Samuel Johnson*, 4: 78.

47. S. Johnson to Mrs. William Samuel Johnson, Sept. 28, 1761, *Samuel Johnson*, 1: 312; S. Johnson to William Samuel Johnson, Oct. 12, 1761, *ibid.*, 1: 314; S. Johnson to Edward Winslow, May 3, 1762, *ibid.*, 1: 321.

48. Humphrey, "King's College," pp. 167–72; S. Johnson to William Samuel Johnson, Oct. 18, 1762, *Samuel Johnson*, 1: 324.

49. S. Johnson to William Samuel Johnson, Sept. 9, 1762, College Papers; S. Johnson to Archbishop of Canterbury, Dec. 5, 1762, *Samuel Johnson*, 1: 327; S. Johnson to Governors, [Nov. 1762?], *ibid.*, 4: 85.

50. William Samuel Johnson to Daniel Horsmanden, Nov. 18, 1762, *Samuel Johnson*, 4: 87; Memorandum Book #5, 1762/1763, entries for Nov. 25–28, 1762, William Samuel Johnson Papers, Connecticut Historical Society.

51. William Samuel Johnson to Daniel Horsmanden, Nov. 18, 1762, *Samuel Johnson*, 4: 87; Sir James Jay's Answer to the Governors' Bill of Complaint, May 6, 1767, Public Record Office, C12 855/19B, #1, photostats, James Jay Papers, SCCU.

52. S. Johnson to SPG, July 5, 1766, *Samuel Johnson*, 1: 366.

8.   MYLES COOPER TAKES THE REINS

1. Thomas Jones, *History of New York during the Revolutionary War* . . . , ed. Edward F. De Lancey (New York, 1879), 1: 61.

2. Samuel Auchmuty to S. Johnson, March 27, 1771, Hawks Papers, Church Historical Society (cited hereafter as CHS).

3. John Moore, "Catalogue of Books Lately Published, A Facetious List," Misc. MSS: John Moore, New-York Historical Society (cited hereafter as NYHS); Franklin B. Dexter, ed., *The Literary Diary of Ezra Stiles* . . . (New York: Scribners, 1901), 2: 339.

4. Clarence H. Vance, "Myles Cooper," *Columbia University Quarterly* 22 (Sept. 1930): 261–63. Cooper's date of birth is not known. He was christened Feb. 19, 1737.

5. Peter Bard to Samuel Bard, April 28, 1763, Bard Collection, Bard College Library.

6. Dexter, *Literary Diary of Ezra Stiles*, 2: 339; Vance, "Myles Cooper," pp. 265, 269.

7. Jones, *History of New York*, 1: 61.

8. Myles Cooper to John Vardill, Aug. 3, 1774, quoted in Vance, "Myles Cooper," p. 277; Dexter, *Literary Diary of Ezra Stiles*, 2: 339.

9. *Early Minutes of the Trustees: Vol. I, 1755–1770* (New York, 1932), Nov. 16, 1762, March 1, 2, 1763 (cited hereafter as *Governors Minutes*); Myles Cooper to Jonathan Boucher, March 22, 1773 (misdated 1770), Herbert B. Howe, "Colonel

George Washington and King's College," *Columbia University Quarterly* 24 (June 1932): 141.

10. Myles Cooper to Archbishop of Canterbury, June 23, 1763, Herbert and Carol Schneider, eds., *Samuel Johnson, President of King's College: His Career and Writings* (New York: Columbia University Press, 1929), 4: 101; "Statutes of King's College, 1763," *ibid.*, 4:237–41.

11. Henry Lloyd III to Joseph Lloyd II, Aug. 6, 1764, *Collections of the New-York Historical Society*, 60 (1927): 670 (cited hereafter as *NYHS Colls.*); *Governors Minutes*, May 10, 1763, May 22, Oct. 23, 1764, April 23, Oct. 24, 1765, Nov. 20, 1766, April 7, 1767; "Rules and Orders Relating to the Porter," *Samuel Johnson*, 4: 242–43; "Dr. Smith's Rules for the Better Regulation of the College," Margaret Evans, ed., *Letters of Richard Radcliffe and John James of Queen's College, Oxford, 1755–83* . . . (Oxford, 1888), p. 244.

12. Myles Cooper to Jonathan Boucher, March 22, 1773, Howe, "George Washington and King's College," p. 141.

13. *Governors Minutes*, March 1, April 12, Aug. 24, Nov. 1, 1763.

14. Myles Cooper to Archbishop of Canterbury, Sept. 23, 1763, *Samuel Johnson*, 4: 104; S. Johnson to John Watts, June 1, 1764, *ibid.*, 4: 109–10.

15. *Governors Minutes*, March 1, 1763, Oct. 23, 1764, Dec. 17, 1765; Austin B. Keep, "The Library of King's College," *Columbia University Quarterly* 13 (June 1911): 276; Samuel Auchmuty and Myles Cooper to SPG, n.d., #318, SPG Letters, series B, vol. 2, microfilm, Library of Congress (cited hereafter as LC); Myles Cooper to SPG, Nov. 19, 1766, SPG Letters, series B, vol. 2, microfilm, LC; Myles Cooper to SPG, Sept. 26, 1767, SPG Letters, series B, vol. 3, microfilm, LC.

16. Keep, "Library of King's College," p. 278; Will of James Tucker, *NYHS Colls.* 31 (1898): 236–37; List of Benefactors to King's College, *Samuel Johnson*, 4: 262; J. Hector St. John Crèvecoeur, *Letters from an American Farmer* (New York: Fox, Duffield & Co., 1904), p. 351.

17. Crèvecoeur, *Letters from an American Farmer*, p. 351; Samuel E. Morison, *The Founding of Harvard College* (Cambridge: Harvard University Press, 1935), pp. 269–70; Thomas B. Chandler to S. Johnson, July 7, 1768, *Samuel Johnson*, 1: 443; *New-York Gazette; or the Weekly Post-Boy*, May 19, 1763.

18. Beverly McAnear, "The Raising of Funds by the Colonial Colleges," *Mississippi Valley Historical Review* 38 (March 1952): 600–03, 602n–03n; Bertha S. Fox, "Provost Smith and the Quest for Funds," *Pennsylvania History*, 2 (Oct. 1935): 231; William Smith to Richard Peters, May 21, Aug. 16, 1763, quoted in *ibid.*, pp. 233–34, 236; James Jay's Bill, Nov. 16, 1767, To Charles Lord Camden, P.R.O., Chancery, 12:1310, 13A, photostats, James Jay Papers, Special Collections, Columbia University Library (cited hereafter as SCCU).

19. McAnear, "Raising of Funds," pp. 600n, 603n, 606n. The usual conversion ratio was £100 sterling to £180 New York Currency. However this ratio varied. Some of the money was converted at a ratio of £100 sterling to £190 New York currency. See *Governors Minutes*, May 8, 1764.

20. Samuel Auchmuty to S. Johnson, March 21, 1769, Hawks Papers, CHS. For a fuller discussion of the controversy between the Governors and Jay see David C. Humphrey, "King's College in the City of New York, 1754–1776" (Ph.D. diss., Northwestern University, 1968), pp. 219–26.

21. Franklin B. Dexter, ed., *Extracts from the Itineraries and Other Miscellanies of Ezra Stiles* . . . (New Haven: Yale University Press, 1916), p. 205.

22. For a fuller discussion of finances during the 1760s and 1770s, see Humphrey, "King's College," pp. 226–28, 305–07. Figures in most cases are estimates, due to the skimpiness of financial records. The best data cover the years at the opening of the Revolution. In 1775 the treasurer reported to the governors that the college held good bonds worth £16,286 (exclusive of interest due). The treasurer also held a large amount of cash, probably more than £1,000. The account book of Augustus Van Horne, who became treasurer in 1779, indicates that the college held bonds worth £18,335 in principal in 1779, the last of which had been given in July 1776 and at least two of which (worth £540) were bad. Also, according to the account book in 1779, £5,590 was due in interest on the bonds, and the former treasurer still held £2,857 in cash. "Minutes of the Governors of King's College, 1770–1781," Aug. 31, 1775, photostats, Columbiana, Columbia University (the minutes for these years exist only in draft and will be cited hereafter as "Governors Minutes," draft); Deposit of Leonard Lispenard, Dec. 2, 1776, College Papers, SCCU; Account Book of Augustus Van Horne, NYHS.

23. "Myles Cooper's Report to the Governors," Oct. 12, 1772, College Papers; *Governors Minutes*, Nov. 1, 1763; John Watts to General Monckton, Oct. 30, 1763, *NYHS Colls.*, 61 (1928): 189–90; W. L. Grant and J. Munro, eds., *Acts of the Privy Council of England, Colonial Series* . . . (Hereford and London: H. M. Stationery Office, 1908–12), 4: 681, 6: 369; "King's Mandamus for 20,000 acres," March 29, 1765, copy, James Jay Papers, SCCU.

24. *Governors Minutes*, Nov. 20, 1766, March 20, 1770; "Governors Minutes," draft, Feb. 17, April 10, 1772; "New York Council Minutes," Feb. 4, 12, 1767, Feb. 7, March 14, 1770, 29: 213, 214, 353–54, 372, New York State Library; Dixon Ryan Fox, *Yankees and Yorkers* (New York: New York University Press, 1940), pp. 154–67, 173–74; "Inhabitants in County of Gloucester, 1771," E. B. O'Callaghan, ed., *The Documentary History of the State of New-York* (Albany, 1849–51), 4: 708.

25. "New York Land Grants in Vermont," *Collections of the Vermont Historical Society*, 1 (1870): 156, 157; *New York Gazette; and the Weekly Mercury*, April 4, 1774. Columbia lost all this land when Vermont became a separate state.

26. Peter Bard to Samuel Bard, April 28, 1763, Bard Collection, Bard College Library; John Watts to Moses Franks, Nov. 24, 1763, *NYHS Colls.*, 61 (1928): 201; Samuel Auchmuty to S. Johnson, Oct. 26, 1764, Hawks Papers, CHS.

27. Samuel Auchmuty to S. Johnson, Oct. 26, 1764, Hawks Papers, CHS; *Governors Minutes*, Nov. 1, 1763; S. Johnson, "Autobiography," *Samuel Johnson*, 1: 43.

28. Morris Saffron, *Samuel Clossy, M. D.* (*1724–1786*), *Professor of Anatomy at King's College: The Existing Works* . . . (New York: Hafner, 1967), pp. xi–xxi; Clossy to George Cleghorn, received Aug. 1, 1764, *ibid.*, pp. xxx–xxxi; *New York Mercury*, Aug. 13, 1764, Sept. 30, 1765.

29. Samuel Auchmuty to S. Johnson, March 21, 1769, Hawks Papers, CHS.

30. *Governors Minutes*, Nov. 20, 1766, Aug. 14, 1767; "Governors Minutes," draft, May 14, Sept. 17, 1771; [Hugh Gaine], *The New-York Pocket Almanack, For the Year 1774* . . . (New York, n. d.), p. 54; Hugh Gaine, *Gaine's Universal Register, or, American and British Kalendar, For the Year 1775* (New York, n. d.), p. 104.

31. Samuel Auchmuty to S. Johnson, March 21, 1769, Hawks Papers, CHS; Myles Cooper to William Smith, April 10, 1769, Protestant Episcopal Church Archives, CHS.

32. "Address of Governors, President, and Professors of King's College to Governor Tryon," March 31, 1774, Public Record Office, Colonial Office 5, America and West Indies, vol. 1106, p. 255, transcript, LC; Myles Cooper to Jonathan Boucher, March 22, 1773, Howe, "George Washington and King's College," p. 141; Charles Inglis to William Johnson, July 11, 1772, James Sullivan et al., eds., *The Papers of Sir William Johnson* (Albany: University of the State of New York, 1921–65), 8: 542.

33. *Governors Minutes*, March 20, 1770; "Governors Minutes," draft, April 12, Nov. 1, 1770, May 14, Oct. 8, 1771.

34. Charles Inglis to S. Johnson, Nov. 6, 1771, John W. Lydekker, *The Life and Letters of Charles Inglis* . . . (London and New York: Macmillan, 1936), p. 137.

9. THE COMING OF THE REVOLUTION

1. Quoted in Lorenzo Sabine, *Biographical Sketches of Loyalists of the American Revolution, with An Historical Essay* (Boston, 1864), 1: 207.

2. Myles Cooper to William Smith, Jan. 26, 1771, Protestant Episcopal Church Archives, Church Historical Society (cited hereafter as CHS); "Minutes of Meeting of Committee for Considering Ways and Means for Promoting the Interest of the College," Sept. 18, 1771, College Papers, Special Collections, Columbia University Library (cited hereafter as College Papers); "Minutes of the Governors of King's College, 1770–1781," Sept. 30, 1771, photostats, Columbiana, Columbia University (minutes for most of 1770 and for 1771 through 1781 exist only in draft and will be cited hereafter as "Governors Minutes," draft).

3. "Draft Address of the Governors of the College to the Public," College Papers, Box 1.

4. Copies or drafts of the addresses, all dated Oct. 12, 1771, are in the College Papers.

5. Myles Cooper to Jonathan Boucher, March 22, 1773 (misdated 1770), Herbert B. Howe, "Colonel George Washington and King's College," *Columbia University Quarterly* 24 (June 1932): 141; Samuel Auchmuty to S. Johnson, Wednes-

NOTES FOR PAGES 142-149

day or rather Thursday morning, Hawks Papers, CHS; Charles Inglis to William Johnson, July 11, 1772, James Sullivan et al., eds., *The Papers of Sir William Johnson* (Albany: University of the State of New York, 1921–65), 8: 542.

6. Bruce Steiner describes their efforts well in *Samuel Seabury, 1729–1796: A Study in the High Church Tradition* (Athens, Ohio: Ohio University Press, 1971), pp. 101ff.

7. Herbert L. Osgood, "The Society of Dissenters founded at New York in 1769," *American Historical Review* 6 (April 1901): 505; "Governors' Address to the King," Oct. 12, 1771, draft (crossed out), College Papers.

8. "Governors' Address to Lord North," Oct. 12, 1771, copy, College Papers.

9. Steiner, *Samuel Seabury*, pp. 128–29; *New York Gazette; and the Weekly Mercury*, May 16, 1768; Samuel Auchmuty to SPG, Oct. 17, 1767, SPG Letters, series B, vol. 2, transcript, Library of Congress.

10. Patricia Bonomi, *A Factious People: Politics and Society in Colonial New York* (New York and London: Columbia University Press, 1971), pp. 266–78; Carl Becker, *The History of Political Parties in the Province of New York, 1760–1776* (Madison, Wis.: University of Wisconsin Press, 1960), pp. 79–94; Samuel Auchmuty to S. Johnson, June 12, 1766, Herbert and Carol Schneider, eds., *Samuel Johnson, President of King's College: His Career and Writings* (New York: Columbia University Press, 1929), 1: 363.

11. Charles Inglis to S. Johnson, Nov. 6, 1771, John W. Lydekker, *The Life and Letters of Charles Inglis . . .* (London and New York: Macmillan, 1936), pp. 136–37; "Myles Cooper's Report to the Governors," Oct. 12, 1772, College Papers; *Journal of the Commissioners for Trade and Plantations . . .* (London: H. M. Stationery Office, 1920–38), 13 (Jan. 1768–Dec. 1775): 304–06; A. Atkinson to Myles Cooper, May 6, 1772, General MSS Collection, Special Collections, Columbia University Library (cited hereafter as SCCU); Dr. Berkeley to S. Johnson, March 14, 1772, Bancroft Transcripts, Letters of Samuel Johnson and William Samuel Johnson, 1760–1775, New York Public Library (cited hereafter as NYPL).

12. Charles Inglis to William Johnson, [Oct. 27, 1772], *Papers of Sir William Johnson*, 8: 621; Joseph Lamson to [S. Johnson], [1771], Samuel Johnson Correspondence, SCCU; *N. Y. Gazette; and the Weekly Mercury*, Oct. 5, 1772.

13. "Myles Cooper's Report to the Governors," Oct. 12, 1772, College Papers; "Governors Minutes," draft, Oct. 12, 1772, Aug. 4, 1774.

14. "Draft of Charter for the American University in the Province of New York," Public Record Office, Colonial Office 5, America and West Indies, vol. 1106, pp. 63–122. Transcripts can be found at the Library of Congress and at Columbiana. Quotations are from the Columbiana transcript.

15. W. R. Ward, *Georgian Oxford: University Politics in the Eighteenth Century* (Oxford: Clarendon Press, 1958), pp. 3–7.

16. "Memorial Concerning the Iroquois," Oct. 1, 1771, E. B. O'Callaghan, ed., *The Documentary History of the State of New-York* (Albany, 1849–51), 4: 1102–06, 1116; Myles Cooper to William Johnson, Nov. 29, 1766, *Papers of Sir*

William Johnson, 5: 431; Samuel Auchmuty to William Johnson, Jan. 5, 1767, *ibid.*, 5: 464; William Johnson to Myles Cooper, Dec. 27, 1766, *ibid.*, 5: 455; William Johnson to Henry Barclay, March 30, 1763, *ibid.*, 4: 72–73; Charles Inglis to S. Johnson, Nov. 6, 1771, Lydekker, *Life and Letters of Charles Inglis*, pp. 137–38; Frank J. Klingberg, *Anglican Humanitarianism in Colonial New York* (Philadelphia: Church Historical Society, 1940), pp. 93–118.

17. "Governors Minutes," draft, March 29, 1774; "Account of James Downes," April 12, 1774, College Papers; *N. Y. Gazette; and the Weekly Mercury*, April 4, 11, 1774.

18. *N. Y. Gazette; and the Weekly Mercury*, April 11, 1774.

19. "Governors Minutes," draft, Nov. 11, Dec. 28, 1773; "Memorial of John Vardill," American Loyalist Transcripts, vol. 42, pp. 38, 39, NYPL; *Dictionary of American Biography*, s.v. "John Vardill."

20. Bernard Mason, *The Road to Independence: The Revolutionary Movement in New York, 1773–1777* (Lexington, Ky.: University of Kentucky Press, 1966), pp. 49–50.

21. John Vardill to James Duane, Sept. 15, 1774, James Duane Papers, 1772–1774, New-York Historical Society; "Warrant for appointment of John Vardill," Jan. 9, 1778, Grants and Warrants From Aug. 18, 1777 to Feb. 20, 1783, vol. 2, Public Record Office, Colonial Office 324/44, pp. 28–29; *N. Y. Gazette; and the Weekly Mercury*, Dec. 12, 1774, Jan. 9, 1775; Franklin B. Dexter, *The Literary Diary of Ezra Stiles . . .* (New York: Scribners, 1901), 1: 502–03. My thanks to Mark N. Brown for checking the warrant for the appointment of John Vardill and several other documents at the Public Record Office while doing research in London in 1967.

22. William Tryon to Earl of Dartmouth, Feb. 17, 1775, P.R.O., C.O. 5, vol. 1106, p. 55, transcript, Papers Concerning the Royal Charter of 1774, Columbiana; Earl of Dartmouth to William Tryon, May 4, 1775, E. B. O'Callaghan and B. Fernow, eds., *Documents Relative to the Colonial History of the State of New-York . . .* (Albany, 1853–87), 8: 573–74.

23. [Ambrose Serle] to Earl of Dartmouth, Nov. 8, 1776, B. F. Stevens, *Facsimiles of Manuscripts in European Archives Relating to America, 1773–1783 . . .* (London, 1889–98), 24: #2045; Samuel Bard to John Bard, 1773, Bard Collection, New York Academy of Medicine; Clarence H. Vance, "Myles Cooper," *Columbia University Quarterly* 22 (Sept. 1930): 274–75, 278.

24. Myles Cooper, *National Humiliation and Repentance recommended . . .* (Oxford, 1777), pp. 18, 20.

25. *N. Y. Gazette; and the Weekly Mercury*, Dec. 7, 1772, reprinted in *New Jersey Archives*, 1st series, 28 (1916): 349, 353–54; *New York Journal; or the General Advertiser*, Oct. 4, 1770 and *Pennsylvania Gazette*, Oct. 18, 1770, reprinted in *New Jersey Archives*, 1st series, 27 (1905): 268, 292.

26. Morris Saffron, *Samuel Clossy, M.D. (1724–1786), Professor of Anatomy at King's College, New York: The Existing Works . . .* (New York: Hafner, 1967), pp. lv–lvii; *Dictionary of American Biography*, s.v. "Robert Harpur."

27. M. Halsey Thomas, ed., "King's College Commencement in the Newspapers," *Columbia University Quarterly* 22 (June 1930): 230, 233, 235, 242–46.

28. Broadus Mitchell, *Alexander Hamilton: Youth to Maturity, 1755–1788* (New York: Macmillan, 1957), p. 77; Thomas J. Wertenbaker, *Princeton, 1746–1896* (Princeton, N.J.: Princeton University Press, 1946), p. 57.

29. *A History of Columbia University, 1754–1904* . . . (New York: Columbia University Press, 1904), p. 48; Vance, "Myles Cooper," pp. 278–79; Mitchell, *Alexander Hamilton*, pp. 75, 510–12; Cadwallader Colden to Lord Dartmouth, June 7, 1775, *Collections of the New-York Historical Society*, 10 (1877): 421; *Pennsylvania Journal; and the Weekly Advertiser*, May 17, 1775. Tradition has it that Cooper escaped while Alexander Hamilton held off the mob, haranguing it on the impropriety of its conduct and on the disgrace it would bring to the cause of liberty. This popular story may well be true, but it rests on two doubtful pieces of evidence. The major source is a personal reminiscence of Hamilton written forty-six years after the event by Robert Troup, a graduate of King's College in 1774, who claimed that he stood by Hamilton's side during the harangue. Hamilton's harangue is also mentioned in a reminiscence of Hamilton written thirty-five to forty years after the event by Hercules Mulligan, who was a good friend of Hamilton's in 1775. Not only did both men write their reminiscences several decades after the event, but both did so at the request of Hamilton's son (who was preparing a filiopietistic biography of his father) at a time when both men were getting along in years (Mulligan was in his seventies, Troup was sixty-four). Moreover, both men idolized Hamilton. Not surprisingly, their reminiscences contain inaccuracies on other aspects of Hamilton's life. And Troup was not above embellishing his story of Hamilton's harangue in another telling of it, adding details about how Cooper, "at first imagining he [Hamilton] was exciting the mob, exclaimed from an upper window, 'Don't listen to him, gentlemen, he is crazy, he is crazy.' " The two men's recollections of Hamilton's harangue are not confirmed by other sources, including two narratives of the event written shortly after it occurred. Cadwallader Colden described the advance of the mob and Cooper's flight in a letter written a month after they took place, but he did not mention either Hamilton or the harangue. Nor did Myles Cooper mention them in a poem which he wrote about the event in 1776, though he did indicate that a student (unnamed) wakened him as the mob approached and fled with him. See Mitchell, *Alexander Hamilton*, pp. 74–76, 510–12, and Nathan Schachner, ed., "Alexander Hamilton Viewed by His Friends: The Narratives of Robert Troup and Hercules Mulligan," *William and Mary Quarterly*, 3d series, 4 (April 1947): 203–08, 211, 219.

30. "Matricula of King's College," *Samuel Johnson*, 4: 260–61; *Journals of the Provincial Congress, Provincial Convention, Committee of Safety and Council of Safety of the State of New-York, 1775–1776–1777* (Albany, 1842), 1: 400.

31. *N. Y. Gazette; and the Weekly Mercury*, May 20, 1776, June 2, 1777; "Matricula of King's College," *Samuel Johnson*, 4: 261.

32. Committee of Governors to Myles Cooper, June 13, 1781, draft, College

NOTES FOR PAGES 155–162 345

Papers; Myles Cooper to Isaac Wilkins, Feb. 26, 1779, extracted in George A. Ward, *Journal and Letters of the Late Samuel Curwen* . . . (New York, 1842), p. 540.

33. Theodore Frelinghuysen to Classis of Amsterdam, Feb. 20, 1756, E. T. Corwin, ed., *Ecclesiastical Records, State of New York* (Albany: James B. Lyon, 1901–16), 5: 3648–49; [Theodore Frelinghuysen], *A Remark on the Disputes and Contentions in This Province* (New York, 1755), pp. 11–12; Donald G. Tewksbury, *The Founding of American Colleges and Universities Before the Civil War* . . . (New York: Teachers College, Columbia University, 1932), pp. 28, 69, 90; Natalie A. Naylor, "The Ante-Bellum College Movement: A Reappraisal of Tewksbury's *Founding of American Colleges and Universities*," *History of Education Quarterly* 13 (Fall 1973): 261–71.

10. THE EDUCATION OF WISE AND GOOD MEN

1. David Fordyce, *Dialogues Concerning Education*, 2d ed. (Glasgow, 1768), 2: 301.

2. Myles Cooper, *Ethices Compendium* . . . (New York, 1774), passim; S. Johnson, *Elementa Philosophica* . . . , Herbert and Carol Schneider, eds., *Samuel Johnson, President of King's College: His Career and Writings* (New York: Columbia University Press, 1929), 2: 361–67, 446–53, 485–514; S. Johnson, "Raphael: or The Genius of the English America," *ibid.*, 2: 569–70; George C. Brauer, Jr., *The Education of a Gentleman: Theories of Gentlemanly Education In England, 1660–1775* (New York: Bookman Associates, 1959), pp. 13–30, 34–42; Norman S. Fiering, "President Samuel Johnson and the Circle of Knowledge," *William and Mary Quarterly*, 3d series, 28 (April 1971): 231–35.

3. S. Johnson, "A Paper to Be Read at My Decease or Dismission," [1759 ?], *Samuel Johnson* 4: 115–16 (cited hereafter as "A Paper"); *New-York Gazette; or the Weekly Post-Boy*, June 3, 1754, *ibid.*, 4: 222–24; S. Johnson to William Samuel Johnson, Nov. 30, 1761, Samuel Johnson Correspondence, vol. 2, Special Collections, Columbia University Library (cited hereafter as SCCU).

4. *Elementa Philosophica, Samuel Johnson*, 2: 362–65, 431–32; S. Johnson, "Raphael," *ibid.*, 2: 567; S. Johnson, "Advertisement," *ibid.*, 2: 314; Fordyce, *Dialogues Concerning Education*, 2: 294, 307.

5. *Elementa Philosophica, Samuel Johnson*, 2: 490–501.

6. "Form of Morning and Evening Prayers for the College," *ibid.*, 4: 265–71; S. Johnson, "A Paper," *ibid.*, 4: 115; "Short Prayer for the Pupils," *ibid.*, 4: 272–73.

7. "Laws and Orders of King's College, 1755," *ibid.*, 4: 226–28.

8. S. Johnson to William Samuel Johnson, Feb. 16, 1761, *ibid.*, 1: 305–06; S. Johnson, "Raphael," *ibid*, 2: 568–69.

9. "Laws and Orders of King's College, 1755," *ibid.*, 4: 225–26, 229; S. Johnson to East Apthorp, Dec. 1, 1759, *ibid.*, 4: 57; "Statutes of King's College, 1763," *ibid.*, 4: 238–41. The Easter vacation was a vacation from classes only, not from other college functions, such as morning and evening prayers. Under Coo-

per the fall vacation was two weeks, and commencement took place in May, with the new school year beginning in June. Cooper usually examined candidates for admission late in June.

10. The discussion of Johnson's curriculum is based mainly on three sources: S. Johnson to Edward Antill, drafted on letter of Antill to Johnson, Jan. 16, 1759, College Papers, SCCU; S. Johnson to East Apthorp, Dec. 1, 1759, *Samuel Johnson*, 4: 56–57; S. Johnson, "A Paper," *ibid.*, 4: 115–16. The original of the 12/1/59 letter (Samuel Johnson Correspondence, SCCU) indicates, unlike the printed version, that the sophomores read Dionysius Periegetes, and John Locke's *An Essay Concerning Human Understanding*. Unless otherwise noted, quotations and information which follow come from the three sources above.

11. "Laws and Orders of King's College, 1755," *Samuel Johnson*, 4: 225. The laws specified that students be "expert in arithmetic so far as the rule of reduction," although Johnson omitted this requirement in explaining the admission requirements to East Apthorp.

12. Jean Heuzet, *Selectae E Profanis Scriptoribus Historiae* . . . , 3d ed. (London, 1758), p. vii, passim.

13. John Clarke, *An Introduction to the Making of Latin* . . . (Worcester, Mass., 1786), passim; S. Johnson to Bishop Lowth, June 25, 1767, *Samuel Johnson*, 1: 409.

14. *Elementa Philosophica, Samuel Johnson*, 2: 365; William Duncan, *The Elements of Logic. In Four Books* . . . (Philadelphia, 1792), p. x; Wilbur Samuel Howell, *Logic and Rhetoric in England, 1500–1700* (Princeton, N.J.: Princeton University Press, 1956), pp. 350–61. The discussion of Duncan in this and the next three paragraphs draws heavily on Wilbur Samuel Howell's excellent analysis in *Eighteenth-Century British Logic and Rhetoric* (Princeton, N.J.: Princeton University Press, 1971), pp. 349–61.

15. Howell, *Eighteenth-Century British Logic and Rhetoric*, pp. 352–53; Duncan, *Elements of Logic*, p. 215; Howell, *Logic and Rhetoric, 1500–1700*, pp. 346–57.

16. Howell, *Eighteenth-Century British Logic and Rhetoric*, pp. 353–55, 360; M. Halsey Thòmas, ed., "King's College Commencement in the Newspapers," *Columbia University Quarterly* 22 (June 1930): 229.

17. *Elementa Philosophica, Samuel Johnson*, 2: 353, 362; Howell, *Logic and Rhetoric, 1500–1700*, p. 66; Howell, *Eighteenth-Century British Logic and Rhetoric*, pp. 79–81, 137–39, 142, 697.

18. John Sterling, *A System of Rhetorick* . . . (New York, 1788), pp. 1–12; [Anthony Blackwall], *Rhetoric and Poetry, Extracted from the Preceptor* . . . (Boston, 1796), p. 19, passim. Blackwall's work was originally entitled *An Introduction to the Classics* and was also included in Robert Dodsley's *The Preceptor* . . . (London, 1748).

19. *Elementa Philosophica, Samuel Johnson*, 2: 363; Howell, *Eighteenth-Century British Logic and Rhetoric*, p. 697.

20. Walter Miller, ed., *Xenophon, Cyropaedia* (Cambridge: Harvard University Press, 1960), 1: viii, ix, xii; George H. Sabine, *A History of Political Theory*, 3d ed.

(New York: Holt, Rinehart & Winston, 1961), pp. 430–31; Joseph J. Ellis, *The New England Mind in Transition: Samuel Johnson of Connecticut, 1696–1772* (New Haven and London: Yale University Press, 1973), pp. 226–27; Peter Van Schaack to Henry Van Schaack, Jan. 2, 1769, Peter Van Schaack Papers, SCCU.

21. Howell, *Eighteenth-Century British Logic and Rhetoric*, p. 267.

22. Samuel Bayard's workbook (identified as Robert Harpur's), Columbiana, Columbia University; Edmund Stone, *Euclid's Elements of Geometry, The First Six, the Eleventh and Twelfth Books . . .* (London, 1752), p. xii.

23. John Rowning, *A Compendious System of Natural Philosophy . . .* (London, 1744), p. iv; Samuel E. Morison, *Harvard College in the Seventeenth Century* (Cambridge: Harvard University Press, 1936), p. 243.

24. *Early Minutes of the Trustees: Vol. I, 1755–1770* (New York, 1932), May 8, 1759, Aug. 24, 1763 (cited hereafter as *Governors Minutes*); "Minutes of the Governors of King's College, 1770–1781," Nov. 15, 1774, photostats, Columbiana; J. Hector St. John Crèvecoeur, *Letters from an American Farmer* (New York: Fox, Duffield & Co., 1904), p. 351.

25. Penned in Johnson's personal copy of *Elementa Philosophica*, Columbiana.

26. *Ibid.*

27. S. Johnson, "Autobiography," *Samuel Johnson*, 1: 6–7, 23; S. Johnson to William Samuel Johnson, Jan. 20, 1755, *ibid.*, 1: 209.

28. Several perceptive studies of Johnson's thought have recently been completed. The discussion which follows has benefited particularly by Joseph J. Ellis, *The New England Mind in Transition* and Norman S. Fiering, "Moral Philosophy in America, 1650 to 1750, and Its British Context" (Ph.D. diss., Columbia University, 1969). Still valuable is Theodore Hornberger's article, "Samuel Johnson of Yale and King's College: A Note on the Relation of Science and Religion in Provincial America," *New England Quarterly* 8 (Sept. 1935): 378–97. Another perceptive work, which I had an opportunity to see only after I had completed all but a fraction of this book, is Donald F. M. Gerardi, "The American Doctor Johnson: Anglican Piety and the Eighteenth-Century Mind" (Ph.D. diss., Columbia University, 1973).

29. Ellis, *New England Mind*, pp. 154–55; *Elementa Philosophica, Samuel Johnson*, 2: 375.

30. *Elementa Philosophica, Samuel Johnson*, 2: 446, 483; S. Johnson, "Exhortation to the Graduates," *ibid.*, 4: 278–79; Fiering, "Moral Philosophy in America," pp. 339–46.

31. S. Johnson, "Autobiography," *Samuel Johnson*, 1: 45; Hornberger, "Samuel Johnson of Yale and King's College," pp. 393–96; Ellis, *New England Mind*, pp. 228–30.

32. Ellis, *New England Mind*, pp. 231–32; S. Johnson to George Berkeley, Jr., Dec. 10, 1756, *Samuel Johnson*, 2: 338.

33. "State of the Case between Dr. Johnson and the Governors," [Jan. 31, 1763?], *Samuel Johnson*, 4: 94; Hornberger, "Samuel Johnson of Yale and King's College," p. 396.

34. Samuel E. Morison, *The Founding of Harvard College* (Cambridge: Harvard University Press, 1935), pp. 50–57; Fiering, "President Samuel Johnson and the Circle of Knowledge," p. 223.

35. S. Johnson, "A Catalogue of Books," *Samuel Johnson*, 1: 522–24; S. Johnson to Benjamin Franklin, [Nov. 1750], Leonard W. Labaree et al., eds., *The Papers of Benjamin Franklin* (New Haven: Yale University Press, 1959–), 4: 74–75; S. Johnson to Cadwallader Colden, June 7, 1747, *Samuel Johnson*, 2: 299. The works in question are John Locke, *Some Thoughts Concerning Education* (London, 1693); Robert Dodsley, *The Preceptor . . .* , 2 vols. (London, 1748), which was actually a compilation of texts on several subjects which together formed "A General Course of Education"; Fordyce, *Dialogues Concerning Education;* Benjamin Franklin, *Proposals Relating to the Education of Youth in Pennsilvania* (Philadelphia, 1749), and "The Idea of the English School"; and William Smith, *A General Idea of the College of Mirania . . .* (New York, 1753). The best edition of Locke's work is James L. Axtell, ed., *The Educational Writings of John Locke . . .* (Cambridge: Cambridge University Press, 1968). Franklin's two essays are in *Papers of Benjamin Franklin*, vols. 3, 4.

36. *N. Y. Gazette; or the Weekly Post-Boy*, June 3, 1754, *Samuel Johnson*, 4: 223–24; S. Johnson, "Advertisement," *ibid.*, 2: 314–15; S. Johnson to Benjamin Franklin, [Nov. 1750], *Papers of Benjamin Franklin*, 4: 75. See also Johnson's discussion of subjects in *Elementa Philosophica*, *Samuel Johnson*, 2: 361–67, especially 366.

37. Myles Cooper to Jonathan Boucher, March 22, 1773 (misdated 1770), Herbert B. Howe, "Colonel George Washington and King's College," *Columbia University Quarterly* 24 (June 1932): 141. Cooper's plan of education can be found in the *Governors Minutes*, March 1, 1763. For the curriculum at Queen's College, Oxford, see Timothy L. S. Sprigge, ed., *The Correspondence of Jeremy Bentham, Volume 1: 1754–76* (London: Athlone Press, 1968), pp. 19, 21–22, 37, 46–47, 50, 60, 61, 67, 69, 70; and Margaret Evans, ed., *Letters of Richard Radcliffe and John James of Queen's College, Oxford, 1755–1783 . . .* (Oxford, 1888), pp. 45–81, 110–11, 142–43.

38. Helpful clues on the curriculum can be found in: M. Halsey Thomas, ed., "The Black Book of King's College," *Columbia University Quarterly* 23 (March 1931): 1–18; sources at the New-York Historical Society (cited hereafter as NYHS) on the literary society which was formed by supporters of the college, especially *For the Encouragement of Learning, in King's-College, New-York*, Broadside Collection, and the "Minutes and Accounts of the Literary Society"; Robert Harpur's Account Book, photostats, Columbiana; Hugh Gaine's annual *Registers* and *Almanacks;* John Parke Custis to George Washington, July 5, 1773, Howe, "George Washington and King's College," p. 151; Thomas, "King's College Commencement in the Newspapers," pp. 230–47; and various books at Columbiana once owned by King's College students.

39. Robert Harpur officially resigned as professor of mathematics in 1767. However, he continued to teach at the college until the Revolution. His financial

accounts show that in the 1770s he tutored students in mathematics and related fields on a private basis charging an extra fee. Yet less than half the matriculated students arranged for his instruction. Whether and how the other students were tutored in mathematics cannot be determined. On James Ferguson's book, see the copy owned by Philip Pell, class of 1770, now at Columbiana.

40. Cooper, *Ethices Compendium*, p. 78; Howell, *Eighteenth-Century British Logic and Rhetoric*, pp. 13–14, 259–60; John James, Jr., to John James, Sr., Nov. 21, 1778, Evans, *Letters of Radcliffe and James*, p. 50.

41. I am grateful to James McCabe, formerly of Carnegie-Mellon University, who translated Cooper's text for me and enlightened me on its contents. Cooper's personal copy of Whitby's *Ethices Compendium* is at Columbiana.

42. Samuel Clossy, *Observations On some of the Diseases Of the Parts of the Human Body* . . . (London, 1763), p. iv, in Morris H. Saffron, *Samuel Clossy, M.D. (1724–1786)* . . . (New York: Hafner, 1967); Lyman H. Butterfield, ed., *Diary and Autobiography of John Adams* (Cambridge: Harvard University Press, 1961), 2: 110; "Notes on Samuel Clossy's Lectures," College Papers, SCCU.

43. *For the Encouragement of Learning, in King's-College, New-York*, Broadside Collection, NYHS; "Minutes and Accounts of the Literary Society," NYHS; Hugh Gaine, *Gaine's Universal Register, or, American and British Kalendar, For the Year 1775* (New York, n. d.), p. 104; *New York Gazette; and the Weekly Mercury*, Sept. 14, 1772.

44. Thomas, "King's College Commencement in the Newspapers," p. 243; Gulian Verplanck to his brother, March 12 and April 5, 1775, Gulian C. Verplanck Papers, Box 8, NYHS.

45. Myles Cooper, *Poems on Several Occasions* (Oxford, 1761), passim; Nathan Schachner, ed., "Alexander Hamilton Viewed by His Friends: The Narratives of Robert Troup and Hercules Mulligan," *William and Mary Quarterly*, 3d series, 4 (April 1947): 214; College Exercise, "Virse," Robert R. Livingston Papers, Box 2, NYHS.

46. Thomas, "King's College Commencement in the Newspapers," pp. 235, 243; Myles Cooper to William Smith, Aug. 14, 1773, Hawks Papers, Church Historical Society; John Moore, "Catalogue of Books Lately Published, A Facetious List," Misc. MSS: John Moore, NYHS; S. Johnson to William Samuel Johnson, Nov. 15, 1762, *Samuel Johnson*, 1: 324.

11. THE UNDERGRADUATE EXPERIENCE

1. William B. Sprague, *Annals of the American Pulpit* . . . (New York, 1865–69), 5: 463; Myles Cooper to Samuel Peters, July 18, 1785, Samuel Peters Papers, vol. 2, microfilm, New-York Historical Society (cited hereafter as NYHS); Peter Van Schaack to Henry Walton, Oct. 1, 1784, Peter Van Schaack Papers, Box 2, Special Collections, Columbia University Library (cited hereafter as SCCU).

2. *New-York Gazette; or the Weekly Post-Boy*, June 3, 1754, Herbert and Carol Schneider, eds., *Samuel Johnson, President of King's College: His Career and Writings*

(New York: Columbia University Press, 1929), 4: 223; [John Vardill], *Candid Remarks on Dr. Witherspoon's Address To the Inhabitants of Jamaica* . . . (Philadelphia, 1772), pp. 28–29; Samuel Bard to his brother, June 2, 1764, Bard Collection, New York Academy of Medicine.

3. Vardill, *Candid Remarks*, pp. 27–30; George Rapalje to Governors of King's College, 1774, College Papers, SCCU (cited hereafter as College Papers); "Benjamin Moore's Testimonial for John Nicoll," Sept. 6, 1775, College Papers.

4. S. Johnson, "Raphael, or The Genius of the English America: A Rhapsody," *Samuel Johnson*, 2: 556; Vardill, *Candid Remarks*, p. 27.

5. M. Halsey Thomas, ed., "The Black Book of King's College," *Columbia University Quarterly* 23 (March 1931): 4–5, 6, 8–9 (cited hereafter as "Black Book"); "Minutes of the Governors of King's College, 1770–1781," Nov. 11, 1773, photostats, Columbiana, Columbia University (cited hereafter as "Governors Minutes," draft).

6. "Black Book," pp. 2–17; "Matricula of King's College," *Samuel Johnson*, 4: 247; "Petition of John Rutgers Marshall to Governors of King's College," Sept. 6, 1770, College Papers; S. Johnson to [Myles Cooper], Aug. 24, 1770, College Papers; "Governors Minutes," draft, Nov. 1, 1770.

7. "Black Book," pp. 2–17; "Governors Minutes," draft, Sept. 2, 1773; S. Johnson, "Raphael," *Samuel Johnson*, 2: 559–60.

8. "Black Book," p. 16; "Governors Minutes," draft, Aug. 31, 1775; "Matricula of King's College," *Samuel Johnson*, 4: 250; "Statutes of King's College, 1763," *ibid.*, 4: 240–41; "Minutes and Accounts of the Literary Society," NYHS; *For the Encouragement of Learning, in King's-College, New-York*, Broadside Collection, NYHS; Charles Inglis, "Address to the Students of King's College," Journals and Correspondence, vol. 1, Nova Scotia Archives, Halifax, transcript at Columbiana (cited hereafter as Inglis, "Address to Students").

9. Inglis, "Address to Students"; "Short Prayer for the Pupils," *Samuel Johnson*, 4: 272; "Laws and Orders of King's College, 1755," *ibid.*, 4: 227; "Matricula of King's College," *ibid.*, 4: 249; *Early Minutes of the Trustees: Vol. I, 1755–1770* (New York, 1932), March 1, 1763 (cited hereafter as *Governors Minutes*).

10. Inglis, "Address to the Students."

11. *Dictionary of American Biography*, s.v. "Benjamin Moore"; Benjamin Moore to Henry De Wint, July 13, 1771, General MSS Collection, SCCU; "Minutes and Accounts of the Literary Society," May 5, 1767, May 17, 1768, NYHS; Sprague, *Annals of American Pulpit*, 5: 300.

12. "Records of Trinity Church Parish, New York City," *New York Genealogical and Biographical Record 68* (Jan. 1937): 66; *New-York Gazette; and the Weekly Mercury*, Jan. 16, 1775; Will of John Davan, Sr., *New Jersey Archives*, 1st series, 38 (1944): 97; *New York Mercury*, March 24, 1760, extracted in *New Jersey Archives*, 1st series, 20 (1898): 416.

13. "Black Book," pp. 6–17; "Governors Minutes," draft, July 21, 1774.

14. "Governors Minutes," draft, March 29, 1774. The youngest entrant was probably a few months short of twelve.

15. Frank Monaghan, *John Jay* . . . (New York and Indianapolis: Bobbs-Merrill, 1935), pp. 23–26; Paul M. Hamlin, "Peter Van Schaack," *Columbia University Quarterly* 24 (March 1932): 67–68; William Moore, *History of St. George's Church, Hempstead, Long Island, N.Y.* (New York, 1881), pp. 103–04. In a few cases, mostly where an undergraduate transferred from another college, the problem was mitigated by admitting a student into an advanced class or otherwise permitting him to receive a degree in less than four years.

16. "Matricula of King's College," *Samuel Johnson*, 4: 244–61. The median period of stay for those not graduating is based on those students who entered from 1754 through 1772. My list of 108 B.A. recipients is the same as that in M. Halsey Thomas, *Columbia University Officers and Alumni, 1754–1857* (New York: Columbia University Press, 1936), pp. 97–105, except for the following: I have omitted John Nicoll, '76, who received his degree in 1793, as well as Isaac Ogden, '58, Joseph Reade, '58, William Hanna, '59, and Richard Clarke, '62, who never actually studied at King's College, despite receiving degrees. I have added John Van Beuren, '75, who definitely received his B.A. in 1775, as well as John Colden, Frederick Dibblee, Thomas Reid, and John Watkin Watkins, all '76, who completed all academic requirements for their degrees by May 1776 and in all likelihood received degrees before the college was closed by the American Revolution. On Van Beuren, see M. Halsey Thomas, ed., "King's College Commencement in the Newspapers," *Columbia University Quarterly* 22 (June 1930): 247. On the four members of the class of '76, see "List of Graduates in May 1776," College Papers.

17. Albert Welles, *Watts (Watt)* . . . ([New York, 1882?]), pp. 1–7; Memorandum Book #5, Nov. 25, 1762, William Samuel Johnson Papers, Connecticut Historical Society; Richard H. Greene, "King's (Now Columbia) College and Its Earliest Alumni," *New York Genealogical and Biographical Record* 25 (Oct. 1894): 180–81.

18. "Matricula of King's College," *Samuel Johnson*, 4: 244–61; "Laws of Yale College, 1745," Franklin B. Dexter, *Biographical Sketches of the Graduates of Yale College* . . . (New York: Henry Holt & Co., 1885–1911), 2: 3. The ordering of some of the better-known family names does not always correspond exactly to what one would expect if Johnson used social status as the sole criterion, but undoubtedly the names were ordered and ordered with family social position in mind.

19. Nathaniel Dubois, Jr. to Robert R. Livingston, Jr., Sept. 7, 1763, Robert R. Livingston Papers, Box 1, NYHS; John Moore," List of Members of the Social Club, New York," Misc. MSS: John Moore, NYHS; Thomas, "King's College Commencement in the Newspapers," p. 234.

20. William M. MacBean, *Biographical Register of St. Andrew's Society of the State of New York* (New York: St. Andrew's Society of the State of New York, 1922–25), 1: 252–53; Thomas, *Columbia University Officers and Alumni*, p. 100.

21. Micajah Townsend to Governors of King's College, n.d., College Papers; Will of Micajah Townsend, *Collections of the New-York Historical Society*, 34 (1901):

231–33 (cited hereafter as *NYHS Colls.*); "Warrant for Collecting Tax of Queens Village," 1757, *ibid.*, 60 (1927): 543–44; "Matricula of King's College," *Samuel Johnson*, 4: 244.

22. "Matricula of King's College," *Samuel Johnson*, 4: 244, 247; S. Johnson to Archbishop of Canterbury, Sept. 25, 1767, *ibid.*, 1: 419; Micajah Townsend to Governors of King's College, n. d., College Papers; Leonhard F. Fuld, "King's College Alumni–II," *Columbia University Quarterly* 9 (Dec. 1907): 54.

23. Myles Cooper to Jonathan Boucher, March 22, 1773 (misdated 1770), Herbert B. Howe, "Colonel George Washington and King's College," *Columbia University Quarterly* 24 (June 1932): 141.

24. *Ibid.*, pp. 148, 152, 157; William Lamson to SPG, Oct. 9, 1773, SPG Letters, Misc. Unbound MSS, Connecticut, part 1, photostats, Library of Congress (cited hereafter as LC); Herbert A. Johnson, "When John Jay was Jack," *Columbia College Today* 10 (Spring/Summer 1963): 51; Julius Goebel, Jr., *The Law Practice of Alexander Hamilton: Documents and Commentaries* (New York and London: Columbia University Press, 1964–), 1: 5–6, 48; Nathan Schachner, ed., "Alexander Hamilton Viewed by His Friends: The Narratives of Robert Troup and Hercules Mulligan," *William and Mary Quarterly*, 3d series, 4 (April 1947): 212–13.

25. Julia C. Andrews, "Memorandum on Robert Harpur's life," Material Concerning Robert Harpur, New York State Library.

26. A: B to John Tabor Kempe, received May 23, 1765, Sedgwick Papers II, Box 2, Massachusetts Historical Society.

27. "College Intrigues or the Amors of Patrick," and "Advertisement," April 18, 1766, College Papers.

28. *Governors Minutes*, May 13, 1766, Feb. 26, 1767; "Black Book," p. 7; Robert Harpur to Governors of King's College, July 21, 1774, College Papers.

29. "Statutes of King's College, 1763," *Samuel Johnson*, 4: 239, 240; "Black Book," pp. 2–17; MS of Andrew P. Skene, Oct. 25, 1770, Skene Papers, Fort Ticonderoga Library, transcript in Andrew P. Skene Folder, Columbiana; "Governors Minutes," draft, Sept. 17, 1771.

30. "Black Book," pp. 2–17.

31. Samuel Auchmuty to S. Johnson, March 27, 1771, Hawks Papers, Church Historical Society; "Report of Committee of Visitation," filed Sept. 17, 1771, College Papers.

32. "Report of Committee of Visitation," filed Sept. 17, 1771, College Papers; Johnson, "When John Jay was Jack," p. 50; Myles Cooper to Jonathan Boucher, March 22, 1773 (misdated 1770), Howe, "George Washington and King's College," p. 141.

33. "Minutes of Committee of Visitation," May 22, 1772, College Papers; Nathaniel Dubois, Jr. to Robert R. Livingston, Jr., Sept. 7, 1763, Robert R. Livingston Papers, Box 1, NYHS; "Black Book," p. 2.

34. John Parke Custis to Martha Washington, July 5, 1773, Howe, "George Washington and King's College," p. 152; "Laws and Orders of King's College, 1755," *Samuel Johnson*, 4: 228; "Statutes of King's College, 1763," *ibid.*, 4: 238.

35. *New York Gazette*, June 20, 1763, extracted in I. N. Phelps Stokes, *The Iconography of Manhattan Island, 1498–1909* (New York: R. H. Dodd, 1915–28), 4: 735; Henry Lloyd III to Joseph Lloyd II, Aug. 6, 1764, *NYHS Colls.*, 60 (1927): 670; John Barent Johnson, MS Diary, Columbiana, passim; Nathaniel Dubois, Jr., to Robert R. Livingston, Jr., Sept. 17, 1763, quoted in George Dangerfield, *Chancellor Robert R. Livingston of New York, 1746–1813* (New York: Harcourt, Brace & Co., 1960), p. 45.

36. John Parke Custis to George Washington, July 5, 1773, Howe, "George Washington and King's College," p. 151; Carl Abbott, "The Neighborhoods of New York, 1760–1775," *New York History* 55 (Jan. 1974): 49–50; Carl Bridenbaugh, *Cities in Revolt: Urban Life in America, 1743–1776* (New York: Knopf, 1955), p. 316; Carl Bridenbaugh, ed., "Patrick M'Robert's Tour Through Part of the North Provinces of America," *Pennsylvania Magazine of History and Biography* 59 (April 1935): 139, 142.

37. "Remarks on the Description of Columbia College," *New-York Magazine; or Literary Repository* 1 (June 1790): 341; "Black Book," p. 15.

38. "Photostat: 1763–64," College Papers; *Governors Minutes*, March 1, 1763; S. Johnson to SPG, April 15, 1765, SPG Letters, series B, vol. 23, microfilm, LC; S. Johnson to SPG, April 30, 1761, SPG Letters, series B, vol. 2, transcript, LC; S. Johnson to SPG, Jan. 10, 1762, SPG Letters, series B, vol. 2, transcript, LC; *N.Y. Gazette; or the Weekly Post-Boy*, June 26, 1766, "Black Book," p. 6; Robert Harpur, Account Book, photostats, Columbiana.

39. John S. Brubacher and Willis Rudy, *Higher Education in Transition: A History of American Colleges and Universities, 1636–1968*, rev. ed. (New York: Harper & Row, 1968), p. 51.

40. The venerable history of the collegiate way of living and its success at colonial Harvard, Yale, and Princeton have led to the assumption that the collegiate way was a pervasive aspect of colonial higher education. Actually, the collegiate way had a spotty history in the middle colonies, and the strength with which it took root at each college varied closely with the extent to which alumni of Harvard and Yale had a say in the running of the college. The collegiate way of living flourished at Princeton. It worked moderately well at King's College but was abandoned after the American Revolution. It had a short, very unhappy history at the College of Philadelphia, whose leaders also abandoned it after the Revolution, and it did not take root at Queen's College, which built its first residence building for students near the end of the nineteenth century. Princeton, in contrast to the other three colleges, combined the major ingredients which sustained the collegiate way in the eighteenth century: a non-urban location, which meant that most students did not live nearby and that the opportunities for rooming in town were limited; leaders whose religious inspiration, deep sense of community, and personal experiences as youths with the collegiate way made it seem imperative that students live in a communal setting; and the funds which permitted the construction of adequate housing. Even Princeton maintained the collegiate way only by crowding students in Nassau Hall. And at Harvard and Yale the shortage of housing space for students often resulted in some of them

living in town. Indeed, in 1761 Harvard was so crowded that over ninety students lodged in town. Soon after, the college constructed a new residence building. On the last point see Samuel E. Morison, *Three Centuries of Harvard, 1636–1936* (Cambridge: Harvard University Press, 1965), p. 94.

12. THE INTELLECTUAL AND POLITICAL LEGACY

1. John Jay to [Alexander McDougall], Feb. 17, 1776, drafted on letter of Edward Nicoll to John Jay, John Jay Papers, Special Collections, Columbia University Library (cited hereafter as SCCU).

2. "Statutes of King's College, 1763," Herbert and Carol Schneider, eds., *Samuel Johnson, President of King's College: His Career and Writings* (New York: Columbia University Press, 1929), 4: 240; John Parke Custis to Martha Washington, July 5, 1773, Herbert B. Howe, "Colonel George Washington and King's College," *Columbia University Quarterly* 24 (June 1932): 152; [John Vardill], *Candid Remarks on Dr. Witherspoon's Address To the Inhabitants of Jamaica . . .* (Philadelphia, 1772), pp. 41–42.

3. Catherine S. Crary, *The Price of Loyalty: Tory Writings from the Revolutionary Era* (New York: McGraw-Hill, 1973), pp. 93–96, 419, 420; Edward Antill to S. Bauman, July 7, 1783, quoted in John Schuyler, *Institution of the Society of the Cincinnati . . .* (New York, 1886), pp. 153–55; John Moore, "List of Members, The Social Club, New York," copy, Misc. MSS: John Moore, New-York Historical Society (cited hereafter as NYHS); Richard H. Greene, "King's (Now Columbia) College and Its Earliest Alumni," *New York Genealogical and Biographical Record 25* (July 1894): 127–28; Rudolph Ritzema to Alexander McDougall, Nov. 19, 1775, quoted in Bernard Mason, *The Road to Independence: The Revolutionary Movement in New York, 1773–1777* (Lexington, Ky.: University of Kentucky Press, 1966), p. 108.

4. Samuel E. Morison, *Three Centuries of Harvard, 1636–1936* (Cambridge: Harvard University Press, 1936), p. 147n; Sheldon S. Cohen and Larry R. Gerlach, "Princeton in the Coming of the American Revolution," *New Jersey History* 92 (Summer 1974): 83–84. I do not know the exact percentage of loyalists among the King's College alumni. I have data on more than half the students living in 1776 (graduates and nongraduates). About two-thirds of these were loyalists, most of the rest patriots. Based on this data it seems reasonable to say that probably half or more of all the alumni living in 1776 became loyalists, but the number of students whose Revolutionary sentiments I have not uncovered is too large to justify a more precise statement. Morison's data include only graduates of Harvard.

5. Alfred F. Young, *The Democratic Republicans of New York: The Origins, 1763–1797* (Chapel Hill, N.C.: University of North Carolina Press, 1967), pp. 14–15, 32, 48, 238, 254, 334, 432, 566–67.

6. Gouverneur Morris to [first name not given] Penn, May 20, 1774, quoted in Max M. Mintz, *Gouverneur Morris and the American Revolution* (Norman, Okla.: University of Oklahoma Press, 1970), p. 44; Gouverneur Morris to John Jay,

Jan. 1, 1783, quoted in Staughton Lynd, "A Governing Class on The Defensive: The Case of New York," in Staughton Lynd, *Class Conflict, Slavery, and the United States Constitution: Ten Essays* (Indianapolis and New York: Bobbs-Merrill, 1967), p. 115.

7. Gordon S. Wood, *The Creation of the American Republic, 1776–1787* (Chapel Hill, N.C.: University of North Carolina Press, 1969), pp. 476–99; Robert R. Livingston, "An Oration Delivered July 4, 1787 . . . ," and John Jay to Alexander Hamilton, May 8, 1778, both quoted in *ibid.*, pp. 477, 493.

8. John Vardill to Peter Van Schaack, Dec. 10, 1774, Peter Van Schaack Papers, Box 1, SCCU.

9. Young, *Democratic Republicans of New York*, pp. 206n, 334, 567; Rick J. Ashton, "The Loyalist Experience: New York, 1763–1789" (Ph.D. diss., Northwestern University, 1973), p. 201.

10. Ashton, "The Loyalist Experience," p. 91; Wood, *Creation of American Republic*, pp. 16–17; [Isaac Wilkins], *Short Advice To the Counties of New-York* (New York, 1774), p. 6.

11. William H. Nelson, *The American Tory* (Oxford: Clarendon Press, 1961), pp. 178–81; Benjamin Moore, *A Sermon Occasioned by the Death of the Revd. Dr. Auchmuty* . . . (New York, 1777), p. 8; John Vardill to Peter Van Schaack, Sept. 15, 1774, Peter Van Schaack Papers, Box 1, SCCU.

12. Alexander Hamilton, *A Full Vindication of the Measures of the Congress* . . . (New York, 1774), in Harold C. Syrett and Jacob E. Cooke, eds., *The Papers of Alexander Hamilton* (New York and London: Columbia University Press, 1961–), 1: 50; Richard B. Morris, *Seven Who Shaped Our Destiny: The Founding Fathers as Revolutionaries* (New York: Harper & Row, 1973), p. 173.

13. Wood, *Creation of American Republic*, p. 520.

14. Douglas Sloan, *The Scottish Enlightenment and the American College Ideal* (New York: Teachers College Press, 1971), p. 93; "William Smith's Proposed Curriculum for the College of Philadelphia," Lawrence A. Cremin, *American Education: The Colonial Experience, 1607–1783* (New York: Harper & Row, 1970), p. 383.

15. Bernard Bailyn, *The Origins of American Politics* (New York: Knopf, 1968), pp. 35–51, 56.

16. *Ibid.*, pp. 39–44, 56; Bernard Bailyn, "The Transforming Radicalism of the American Revolution," *Pamphlets of the American Revolution, 1750–1776: Volume I, 1750–1765* (Cambridge: Harvard University Press, 1965), pp. 39, 43–44; Wood, *Creation of American Republic*, p. 15; *Cato's Letters*, April 15, 1721, Sept. 22, 1722, David L. Jacobson, ed., *The English Libertarian Heritage* . . . (Indianapolis: Bobbs-Merrill, 1965), pp. 71, 224.

17. "Address of Governors to Lord Sandys," May 14, 1762, *Early Minutes of the Trustees: Vol. I, 1755–1770* (New York, 1932), Nov. 16, 1762.

18. Myles Cooper to William Smith, Aug. 14, 1773, Hawks Papers, Church Historical Society; *New York Mercury*, Aug. 27, Sept. 17, 24, 1753; Myles Cooper, *National Humiliation and Repentance recommended* . . . (Oxford, 1777), p. 22;

S. Johnson, *Elementa Philosophica* . . . , *Samuel Johnson*, 2: 501; Essay by "Popli-cola," *Rivington's New York Gazetteer*, Dec. 2, 1773; Joseph J. Ellis, *The New England Mind in Transition: Samuel Johnson of Connecticut, 1696–1772* (New Haven: Yale University Press, 1973), pp. 227, 261.

19. *New York Gazette; and the Weekly Mercury*, Dec. 7, 1772, reprinted in *New Jersey Archives*, 1st series, 28 (1916): 354–55.

20. John Witherspoon, *The Dominion of Providence over the Passions of Men* . . . , quoted in Cohen and Gerlach, "Princeton in the Coming of American Revolution," p. 82; Cooper, *National Humiliation*, pp. 7, 14–15; Ellis, *New England Mind in Transition*, pp. 253–55.

21. Bailyn, "Transforming Radicalism of American Revolution," pp. 60–62.

22. See pp. 82–86, 90–91.

23. "Whip for the American Whig," *N. Y. Gazette; and the Weekly Mercury*, Oct. 24, 1768. On Princeton's founders see Alan Heimert, *Religion and the American Mind: From the Great Awakening to the Revolution* (Cambridge: Harvard University Press, 1966), pp. 183–93; and Guy H. Miller, "A Contracting Community: American Presbyterians, Social Conflict, and Higher Education, 1730–1820" (Ph.D. diss., University of Michigan, 1970), Part One.

24. Cooper, *National Humiliation*, pp. 22–23; S. Johnson, "Raphael, or The Genius of English America: A Rhapsody," *Samuel Johnson*, 2: 574–75, 578; S. Johnson, "Proposals Regarding the Government of Connecticut," [1748–49?], *ibid.*, 1: 149; Essay by "Poplicola," *Rivington's N.Y. Gazetteer*, Dec. 2, 1773.

25. "Memorial of John Vardill," American Loyalist Transcripts, vol. 42, p. 54, New York Public Library.

26. For discussions of this shift, see Edmund S. Morgan, "The American Revolution Considered as an Intellectual Movement," in Arthur M. Schlesinger, Jr., and Morton White, eds., *Paths of American Thought* (Boston: Houghton Mifflin, 1963), pp. 11–33; and Heimert, *Religion and American Mind*, pp. 182–83, 451.

27. I have counted as non-Anglican clerical alumni Brandt Schuyler Lupton and, possibly, David Brooks. However, Brooks, who came to King's College from Yale in 1761 as a sophomore and stayed two years, should not be counted if he is not the same David Brooks who graduated from Yale in 1768. I have no direct evidence that the two David Brooks are the same person.

28. Samuel Auchmuty to S. Johnson, Aug. 6, 1754, *Samuel Johnson*, 1: 340; Edward Antill to S. Johnson, [1762?], *ibid.*, 1: 331; S. Johnson to Edward Antill, [1762?], *ibid.*, 1: 332; John M. Murrin, "The Legal Transformation: The Bench and Bar of Eighteenth-Century Massachusetts," in Stanley N. Katz, ed., *Colonial America: Essays in Politics and Social Development* (Boston: Little, Brown, 1971), pp. 427, 427n; Frank Monaghan, *John Jay* . . . (New York and Indianapolis: Bobbs-Merrill, 1935), p. 29; Greene, "King's College and Its Earliest Alumni," p. 127; Paul Hamlin, *Legal Education in Colonial New York* (New York: New York University Press, 1939), pp. 116–17, 118n–19n, 134–35. Hamlin lists forty-one alumni who were admitted to the bar of New York, but three of these, Isaac Ogden, Joseph Reade, and William Hanna, were never students at King's College, despite receiving degrees.

29. Harry Carman, "The Professions in New York in 1800," *Columbia University Quarterly* 23 (June 1931): 160–61.
30. Edmund P. Willis, "Social Origins of Political Leadership in New York City from the Revolution to 1815" (Ph.D. diss., University of California, Berkeley, 1967), pp. 21, 96.
31. *Ibid.*, pp. 334–56.

3. King's College Medical School

INTRODUCTION

1. *Constitutional Gazette*, Oct. 18, 1775, March 9, 1776.
2. The thirteen names are listed by Claude E. Heaton, "Medicine in New York during the English Colonial Period," *Bulletin of the History of Medicine* 17 (Jan. 1945): 25–26; Cadwallader Colden to John Mitchell, Nov. 7, [1745], *Collections of the New-York Historical Society*, 67 (1934): 329.

13. EDUCATION AND THE PROFESSIONALIZATION OF MEDICINE

1. Richard Shryock, *Medicine and Society in America, 1660–1860* (New York: New York University Press, 1960), p. 31. I have found the works of Richard Shryock, Lester King, and Whitfield J. Bell, Jr., continuingly helpful in writing this chapter and the next one, especially Shryock's *Medicine and Society in America* and *The Development of Modern Medicine . . .* , rev. ed. (New York: Knopf, 1947); King's *The Medical World of the Eighteenth Century* (Chicago: University of Chicago Press, 1958); and Bell's "Medical Practice in Colonial America," *Bulletin of the History of Medicine* 31 (Sept.–Oct. 1957): 442–53 and "A Portrait of the Colonial Physician," *Bulletin of the History of Medicine* 44 (Nov.–Dec. 1970): 497–517. I have also used extensively Francisco Guerra's *American Medical Bibliography, 1639–1783* (New York: Lathrop C. Harper, 1962).
2. Franklin to Cadwallader Colden, Nov. 28, 1745, Leonard W. Labaree et al., eds., *The Papers of Benjamin Franklin* (New Haven: Yale University Press, 1959–), 3: 49; *Dictionary of American Biography*, s.v. "Peter Middleton"; Richard Bayley, *Cases of Angina Trachealis . . . To which is added, a Letter from Peter Middleton, M. D. To the Author* (New York, 1781), p. 19; James Mease, ed., *The Surgical Works of the Late John Jones, M. D. . . .* (Philadelphia, 1795), pp. 7–8.
3. Samuel Bard, "Biographical account of his father," n.d., Bard Collection, Bard College Library (collection and library cited hereafter as BCL).
4. Contemporary estimates ranged from "upwards of Thirty" to "*upwards of* 40." See *New York Gazette Revived in the Weekly Post-Boy*, April 27, 1752, Feb. 5, 1753; Milton M. Klein, ed., *The Independent Reflector . . .* (Cambridge: Harvard University Press, 1963), p. 139 (Feb. 15, 1753).
5. *New York Mercury*, May 17, 1756; Mease, *Surgical Works of John Jones*, p. 10; *Medical Observations and Inquiries*, 2 (1757–61): 369–72, quoted in Byron Stookey, *A History of Colonial Medical Education: in the Province of New York, with its Subsequent Development (1767–1830)* (Springfield, Ill.: Charles C. Thomas, 1962),

p. 33; Robert Whytt to Cadwallader Colden, March 17, 1761, *Collections of the New-York Historical Society*, 55 (1922): 16 (cited hereafter as *NYHS Colls.*).

6. Morris Saffron, *Samuel Clossy, M. D. (1724–1786), Professor of Anatomy at King's College, New York: The Existing Works* . . . (New York: Hafner, 1967), pp. xi–xxi; Samuel Bard to John Bard, Nov. 14, 1762, Feb. 16, 1764, BCL; Samuel Bard to John Bard, Dec. 29, 1762, Bard Collection, New York Academy of Medicine (collection and library cited hereafter as NYAM).

7. I have used the following sources in piecing together the scientific and ethical conceptions of the five men. Samuel Clossy: Saffron's collection of Clossy's writings (see n. 6), especially Clossy's lecture, "The Uses of Anatomy," and the "Preface" to his *Observations On some of the Diseases Of the Parts of the Human Body;* Peter Middleton: Middleton's *A Medical Discourse, or an Historical Inquiry Into the Ancient and Present State of Medicine* . . . (New York, 1769); Samuel Bard: Bard's *A Discourse upon the Duties of a Physician* . . . (New York, 1769), and Bard's letters to his father in the NYAM and BCL; John Bard: Bard's letters to his son in NYAM and BCL, Bard's "An Essay on the Nature and Cause of the Malignant Pleurisy . . . ," *American Medical and Philosophical Register* . . . , 2d ed. (New York, 1814), 1: 409–21, and Samuel Bard's "Biographical account of his father," n.d., BCL; John Jones: W. B. McDaniel II, ed., "John Jones' Introductory Lecture to His Course in Surgery (1769), King's College, Printed from the Author's Manuscript," *Transactions & Studies of the College of Physicians of Philadelphia,* 4th series, 8 (1940–41): 180–90, and Jones's *Plain Concise Practical Remarks on the Treatment of Wounds and Fractures* . . . (New York, 1775), especially the preface. To avoid constant repetition, for the discussion which follows in the next seven paragraphs I have restricted footnotes which cite material in the above sources largely to quotations.

8. John Bard to Samuel Bard, Jan. 17, 1764, BCL; John Bard to Samuel Bard, Dec. 11, 1765, NYAM.

9. King, *Medical World of the Eighteenth Century*, ch. 2, and King, "Rationalism in Early Eighteenth Century Medicine," *Journal of the History of Medicine and Allied Sciences* 18 (July 1963): 257–71 have provided helpful background material for the discussion in this and the following two paragraphs.

10. Middleton, *Medical Discourse*, p. 53.

11. *N. Y. Weekly Post-Boy*, July 22, 1745, quoted in John Duffy, *A History of Public Health in New York City, 1625–1866* (New York: Russell Sage Foundation, 1968), p. 64; Carl Bridenbaugh, ed., *Gentleman's Progress: The Itinerarium of Dr. Alexander Hamilton, 1744* (Chapel Hill, N.C.: University of North Carolina Press, 1948), p. 65.

12. *Medical Discourse*, p. 54; "Uses of Anatomy," Saffron, *Samuel Clossy*, p. cxvi.

13. Although John Bard, unlike the other four men, did not study in Europe, he shared thoroughly the ideas discussed here. His son wrote of him, for instance, in "his profession he read all the best authors of his day but his studies were rather select than general—Sydenham & Huxham were his favorites, [and]

he formed himself in their plan. . . . ." John Bard not only dispatched his son to Edinburgh for a medical education—at heavy expense—but emphasized how important it was that Samuel investigate the "original" principles upon which medical science was founded. See Samuel Bard, "Biographical account of his father," n.d., and John Bard to Samuel Bard, draft, n.d., BCL.

14. Samuel Clossy and Peter Middleton placed the greatest emphasis on the value of these principles, though the others by no means disregarded them. See Clossy, "Uses of Anatomy," Saffron, *Samuel Clossy*, pp. civ–cv; *New York Gazette; and the Weekly Mercury*, Oct. 21, 1771; Middleton, *Medical Discourse*, p. 57; Samuel Bard to John Bard, Dec. 29, 1762, NYAM; Benjamin Rush to John Morgan, Jan. 20, 1768, L. H. Butterfield, ed., *Letters of Benjamin Rush* (Princeton, N.J.: Princeton University Press, 1951), 1: 50; McDaniel, "John Jones' Introductory Lecture," pp. 183–84.

15. Middleton, *Medical Discourse*, pp. 17, 50, 54; McDaniel, "John Jones' Introductory Lecture," pp. 184–85.

16. Bard, *Discourse upon the Duties*, p. 9.

17. *Ibid.*, pp. 9–10; Middleton, *Medical Discourse*, pp. 66–67.

18. Middleton, *Medical Discourse*, pp. 50–51.

19. *Ibid.*, p. 69; Bard, *Discourse upon the Duties*, p. i. The 1749 date is widely accepted. See, for example, Duffy, *Public Health in New York City*, p. 65; Raymond P. Stearns, *Science in the British Colonies of America* (Urbana, Ill.: University of Illinois Press, 1970), p. 671; Stookey, *Colonial Medical Education*, pp. 12, 75. It has also been criticized: W. B. McDaniel II, "A Brief Sketch of the Rise of American Medical Societies," Felix Marti-Ibanez, ed., *History of American Medicine: A Symposium* (New York: M.D. Publications, 1959), p. 134. The 1749 date rests on one piece of evidence. John Bard read a medical essay to a "weekly society of gentlemen in New-York" in January 1749 (see n. 7). However, there is no evidence that this was a society of medical men, or that it was founded in 1749, or that it remained in existence during the 1750s, or that there is any continuity between this group and the medical society referred to by Samuel Bard and Middleton in 1769. Nor is it at all clear just who could have belonged to it if it was a medical group, since the ranks of the professional medical community in 1749 were so thin. On the other hand, scientific and literary groups with an interest in medical topics were not uncommon. A "Society for the Promotion of Useful Knowledge" met regularly in New York City in 1748 and 1749. Leading members included William Smith, Sr. and Jr., William Livingston, and James Alexander, all lawyers (*Independent Reflector*, pp. 18, 18n). There are no other indications that a medical society existed in New York at mid-century. In *Old New York: or, Reminiscences of The Past Sixty Years* (New York, 1866), p. 288, John W. Francis mentions a "club of professional gentlemen in New York about 1750." But Francis's list of members indicates that the club was clearly not a medical group. Nor is Francis a contemporary source. He was born almost forty years after the event. The references to a medical society made by Samuel Bard and Middleton in 1769 (see above), the development of the professional medical com-

munity discussed in this essay, and the organization of medical societies in Philadelphia and New Jersey about 1766 all point to the mid-1760s as the date of origin of the medical society out of which grew the King's College Medical School and the city's first hospital. Probably this was the city's first medical society.

20. *N. Y. Gazette; or the Weekly Post-Boy*, Nov. 17, 1763, May 9, 1765; John Bard to Samuel Bard, Jan. 17, 1764, BCL; John Watts to General Monckton, May 16, 1764, *NYHS Colls.*, 61 (1928): 254–55; *N. Y. Mercury*, Aug. 13, 1764, Sept. 30, 1765.

21. *The Colonial Laws of New York from the Year 1664 to the Revolution . . .* (Albany, 1894), 4: 455–56.

22. *N. Y. Gazette Revived in the Weekly Post-Boy*, Feb. 12, 1750, May 20, 1754; *Independent Reflector*, p. 139 (Feb. 15, 1753), pp. 225–27 (May 10, 1753). See also the *New-York Evening Post*, April 3, 1749.

23. *N. Y. Mercury*, May 13, 1754, supplement. See also *N. Y. Evening Post*, Dec. 9, 1751.

24. Middleton, *Medical Discourse*, p. 64; *Journal of the Votes and Proceedings of the General Assembly Of the Colony of New-York . . . [1691–1765]* (New York, 1764–66), 2: 608, 613, 614.

25. *N. Y. Mercury*, Jan. 10, 1763; *New-York Journal; or the General Advertiser*, March 14, 1771. I have not, anyway, come across a public or private statement by anyone during these years that he had been licensed under the provisions of the 1760 act. In contrast, midwives, who were not covered by the 1760 act but who were required by a 1731 city law to take an oath regarding their practice, did occasionally advertise that they had been examined by the "Faculty in this City." See the *N. Y. Gazette; and the Weekly Mercury*, July 4, 1768; *N. Y. Journal; or the General Advertiser*, May 30, 1771.

26. Duffy, *Public Health in New York City*, p. 66.

27. *N. Y. Journal; or the General Advertiser*, Aug. 23, 1770, July 29, 1773; Grete de Francesco, *The Power of the Charlatan*, trans. Miriam Beard (New Haven: Yale University Press, 1939), pp. 202–04; King, *Medical World of the Eighteenth Century*, p. 53.

28. Middleton, *Medical Discourse*, p. 64; Joseph F. Kett, *The Formation of the American Medical Profession: The Role of Institutions, 1780–1860* (New Haven and London: Yale University Press, 1968), pp. 16–17, 20–22. An essayist in the *N. Y. Mercury* (Aug. 25, 1766) stated flatly that "no Law" had been "put in Execution to bring them [charlatans and empirics] to the Bar of Examination, but uncontroul'd they proceed. . . ."

29. Bell, Jr., "Portrait of the Colonial Physician," p. 510.

30. Middleton, *Medical Discourse*, pp. 61–64; Clossy, "Uses of Anatomy," Saffron, *Samuel Clossy*, pp. cxv–cxvi; *N. Y. Mercury*, Aug. 25, 1766.

31. John Watts to Isaac Barré, Nov. 15, 1763, *NYHS Colls.*, 61 (1928): 198; *Independent Reflector*, p. 140 (Feb. 15, 1753); *N. Y. Mercury*, Dec. 14, 1761; Thomas J. Wertenbaker, *The Golden Age of Colonial Culture*, 2d ed. (New York: New York University Press, 1949), p. 53; Saffron, *Samuel Clossy*, p. lvi; David C.

Humphrey, "King's College in the City of New York, 1754–1776" (Ph.D. diss., Northwestern University, 1968), pp. 347–49, 356, 362, 588–89.

32. Middleton, *Medical Discourse*, p. 63; *N. Y. Mercury*, Aug. 25, 1766.

33. At least such is suggested by the popular support of a doctor like Roelof Kierstede (see n. 11) and the durability of a doctor like Engelbart Kemmena (see Heaton, "Medicine in New York," p. 26; and *N. Y. Journal; or the General Advertiser*, Nov. 23, 1775).

34. Middleton, *Medical Discourse*, p. 63; John Bard to Samuel Bard, Jan. 17, 1764, BCL.

35. By and large, however, professional physicians appear to have established fairly lucrative practices. See Jackson Turner Main, *The Social Structure of Revolutionary America* (Princeton, N.J.: Princeton University Press, 1965), pp. 99–100, 145–46.

36. Middleton, *Medical Discourse*, 51; Samuel Bard to John Bard, Dec. 29, 1762, NYAM; Whitfield Bell, Jr., *John Morgan, Continental Doctor* (Philadelphia: University of Pennsylvania Press, 1965), pp. 70–73. Historians often give Samuel Bard most of the credit for founding the medical school (see, for instance, Daniel H. Calhoun, *Professional Lives in America: Structure and Aspiration, 1750–1850* [Cambridge: Harvard University Press, 1965], pp. 27–28; and Shryock, *Medicine and Society*, p. 25). There is no reason for doing so. Morris Saffron justifiably attacks the "Bardian legend" in *Samuel Clossy*, p. lxxvi.

37. Middleton, *Medical Discourse*, p. 51.

38. Samuel Clossy, John Jones, and Samuel Bard to the College Governors, read at governors meeting of Nov. 15, 1774, College Papers, Special Collections, Columbia University Library (cited hereafter as SCCU); Middleton, *Medical Discourse*, p. 64; *N. Y. Mercury*, Nov. 9, 1767.

39. *N. Y. Mercury*, Nov. 9, 1767; Middleton, *Medical Discourse*, p. 64; Clossy, "Uses of Anatomy," Saffron, *Samuel Clossy*, p. cxvi; McDaniel, "John Jones' Introductory Lecture," p. 187. See also, especially on the effort to gain public support for professional physicians, an anonymous, three-part essay, entitled "The Duties of Patients and Physicians considered," which appeared in the *N. Y. Gazette; or the Weekly Post-Boy*, May 21, May 28, June 4, 1767.

40. Vern and Bonnie Bullough, "The Causes of the Scottish Medical Renaissance of the Eighteenth Century," *Bulletin of the History of Medicine* 45 (Jan.–Feb. 1971): 23–26.

41. John Morgan, *A Discourse Upon the Institution of Medical Schools in America* . . . (Philadelphia, 1765), pp. xv–xviii, 14, 18, 30, 40–45; Bell, Jr., *John Morgan*, p. 71.

42. John Bard to Samuel Bard, Dec. 11, 1765, NYAM; Samuel Bard, *Discourse upon the Duties*, p. 12; Samuel Bard to John Morgan, Jan. 21, 1767, Autograph File, College of Physicians of Philadelphia (cited hereafter as COPOP); Middleton, *Medical Discourse*, pp. 60–61, 66; McDaniel, "John Jones' Introductory Lecture," pp. 183–87; Clossy, "Uses of Anatomy," Saffron, *Samuel Clossy*, pp. cvii–cxv.

43. *N. Y. Mercury*, Aug. 25, 1766.

44. Unless otherwise noted, figures throughout the essay refer to pounds New York currency. Statements on the cost, duration, and character of medical apprenticeship are based on apprenticeship practices in New Jersey, Pennsylvania, and Virginia as well as New York, since the data on New York is very spotty. See especially Samuel McKee, *Labor in Colonial New York, 1664–1776* (New York: Columbia University Press, 1935), pp. 86–87; Stephen Wickes, *History of Medicine in New Jersey* . . . (Newark, N.J., 1879), pp. 36, 100–02; Wyndham Blanton, *Medicine in Virginia in the Eighteenth Century* (Richmond: Garrett & Massie, 1931), pp. 76–81; Bell, Jr., *John Morgan*, pp. 118–19, 154; Benjamin Rush to Mrs. Rush, [July 23, 1776], Butterfield, *Letters of Benjamin Rush*, 1: 106.

45. Samuel Clossy et al. to Governors of King's College, Aug. 4, 1767, and Tennent to Governors of King's College, Aug. 5, 1767, both reproduced in Stookey, *Colonial Medical Education*, pp. 48–51. Just why John Bard did not serve on the medical faculty is not known, but "the confined circumstances of his Education" (Samuel Bard, "Biographical account of his father," n.d., BCL) and his lack of a medical degree militated against his participation.

46. Sir James Jay to Committee of College Governors, April 19, 1763, James Jay Papers, SCCU.

47. *Early Minutes of the Trustees: Vol. I, 1755–1770* (New York, 1932), June 22, 1763 (cited hereafter as *Governors Minutes*); John Watts to General Monckton, May 16, 1764, *NYHS Colls.*, 61 (1928): 254; Samuel Bard to John Bard, Sept. 4, [1763?], NYAM. Early in 1764 Jay was still seeking out "2 or 3 Physicians" for professorships in the school. Sir James Jay to James Duane, March 12, 1764, Duane Papers (1683–1765), New-York Historical Society.

48. *Governors Minutes*, Aug. 14, 1767.

49. *N. Y. Mercury*, Oct. 12, 1767; Samuel Clossy et al. to the College Governors, read at meeting of Nov. 15, 1774, College Papers; Frederick C. Waite, "The Degree of Bachelor of Medicine in the American Colonies and the United States," *Yale Journal of Biology and Medicine* 10 (March 1938): 310–14.

50. *N. Y. Mercury*, Nov. 9, 1767.

51. Samuel Bard to John Bard, Dec. 29, 1762 and John Bard to Samuel Bard, April 9, 1763, copy, NYAM.

14. THE LIMITS OF ACADEMIC MEDICAL TRAINING

1. Robert J. Samuelson, "Mt. Sinai: How a Hospital Builds a Medical School," *Science* 158 (Nov. 1967): 618; "M.D.'s Needed," *New York Times*, May 26, 1970, p. 40.

2. *Medical School Admission Requirements, U.S.A. and Canada, 1971–72, 22nd Edition* (Washington, D.C.: Association of American Medical Colleges, 1971), p. 197; *Mount Sinai School of Medicine Bulletin, 1971–72* (New York, 1971), pp. 12, 20.

3. Peter Middleton, *A Medical Discourse, or an Historical Inquiry Into the Ancient and Present State of Medicine* . . . (New York, 1769), pp. 52–53, 59–60; Samuel

Bard, *A Discourse upon the Duties of a Physician* . . . (New York, 1769), pp. i–iii, 15–17; Byron Stookey, *A History of Colonial Medical Education: in the Province of New York, with its Subsequent Development (1767–1830)* (Springfield, Ill.: Charles C. Thomas, 1962), pp. 68–74.

4. "Matricula of King's College," Herbert and Carol Schneider, eds., *Samuel Johnson, President of King's College: His Career and Writings* (New York: Columbia University Press, 1929), 4: 253–60. The evidence suggests that John Augustus Graham, who received an M.B. in 1772, matriculated in 1768 or 1769, although he is not listed as a matriculant. There is no concrete evidence that the Revolutionary climate of the early 1770s accounted in part for the decline in matriculants, although it is possible. The number of matriculants in the liberal arts college increased dramatically in the early 1770s.

5. "Claim of Samuel Clossy," American Loyalist Transcripts, printed in Morris Saffron, *Samuel Clossy, M.D. (1724–1786), Professor of Anatomy at King's College, New York: The Existing Works* . . . (New York: Hafner, 1967), pp. lxxxix, xci; *New York Mercury*, Sept. 30, 1765, Nov. 2, 1767; *New York Journal; or the General Advertiser*, Sept. 28, 1769; "Minutes of the Governors of King's College, 1770–1781," May 12, 1772, photostats, Columbiana, Columbia University (cited hereafter as "Governors Minutes," draft). Liberal arts students, who paid tuition, may have received some credit toward fees for medical courses.

6. Nathan Schachner, ed., "Alexander Hamilton Viewed by His Friends: The Narratives of Robert Troup and Hercules Mulligan," *William and Mary Quarterly*, 3d series, 4 (April 1947): 212.

7. *N. Y. Mercury*, Sept. 30, 1765, Nov. 2, 1767; *New York Gazette; and the Weekly Mercury*, May 28, 1770, July 25, 1774; *N. Y. Journal; or the General Advertiser*, Sept. 28, 1769; Beverly McAnear, "The Selection of an Alma Mater by Pre-Revolutionary Students," *Pennsylvania Magazine of History and Biography* 73 (Oct. 1949): 432–34. See ch. 6 for data on income of New Yorkers in the Revolutionary era.

8. Quoted in Frederick C. Waite, "The Degree of Bachelor of Medicine in the American Colonies and the United States," *Yale Journal of Biology and Medicine* 10 (March 1938): 314.

9. Stephen Wickes, *History of Medicine in New Jersey* . . . (Newark, N.J., 1879), p. 36; David L. Cowen, *Medicine and Health in New Jersey: A History* (Princeton, N.J.: Van Nostrand, 1964), p. 7.

10. Whitfield J. Bell, Jr., "Medical Practice in Colonial America," *Bulletin of the History of Medicine* 31 (Sept.–Oct. 1957): 446, 447; Jackson Turner Main, *The Social Structure of Revolutionary America* (Princeton, N.J.: Princeton University Press, 1965), pp. 99, 145.

11. Samuel Clossy et al. to College Governors, read at meeting of Nov. 15, 1774, College Papers, Special Collections, Columbia University Library (cited hereafter as SCCU); "Governors Minutes," draft, Nov. 15, 1774. In 1772 the governors considered making a B.A. a prerequisite to admission into the medical school. See *ibid.*, May 12, 1772.

12. Richard Shryock, *The Development of Modern Medicine* . . . , rev. ed. (New York: Knopf, 1947), ch. 2.

13. Middleton, *Medical Discourse,* p. 54.

14. *N. Y. Mercury,* Oct. 12, Nov. 2, Nov. 9, 1767; *N. Y. Gazette; and the Weekly Mercury,* Oct. 31, 1768, Sept. 25, 1769, Jan. 8, May 28, Sept. 10, Nov. 5, 1770, Nov. 4, 1771, May 4, Oct. 19, Nov. 9, 1772, Nov. 1, 1773, supplement, Jan. 10, July 25, Sept. 5, 1774, Jan. 16, Sept. 25, 1775; *N. Y. Journal; or the General Advertiser,* Oct. 17, 1771, Oct. 22, 1772, April 25, 1776; James Graham's Lecture Tickets, 1773-75, New-York Historical Society; *Early Minutes of the Trustees: Vol. I, 1755-1770* (New York, 1932), March 20, 1770; Hugh Gaine, *Gaine's Universal Register, or, American and British Kalendar, For the Year 1775* (New York, n.d.), p. 105. I have not been able to confirm that other courses besides Clossy's were offered in 1775-76.

15. "John Hodge's notes on John Morgan's chemistry lectures for 1766," College of Physicians of Philadelphia (cited hereafter as COPOP).

16. Andrew Kent, "William Cullen's History of Chemistry," and Douglas Guthrie, "William Cullen, M. D., and his Times," both in Andrew Kent, ed., *An Eighteenth Century Lectureship in Chemistry* . . . (Glasgow: Jackson, Son & Co., 1950), pp. 15, 27, 60; Whitfield J. Bell, Jr., "Some American Students of 'That Shining Oracle of Physic,' Dr. William Cullen of Edinburgh, 1755-1766," *Proceedings of the American Philosophical Society* 94 (June 1950): 275-76, 279.

17. *N. Y. Gazette; and the Weekly Mercury,* July 25, 1774; Samuel Bard, "Syllabus," Bard Collection, Bard College Library (collection and library cited hereafter as BCL); Samuel Bard to John Bard, March 6, 1763, Bard Collection, New York Academy of Medicine (collection and library cited hereafter as NYAM).

18. Samuel Bard, "Syllabus," BCL; Samuel Bard to John Bard, Dec. 29, 1762, NYAM.

19. "James Graham's notes on Samuel Bard's lectures on the practice of medicine," College of Physicians and Surgeons Papers (cited hereafter as College of P. and S. Papers), SCCU; Bard, *Discourse upon the Duties,* p. 17.

20. Lester King, *The Medical World of the Eighteenth Century* (Chicago: University of Chicago Press, 1958), ch. 3; Alexander Grant, *The Story of the University of Edinburgh During Its First Three Hundred Years* (London, 1884), 2: 411; Bell, Jr., "Some American Students of William Cullen," p. 279.

21. "James Graham's notes on Bard's lectures," College of P. and S. Papers, SCCU; Bard, *Discourse upon the Duties,* p. 8.

22. Richard Shryock, *Medicine and Society in America, 1660-1860* (New York: New York University Press, 1960), pp. 66-67; John Jones's lectures on surgery, COPOP; "James Graham's notes on Bard's lectures," College of P. and S. Papers, SCCU.

23. "James Graham's notes on Bard's lectures," College of P. and S. Papers, SCCU; Shryock, *Medicine and Society,* p. 52.

24. Saffron, *Samuel Clossy,* pp. xvi-xix; Clossy, "Uses of Anatomy," *ibid.,*

pp. xciii–cxv; George W. Corner, *Anatomy* (New York: Paul B. Hoeber, 1930), pp. 37–38.

25. "Uses of Anatomy," Saffron, *Samuel Clossy*, p. xcix; *N. Y. Mercury*, Nov. 2, 1767; *N. Y. Gazette; and the Weekly Mercury*, Sept. 10, 1770, Oct. 21, 1771.

26. *N. Y. Gazette; and the Weekly Mercury*, Oct. 21, 1771; *N. Y. Mercury*, Nov. 2, 1767; "Claim of Samuel Clossy," American Loyalist Transcripts, printed in Saffron, *Samuel Clossy*, p. xc.

27. Shryock, *Medicine and Society*, p. 49.

28. The work was published in New York in 1775, in Philadelphia in 1776, and (under the title *The Surgical Works of the Late John Jones, M.D.* . . .) in Philadelphia in 1795.

29. W. B. McDaniel II, ed., "John Jones' Introductory Lecture to His Course in Surgery (1769), King's College, Printed from the Author's Manuscript," *Transactions & Studies of the College of Physicians of Philadelphia*, 4th series, 8 (1940–41): 181–88; John Jones's lectures on surgery, COPOP.

30. John Jones's lectures on surgery, COPOP.

31. McDaniel, "John Jones' Introductory Lecture," pp. 183–87; Shryock, *Medicine and Society*, p. 59.

32. Cowen, *Medicine and Health in New Jersey*, pp. 7, 10–14.

33. *N. Y. Journal; or the General Advertiser*, March 14, July 25, 1771; *N. Y. Gazette; and the Weekly Mercury*, Aug. 8, Aug. 8, supplement, Aug. 22, 1774.

34. M. Halsey Thomas, *Columbia University Officers and Alumni, 1754–1857* (New York: Columbia University Press, 1936), 178–84; Stookey, *Colonial Medical Education*, chs. 2–4. In *Professional Lives in America: Structure and Aspiration, 1750–1850* (Cambridge: Harvard University Press, 1965), pp. 27–28, Daniel H. Calhoun reads the medical factionalism of the post-Revolutionary period back into the pre-Revolutionary years. However, whatever rivalry existed before the Revolution among Samuel Bard, Sir James Jay, Samuel Clossy, and others was of minor consequence, unlike the rivalries of the post-Revolutionary years.

35. See, for example, the writings of Richard Shryock and Whitfield J. Bell, Jr.

36. Byron Stookey, "America's Two Colonial Medical Schools," *Bulletin of the New York Academy of Medicine* 40 (April 1964): 270; Waite, "Degree of Bachelor of Medicine," p. 314.

4. *King's College Becomes Columbia*

INTRODUCTION

1. J. Franklin Jameson, *The American Revolution Considered as a Social Movement* (Boston: Beacon Press, 1956), pp. 9, 82–83. For lists of students, faculty, and trustees see M. Halsey Thomas, *Columbia University Officers and Alumni, 1754–1857* (New York: Columbia University Press, 1936), pp. 13–14, 25–27, 111–14. Biographical data has been drawn from a large number of sources. "Ac-

tive" trustees refers to those who attended thirteen or more trustees meetings from 1787 through 1789.

2. "Minutes of the Trustees of Columbia College," Nov. 26, 1787, Aug. 25, 1788, typescripts, Columbiana, Columbia University; "Report of Committee on Plan of Education," April 25, 1791, College Papers, Special Collections, Columbia University Library.

15. RESHAPING KING'S COLLEGE

1. Charles Inglis, "Sermon to the Troops," Sept. 1777, extracted in John W. Lydekker, *The Life and Letters of Charles Inglis* . . . (London and New York: Macmillan, 1936), p. 257; Charles Inglis to William Morice, May 6, 1782, *ibid.*, p. 208; SPG Journals, 23: 181 et seq., *ibid.*, pp. 213–14; Petition of Charles Inglis et al. to Sir Guy Carleton, Oct. 18, 1783, "King's College and Episcopate in Nova Scotia," *Collections of the Nova Scotia Historical Society*, 6 (1887–88): 123–24.

2. Charles Inglis to Archbishop of Canterbury, April 1789, quoted in Thomas B. Akins, *A Brief Account of the Origin, Endowment and Progress of the University of King's College, Windsor, Nova Scotia* (Halifax, 1865), p. 8; Charles Inglis to Richard Cumberland, May 5, 1790, quoted in M. Halsey Thomas, ed., "The Memoirs of William Cochran," *New-York Historical Society Quarterly* 38 (Jan. 1954): 76n.

3. "Petition of Governors of King's College," March 24, 1784, Daniel J. Pratt, "Annals of Public Education in the State of New York," *Proceedings of the Twelfth Anniversary of the University Convocation of the State of New York* (Albany, 1876), p. 199 (cited hereafter as "Annals").

4. *Ibid.*, pp. 197–99.

5. Sidney Sherwood, *The University of the State of New York: History of Higher Education in the State of New York*, United States Bureau of Education, Circular of Information No. 3, 1900 (Washington, D.C., 1900), p. 50. Sherwood's study is in many respects an excellent one. See also John B. Pine, "The Origin of the University of the State of New York," *Columbia University Quarterly* 11 (March 1909): 155–60. Some insight into the areas of disagreement over Duane's bill can be gained by reading the letter of John Henry Livingston to James Duane, [1784?], James Duane Papers, New-York Historical Society.

6. "Annals," p. 208n. The act is printed in "Annals," pp. 203–09.

7. The governor, lieutenant governor, secretary, and attorney general of New York State, the president of the senate, and the speaker of the assembly were ex officio regents. The two residents from each of New York's twelve counties were listed by name in the act but were to be replaced at their death, resignation, or removal from the state by the governor with the consent of the council of appointment.

8. "Constitution of 1777" quoted in John W. Pratt, *Religion, Politics, and Diversity: The Church-State Theme in New York History* (Ithaca, N.Y.: Cornell University Press, 1967), p. 89.

9. "Minutes of the Governors of King's College, 1770–1781," Oct. 12, 1772,

photostats, Columbiana, Columbia University; "Senate Journal," Jan. 26, Feb. 19, 1784, "Annals," pp. 198, 199.

10. "Regents Minutes," May–August 1784, "Annals," pp. 209–16.

11. "Annals," pp. 216–22; Sherwood, *University of the State of New York*, pp. 55, 56.

12. I have counted all meetings from May 4, 1784 to March 29, 1787, "Annals," pp. 209–59.

13. For definition of terms "well-to-do," etc., see Jackson T. Main, *Political Parties before the Constitution* (Chapel Hill, N.C.: University of North Carolina Press, 1973), pp. 29–30, 35.

14. *New York Journal and State Gazette*, Nov. 4, 1784, extracted in Thomas F. Devoe, "King's College—Columbia College: Extracts from Old Newspapers, 1755–1835," p. 27, Columbiana; "Committee Report on Plan of Education," 1784, College Papers, Special Collections, Columbia University Library (cited hereafter as College Papers); *Dictionary of National Biography*, s.v. "Joseph Priestly," "Richard Price," "John Jebb."

15. "Regents Minutes," May 5, 1784, Dec. 14, 1784–Jan. 26, 1785, "Annals," pp. 210, 226–32; "Minutes of the Trustees of Columbia College," Nov. 26, 1787, typescripts, Columbiana (cited hereafter as "Trustees Minutes").

16. "Regents Minutes," May 5, 1784, "Annals," p. 211; "Memorial of Regents to Legislature," 1784, draft, College Papers; M. Halsey Thomas, "The King's College Building: with some notes on its later tenants," *New-York Historical Society Quarterly* 39 (Jan. 1955), p. 47.

17. "Trustees Minutes," Nov. 26, 1787; *New York Journal and Weekly Register*, April 13, 1786, quoted in *A History of Columbia University, 1754–1904* (New York: Columbia University Press, 1904), p. 66.

18. "Senate Journal," Nov. 19, 1784, "Annals," p. 218; "Annals," p. 221n; "Regents Minutes," Feb. 28, 1786, Feb. 16, 1787, "Annals," pp. 243, 253; Sherwood, *University of the State of New York*, p. 59.

19. "Regents Minutes," Feb. 16, 1787, "Annals," pp. 252–53; Sherwood, *University of the State of New York*, pp. 63–67.

20. Sherwood, *University of the State of New York*, pp. 68–73. Sherwood's discussion of the two bills is extremely helpful.

21. "Regents Minutes," March 8, 1787, "Annals," pp. 255–56.

22. The act is printed in "Annals," pp. 262–70.

23. John S. Whitehead, *The Separation of College and State: Columbia, Dartmouth, Harvard, and Yale, 1776–1876* (New Haven and London: Yale University Press, 1973), pp. 4–6, 51.

24. *Ibid.*, pp. 28, 108.

25. M. Halsey Thomas, *Columbia University Officers and Alumni, 1754–1857* (New York: Columbia University Press, 1936), pp. 14, 17, 25–27; *History of Columbia University*, pp. 87–93, 97–98.

26. Charles Inglis to William Samuel Johnson, June 13, 1796, Samuel Johnson

Papers, Special Collections, Columbia University Library; *N. Y. Journal and Weekly Register*, May 7, 1789; E. Edwards Beardsley, *Life and Times of William Samuel Johnson* . . . (New York, 1876), pp. 141–45.

27. George C. Groce, Jr., *William Samuel Johnson: A Maker of the Constitution* (New York: Columbia University Press, 1937), pp. 193–94. Groce's chapter on Johnson's presidency of Columbia is well done and very helpful.

28. Whitehead, *Separation of College and State*, pp. 28, 28n; *History of Columbia University*, pp. 97–98. It was probably for this reason as much as for financial considerations that the regents had earlier postponed the appointment of a president. If they named an Episcopal clergyman they could alienate those very religious groups whose support they needed to create an effective institution. But were they to appoint a non-Episcopalian, they would have to contend with Trinity Church.

29. Groce, *William Samuel Johnson*, pp. 181–82, 181n; Alexander Hamilton to James Ashton Bayard, Aug. 6, 1800, Henry Cabot Lodge, ed., *The Works of Alexander Hamilton*, 2d edition (New York: Putnam, 1904), 10: 385.

16. THE FLOWERING OF AN URBAN INSTITUTION

1. John Barent Johnson, MS Diary, Feb. 5, April 24, May 2, 1792, Columbiana, Columbia University (cited hereafter as John Barent Johnson, Diary).

2. "Regents Minutes," May 15, 17, 26, June 15, Aug. 25, Dec. 7, 1784, March 29, 1787, Daniel J. Pratt, "Annals of Public Education in the State of New York," *Proceedings of the Twelfth Anniversary of the University Convocation of the State of New York* (Albany, 1876), pp. 211–16, 224, 259 (cited hereafter as "Annals"); "Treasurer's Financial Notes," 1780s, College Papers, Special Collections, Columbia University Library (cited hereafter as College Papers); "Public Notice of Columbia Professors," May 14, 1785, clipping from unidentified New York newspaper, College Papers; "Minutes of the Trustees of Columbia College," April 5, Nov. 26, Dec. 4, 1787, June 25, 1792, typescripts, Columbiana, Columbia University (cited hereafter as "Trustees Minutes"); John Maclean, *History of the College of New Jersey, From Its Origin in 1746 to the Commencement of 1854* (Philadelphia, 1877), 1: 330–31, 343, 2: 6; "Minutes of Faculty Meeting," Feb. 19, 1795, College Papers.

3. Jonathan Baldwin to Brockholst Livingston, Dec. 7, 1784, College Papers; "Public Notice of Columbia Professors," May 14, 1785, clipping from unidentified New York newspaper, College Papers.

4. "List of Students," 1791, College Papers; Franklin B. Hough, *Historical and Statistical Record of the University of the State of New York During the Century from 1784 to 1884* (Albany, 1885), p. 103; M. Halsey Thomas, *Columbia University Officers and Alumni, 1754–1857* (New York: Columbia University Press, 1936), pp. 111–17. Two hundred and seventy-one students entered in the classes of 1786 through 1800. Two hundred and eight of them earned B.A.'s. These figures do not include Brandt Schuyler Lupton, '88, who actually attended the college before the American Revolution.

5. Thomas, *Columbia University Officers and Alumni*, pp. 111–14; "Matriculation Book," 1784–1788, MS, Columbiana. The profile which follows is based on a large number of primary and secondary sources.

6. This is my impression of the social class background based on the data I have. My data do not justify an elaborate comparison. The matriculation book lists a place of residence for each student included therein, which helps immensely in finding additional data on them. However, not every student is included in the matriculation book, and in a handful of cases there is a question about the correctness of the residence listed. The King's College matriculation book did not list places of residence.

7. Samuel L. Mitchill to William Samuel Johnson, Feb. 29, 1796, E. Edwards Beardsley, *Life and Times of William Samuel Johnson* . . . (New York, 1876), p. 152.

8. "List of undergraduates in 1800," "Matriculation Book," MS, Columbiana.

9. DeWitt Clinton, "Address to the Alumni, May, 1827," William W. Campbell, *The Life and Writings of De Witt Clinton* (New York, 1849), pp. 8–9; "Trustees Minutes," Nov. 26, 1787.

10. Moreau de Saint-Méry, *Voyage aux États-Unis de L'Amérique, 1793–1798*, ed. by Stewart L. Mims (New Haven: Yale University Press, 1913), p. 167; John Drayton, *Letters Written During A Tour Through the Northern and Eastern States of America* (Charleston, S.C., 1794), p. 25; Clement C. Moore, *The Early History of Columbia College*, ed. by M. Halsey Thomas (New York: Columbia University Press, 1940), p. xii.

11. *The Statutes of Columbia College, in New-York* (New York, 1785), pp. 7–9; *The Statutes of Columbia College, in New-York* (New York, 1788), pp. 6–8.

12. "Petition of Students to Trustees," Aug. 19, 1788, College Papers; "Trustees Minutes," Dec. 3, 1787, Aug. 25, 1788, April 9, 1789; "Report of Committee on Plan of Education," April 25, 1791, College Papers; George C. Groce, Jr., *William Samuel Johnson: A Maker of the Constitution* (New York: Columbia University Press, 1937), p. 175n; "List of delinquent students," March 30, 1793, College Papers.

13. *New-York Evening Post*, May 6, 1825, extracted in Thomas, Clement Moore's *Early History of Columbia College*, p. viii; Francis Silvester to DeWitt Clinton, Feb. 12, 1788, DeWitt Clinton Papers, vol. 1, Special Collections, Columbia University Library (cited hereafter as SCCU); Alexander Hamilton to James Ashton Bayard, Aug. 6, 1800, Henry Cabot Lodge, ed., *The Works of Alexander Hamilton*, 2d edition (New York: Putnam, 1904), 10: 385.

14. "Memorial of Regents to Legislature," 1784, draft, College Papers; "Trustees Minutes," March 5, 1792; *A History of Columbia University, 1754–1904* (New York: Columbia University Press, 1904), p. 101.

15. "Regents Minutes," Aug. 25, 1784, "Annals," p. 216.

16. *Ibid.;* Abraham Hun to DeWitt Clinton, June 27, 1786, DeWitt Clinton Papers, vol. 1, SCCU.

17. John Barent Johnson, Diary, passim; Ray W. Irwin and Edna L. Jacob-

son, eds., *A Columbia College Student in the Eighteenth Century: Essays by Daniel D. Tompkins* . . . (New York: Columbia University Press, 1940), pp. 12, 38–40.

18. Irwin and Jacobson, *Essays by Daniel D. Tompkins*, p. 41; Helen P. Roach, *History of Speech Education at Columbia College, 1754–1940* (New York: Teachers College, Columbia University, 1950), pp. 34–35; John F. Roche, "The Uranian Society: Gentlemen and Scholars in Federal New York," *New York History* 52 (April 1971): 121–32.

19. John Barent Johnson, Diary, *passim*. One must be cautious in generalizing from Johnson's diary, since he was three years older than the average Columbia student, more mature, and did not live with his family. However, there is nothing to suggest that his experiences were unique.

20. "Trustee Minutes," Nov. 26, 1787.

21. *Ibid.*, Jan. 12, Feb. 13, 14, June 25, July 9, Oct. 2, 1792, May 5, 8, 9, 1795; Samuel Latham Mitchill, *The Present State of Learning in the College of New-York* (New York, 1794), pp. 3–16; Thomas, *Columbia University Officers and Alumni*, pp. 25–27, 178; Byron Stookey, *A History of Colonial Medical Education: in the Province of New York, with its Subsequent Development (1767–1830)* (Springfield, Ill.: Charles C. Thomas, 1962), pp. 88–102.

22. James Kent, *An Introductory Lecture to a Course of Law Lectures, Delivered November 17, 1794* (New York, 1794), pp. 8, 19–20; Samuel Latham Mitchill, *Outline of the Doctrines in Natural History, Chemistry, and Economics* . . . (New York, 1792), pp. 5–31; "Trustees Minutes," Dec. 27, 1792.

23. Anthony Villette de Marcellin to Trustees, Aug. 5, 1793, College Papers; John Christopher Kunze to Trustees, Aug. 2, 1793, College Papers; Mitchill, *Present State of Learning*, p. 8; *Dictionary of American Biography*, s.v. "James Kent"; *History of Columbia University*, p. 81.

24. The best general sources on the curriculum are the plans of education published in 1785 and 1788 with the *Statutes of Columbia College;* Mitchill, *Present State of Learning*, pp. 3–11; and the detailed MS diary of John Barent Johnson at Columbiana. Johnson was an undergraduate from 1788 to 1792. He kept his diary throughout his undergraduate years, but the portion covering the period from late November 1790 to late September 1791 has been lost. The diary suggests that the plan of education was followed fairly closely.

25. *Statutes of Columbia College, 1788*, following p. 15; William Cochran, "Observations on the Plan of Education," March 19, 1788, College Papers. The readings varied somewhat when Elijah Rattoone was teaching Latin and Greek (1792–97).

26. William Cochran, "Observations on the Plan of Education," March 19, 1788, College Papers.

27. Irwin and Jacobson, *Essays by Daniel D. Tompkins*, p. 27; M. Halsey Thomas, ed., "The Memoirs of William Cochran," *New-York Historical Society Quarterly* 38 (Jan. 1954): 70.

28. *New-York Packet*, Nov. 14, 17, 1789. For other essays attacking the study of Latin and Greek, see *ibid.*, Aug. 15, Sept. 3, 1789, March 13, April 24, 1790; *New York Daily Advertiser*, Dec. 24, 1789. The main defense of the classics,

"Thoughts on Education," appeared in *N. Y. Packet*, Nov. 17, 19, 21, 24, 1789. For a general discussion of anticlassical sentiment during the Revolutionary and post-Revolutionary years, see Meyer Reinhold, "Opponents of Classical Learning in America During the Revolutionary Period," *Proceedings of the American Philosophical Society*, 112 (No. 4, 1968): 221–34.

29. "Report of Committee on Plan of Education," April 25, 1791, College Papers; Mitchill, *Outline of Doctrines in Natural History*, pp. 21, 25–26.

30. George Rapelje, *A Narrative of Excursions, Voyages, and Travels, Performed at Different Periods in America, Europe, Asia, and Africa* (New York, 1834), pp. 16–17; Henry Suydam, *History and Reminiscences of the Mesier Family* . . . ([New York], 1882), pp. 11–14.

31. Richard B. Davis, *Poems by Richard B. Davis; with A Sketch of His Life* (New York, 1807), p. xvii.

32. Mitchill, *Present State of Learning*, pp. 3–4; *Statutes of Columbia College, 1788*, following p. 15; John Barent Johnson, Diary, Jan. 23, 1789, April 3, 1790, Nov. 17, 22, 1791; Wilbur Samuel Howell, *Eighteenth-Century British Logic and Rhetoric* (Princeton, N.J.: Princeton University Press, 1971), pp. 125–38, 647–71, 675, 696–98; Mitchill, *Present State of Learning*, p. 3.

33. "Trustees Minutes," April 9, 1789; Rapelje, *Narrative of Excursions*, p. 17; Theodore Hornberger, *Scientific Thought in the American Colleges, 1638–1800* (New York: Octagon Books, 1968), pp. 49–57.

34. Mitchill, *Present State of Learning*, p. 6; "Notes on John Kemp's lectures in Natural and Experimental Philosophy," 1791, MS, Columbiana; W. P. and J. P. Cutler, eds., *Life, Journals, and Correspondence of Rev. Manasseh Cutler* (Cincinnati, 1888), 2: 239. Samuel Bard taught natural philosophy briefly before Kemp. See Byron Stookey, "Samuel Bard's Course on Natural Philosophy and Astronomy, 1785–1786: Required for a Medical Degree at Columbia," *Journal of Medical Education* 39 (April 1964): 397–406.

35. *Dictionary of American Biography*, s.v. "John Daniel Gros"; *Statutes of Columbia College, 1788*, following p. 15.

36. Lawrence A. Cremin, *American Education: The Colonial Experience, 1607–1783* (New York: Harper & Row, 1970), pp. 460–66; John Daniel Gros, *Natural Principles of Rectitude, for the Conduct of Man in All States and Situations of Life* . . . (New York, 1795), pp. xii, 362; Mitchill, *Present State of Learning*, p. 5.

37. Gros, *Natural Principles*, pp. 10–11; Wilson Smith, *Professors & Public Ethics: Studies of Northern Moral Philosophers before the Civil War* (Ithaca, N.Y.: Cornell University Press, 1956), p. 86.

38. Gros, *Natural Principles*, pp. 253, 297, 319, 331, 359.

39. *Ibid.*, pp. 283–84, 292, 413; Francis Silvester to DeWitt Clinton, Feb. 12, 1788, DeWitt Clinton Papers, vol. 1, SCCU; Clinton, "Address to the Alumni," Campbell, *Life and Writings of De Witt Clinton*, p. 10; Roach, *History of Speech Education*, p. 27.

40. Gros, *Natural Principles*, p. 362; Smith, *Professors & Public Ethics*, pp. 83–90.

41. Gerard Beekman, Ticket to J. D. Gros's Course in Logic, Beekman Pa-

pers, New-York Historical Society; Gros, *Natural Principles*, pp. 208–14; Howell, *Eighteenth-Century British Logic and Rhetoric*, pp. 350–51, 695–96; Roach, *History of Speech Education*, p. 26.

42. Thomas, *Columbia University Officers and Alumni*, pp. 180–81; John Barent Johnson, Diary (Johnson attended medical lectures while a senior); Alexander Hamilton to James Ashton Bayard, Aug. 6, 1800, Lodge, *Works of Alexander Hamilton*, 10: 385; Hornberger, *Scientific Thought in American Colleges*, pp. 73–74.

43. Douglas Sloan, *The Scottish Enlightenment and the American College Ideal* (New York: Teachers College Press, 1971), pp. 112–13.

44. Beardsley, *William Samuel Johnson*, p. 144; Irwin and Jacobson, *Essays by Daniel D. Tompkins*, p. 32.

45. Irwin and Jacobson, *Essays by Daniel D. Tompkins*, p. 16; Groce, *William Samuel Johnson*, p. 182n; Thomas, "Memoirs of William Cochran," p. 68.

46. Beardsley, *William Samuel Johnson*, p. 145.

47. John Barent Johnson, Diary, passim; "Trustees Minutes," May 5, 1791.

48. "Trustees Minutes," May 5, 1791; "Report of Committee on Plan of Education," April 25, 1791; *Statutes of Columbia College, 1785*, pp. 17–18; *Statutes of Columbia College, 1788*, pp. 14–15; John Barent Johnson, Diary, passim.

49. Irwin and Jacobson, *Essays by Daniel D. Tompkins*, p. 49.

RETROSPECT: CROSSCURRENTS IN EIGHTEENTH-CENTURY AMERICA

1. Jack P. Greene, "Autonomy and Stability: New England and the British Colonial Experience in Early Modern America," *Journal of Social History* 7 (Winter 1974): 192–93.

2. Milton M. Klein, "New York in the American Colonies: A New Look," *New York History* 53 (April 1972): 135, 138.

3. *Ibid.*, pp. 154–55.

4. Lawrence Stone, "The Ninniversity?" *New York Review of Books* 16 (Jan. 28, 1971): 22; Michael Kammen, "Biformity: A Frame of Reference," in Kammen, ed., *The Contrapuntal Civilization: Essays Toward a New Understanding of the American Experience* (New York: Thomas Y. Crowell, 1971), pp. 5, 20, 26–28.

BIBLIOGRAPHY

THE SOURCES for a study of King's College and Columbia College are plentiful on some subjects, virtually nonexistent on others. The controversies over the founding of King's College produced a substantial body of newspaper essays, pamphlets, and private letters. However, these were written largely by the Anglican clerics and the triumvirate. The Anglican and Dutch Reformed laymen who participated in the founding of the college left little record of their views. Nor, of course, did most other New Yorkers. One has to be very careful about generalizing on the basis of records left by both the Anglican clerics and the triumvirate, since there are several reasons to believe that both their associates and their followers viewed the issues differently. A thorough investigation of the SPG Archives turned up a few relevant letters, but it was especially interesting to see how rarely the college was ever mentioned.

Sources on King's College in operation are similarly uneven. The College Papers are helpful but thin. Financial records are particularly slim. The Governors Minutes are indispensable, but, like most minutes of their kind, they hide as much as they reveal. I turned up only a small number of private letters by the governors which bear on the college. Samuel Johnson's writings are plentiful and rich, but sources on Myles Cooper and his presidency are scarce. The other faculty members left few records, and the students and their parents are virtually a wasteland as far as sources go. There are few letters by undergraduates and almost nothing in the way of student workbooks, lecture notes, and diaries, or of recollections of undergraduate days by alumni. The sources I used to track down biographical data on the students, contributors, and governors are too extensive to list here. The Genealogy Room of the New York Public Library is an especially fruitful place to hunt for biographical data. A bibliography of most of the sources used in compiling the group profile of the King's College students (but not the Columbia students) can be found in David C. Humphrey, "King's College in the City of New York, 1754–1776" (Ph.D. diss., Northwestern University, 1968), pp. 642–61. Various key sources on King's College are scattered among the many manuscript and printed sources listed below, among which the most useful are the New York newspapers and the collections at Columbia, the New-York Historical Society, and the Church Historical Society.

The chapters on the King's College Medical School benefited greatly by the Bard family papers. However, the other doctors who participated in the project left few letters, memoirs, or the like, which is one reason why the Bards usually get more credit than they deserve for founding the medical school. At the opening of the medical school each of the four major professors—Clossy, Jones, S. Bard, and Middleton—gave a general lecture on medical science and medical education. All but Clossy's lecture are enlightening (see p. 358, note 7). Also very helpful are Bard's lecture notes on chemistry, Jones's on surgery, and a student's notes on Bard's lectures in the practice of medicine. The latter is one of the few valuable items from this period in the College of Physicians and Surgeons Papers at Columbia. Notices of medical courses in the New York newspapers help immensely in pinning down yearly course offerings and their content.

Sources on post-Revolutionary Columbia suffer from some of the same deficiencies as those on King's College, yet there are also some pleasant surprises. The College Papers are fuller. The matricula includes information on the parents and the place of residence of the students, which makes tracking down the students much easier. There are informative sources on a number of courses. And John Barent Johnson's diary, Daniel Tompkins's undergraduate essays, and some scattered recollections by alumni help a great deal in writing about the curriculum and undergraduate life.

I have remarked at appropriate places in the footnotes on a number of primary and secondary sources which were especially valuable. I would particularly like to acknowledge here the work of Milton M. Klein, Beverly McAnear, M. Halsey Thomas, Whitfield J. Bell, Jr., Richard Shryock, and Bernard Bailyn.

Manuscript Sources

Bard College Library (Annandale-on-Hudson, New York)
    Bard Collection
Church Historical Society (Austin, Texas)
    Hawks Papers
    Protestant Episcopal Church Archives
College of Physicians of Philadelphia (Philadelphia, Pennsylvania)
    Autograph File
    John Hodge, Notes on John Morgan's lectures
    John Jones, Lectures on surgery
Columbia University-Columbiana (New York, New York)
    Samuel Bayard, Workbook
    Thomas F. Devoe, King's College—Columbia College; Extracts from Old Newspapers, 1755–1835
    Robert Harpur, Account Book, photostats

Individual folders on King's College and Columbia alumni
Charles Inglis, Address to Students, transcript
John Barent Johnson, Diary
John Kemp, Lectures on natural philosophy, student notes
Matriculation Books
Minutes of the Governors of King's College, 1770–1781, photostats
Minutes of the Trustees of Columbia College, transcripts
Papers Concerning the Royal Charter of 1774, transcripts
Columbia University-Special Collections
DeWitt Clinton Papers
College of Physicians and Surgeons Papers
College Papers
General Manuscripts Collection
James Jay Papers
John Jay Papers
Samuel Johnson Papers and Correspondence
Charity Clarke and Clement Moore Papers
Gouverneur Morris Papers
Peter Van Schaack Papers
Connecticut Historical Society (Hartford, Connecticut)
William Samuel Johnson Papers
Library of Congress (Washington, D.C.)
Lambeth Palace Library, 1123, transcripts
Public Record Office, Colonial Office 5, America and West Indies, vol.
1106, transcripts
Society for the Propagation of the Gospel in Foreign Parts, Journals and
Letters, transcripts, photostats, and microfilm
Massachusetts Historical Society (Boston, Massachusetts)
William Livingston Papers
Sedgwick Papers
Museum of the City of New York (New York, New York)
Receipt book of Joseph Murray's estate
New York Academy of Medicine (New York, New York)
Bard Collection
New-York Historical Society (New York, New York)
Goldsbrow Banyar Papers
Beekman Papers
Broadside Collection
James Duane Papers
James Graham, Lecture Tickets
Peter Jay, Ledger
John Tabor Kempe Papers
Literary Society, Minutes and Accounts
Robert R. Livingston Papers

Misc. MSS: John Moore
John Moore, Autobiography, transcript
New York City Papers-Churches
Samuel Peters Papers, microfilm
Augustus Van Horne, Account Book
Gulian Verplanck Papers
John Watts Papers
New York Public Library (New York, New York)
American Loyalist Transcripts
Bancroft Transcripts, Letters of Samuel Johnson and William Samuel John-
son
William Smith Papers
New York State Library (Albany, New York)
Catalogue of John Chambers's Library
Material concerning Robert Harpur
Misc. MSS: Edward Antill
New York Council Minutes
Skene Papers
Public Record Office (London)
Grants and Warrants From 8/18/1777 to 2/20/1783, vol. 2, C. O. 324/44
Princeton University-Archives (Princeton, New Jersey)
College Papers
Minutes of Trustees of College of New Jersey
Princeton University-Special Collections
Aaron Burr Collection (1716–1757)
Yale University (New Haven, Connecticut)
Livingston-Welles Correspondence, Johnson Family Papers

Newspapers and Essay Journals (with publishers and dates published)

Constitutional Gazette (New York: John Anderson, 1775–76)
John Englishman, In Defence of the English Constitution (1st issue entitled John English-
man's true Notion of Sister-Churches; New York: James Parker et al., 1755)
New York Daily Advertiser (title varies; Francis Childs et al., 1785–1806)
New-York Evening Post (Henry DeForeest, 1744–53)
New York Gazette; and the Weekly Mercury (Hugh Gaine, 1768–83)
New-York Gazette; or the Weekly Post-Boy (entitled New-York Gazette Revived in the
Weekly Post-Boy from 1747 through 1752; James Parker, John Holt et al.,
1747–73)
New York Journal and Weekly Register (title varies; Thomas Greenleaf et al.,
1784–93)
New-York Journal; or the General Advertiser (John Holt, 1766–76)
New York Mercury (Hugh Gaine, 1752–68)
New-York Packet (Samuel and John Loudon, 1783–92)

New-York Weekly Journal (John Peter Zenger et al., 1733–51)
Occasional Reverberator (New York: James Parker, 1753)
Pennsylvania Journal; and the Weekly Advertiser (title varies; William and Thomas Bradford et al., 1742–93)
Rivington's New York Gazetteer (James Rivington, 1773–75)

Printed Primary Sources

Bard, John. "An Essay on the Nature and Cause of the Malignant Pleurisy. . . ." In *American Medical and Philosophical Register; or, Annals of Medicine, Natural History, Agriculture, and the Arts.* 2d ed. New York, 1814.

Bard, Samuel. *A Discourse upon the Duties of a Physician, with Some Sentiments, on the Usefulness and Necessity of a Public Hospital: Delivered before the President and Governors of King's College, at the Commencement, Held on the 16th of May, 1769. . . .* New York, 1769.

Bayley, Richard. *Cases of Angina Trachealis, with the Mode of Cure, in a Letter to William Hunter By Richard Bayley. To Which Is Added, A Letter from Peter Middleton to the Author.* New York, 1781.

[Blackwall, Anthony.] *Rhetoric and Poetry. Extracted from the Preceptor. For the Use of the University of Cambridge.* Boston, 1796.

Bridenbaugh, Carl, ed. *Gentleman's Progress: The Itinerarium of Dr. Alexander Hamilton, 1744.* Chapel Hill, N.C.: University of North Carolina Press, 1948.

———. ed. "Patrick M'Robert's Tour Through Part of the North Provinces of America." *Pennsylvania Magazine of History and Biography* 59 (1935): 134–80.

Butterfield, L. H., ed. *Diary and Autobiography of John Adams.* 4 vols. Cambridge: Harvard University Press, 1961.

———. ed. *Letters of Benjamin Rush.* 2 vols. Princeton, N.J.: Princeton University Press, 1951.

Campbell, William W. *The Life and Writings of De Witt Clinton.* New York, 1849.

Chandler, Thomas Bradbury. *The Life of Samuel Johnson, D.D., The first President of King's College, in New-York. . . .* New York, 1805.

Clarke, John. *An Introduction to the Making of Latin. Comprising, After an Easy, Compendious Method, The Substance of Latin Syntax, with Proper English Examples. . . .* Worcester, Mass., 1786.

Collections of the New-York Historical Society. Publication Fund Series. 85 vols. to date. New York, 1868—.

The Colonial Laws of New York from the Year 1664 to the Revolution. 5 vols. Albany, 1894.

Cooper, Myles. *Ethices Compendium, in Usum Collegiorum Americanorum, Emendatius Editum.* New York, 1774.

———. *National Humiliation and Repentance recommended, and the Causes of the present Rebellion in America assigned, in A Sermon preached before the University of Oxford, on Friday, December 13, 1776.* Oxford, 1777.

———. *Poems on Several Occasions.* Oxford, 1761.

Corwin, E. T., ed. *Ecclesiastical Records, State of New York.* 7 vols. Albany: James B. Lyon, 1901–16.

The Craftsmen: A Sermon, from The Independent Whig. . . . 5th ed. New York, 1753.

Crary, Catherine S., ed. *The Price of Loyalty: Tory Writings from the Revolutionary Era.* New York: McGraw-Hill, 1973.

Crèvecoeur, J. Hector St. John. *Letters from an American Farmer.* New York: Fox, Duffield & Co., 1904.

Cutler, W. P. and J. P., eds. *Life, Journals, and Correspondence of Rev. Manasseh Cutler, LL.D.* 2 vols. Cincinnati, 1888.

Davis, Richard B. *Poems by Richard B. Davis; with A Sketch of His Life.* New York, 1807.

Dexter, Franklin B., ed. *Extracts from the Itineraries and Other Miscellanies of Ezra Stiles, D.D., LL.D., 1755–1794, with a Selection from his Correspondence.* New Haven: Yale University Press, 1916.

———. ed. *The Literary Diary of Ezra Stiles, D.D., LL.D., President of Yale College.* 3 vols. New York: Scribners, 1901.

Dodsley, Robert, comp. *The Preceptor: Containing A General Course of Education. Wherein the First Principles of Polite Learning Are Laid Down in a Way Most Suitable for Trying the Genius, and Advancing the Instruction of Youth.* 5th ed. 2 vols. London, 1769.

Drayton, John. *Letters Written During A Tour Through the Northern and Eastern States of America.* Charleston, S.C., 1794.

Duncan, William. *The Elements of Logic. In Four Books.* . . . Philadelphia, 1792.

Early Minutes of the Trustees: Vol. I, 1755–1770. New York, 1932.

Evans, Margaret, ed. *Letters of Richard Radcliffe and John James of Queen's College, Oxford, 1755–83, with Additions, Notes, and Appendices.* Oxford, 1888.

Fordyce, David. *Dialogues Concerning Education.* 2d ed. 2 vols. Glasgow, 1768.

[Frelinghuysen, Theodore.] *A Remark on the Disputes and Contentions in This Province.* New York, 1755.

Gaine, Hugh. *Gaine's Universal Register, or, American and British Kalendar, For the Year 1775.* New York, n.d.

[———.] *The New-York Pocket Almanack, For the Year 1774.* . . . New York, n.d.

Grant, W. L., and Munro, J., eds. *Acts of the Privy Council of England, Colonial Series, v, A.D. 1766–1783.* 6 vols. Hereford and London: H. M. Stationery Office, 1908–12.

Gros, John Daniel. *Natural Principles of Rectitude, for the Conduct of Man in All States and Situations of Life; Demonstrated and Explained in a Systematic Treatise on Moral Philosophy.* . . . New York, 1795.

Hawks, Francis L., and Perry, William S., eds. *Documentary History of The Protestant Episcopal Church in the United States of America. Containing Numerous Hitherto Unpublished Documents Concerning the Church in Connecticut.* 2 vols. New York, 1863–64.

Heuzet, Jean. *Selectae E Profanis Scriptoribus Historiae; Quibus Admista Sunt Varia*

Honeste Vivendi Praecepta, ex Iisdem Scriptoribus Depromta. 3d ed. London, 1758.

Howe, Herbert B. "Colonel George Washington and King's College," *Columbia University Quarterly* 24 (1932): 137–57.

Irwin, Ray W., and Jacobson, Edna L., eds. *A Columbia College Student in the Eighteenth Century: Essays by Daniel D. Tompkins. . . .* New York: Columbia University Press, 1940.

Jacobson, David L., ed. *The English Libertarian Heritage: From the Writings of John Trenchard and Thomas Gordon in The Independent Whig and Cato's Letters.* Indianapolis: Bobbs-Merrill, 1965.

Jones, John. *Plain Concise Practical Remarks on the Treatment of Wounds and Fractures. To Which Is Added, a Short Appendix on Camp and Military Hospitals: Principally Designed for the Use of Young Military Surgeons in North-America.* New York, 1775.

Jones, Thomas. *History of New York during the Revolutionary War, and of the Leading Events in the Other Colonies at That Period,* edited by Edward F. De Lancey. New York, 1879.

Journal of the Commissioners for Trade and Plantations. . . . 14 vols. London: H. M. Stationery Office, 1920–38.

Journal of the Votes and Proceedings of the General Assembly Of the Colony of New-York. Began the 9th day of April, 1691; and Ended the [23d of December, 1765]. 2 vols. New York, 1764–66.

Journals of the Provincial Congress, Provincial Convention, Committee of Safety and Council of Safety of the State of New York, 1775–1776–1777. 2 vols. Albany, 1842.

[Kennedy, Archibald.] *A Speech Said to have been Delivered Some Time Before the Close of the Last Session, By a Member Dissenting from the Church.* [New York], 1755.

Kent, James. *An Introductory Lecture to a Course of Law Lectures, Delivered November 17, 1794.* New York, 1794.

"King's College and Episcopate in Nova Scotia," *Collections of the Nova Scotia Historical Society.* 6 (1887–88): 123–35.

Klein, Milton M., ed. *The Independent Reflector or Weekly Essays on Sundry Important Subjects More particularly adapted to the Province of New-York.* Cambridge: Harvard University Press, 1963.

Labaree, Leonard W. et al., eds. *The Papers of Benjamin Franklin.* 18 vols. to date. New Haven: Yale University Press, 1959–.

"Letter to Dr. Stuber, of Philadelphia, concerning the learned Languages, from Dr. John C. Kunze," *New-York Magazine; or Literary Repository* 1 (1790): 212–18.

[Livingston, William.] *An Address to His Excellency Sir Charles Hardy, Knt., Captain General and Governor in Chief of the Province of New-York, and territories thereon depending in America, and Vice-Admiral of the same.* New York, 1755.

[———.] *Some Serious Thoughts on The Design of erecting a College in the Province of*

380 BIBLIOGRAPHY

New-York. Shewing The eminent Advantages of a liberal Education, more especially with Regard to Religion and Politicks. . . . New York, 1749.

Locke, John. *John Locke: On Politics and Education.* Roslyn, New York: Walter J. Black, 1947.

Lodge, Henry Cabot, ed. *The Works of Alexander Hamilton.* 2d ed. 12 vols. New York: Putnam, 1904.

Lydekker, John W. *The Life and Letters of Charles Inglis: His Ministry in America and Consecration as First Colonial Bishop, from 1759 to 1787.* London and New York: Macmillan, 1936.

McDaniel, W. B. II, ed. "John Jones' Introductory Lecture to His Course in Surgery (1769), King's College, Printed from the Author's Manuscript," *Transactions & Studies of the College of Physicians of Philadelphia,* 4th series, 8 (1940–41): 180–90.

Macsparran, James. *America Dissected, Being a Full and True Account of All the American Colonies.* . . . In *History of the Episcopal Church in Narragansett, Rhode Island.* . . , by Wilkins Updike. New York, 1847.

Manross, William W. *The Fulham Papers in the Lambeth Palace Library; American Colonial Section, Calendar and Indexes.* Oxford: Clarendon Press, 1965.

Mease, James, ed. *The Surgical Works of the Late John Jones, M.D.* . . . Philadelphia, 1795.

Middleton, Peter. *A Medical Discourse, or an Historical Inquiry Into the Ancient and Present State of Medicine: The Substance of Which Was Delivered at Opening the Medical School In the City of New-York.* New York, 1769.

Miller, Walter, tr. and ed. *Xenophon, Cyropaedia.* 2 vols. Cambridge: Harvard University Press, 1960.

Mitchill, Samuel Latham. *Outline of the Doctrines in Natural History, Chemistry, and Economics, which, under the patronage of the state, are now delivering in the College of New-York.* New York, 1792.

———. *The Present State of Learning in the College of New-York.* New York, 1794.

Monaghan, Frank. "Dr. Samuel Johnson's Letters to Peter Jay," *Columbia University Quarterly* 25 (1933): 85–94.

Moore, Benjamin. *A Sermon Occasioned by the Death of the Revd. Dr. Auchmuty, Rector of Trinity Church in the City of New-York. Preached March 9, 1777.* New York, 1777.

Morgan, John. *A Discourse Upon the Institution of Medical Schools in America.* . . . Philadelphia, 1765.

New Jersey Archives (Archives of the State of New Jersey). 1st series. 42 vols. Imprint varies, 1880–1949.

Nichols, John. *Illustrations of the Literary History of the Eighteenth Century. Consisting of Authentic Memoirs and Original Letters of Eminent Persons; and Intended as a Sequel to the Literary Anecdotes.* 8 vols. London, 1817–58.

North, Douglass C., and Thomas, Robert Paul, eds. *The Growth of the American Economy to 1860.* New York: Harper & Row, 1968.

O'Callaghan, Edmund B., ed. *The Documentary History of the State of New-York.* 4 vols. Albany, 1849–51.

——— and Fernow, B., eds. *Documents Relative to the Colonial History of the State of New-York*. . . . 15 vols. Albany, 1853–87.

Osgood, Herbert L. "The Society of Dissenters founded at New York in 1769," *American Historical Review* 6 (1901): 498–507.

Perry, William S., ed. *Historical Collections Relating to the American Colonial Church*. 3 vols. Hartford, 1870–73.

Pilcher, George W. *Samuel Davies: Apostle of Dissent in Colonial Virginia*. Knoxville, Tenn.: University of Tennessee Press, 1971.

Pratt, Daniel J. "Annals of Public Education in the State of New York," *Proceedings of the Twelfth Anniversary of the University Convocation of the State of New York*. Albany, 1876.

Rapelje, George. *A Narrative of Excursions, Voyages, and Travels, Performed at Different Periods in America, Europe, Asia, and Africa*. New York, 1834.

Records of the Presbyterian Church in the United States of America. Philadelphia, 1841.

"Records of Trinity Church Parish, New York City," *New York Genealogical and Biographical Record* 68 (1937): 66–81; 69 (1938): 146–62.

"Remarks on the Description of Columbia College," *New-York Magazine; or Literary Repository* 1 (1790): 340–41.

Rowning, John. *A Compendious System of Natural Philosophy: With Notes Containing the Mathematical Demonstrations, and Some Occasional Remarks*. London, 1744.

Saffron, Morris. *Samuel Clossy, M.D. (1724–1786), Professor of Anatomy at King's College, New York: The Existing Works, with a Biographical Sketch*. New York: Hafner, 1967.

Saint-Méry, Moreau de. *Voyage aux États-Unis de L'Amérique, 1793–1798*. Edited by Stewart L. Mims. New Haven: Yale University Press, 1913.

Schneider, Herbert and Carol, eds. *Samuel Johnson, President of King's College: His Career and Writings*. 4 vols. New York: Columbia University Press, 1929.

Schachner, Nathan, ed. "Alexander Hamilton Viewed by His Friends: The Narratives of Robert Troup and Hercules Mulligan," *William and Mary Quarterly*, 3d series, 4 (1947): 203–25.

Smith, Horace W. *Life and Correspondence of the Rev. William Smith, D.D.* 2 vols. Philadelphia, 1879–80.

Smith, William. *Discourses on Public Occasions in America*. 2d ed. London, 1762.

[———.] *A General Idea of the College of Mirania; with A Sketch of the Method of teaching Science and Religion, in the several Classes: and Some Account of its Rise, Establishment and Buildings*. . . . New York, 1753.

[———.] *Some Thoughts on Education: with Reasons for Erecting a College in this Province, and fixing the same at the City of New-York*. . . . New York, 1752.

Smith, William, Jr. *The History of the Province of New-York*, edited by Michael Kammen. 2 vols. Cambridge: Harvard University Press, 1972.

Sprigge, Timothy L. S., ed. *The Correspondence of Jeremy Bentham*. 2 vols. to date. London: Athlone Press, 1968–.

The Statutes of Columbia College, in New-York. New York, 1785.

The Statutes of Columbia College, in New-York. New York, 1788.

Sterling, John. *A System of Rhetorick, In a Method entirely New. Containing All the*

Tropes and Figures necessary to Illustrate the Classicks, both Poetical and Historical. New York, 1788.

Stevens, B. F. *Facsimiles of Manuscripts in European Archives Relating to America, 1773–1783, with Descriptions, Editorial Notes, Collations, References, and Translations.* 25 vols. London, 1889–98.

Stone, Edmund. *Euclid's Elements of Geometry. The First Six, The Eleventh and Twelfth Books; Translated into English from Dr. Gregory's Edition: With Notes and Additions.* London, 1752.

Stookey, Byron. "Samuel Bard's Course on Natural Philosophy and Astronomy, 1785–1786: Required for a Medical Degree at Columbia," *Journal of Medical Education* 39 (1964): 397–406.

Sullivan, James et al., eds. *The Papers of Sir William Johnson.* 14 vols. Albany: University of the State of New York, 1921–65.

Syrett, Harold C., and Cooke, Jacob E., eds. *The Papers of Alexander Hamilton.* 19 vols. to date. New York and London: Columbia University Press, 1961–.

Thomas, M. Halsey, ed. "The Black Book of King's College," *Columbia University Quarterly* 23 (1931): 1–18.

————. ed. "King's College Commencement in the Newspapers," *Columbia University Quarterly* 22 (1930): 226–47.

————. ed. "The Memoirs of William Cochran," *New-York Historical Society Quarterly* 38 (1954): 55–83.

[Vardill, John.] *Candid Remarks on Dr. Witherspoon's Address To the Inhabitants of Jamaica, And the other West-India Islands, &c. In a Letter to those Gentlemen.* Philadelphia, 1772.

Ward, George A. *Journal and Letters of the Late Samuel Curwen, Judge of Admiralty, Etc., An American Refugee in England, from 1775 to 1784. . . .* New York, 1842.

[Wilkins, Isaac.] *Short Advice to the Counties of New-York.* New York, 1774.

"The Will of James Alexander," *New York Genealogical and Biographical Record* 18 (1887): 173–81.

Wilson, Rufus R., ed. *Burnaby's Travels Through North America.* New York: A. Wessels Co., 1904.

Secondary Sources

Abbott, Carl. "The Neighborhoods of New York, 1760–1775," *New York History* 55 (1974): 35–54.

Akins, Thomas B. *A Brief Account of the Origin, Endowment and Progress of the University of King's College, Windsor, Nova Scotia.* Halifax, 1865.

Alexander, Samuel D. *Princeton College during the Eighteenth Century.* New York, 1872.

Allen, Robert J. "William Oldisworth: 'the Author of *The Examiner*,' " *Philological Quarterly* 26 (1947): 159–80.

Ashley Smith, J. W. *The Birth of Modern Education: The Contribution of the Dissenting Academies, 1660–1800.* London: Independent Press, 1954.

Ashton, Rick J. "The Loyalist Experience: New York, 1763–1789." Ph.D. dissertation, Northwestern University, 1973.

Axtell, James L. "Coming of Age in Colonial America: A New Look." Paper read at American Historical Association, Boston, Mass., Dec. 30, 1970. Mimeographed.

Bailyn, Bernard. *Education in the Forming of American Society: Needs and Opportunities for Study.* Chapel Hill, N. C.: University of North Carolina Press, 1960.

———. *The Origins of American Politics.* New York: Knopf, 1968.

———. "The Transforming Radicalism of the American Revolution," *Pamphlets of the American Revolution, 1750–1776: Volume I, 1750–1765.* Cambridge: Harvard University Press, 1965.

Beardsley, E. Edwards. *Life and Times of William Samuel Johnson, LL. D., First Senator in Congress from Connecticut, and President of Columbia College, New York.* New York, 1876.

Becker, Carl. *The History of Political Parties in the Province of New York, 1760–1776.* Madison, Wis.: University of Wisconsin Press, 1960.

Bell, Whitfield J., Jr. *John Morgan, Continental Doctor.* Philadelphia: University of Pennsylvania Press, 1965.

———. "Medical Practice in Colonial America," *Bulletin of the History of Medicine* 31 (1957): 442–53.

———. "A Portrait of the Colonial Physician," *Bulletin of the History of Medicine* 44 (1970): 497–517.

———. "Some American Students of 'That Shining Oracle of Physic,' Dr. William Cullen of Edinburgh, 1755–1766," *Proceedings of the American Philosophical Society* 94 (1950): 275–81.

Blanton, Wyndham. *Medicine in Virginia in the Eighteenth Century.* Richmond: Garrett & Massie, 1931.

Bonomi, Patricia. *A Factious People: Politics and Society in Colonial New York.* New York and London: Columbia University Press, 1971.

Brauer, George C., Jr. *The Education of a Gentleman: Theories of Gentlemanly Education In England, 1660–1775.* New York: Bookman Associates, 1959.

Bridenbaugh, Carl. *Cities in Revolt: Urban Life in America, 1743–1776.* New York: Knopf, 1955.

———. *Mitre and Sceptre: Transatlantic Faiths, Ideas, Personalities, and Politics, 1689–1775.* New York: Oxford University Press, 1962.

Brubacher, John S., and Rudy, Willis. *Higher Education in Transition: A History of American Colleges and Universities, 1636–1968,* rev. ed. New York: Harper & Row, 1968.

Bullough, Vern and Bonnie. "The Causes of the Scottish Medical Renaissance of the Eighteenth Century," *Bulletin of the History of Medicine* 45 (1971): 13–28.

Burr, Nelson, R. *The Anglican Church in New Jersey.* Philadelphia: Church Historical Society, 1954.

Bushman, Richard L. *From Puritan to Yankee: Character and the Social Order in Connecticut, 1690–1765.* Cambridge: Harvard University Press, 1967.
Calhoun, Daniel H. *Professional Lives in America: Structure and Aspiration, 1750–1850.* Cambridge: Harvard University Press, 1965.
Carman, Harry. "The Professions in New York in 1800," *Columbia University Quarterly* 23 (1931): 159–75.
Cheyney, Edward P. *History of the University of Pennsylvania, 1740–1940.* Philadelphia: University of Pennsylvania Press, 1940.
Chroust, Anton-Hermann. *The Rise of the Legal Profession in America.* 2 vols. Norman, Okla.: University of Oklahoma Press, 1965.
Clement, John. "Anglican Clergymen Licensed to the American Colonies, 1710–1744," *Historical Magazine of the Protestant Episcopal Church* 17 (1948): 207–50.
Cohen, Sheldon S., and Gerlach, Larry R., "Princeton in the Coming of the American Revolution," *New Jersey History* 92 (1974): 69–92.
Collins, Varnum L., ed. *General Catalogue of Princeton University, 1746–1906.* Princeton, N.J.: John C. Winston Co., 1908.
Corner, George W. *Anatomy.* New York: Paul B. Hoeber, 1930.
Cowen, David L. *Medicine and Health in New Jersey: A History.* Princeton, N.J.: Van Nostrand, 1964.
Cremin, Lawrence A. *American Education: The Colonial Experience, 1607–1783.* New York: Harper & Row, 1970.
Dangerfield, George. *Chancellor Robert R. Livingston of New York, 1746–1813.* New York: Harcourt, Brace & Co., 1960.
Dexter, Franklin B. *Biographical Sketches of the Graduates of Yale College, with Annals of the College History, Oct. 1701–Sept. 1805.* 5 vols. New York: Henry Holt & Co., 1885–1911.
Dix, Morgan et al. *A History of the Parish of Trinity Church in the City of New York.* 6 vols. New York: Putnam, 1898–1962.
Duffy, John. *A History of Public Health in New York City, 1625–1866.* New York: Russell Sage Foundation, 1968.
Ellis, Joseph J. "Anglicans in Connecticut, 1725–1750: The Conversion of the Missionaries," *New England Quarterly* 44 (1971): 66–81.
———. *The New England Mind in Transition: Samuel Johnson of Connecticut, 1696–1772.* New Haven: Yale University Press, 1973.
Fiering, Norman S. "Moral Philosophy in America, 1650 to 1750, and Its British Context." Ph.D. dissertation, Columbia University, 1969.
———. "President Samuel Johnson and the Circle of Knowledge," *William and Mary Quarterly,* 3d series, 28 (1971): 199–236.
Fox, Bertha S. "Provost Smith and the Quest for Funds," *Pennsylvania History* 2 (1935): 225–38.
Fox, Dixon Ryan. *Yankees and Yorkers.* New York: New York University Press, 1940.
Francesco, Grete de. *The Power of the Charlatan.* Translated by Miriam Beard. New Haven: Yale University Press, 1939.

Francis, John W. *Old New York: or, Reminiscences of The Past Sixty Years.* New York, 1866.

Fuld, Leonhard F. "King's College Alumni-II," *Columbia University Quarterly* 9 (1907): 54–60.

Gaustad, Edwin S. *Historical Atlas of Religion in America.* New York and Evanston: Harper & Row, 1962.

Goebel, Julius, Jr. *The Law Practice of Alexander Hamilton: Documents and Commentaries.* 2 vols. to date. New York and London: Columbia University Press, 1964–.

Goodwin, Gerald. "The Anglican Middle Way in Early Eighteenth-Century America: Anglican Religious Thought in the American Colonies, 1702–1750." Ph.D. dissertation, University of Wisconsin, 1965.

Grant, Alexander. *The Story of the University of Edinburgh During Its First Three Hundred Years.* 2 vols. London, 1884.

Greene, Jack P. "Autonomy and Stability: New England and the British Colonial Experience in Early Modern America," *Journal of Social History* 7 (1974): 171–94.

———. "Search for Identity: An Interpretation of the Meaning of Selected Patterns of Social Response in Eighteenth-Century America," *Journal of Social History* 3 (1970): 189–220.

Greene, Richard H. "King's (Now Columbia) College and Its Earliest Alumni," *New York Genealogical and Biographical Record* 25 (1894): 123–33, 174–81.

Groce, George C., Jr. *William Samuel Johnson: A Maker of the Constitution.* New York: Columbia University Press, 1937.

Guerra, Francisco. *American Medical Bibliography, 1639–1783.* New York: Lathrop C. Harper, 1962.

Hamlin, Paul M. *Legal Education in Colonial New York.* New York: New York University Press, 1939.

———. "Peter Van Schaack," *Columbia University Quarterly* 24 (1932): 66–105.

Harrington, Virginia D. *The New York Merchant on the Eve of the Revolution.* New York: Columbia University Press, 1935.

Heaton, Claude E. "Medicine in New York during the English Colonial Period," *Bulletin of the History of Medicine* 17 (1945): 9–37.

Heimert, Alan. *Religion and the American Mind: From the Great Awakening to the Revolution.* Cambridge: Harvard University Press, 1966.

A History of Columbia University, 1754–1904; Published in Commemoration of the One Hundred and Fiftieth Anniversary of the Founding of King's College. New York: Columbia University Press, 1904.

Hofstadter, Richard, and Metzger, Walter P. *The Development of Academic Freedom in the United States.* New York: Columbia University Press, 1955.

Hornberger, Theodore. "Samuel Johnson of Yale and King's College: A Note on the Relation of Science and Religion in Provincial America," *New England Quarterly* 8 (1935): 378–97.

———. *Scientific Thought in the American Colleges, 1638–1800.* New York: Octagon Books, 1968.

Hough, Franklin B. *Historical and Statistical Record of the University of the State of New York During the Century from 1784 to 1884.* Albany, 1885.

Howell, Wilbur Samuel. *Eighteenth-Century British Logic and Rhetoric.* Princeton, N.J.: Princeton University Press, 1971.

———. *Logic and Rhetoric in England, 1500–1700.* Princeton, N.J.: Princeton University Press, 1956.

Humphrey, David C. "Anglican 'Infiltration' of Eighteenth Century Harvard and Yale," *Historical Magazine of the Protestant Episcopal Church* 43 (1974): 247–51.

———. "British Influences on Eighteenth Century American Education," *History of Education Quarterly* 13 (1973): 65–72.

———. "Colonial Colleges and English Dissenting Academies: A Study in Transatlantic Culture," *History of Education Quarterly* 12 (1972): 184–97.

———. "King's College in the City of New York, 1754–1776." Ph.D. dissertation, Northwestern University, 1968.

———. "The Struggle for Sectarian Control of Princeton, 1745–1760," *New Jersey History* 91 (1973): 77–90.

Jameson, J. Franklin. *The American Revolution Considered as a Social Movement.* Boston: Beacon Press, 1956.

Jencks, Christopher, and Riesman, David. *The Academic Revolution.* Garden City, N.Y.: Doubleday, 1968.

Johnson, Herbert A. "When John Jay was Jack," *Columbia College Today* 10 (1963): 48–51.

Kammen, Michael, ed. *The Contrapuntal Civilization: Essays Toward a New Understanding of the American Experience.* New York: Thomas Y. Crowell, 1971.

———. *People of Paradox: An Inquiry Concerning the Origins of American Civilization.* New York: Knopf, 1972.

Keep, Austin B. "The Library of King's College," *Columbia University Quarterly* 13 (1911): 275–84.

Kemp, William W. *The Support of Schools in Colonial New York by the Society for the Propagation of the Gospel in Foreign Parts.* New York: Teachers College, Columbia University, 1913.

Kent, Andrew, ed. *An Eighteenth Century Lectureship in Chemistry. Essays and Bicentenary Addresses Relating to the Chemistry Department (1747) of Glasgow University (1451).* Glasgow: Jackson, Son & Co., 1950.

Kett, Joseph F. *The Formation of the American Medical Profession: The Role of Institutions, 1780–1860.* New Haven and London: Yale University Press, 1968.

King, Lester. *The Medical World of the Eighteenth Century.* Chicago: University of Chicago Press, 1958.

———. "Rationalism in Early Eighteenth Century Medicine," *Journal of the History of Medicine and Allied Sciences* 18 (1963): 257–71.

Kinloch, Hector G. "Anglican Clergy in Connecticut, 1701–1785." Ph.D. dissertation, Yale University, 1959.

Klein, Milton M. "Church, State, and Education: Testing the Issue in Colonial New York," *New York History* 45 (1964): 291–303.

———. "The Cultural Tyros of Colonial New York," *South Atlantic Quarterly* 66 (1967): 218–32.

———. "New York in the American Colonies: A New Look," *New York History* 53 (1972): 132–56.

———. "The Rise of the New York Bar: The Legal Career of William Livingston," *William and Mary Quarterly*, 3d series, 15 (1958): 334–58.

———. "William Livingston: The *American Whig*." Ph.D. dissertation, Columbia University, 1954.

Klingberg, Frank J. *Anglican Humanitarianism in Colonial New York*. Philadelphia: Church Historical Society, 1940.

Lamb, George W. "Clergymen Licensed to the American Colonies by the Bishops of London: 1745–1781," *Historical Magazine of the Protestant Episcopal Church* 13 (1944): 128–43.

Lynd, Staughton. *Class Conflict, Slavery, and the United States Constitution: Ten Essays*. Indianapolis and New York: Bobbs-Merrill, 1967.

McAnear, Beverly. "American Imprints Concerning King's College," *Papers of the Bibliographical Society of America* 44 (1950): 301–39.

———. "College Founding in the American Colonies, 1745–1775," *Mississippi Valley Historical Review* 42 (1955): 24–44.

———. "Politics in Provincial New York, 1689–1761." Ph.D. dissertation, Stanford University, 1935.

———. "The Raising of Funds by the Colonial Colleges," *Mississippi Valley Historical Review* 38 (1952): 591–612.

———. "The Selection of an Alma Mater by Pre-Revolutionary Students," *Pennsylvania Magazine of History and Biography* 73 (1949): 429–40.

MacBean, William M. *Biographical Register of St. Andrew's Society of the State of New York*. 2 vols. New York: St. Andrew's Society of the State of New York, 1922–25.

McDaniel, W. B. II. "A Brief Sketch of the Rise of American Medical Societies." In *History of American Medicine: A Symposium*, edited by Felix Marti-Ibanez. New York: M D Publications, 1959.

McKee, Samuel. *Labor in Colonial New York, 1664–1776*. New York: Columbia University Press, 1935.

Maclean, John. *History of the College of New Jersey, From Its Origin in 1746 to the Commencement of 1854*. 2 vols. Philadelphia, 1877.

Main, Jackson Turner. *Political Parties before the Constitution*. Chapel Hill, N.C.: University of North Carolina Press, 1973.

———. *The Social Structure of Revolutionary America*. Princeton, N.J.: Princeton University Press, 1965.

Mason, Bernard. *The Road to Independence: The Revolutionary Movement in New York, 1773–1777*. Lexington, Ky.: University of Kentucky Press, 1966.

Masson, Margaret W. "The Premises and Purposes of Higher Education in

388

American Society, 1745–1770." Ph.D. dissertation, University of Washington, 1971.

"M.D.'s Needed," *New York Times.* May 26, 1970, p. 40.

Miller, Guy H. "A Contracting Community: American Presbyterians, Social Conflict, and Higher Education, 1730–1820." Ph.D. dissertation, University of Michigan, 1970.

Mills, Frederick V. "Anglican Resistance to an American Episcopate, 1761–1789." Ph.D. dissertation, University of Pennsylvania, 1967.

Mintz, Max M. *Gouverneur Morris and the American Revolution.* Norman, Okla.: University of Oklahoma Press, 1970.

Mitchell, Broadus. *Alexander Hamilton: Youth to Maturity, 1755–1788.* New York: Macmillan, 1957.

Monaghan, Frank. *John Jay: Defender of Liberty Against Kings & Peoples.* . . . New York and Indianapolis: Bobbs-Merrill, 1935.

Moore, Clement C. *The Early History of Columbia College,* edited by M. Halsey Thomas. New York: Columbia University Press, 1940.

Moore, George H. *Collegium Regale Novi Eboraci: The Origin and Early History of Columbia College.* New York, 1890.

Moore, William. *History of St. George's Church, Hempstead, Long Island, N.Y.* New York, 1881.

Morgan, Edmund S. "The American Revolution Considered as an Intellectual Movement." In *Paths of American Thought,* edited by Arthur M. Schlesinger, Jr., and Morton White. Boston: Houghton Mifflin, 1963.

———. *The Gentle Puritan: A Life of Ezra Stiles, 1727–1795.* New Haven and London: Yale University Press, 1962.

Morison, Samuel E. *The Founding of Harvard College.* Cambridge: Harvard University Press, 1935.

———. *Harvard College in the Seventeenth Century.* Cambridge: Harvard University Press, 1936.

———. *Three Centuries of Harvard, 1636–1936.* Cambridge: Harvard University Press, 1965.

Morris, Richard B. *Seven Who Shaped Our Destiny: The Founding Fathers as Revolutionaries.* New York: Harper & Row, 1973.

Murrin, John M. "The Legal Transformation: The Bench and Bar of Eighteenth-Century Massachusetts." In *Colonial America: Essays in Politics and Social Development,* edited by Stanley N. Katz. Boston: Little, Brown, 1971.

Naylor, Natalie A. "The Ante-Bellum College Movement: A Reappraisal of Tewksbury's Founding of American Colleges and Universities," *History of Education Quarterly* 13 (1973): 261–74.

Nelson, William H. *The American Tory.* Oxford: Clarendon Press, 1961.

Newcombe, Alfred W. "The Appointment and Instruction of S.P.G. Missionaries," *Church History* 5 (1936): 340–58.

"New York Land Grants in Vermont," *Collections of the Vermont Historical Society,* 1 (1870): 147–53.

O'Callaghan, E. B. "John Chambers," *New York Genealogical and Biographical Record* 3 (1872): 57–62.

Olson, Alison B. "The Founding of Princeton University: Religion and Politics in Eighteenth-Century New Jersey," *New Jersey History* 87 (1969): 133–50.

Oviatt, Edwin. *The Beginnings of Yale (1701–1726)*. New Haven: Yale University Press, 1916.

Painter, Borden. "The Anglican Vestry in Colonial America." Ph.D. dissertation, Yale University, 1965.

Persons, Stow. "The Cyclical Theory of History in Eighteenth Century America," *American Quarterly* 6 (1954): 147–63.

Pine, John B. "The Origin of the University of the State of New York," *Columbia University Quarterly* 11 (1909): 155–62.

Pratt, John W. *Religion, Politics, and Diversity: The Church-State Theme in New York History*. Ithaca, N.Y.: Cornell University Press, 1967.

Roach, Helen P. *History of Speech Education at Columbia College, 1754–1940*. New York: Teachers College, Columbia University, 1950.

Roche, John F. "The Uranian Society: Gentlemen and Scholars in Federal New York," *New York History* 52 (1971): 121–32.

Rudolph, Frederick. *The American College and University: A History*. New York: Knopf, 1962.

Sabine, George H. *A History of Political Theory*. 3d ed. New York: Holt, Rinehart & Winston, 1961.

Sabine, Lorenzo. *Biographical Sketches of Loyalists of the American Revolution, with An Historical Essay*. 2 vols. Boston, 1864.

Sachse, William L. *The Colonial American in Britain*. Madison, Wis.: University of Wisconsin Press, 1956.

Samuelson, Robert J. "Mt. Sinai: How a Hospital Builds a Medical School," *Science* 158 (1967): 614–18.

Schuyler, John. *Institution of the Society of the Cincinnati, Formed by the Officers of the American Army of the Revolution, 1783, With Extracts, from the Proceedings of its General Meetings and from the Transactions of the New York State Society*. New York, 1886.

Sherwood, Sidney. *The University of the State of New York: History of Higher Education in the State of New York*. United States Bureau of Education, Circular of Information No. 3, 1900. Washington, D.C., 1900.

Shipton, Clifford K. *Sibley's Harvard Graduates: Biographical Sketches of Those Who Attended Harvard College*. vols. 4–16 to date. Boston, Cambridge: Massachusetts Historical Society, Harvard University Press, 1933–.

Shryock, Richard. *The Development of Modern Medicine: An Interpretation of the Social and Scientific Factors Involved*. rev. ed. New York: Knopf, 1947.

———. *Medicine and Society in America, 1660–1860*. New York: New York University Press, 1960.

Sloan, Douglas. *The Scottish Enlightenment and the American College Ideal*. New York: Teachers College Press, 1971.

Smith, Wilson. *Professors & Public Ethics: Studies of Northern Moral Philosophers before the Civil War.* Ithaca, N.Y.: Cornell University Press, 1956.

Sprague, William B. *Annals of the American Pulpit; or, Commemorative Notices of Distinguished American Clergymen, to 1855.* 9 vols. New York, 1865–69.

Stearns, Raymond P. *Science in the British Colonies of America.* Urbana, Ill.: University of Illinois Press, 1970.

Steiner, Bruce. *Samuel Seabury, 1729–1796: A Study in the High Church Tradition.* Athens, Ohio: Ohio University Press, 1972.

Stokes, I. N. Phelps. *The Iconography of Manhattan Island, 1498–1909.* 6 vols. New York: R. H. Dodd, 1915–28.

Stone, Lawrence. "The Ninniversity?" *New York Review of Books* 16 (Jan. 28, 1971): 21–29.

Stookey, Byron. "America's Two Colonial Medical Schools," *Bulletin of the New York Academy of Medicine* 40 (1964): 269–84.

———. *A History of Colonial Medical Education: in the Province of New York, with its Subsequent Development (1767–1830).* Springfield, Ill.: Charles C. Thomas, 1962.

Suydam, Henry. *History and Reminiscences of the Mesier Family of Wappingers Creek. Together with a Short History of Zion Church. . . .* [New York,] 1882.

Tewksbury, Donald G. *The Founding of American Colleges and Universities Before the Civil War, with Particular Reference to the Religious Influences Bearing upon the College Movement.* New York: Teachers College, Columbia University, 1932.

Thomas, M. Halsey. *Columbia University Officers and Alumni, 1754–1857.* New York: Columbia University Press, 1936.

———. "The King's College Building: with some notes on its later tenants," *New-York Historical Society Quarterly* 39 (1955): 23–61.

———. "The Reverend Samuel Johnson's 'Collection of Prayers' (1759)," *Papers of the Bibliographical Society of America* 48 (1954): 416–21.

Tucker, Louis L. *Puritan Protagonist: President Thomas Clap of Yale College.* Chapel Hill, N.C.: University of North Carolina Press, 1962.

Turner, Ralph H. "Sponsored and Contest Mobility and the School System," *American Sociological Review* 25 (1960): 855–67.

Upton, L. F. S. *The Loyal Whig: William Smith of New York & Quebec.* Toronto: University of Toronto Press, 1969.

Vance, Clarence H. "Myles Cooper," *Columbia University Quarterly* 22 (1930): 261–86.

Varga, Nicholas. "New York Government and Politics During the Mid-Eighteenth Century." Ph.D. dissertation, Fordham University, 1960.

Waite, Frederick C. "The Degree of Bachelor of Medicine in the American Colonies and the United States," *Yale Journal of Biology and Medicine* 10 (1938): 309–33.

Wall, Alexander J. "The Controversy in the Dutch Church in New York Concerning Preaching in English, 1754–1768," *New York Historical Society Quarterly Bulletin* 12 (1928): 39–58.

Ward, W. R. *Georgian Oxford: University Politics in the Eighteenth Century*. Oxford: Clarendon Press, 1958.

Welles, Albert. *Watts (Watt). Also Watts, Wattes, Wattys, Wathes, de Wath, Le Fleming, (In England)*. New York, 1898.

Wertenbaker, Thomas J. *The Golden Age of Colonial Culture*. 2d ed. New York: New York University Press, 1949.

———. *Princeton, 1746–1896*. Princeton, N.J.: Princeton University Press, 1946.

Whitehead, John S. *The Separation of College and State: Columbia, Dartmouth, Harvard, and Yale, 1776–1876*. New Haven and London: Yale University Press, 1973.

Wickes, Stephen. *History of Medicine in New Jersey, and of Its Medical Men, from the Settlement of the Province to A.D. 1800*. Newark, N.J., 1879.

Willis, Edmund P. "Social Origins of Political Leadership in New York City from the Revolution to 1815." Ph.D. dissertation, University of California, Berkeley, 1967.

Wood, Gordon S. *The Creation of the American Republic, 1776–1787*. Chapel Hill, N.C.: University of North Carolina Press, 1969.

Young, Alfred F. *The Democratic Republicans of New York: The Origins, 1763–1797*. Chapel Hill, N.C.: University of North Carolina Press, 1967.

INDEX

Faculty (*Continued*)
200; religious composition of, 106,
123, 152, 248, 267, 279, 298; under
Myles Cooper, 134–35, 146, 150,
176, 200–02, 348–49; of American
University, 140, 147–48, 150;
loyalism and, 140, 151–52; professorships in municipal law and Christian
religion, 150; political views of,
151–52, 216–24, 267, 282, 300,
302–03, 311; in 1776, 153–54; medical, 246–47, 250–55, 261, 262, 275,
294; on board of regents, 272, 274,
278; at Columbia, 275–76, 279, 284,
290, 291, 293–303, 371; *see also* Curriculum; Dutch professor of divinity;
individual faculty members
Family relationships, *see* King's College,
and family relationships
Farmers: as fathers of students, 94, 95,
97; among alumni, 226
Farquhar, William, 234
Federalist Papers, 216
Federalists, 210–12, 214, 216, 224, 282
Ferguson, James, *Lectures on Select
Subjects*, 177
Finances: private gifts and contributions, 3, 16, 32, 55, 65, 75, 87, 96–97,
115, 123, 131–33, 150, 332; public
support, 46, 65, 70, 115, 132, 276,
294, 326; endowment, 70, 92, 115,
133, 138, 247, 333, 340; group profile
of subscribers of 1755, 96–97; at
King's College, 115, 119, 120,
131–34, 340; fund raising in England,
121–22, 123, 131–33; landholdings,
133–34, 140, 146, 150, 340; at medical
school, 247, 250–51; at Columbia,
276, 290, 294; *see also* Costs; Lotteries
Firewood, 10, 13
First commissioner for trade and plantations, 69
Fordyce, David, 157, 159, 172, 174–75;
Dialogues Concerning Education, 174

Fothergill, John, 257
Founders, *see* King's College, goals of
founders, principal founders of
Franklin, Benjamin, 11, 22, 24, 34,
174–75, 233, 316
Freethinking, Samuel Johnson's fears
of, 19, 20–21, 28, 42, 170
Frelinghuysen, Theodore, 60–66, 71,
155
French and Indian War, 62, 123, 240;
impact on King's College, 75–76, 92,
119, 120, 198
French church, 67, 68, 69
French language, as academic subject,
181, 275, 294, 295, 301, 302
Fund raising, *see* Finances

Galen, 258
Gardening, as academic subject, 175
General Assembly, of New York, *see*
New York General Assembly
Gentility, as educational goal, 7, 11, 13,
82–83, 157, 158, 183
Geography, as academic subject, 83,
158, 168, 175, 294, 298
Geology, as academic subject, 294
Geometry, as academic subject, 83,
167–68, 177, 298
George II (King of Great Britain and
Ireland, 1727–1760), 8
George III (King of Great Britain and
Ireland, 1760–1820), 123, 141, 150
German language, as academic subject,
275, 301
German Reformed church, 286, 298
Glasgow, University of, 123, 135, 245
Gloucester County, N.Y., 133–34
Goldsmith, Oliver, 297; *History of
England*, 181
Gordon, Thomas, 44, 219; *The
Craftsmen*, 44; *Independent Whig*, 44
Government officials, *see* Politicians and
government officials
Governors of King's College, 63–65,

Merchants, 11, 85, 96, 123, 175, 274, 311; as fathers of students, 94–95, 97, 252, 286; as alumni, 195, 226–27, 286
Metaphysics, as academic subject, 128, 135, 169–71, 175, 176, 177, 180, 208
Meteorology, as academic subject, 294
Middleton, Peter, 233–48, 251, 254–55, 262
Midwifery, as academic subject, 247, 255
Military officers, 97, 226
Milton, John, 176; *Paradise Lost*, 181
Mineralogy, as academic subject, 294
Ministers: among college alumni, 24, 73–74, 225, 285–86, 356; education of and King's College, 27, 55, 59–66, 73–74, 82, 84–85, 163; as college governors, trustees, regents, 28, 29–30, 67–69, 77, 121, 137, 143, 272, 274, 279–80; versus laymen, 32–34, 42, 45, 47, 67–69, 76, 77, 137, 373; as fathers of students, 56, 74, 94–95, 97, 252, 286; *see also* Episcopal clergy
Ministry Act of 1693, 28–29
Mitchill, Samuel Latham, 294, 296, 301
Mobility, social, *see* Social mobility
Mobility, sponsored, *see* Sponsored mobility
Modernization, 307–13
Mohawk River valley, 149
Moore, Benjamin, 153–54, 191, 192–93, 216, 225, 269; portrait of, 193
Moral philosophy, as academic subject: at King's College, 158, 163, 169–70, 172, 174, 177, 180–81, 216, 221; at Columbia, 294, 298–300, 302; *see also* Ethics; Politics
Moravians, 98
Morgagni, Giovanni Battista, 237, 258
Morgan, John, 242, 245, 255, 260, 261, 262
Morningside Heights, 16
Morris, Gouverneur, 139, 182, 196,

225; as conservative Whig, 210–16; portrait of, 213
Morris, Richard B., 216
Mount Sinai School of Medicine, 250
Murray, Joseph, 11, 31–32, 33, 34, 38, 48, 50, 52, 83–84, 115, 130
Music, as academic subject, 275

Natural history, as academic subject, 294, 296, 301
Natural philosophy, as academic subject, 236; at King's College, 108, 120, 123, 135, 158, 168–69, 176, 177, 180, 206; at Columbia, 294, 298; *see also* Science
Natural rights, 180–81, 221, 223, 299, 311
Navigation, as academic subject, 207, 298
Newark, N.J., 23, 26, 32
New Brunswick, 214, 226
New Brunswick, N.J., 23, 26
Newburgh, N.Y., 6–9, 316
New Haven, Conn., 24, 25
New Jersey: Anglican clerics in, 23, 26, 72, 127, 145; as residence of students, 97, 287; *see also* College of New Jersey
New Jersey, College of, *see* College of New Jersey
New Jersey Medical Society, 253, 261
New Learning, 170–75, 180, 183
New Lights, 25, 27, 60, 74, 280
New Sides, 25, 74, 155, 223; *see also* Presbyterians
New Testament, as text, 163, 177
Newton, Sir Isaac, 20, 170, 174, 309; *Principia*, 254
Newtonianism, 22, 168, 170, 173
Newtown, N.Y., 191
New Windsor, N.Y., 316
New York: rural New Yorkers and King's College, 5–12, 51, 59, 71,